A Pragmatic Approach to the Generation and Gender
Gap in Japanese Politeness Strategies

Hituzi Linguistics in English

No.1　Lexical Borrowing and its Impact on English　Makimi Kimura-Kano
No.2　From a Subordinate Clause to an Independent Clause
　　　　　　　　　　　　　　　　　　　　　　　　Yuko Higashiizumi
No.3　ModalP and Subjunctive Present　　　　　　　　Tadao Nomura
No.4　A Historical Study of Referent Honorifics in Japanese
　　　　　　　　　　　　　　　　　　　　　　　　　Takashi Nagata
No.5　Communicating Skills of Intention　　　　Tsutomu Sakamoto
No.6　A Pragmatic Approach to the Generation and Gender
　　　Gap in Japanese Politeness Strategies　　　Toshihiko Suzuki
No.7　Japanese Women's Listening Behavior in Face-to-face Conversation
　　　　　　　　　　　　　　　　　　　　　　　　Sachie Miyazaki

Hituzi Linguistics in English No. 6

A Pragmatic Approach to the Generation and Gender
Gap in Japanese Politeness Strategies

Toshihiko Suzuki

Hituzi Syobo Publishing

Copyright © Toshihiko Suzuki 2007
First published 2007

Author: Toshihiko Suzuki

All rights reserved. Except for the quotation of short passages for the purposes of criticism and review, no part of this publication may be reduced, stored in a retrieval system, or transmitted in any form or by any means, electronic, mechanical, photocopying, recording or otherwise, without the written prior permission of the publisher.
In case of photocopying and electronic copying and retrieval from network personally, permission will be given on receipts of payment and making inquiries. For details please contact us through e-mail. Our e-mail address is given below.

Book Design © Hirokazu Mukai (glyph)

Hituzi Syobo Publishing
5-21-5 Koishikawa Bunkyo-ku Tokyo, Japan 112-0002

phone +81-3-5684-6871 fax +81-3-5684-6872
e-mail: toiawase@hituzi.co.jp
http://www.hituzi.co.jp/
postal transfer 00120-8-142852

ISBN978-4-89476-330-2
Printed in Japan

Abstract

This publication, based on my thesis for the Ph.D. degree of Lancaster University, U.K. has been awarded **Grant-in-Aid for Publication of Scientific Research Results**, part of **Grant-in-Aid for Scientific Research (KAKENHI)**. I would like to express my deepest gratitude to **Japan Society for the Promotion of Science (JSPS)** for its generous offer of the grant that has made this publication possible.

This study investigates the 'generation gap' in linguistic politeness strategies in contemporary Japanese, focusing on age–gender differences among the informants as well. My initial hypotheses were that (i) Japanese older and younger people apply different politeness strategies respectively; (ii) older people's language is more polite than younger people's; and (iii) Japanese older women's language is more polite than the others'.

The quantitative and qualitative data analyses have confirmed the three hypotheses presented above. As for the first and second suppositions, the JHA (Japanese higher age group) exhibited a significantly higher degree of **absolute politeness** than the JYA (Japanese younger age group). On the other hand, it should be noted that the difference in **relative politeness** between the two age groups was not statistically significant. In terms of the third assumption, JHAF (Japanese higher age female group) achieved a higher level of performance in both categories (i.e. **politeness** and **appropriateness**) than the other three age–gender groups.

This thesis consists of seven chapters, followed by a bibliography. Appendices are supplied in the form of 'accompanying materials' in a CD-ROM attached to the last page of this thesis.

Chapter 1 is introductory, explaining the general nature of the research and its goals. Chapter 2 provides the theoretical background of this study: Leech's framework is discussed in relation to the other main theories relating to linguistic politeness. Chapter 3 gives a review of previous studies of Japanese politeness and also indicates the new directions in studying it with an examination of current relevant publications.

Chapter 4 provides the methodological background for the data collection of this study. Chapter 5 covers the quantitative and qualitative analyses, and the findings of the research. Chapter 6 describes the supplementary research carried out with spoken data, focusing on the additional 'force' created by prosodic features.

Chapter 7 concludes the thesis by summarising the main findings and pointing the way for future research.

Contents

Abstract	v
LIST OF TABLES AND FIGURES	xi
ABBREVIATIONS	xiii
ACKNOWLEDGEMENTS	xiv

Chapter 1 Introduction	**1**
1.1 The generation gap in Japanese	1
1.2 Showing consideration	2
1.3 Deference versus camaraderie	4
1.4 Politeness and appropriateness scales	5
1.5 A spoken DCT with video prompts	6
1.6 The design of the thesis	6

Chapter 2 Politeness: a survey of theories and approaches	**11**
2.1 Specification of 'politeness' in this study	13
2.1.1 Linguistic politeness and rapport management	13
2.1.2 'Politeness' as defined by the GSP in Leech (2001, 2003) and the PP	16
2.1.2.1 The original PP	17
2.1.2.2 The renewed PP	19
2.1.2.3 The definition of 'politeness' in this study: 'politeness', 'deference', 'camaraderie', 'appropriateness' and 'the scale of politeness'	21
2.1.2.4 The advantage of the GSP and the PP	30
2.1.3 'Politeness1', 'politeness2' and 'politic behaviour'	33
2.1.4 Speech acts and politeness: 'face', 'constraints' and 'semantic formulae'	40
2.2 An overview of related recent politeness theories	48
2.2.1 Fraser's taxonomy	48

2.2.1.1 The social norm view	48
2.2.1.2 The conversational-maxim view	52
2.2.1.3 The face saving view	53
2.2.1.4 The conversational-contract view	53
2.2.2 Eelen's treatment of politeness theories	55
2.2.3 Brown & Levinson	56
2.2.3.1 Politeness and the management of face	56
2.2.3.2 Face-threatening acts and strategies for doing FTAs	58
2.2.3.3 Cross-cultural differences in the framework of 'face'	61
2.2.3.4 Criticisms on B&L's theory	63

Chapter 3 An overview of linguistic politeness in Japanese — 71

3.1 Wakimae/Discernment	73
3.2 Honorifics	76
3.3 Changes in honorifics and politeness strategies	80
3.4 Variables that determine the level of politeness	83
3.5 Supplementary discussions on Japanese politeness	87
3.5.1 Gender issues	88
3.5.2 Interaction of 'wakimae' and 'individual intention' in polite linguistic behaviour	91

Chapter 4 Methodology — 101

4.1 An overview of methodological issues in pragmatic research	102
4.1.1 Classification of methodologies	102
4.1.2 Types of questionnaires	104
4.1.2.1 Rating scales	104
4.1.2.2 DCT (Discourse completion test)	108
4.1.2.3 Interviews	112
4.1.3 Triangulation: combination of research methodologies	114
4.2 Pilot study	115
4.3 Methodology for this study: research procedure	117
4.3.1 Summary of the data collection procedure	117
4.3.2 First-stage data collection: classification of informants	118
4.3.3 First-stage data collection: scenarios	119

4.3.4 First-stage data collection: the spoken DCT with video prompts	119
4.3.5 Some noticeable characteristics of the spoken DCT in this study	122
4.3.6 The second-stage data collection	125

Chapter 5 Results   131

5.1 Summary of findings based on quantitative analysis	131
5.1.1 Overall observations	131
5.1.2 The generation gap in politeness from the quantitative perspective	132
5.1.3 The generation gap in appropriateness from the quantitative perspective	133
5.1.4 Group differences from the quantitative perspective	134
5.1.5 Correlation between politeness and appropriateness	134
5.1.6 Raters' performance	136
5.2 Individual item analyses	136
5.2.1 Item 01	138
5.2.2 Item 02	151
5.2.3 Item 03	162
5.2.4 Item 04	173
5.2.5 Item 05	185
5.2.6 Item 06	196
5.2.7 Item 07	212
5.2.8 Item 08	228

Chapter 6 Further survey: comparisons between written and spoken data   247

6.1 Previous studies on prosodic features of speech act performance and politeness strategies	248
6.2 Supplementary experiment exposing raters to spoken responses	251
6.3 Comparison of raters' evaluation of transcribed and spoken responses	253
6.3.1 Overall observations through quantitative analysis	253
6.3.2 Individual response analysis with instrumental scrutiny	254
6.3.3 Raters' opinions on this experimental survey	272

Chapter 7 Conclusion — 277
  7.1 Summary of findings — 277
  7.2 Retrospective evaluation of this research — 284
    7.2.1 Weaknesses and limitations — 284
    7.2.2 Strengths and advantages over previous research — 286
    7.2.3 Pointers to future research — 287

Bibliography — 289

Index — 301

LIST OF TABLES AND FIGURES

Tables

Table 2.1.1 Components of rapport management presented by Spencer-Oatey (2000c)	14
Table 2.1.2.2 Summary of constraints to pursue the **GSP**	21
Table 3.1 The guideline for address terms in business practices	74
Table 3.4 Variables that determine the level of politeness	84
Table 4.1.1 Focus and procedure in some data collection formats	103
Table 4.1.2.1 Tanaka & Kawabe's list of politeness rank orders	105
Table 5.2-1 Classification of Japanese 1st person pronoun	136
Table 5.2-2 Classification of Japanese verb honorification	137
Table 5.2.1 Summary of statistical data: Item 01	140
Table 5.2.2-1 Summary of statistical data: Item 02	151
Table 5.2.2-2 Summary of humble form usage	161
Table 5.2.3 Summary of statistical data: Item 03	164
Table 5.2.4 Summary of statistical data: Item 04	175
Table 5.2.5 Summary of statistical data: Item 05	187
Table 5.2.6-1 Summary of statistical data: Item 06	198
Table 5.2.6-2 The number of responses with 'lexicogrammatical politeness markers'	211
Table 5.2.7 Summary of statistical data: Item 07	216
Table 5.2.8-1 Summary of statistical data: Item 08	230
Table 5.2.8-2 Summary of the results of the strategy analysis	240
Table 5.2.8-3 Summary of alternative strategies	241

Figures

Figure 2.1.2.3-1 The definition of 'politeness': positive and negative directions	22
Figure 2.1.2.3-2 The scale of politeness	29
Figure 2.2.3.2 Brown & Levinson's (1987) 'Strategies for doing Face-Threatening Acts	59
Figure 3.2-1 The basic model of the Japanese honorific system	77
Figure 3.2-2 Pragmatic and sociolinguistic politeness: their values	79
Figure 4.3.6 The relationship between General pragmatics, Pragmalinguistics and Socio-pragmatics	126

Figure 6.3.2.1   Prosodic features of Response 01 [MJ131 – JYAM02]   256
Figure 6.3.2.2   Prosodic features of Response 02 [MJ222 – JYAF02]   257
Figure 6.3.2.3   Prosodic features of Response 03 [MJ406 – JHAF04]   259
Figure 6.3.2.4   Prosodic features of Response 04 [MJ423 – JYAF04]   260
Figure 6.3.2.5   Prosodic features of Response 05 [MJ627 – JYAF06]   261
Figure 6.3.2.6   Prosodic features of Response 06 [MJ629 – JYAM01]   263
Figure 6.3.2.7   Prosodic features of Response 07 [MJ637 – JYAM06]   265
Figure 6.3.2.8   Prosodic features of Response 08 [MJ808 – JHAF05]   267
Figure 6.3.2.9   Prosodic features of Response 09 [MJ810 – JHAF06]   269
Figure 6.3.2.10 Prosodic features of Response 10 [MJ816 – JHAM05]   270

ABBREVIATIONS

JHA	higher age group
JYA	younger age group
JHAF	higher age female group
JHAM	higher age male group
JYAF	younger age female group
JHAM	younger age male group
HAR	higher age raters
YAR	younger age raters
HFR	higher age female rater
HMR	higher age male rater
YFR	younger age female rater
YMR	younger age male rater
GSP	Grand strategy of politeness
PP	Politeness Principle
s	self/the speaker
o	other(s)
h	the hearer/addressee
EXAL	exalted
FOR	formal
HON	honorific
HUM	humble
POL	polite
ABL	Ablative
ACC	Accusative
ADD	Address term
CJEC	Conjectural
COL	Colloquial
COMP	Complementizer
COND	Conditional
CONJ	Conjunctive
COP	Copula
DAT	Dative

ACKNOWLEDGEMENTS

First and foremost, I would like to express my gratitude to my supervisor Professor Geoffrey Leech for his comments and suggestions on my developing ideas and his unfailing encouragement in my research. Without his dedicated and warm-hearted support, this comprehensive pragmatic study of Japanese politeness would have been impossible.

I am also greatly indebted to Dr Jonathan Culpeper for his valuable advice to improve this thesis and his encouragement to carry out a further survey using spoken data. In Japan, I owe much of this study to aid from Professor Kensaku Yoshida at Sophia University, Professor Hiroshi Matsusaka at Waseda University, Professor Michi Shiina at Hosei University, Professor Yukitaka Tatsumi at Toho University, Professor Asako Kaneko at Showa Women's University, Mr Hikaru Oiji at Midorigaoka Senior High School, Ms Mika Watanabe at Mukoojima Technical High School, Ms Rie Iwahashi formerly at Oxford University Press Japan, Ms Noriko Miyazaki at Kyooiku Doojin-sha, and Ms Mayumi Iritono formerly at Waseda University. I thank them for their support in finding informants and other related issues.

I would like to express my gratitude to my colleagues at my former teaching place, Tokyo Jogakkan Primary, Junior and Senior High School, especially to those who helped me create video prompts and enabled me to organise the first and second-stage researches – Mr Norio Yoshizawa, Mr Tadashi Hosoya, Ms Norie Shimizu, Ms Akiko Koyama, Mr Yuuji Tsunemoto, Mr Takeshi Kitazawa, Ms Tomoko Nakamura and Ms Miyuki Nishizawa. I also thank Mr Hiroshi Hirai at JTB for his cooperation for the video prompts.

Professor Shin'ichiro Torikai at Rikkyo University gave me precious advice in pursuing a Ph.D. and always encouraged me warmly. I am also indebted to Dr Noriko Tanaka at Meikai University for her helpful comments and suggestions in my previous publication about my pilot study.

I am profoundly grateful for the endeavour of Mr Isao Matsumoto, the President of Hitsuzi Syobo Publishing, to enable the publication of this book.

I also thank my colleagues at Lancaster. PASTY (Pragmatics and Stylistics research group at Lancaster University), coordinated by Dr Elena Semino, provided me with new and insightful ideas concerning related issues for this work.

I thank John Heywood for proofreading this thesis and for helpful suggestions for corrections.

And, last but not least, I'd like to dedicate this book to my mother, Yasuko, who has always been supportive to me in my academic pursuits. I would also like to dedicate it to the memory of my late father, Katsumi.

Chapter 1

Introduction

In this chapter I will give an overview of my research. Firstly I will take a general view of the linguistic situation in Japan, focusing on age differences in language use. Secondly I will sketch out some key concepts in this study, which are employed to investigate whether two generations execute linguistic politeness strategies in different/same ways. Thirdly, the procedure in which these concepts are applied will also be presented. Finally I will explicate the design of this thesis and provide a brief summary of each chapter.

1.1 The generation gap in Japanese

Recently there were quite a few newspaper articles and reports on Japanese TV about the government's plan to survey the Japanese-language ability of its citizens. The government's decision came after some conspicuous changes in language in Japanese society, mainly among young people, had been observed. As linguistic attitudes have become more and more liberalised and informal, the proper use of *keigo*, Japanese honorifics, has become less and less important. This tendency has often been regarded as '*kotoba-no midare*' <confusion in language> and summarised as '*wakamono kotoba*' <youth language>. A survey on such 'confusion in language', carried out by a Japanese publishing company *Taishuukan*, suggests that '*-shi*' (a connective particle that implies there's more to say), '*… ja-nai desu-ka*' <(something/someone) is …, isn't it?>, '*bimyoo*' (*lit.* 'subtle', but applied to mean 'not clear'), '*futsuu-ni*' <as a matter of course/as usual>, '*jimi-ni*' <a little, without any outstanding point>, '*yabai*' (*lit.* 'dangerous/too bad' but employed to mean 'splendid') and '*arie-nai*' <impossible/out of the question> are typical expressions in 'youth language'. (There are many more expressions pointed out as 'youth language'.) In this recent research with Japanese senior high school teachers, over 90% of the informants said 'there is confusion in Japanese language', especially among the younger generation.

The governmental research will be undertaken because there have been 'rising worries over the decline in Japanese language competency, especially among younger people' (Daily Yomiuri, 2005/01/08). In this official survey, how *keigo* is used will be scrutinised as one of the key issues: this means that people think the use of polite language has also been changing or 'deteriorating'. It seems that Japanese younger people have been recognised as 'less polite' because of such different attitudes in language. This research is designed to explore such linguistic changes and differences between older and younger people from a pragmatic perspective.

Furthermore, 'gender differences' will also be explored in this study. Although this issue has rarely been mentioned in recent articles or reports, Japanese women are traditionally known as the performers of sophisticated linguistic politeness[1]. This traditional assumption will be examined to learn if it is still the case in present-day Japan. The difference(s) between female informants of different age groups will also be investigated in the age–gender classification research, to see whether the tradition of such linguistic sophistication has been descended from the older generation to the younger or not.

In this study, however, these possible differences will be inspected from a pragmatic point of view: the difference in the 'forces' of informants' responses will be explored with the scales of **absolute politeness** (the degree of politeness created by linguistic features) and **relative politeness** (the degree of appropriateness of an utterance in a certain situation). Previous studies of Japanese politeness have focused only on sociolinguistic differences such as the use of lexical and grammatical devices (i.e. honorific forms or colloquial expressions) in many cases. In this sense such studies belong to the domain of sociolinguistics, which explores 'varieties' within a certain language. This study necessarily treats such sociolinguistic differences as well but the main purpose of doing so is to inspect the differences generated by the holistic 'forces' of utterances, which represent the speakers' intentions. Consequently this is chiefly a study of the 'impressions' that utterances make on addressees, taking a variety of linguistic elements into consideration.

1.2 Showing consideration

'Showing consideration' towards others is a crucial factor in achieving 'social equilibrium'. One question about recent young people's different linguistic attitude is whether such sociolinguistic changes have caused more friction and less harmony in society. How younger people show their consideration towards others may be different, employing strategies of a different sort – but this does not necessarily mean that they are 'less considerate'. For example, compare the following two sample English sentences.

(1) We are very sorry that you are not allowed in because this restaurant is open from 11 o'clock. I would like to suggest that you come back here in ten minutes.

(2) Hi, folks, come in and be seated. We still have ten more minutes before the opening time, but you guys are welcome inside by all means.

It is difficult to tell which of the two above are more 'considerate'. The second remark is quite informal with colloquial expressions, but may be more 'considerate', if we take the propositional content into consideration (the speaker is inviting the customers to come into the restaurant although the opening time is ten minutes later). On the other hand, although the first one demonstrates formality and expresses the speaker's regret, it is still refusing to let the customers come in. Consideration is not only controlled by lexicogrammatical devices but also by the propositional content of an utterance and so on.

Consideration can take various forms in utterances which may be described as 'deference', 'camaraderie', 'cost-benefit', 'optionality' or 'indirectness'. Less polite linguistic features, e.g. the absence of honorific forms, may not lead to less consideration in certain contexts. Showing consideration plays a key role in speech act performance, such as that of 'requesting', 'commiserating' or 'thanking' – consideration may be represented in the forms of 'mitigation of imposition', 'showing a speaker's care and goodwill' or 'intensification of the speaker's gratitude and of the addressee's good deed'. Therefore how successful an utterance is – how polite and appropriate it is – in many cases depends on how consideration of the speaker is communicated. Even if an utterance does not entail any formality, it can be regarded as appropriate as long as it expresses adequate consideration of the speaker in the situation[2]. In this sense a scale that can measure how appropriate an utterance is, judging how consideration is conveyed in an utterance, is necessary.

This necessity of using two scales – one for assessing linguistic features and the other for judging the holistic impression it makes in the context – has led to the employment of the notions of **absolute politeness** and **relative politeness** in this study, which will be discussed later in Section 1.4.

1.3 Deference versus camaraderie

'Deference' (showing respect) and 'camaraderie' (showing solidarity/friendliness) are two major strategies of linguistic politeness for social harmony. These two concepts are realised mainly by lexical and grammatical devices ('deference markers' and 'solidarity markers', which I call 'discernment markers') along with the propositional content. Japan has been known as a society with 'honorific expressions': Matsumoto (1988) and Ide (1989) claimed that *keigo* is one thing missing in Brown & Levinson's theoretical framework for linguistic politeness (1978, 1987). In Japanese society people tend to relate the notion 'politeness' (or its translation *teineisa*) to the use of *keigo*. This means a failure to employ sufficient amount of *keigo* in a proper way leads to the speaker's giving the impression of being impolite and inappropriate. It is for this reason that Japanese younger people's different use of language is likely to evoke a negative impression. *Keigo*, which expresses 'deference' towards the addressee, is a key factor in the discussion of Japanese politeness, but has been discussed rather separately from a pragmatic perspective as stated in Thomas (1995: 150–53). What pragmaticians are interested to see is how a speaker represents his/her intention in the linguistic strategy. Looking only at the presence/absence of honorific forms or the formality/informality of an utterance is not enough to judge if it is truly giving an inconsiderate impression.

'Camaraderie', a concept introduced chiefly by R. Lakoff (e.g. 1990), is another strategy for the establishment or maintenance of social equilibrium. It is an attitude Lakoff described as being expressed through 'first-naming, touching, looking deep into the eyes, and asking *truly caring* questions: "Are you really happy with your life?"' (Lakoff, *ibid*.: 38). It seems this type of 'friendly attitude' is prevailing among younger people in the recent more liberalised society, who employ 'solidarity markers' instead of 'deference markers' to show consideration. 'Camaraderie markers', viz. 'first naming' and other lexicogrammatical devices that show friendliness and closeness between interlocutors, are not supposed to contribute to increasing the degree of **absolute politeness** because of their informal connotations. Still, they could be judged as 'appropriate' in the scale of **relative politeness** especially when they express the 'warmth' of the speaker towards the hearer.

One assumption about the two Japanese age groups is that the older informants are more 'deference-oriented', applying more *keigo* to express their consideration than the younger ones. The younger informants, on the other hand, are supposed to be more 'camaraderie-oriented', applying less *keigo* and more 'camaraderie markers' to show their good intentions than the older ones. A hypothesis that comes from this assumption is, 'The older generation is more polite but there may not be a big difference between the two generations with regard to appropriateness'. This sub-hypothesis will be examined in detail in Chapter 5.

The relation between 'sociolinguistic values', viz. 'deference markers' and 'camaraderie' markers, and 'pragmatic values' to express 'consideration' in the form of linguistic strategies will be presented in Table 2.1.2.3 and discussed in Section 2.1.2.3.

1.4 Politeness and appropriateness scales

In this study of the 'generation gap' in linguistic politeness strategies in contemporary Japanese, I will employ the scales of **politeness** and **appropriateness**. These are useful measures to examine linguistic features and their 'forces' in certain contexts. They relate to **absolute politeness** (a scale based on *pragmalinguistics*) and **relative politeness** (a scale based on *socio-pragmatics*) in Leech's framework (1983; 2002; 2003) respectively. The former measures the 'linguistic features' of utterances, while the latter measures the 'total impression' an utterance makes in context.

In the second-stage data collection, the raters use these scales to evaluate the responses in terms of **politeness** and **appropriateness**. The points scored by the raters using a 5-point scale are calculated to obtain the mean scores of the responses. These scores serve to register a judgement as to which age group is 'more polite' and 'more appropriate' than the other. The raters are also requested to provide a description of the background of their judgement in these two categories. This enables us to learn what factors increase/decrease the degrees of **politeness** and **appropriateness**.

1.5 A spoken DCT with video prompts

In this research, a new research device, 'a spoken DCT with video prompts' is employed. It is a DCT (discourse completion test) with eight different scenarios that (1) elicits spoken responses, not written ones, and (2) is equipped with video prompts. The first function was devised to obtain more natural responses for this research: conventional DCTs in previous pragmatic studies have elicited written responses. The written responses are assumed to be more or less 'manipulated' by the convention for written language and are therefore regarded as 'less authentic' than the responses in natural conversation. The spoken DCT is an attempt to overcome this weakness of conventional DCTs. The second function was devised to allow informants to get immersed in more 'natural' settings. The video prompts contain performers who act as informants' friends, teachers, or an old lady that they happen to meet. The choice of performers on video was made to match the stereotypical images of informants' friends, seniors (*senpai*), juniors (*kohai*) or a restaurant manager. The effectiveness of this new research tool and its advantages over the previous DCTs will be presented in Chapter 4 onwards. It also enabled the researcher to carry out further research using spoken data to investigate the impact of prosody. The results of this experimental study will be provided and discussed in Chapter 6.

1.6 The design of the thesis

Chapter 2 provides the theoretical background of this study. The notion 'politeness' in this study will be specified after examining how it has been treated previously. Some key concepts such as *rapport management, deference, camaraderie, appropriateness* and *constraints* will be explicated to clarify their relevance to this particular study. This study will apply Leech's original and revised *PP* (1983; 2001; 2003) as a theoretical framework for studying linguistic politeness. The *PP* will be discussed in relation to the other main theories in linguistic politeness, such as Brown & Levinson (1978; 1987), Matsumoto (1988), Ide (1989), Fraser (e.g. 1990) and Watts (e.g. 2003). Among them Brown & Levinson's and Watts' frameworks will be treated with due caution, considering their previous and future influence over other studies of linguistic politeness. The difference between Leech's and their frameworks will be focused upon and the advantage of Leech's theory will be presented.

Chapter 3 gives a review of previous studies on Japanese politeness and also indicates the new directions of such studies with an examination of relevant current publications. The key concept *wakimae* (translated as 'discernment' in English) will be discussed in depth in order to explore its implications for a pragmatic study on politeness. This notion has caused controversy over how politeness theories should treat 'relation-acknowledging devices' such as *keigo*, which indicate interlocutors' (relative) social positions. Gender issues in Japanese linguistic politeness will also be presented here, in order to explain the motivation for including this matter as one of the research topics in this study. A description of a pragmatic approach to Japanese politeness with reference to such works as Usami's (2002) and Pizziconi's (2003) as well as my own view will demonstrate a new direction in this area.

Chapter 4 provides the methodological background for the data collection of this study. It starts with a review of the methodologies employed in previous pragmatic studies. The advantages of the new research device of 'a spoken DCT with video prompts' mentioned briefly above will be explicated thoroughly in this chapter. It also provides descriptions of the procedures followed in the first and second-stage data collection. In the first-stage, I obtained spoken responses from Japanese informants with the spoken DCT. 'In-depth guided interviews' were carried out to explore the backgrounds of their responses. In the second-stage, the raters were requested to assess the degrees of **politeness** and **appropriateness** of the responses using a 5-point scale. Interviews with the raters were organised to investigate the factors that determined the levels of these two categories in their evaluation. This study has employed 24 informants in total (12 JHA [6 JHAF and 6 JHAM aged 40-55], 12 JYA [6 JYAF and 6 JYAM aged 18-22]) in the first-stage data collection, and four raters (HFR, HMR, YFR and YMR with the same age bands as the informants) in the second-stage. Their backgrounds are described in detail in this chapter and associated appendices. The DCT of this study has eight different scenarios that allow the researcher to inspect how informants satisfy/dissatisfy the *constraints* in Leech's theory for speech act performance.

Chapter 5 presents the findings of the research and provides quantitative and qualitative analyses of them.. Firstly an overview of the findings obtained through quantitative analysis are presented to discuss the general tendencies of the two age groups and four age-gender groups. After that the results in each item will be inspected from both quantitative and qualitative perspectives. The following is a list of the constraints and speech acts contained in the eight scenarios devised for this research:

Item 01: GENEROSITY (*Place a high value on o's wants*) – offers/invitations;
Item 02: TACT (*Place a low value on s's wants*) – directives (requests);
Item 03: APPROBATION (*Place a high value on o's qualities*) – compliments;
Item 04: MODESTY (*Place a low value on s's qualities*) – self-evaluation (self-depreciation);
Item 05: AGREEMENT (*Place a high value on o's opinions*)/Opinion reticence (*Place a low value on s's opinions*) – agreeing/disagreeing/giving opinions;
Item 06: SYMPATHY (*Place a high value on o's feelings*) – expressing feelings;
Item 07: FEELING-RETICENCE (*Place a low value on s's feelings*)/OBLIGATION (of *o* to *s*) (*Place a low value on o's obligation to s*) – suppressing feelings/response to thanks and apologies;
Item 08: OBLIGATION (of *s* to *o*) (*Place a high value on s's obligation to o*) – apology/thanks.

Chapter 6 describes a supplementary research using spoken data, focusing on the additional 'force' created by prosodic features. Previous studies of politeness have been carried out using only orthographic data. This has prevented researchers from learning about the impact of prosodic features. Since the data for this study was collected in the form of spoken responses, it was possible to conduct an additional experimental study using audio data. I chose ten responses with 'high evaluation' and 'low evaluation' and requested the raters to listen to and evaluate them again. Then interviews were again conducted to probe the factors that made raters change/keep their original assessments. A phonetic analysing instrument *Praat* was employed to explore the causes of the similarities/differences between the first and second ratings by observing relative 'intensity' and 'pitch'. Finally the raters talked about the impressions they had regarding this experimental research with audio data.

Chapter 7 concludes the thesis by summarising the main findings and pointing the way for future research. It provides (a) summary of findings, (b) retrospective evaluation of this research – (i) weaknesses and limitations, (ii) strengths showing advantages over previous studies and (iii) pointers to future research. After looking at the results revealing new facts about the 'generation gap' and 'gender differences' in linguistic politeness strategies, it examines the raters' performance, presents some other noteworthy findings obtained in the qualitative analysis, and evaluates the research methodology applied to this study.

Notes

1. Miller (1967: 289–90, cited in Leech, 1983: 136–37) introduces a case where a high standard of modesty is shown by a Japanese lady in conversation with another Japanese woman about the marvellous garden around her house. In order to show modesty, she keeps refusing to accept any compliments on the garden. Leech observes that '[i]t appears that in Japanese society, and more particularly among Japanese women …, the Modesty Maxim is more powerful than it is as a rule in English-speaking societies…' (Leech, *ibid.*: 137). This may be an old-fashioned and stereotyped example, but it represents the traditional assumptions about Japanese women's sophisticated language use.
2. In saying this, I would like to state that 'polite linguistic features' are still a key factor to make an utterance appropriate. For example, Japanese honorific forms do so by elevating the addressee's or the referent's position and by lowering the interlocutor's.

Chapter 2

Politeness: a survey of theories and approaches

In this chapter I would like to specify the definition and the model of politeness to be employed in this study, and at the same time, to provide an overview of recent theories that have tried to account for politeness from various perspectives. The notion of what has been regarded as politeness varies from one culture to another, from one person to another, and also from one context to another. An attitude, both linguistic and behavioural, that is regarded as polite in one culture, by one person, or in one context may not be considered so in another culture, by another person, or in another situation. Watts (2003) states the following, mentioning the difficulty in employing a uniform criterion to define politeness:

> Most of us are fairly sure we know what we mean when we describe someone's behaviour as 'polite'. To define the criteria with which we apply that description, however, is not quite as easy as we might think. When people are asked what they imagine polite behaviour to be, there is a surprising amount of disagreement. (Watts, *ibid.*: 1)

In the past, pragmatic researchers have approached politeness with their own concepts and definitions of it, without establishing a 'consensus'. Eelen (2001), discussing researchers' various approaches towards politeness, describes how differently politeness has been recognised and treated:

> ... [H]istorically a number of different factors seem to be involved in determining politeness: aspects of social hierarchy (the court) and social status (life in the city), but also a more general notion of 'proper behavioural conduct'. Its meaning is therefore not as straightforwardly clear and simple as may seem at first sight, as during its long historical life, it has gathered a complex of interconnecting associative meanings. (Eelen, *ibid.*: i)

There are cultural, personal and contextual aspects to what politeness means. As for cultural bias, leading politeness theories in the past such as that of Brown & Levinson (henceforth B&L) (1987 [1978]) have been criticised by Japanese researchers such as Matsumoto (1988) and Ide (1989) for being biased towards Western individualistic notions of politeness (for a detailed discussion of this issue see Section 2.2.3.4). With regard to personal differences, Watts (*ibid.*) writes as follows:

> We might make statements like 'He always shows a lot of respect towards his superiors', or 'She's always very helpful and obliging', or 'She speaks really well', or 'He always opens doors for the ladies or helps them on with their coats', etc. Some people feel that polite behaviour is equivalent to socially 'correct' or appropriate behaviour; others consider it to be the hallmark of the cultivated man or woman. Some might characterise a polite person as always being considerate towards other people; others might suggest that a polite person is self-effacing. There are even people who classify polite behaviour negatively, characterising it with such term as 'standoffish', 'haughty', 'insincere', etc.
>
> (Watts, *ibid.*: 1)

As terms for approaching contextual aspects, Leech (1983) uses the concepts of **absolute** and **relative politeness**[1] in order to distinguish the absoluteness of the scale of politeness of an utterance as it appears out of context, and its relativity according to the context. This means that an utterance seemingly polite enough when we hear it or see it on its own can be taken as 'too polite' or 'not polite enough' in a certain context:

> In an absolute sense, [1] *Just be quiet* is less polite than [2] *Would you please be quiet for a moment?* But there are occasions where [1] could be too polite, and other occasions where [2] would not be polite enough. There are even some occasions where [2] would strike one as less polite than [1]; where, for example, [1] was interpreted as a form of banter, and where [2] was used ironically. It is only in a relative sense that we talk of *overpoliteness* and *underpoliteness*.
>
> (Leech, *ibid.*: 102)

In this chapter, I am going to attempt to define the range of what politeness means and establish a comprehensive framework of politeness for this particular study, so that it is possible for me to conduct a rational and consistent discussion based on the same notion of politeness throughout the thesis. I will endeavour to organise a politeness framework for this research into **politeness strategies** in Japanese, mainly employing Leech's original (Leech, 1983) and revised *PP* (Politeness Principle) (Leech, 2001; 2003). Finally in a general survey of linguistic politeness, I will clarify its relationship with other current theories arguing about the nature of politeness systems in social life.

2.1 Specification of 'politeness' in this study

2.1.1 Linguistic politeness and rapport management

Spencer-Oatey, in a recent publication (2000a), presented and discussed her framework of *rapport management* in order to explain the motivational factors in linguistic politeness for social harmony. Her framework of *rapport management* is useful in discussing why and how linguistic politeness is employed to enhance or maintain 'social rapport'. In this publication, however, she avoided using the word 'politeness' because 'the term is so confusing' (Spencer-Oatey, 2000b: 2), a view shared by Watts and Eelen. Instead, she uses the term *rapport management* to refer to 'the use of language to promote, maintain or threaten harmonious social relations' (Spencer-Oatey, 2000b: 3). This up-to-date and innovative attempt explicates the ambiguous concept of what is supposed to contribute to or endanger social rapport. It is also designed to reveal what has not been taken into consideration in the previous pragmatic or sociolinguistic studies concerning a politeness framework. She has introduced certain components of *rapport management* such as (1) '*quality face* – our fundamental desire for people to evaluate us positively in terms of our personal qualities[2]', (2) '*identity face* – our fundamental desire for people to acknowledge and uphold our social identities or roles[3]', (3) '*equity rights* – our fundamental belief that we are entitled to personal consideration from others so that we are treated fairly[4]' and (4) '*association rights* – our fundamental belief that we are entitled to an association with others that is in keeping with the type of relationship that we have with them[5]' (Spencer-Oatey, 2000c: 14). Her framework, using these components, seems to be able to explain more about the relationship and the interactional aspects between personal values and social factors (see Table 2.1.1) than B&L's face management (1987

[1978]), for B&L's notion of face (negative/positive) originates solely in individual motivation, viz. *the wants of every 'competent' adult member* (B&L, 1987: 62). In this sense Spencer-Oatey's framework has been designed to explain social requirements (i.e. norms) for polite behaviour and their prescriptive nature, which Matsumoto (1988) and Ide (1989) claimed to be the main origin of the politeness framework in Japanese society, as well as the factors that relate to *rapport management* at the personal level.

Table 2.1.1 Components of rapport management presented by Spencer-Oatey (2000c)

	face management (personal/social value)	sociality rights management (personal/social entitlements)
personal/independent perspective	quality face (cf. Brown and Levinson's positive face)	equity rights (cf. Brown and Levinson's negative face)
social/interdependent perspective	identity face	association rights

(adapted from Spencer-Oatey, 2000c: 15)

Spencer-Oatey also classifies the directions people take for or against social harmony, naming such directions as *rapport orientation*. The following are the four types of *rapport orientation*:

1. Rapport-enhancement orientation:
   a desire to strengthen or enhance harmonious relations between the interlocutors;
2. Rapport-maintenance orientation:
   a desire to maintain or protect harmonious relations between the interlocutors;
3. Rapport-neglect orientation:
   a lack of concern or interest in the quality of relations between the interlocutors (perhaps because of a focus on self);
4. Rapport-challenge orientation:
   a desire to challenge or impair harmonious relations between the interlocutors.
   (Spencer-Oatey, 2000c: 29–30)

This classification explains where the motives for politeness and impoliteness arise and how they function in *rapport management*. The first and second orientations (*rapport-enhancement* and *rapport maintenance*) appear to involve a polite linguistic attitude and the fourth (*rapport-challenge*) seems to be connected with impolite behaviour, with the third (*rapport-neglect*) possibly being a 'neutral', 'politeness-free' or 'unaware-of-politeness' attitude, as it were. The relationship between this classification of people's motives and the nature of speech acts described by Searle (1979) and Leech (1983) relating to politeness will be discussed later in Section 2.1.4, for these two sets of categories seem to have some significant connections with each other.

Spencer-Oatey also mentions the factors that can be affected by cross-cultural differences when people evaluate the appropriateness of language use and rapport-management outcomes in the following classification:

(1) *Contextual assessment norms*: people from different cultural groups may assess contextual factors somewhat differently;
(2) *Sociopragmatic conventions*: people from different cultural groups may hold differing principles for managing rapport in given contexts;
(3) *Pragmalinguistic conventions*: people from different cultural groups may have differing conventions for selecting strategies and interpreting their use in given context;
(4) *Fundamental cultural values*: research in cross-cultural psychology has identified a small number of universal dimensions of cultural values (e.g. Bond *et al.*, 2000; Gudykunst, 2000 – annotation mine), and found that ethnolinguistic groups differ from each other in terms of their mean location on each of these dimensions;
(5) *Inventory of rapport management strategies*: every language has a very large inventory of rapport-management strategies.   (Spencer-Oatey, 2000c: 42)

Spencer-Oatey has tried to apply this framework of *rapport management* to cross-cultural pragmatic studies to examine and develop her theory and has shown that it is effective in explaining the personal and social factors that caused cross-cultural tensions, particularly in the British–Chinese context (e.g. Spencer-Oatey, 2002; Spencer-Oatey & Xing, 2000).

Spencer-Oatey's framework of *rapport management* thus explicates the background of polite linguistic behaviour. In this study I will utilise her framework partly for examining what motivational factors, both personal and social, affected the production of utterances, and also the scale of politeness that contributes towards social harmony (and also against it[6]). On the other hand, unlike Spencer-Oatey, I will use the term **politeness**, as this study is designed to focus on the linguistic characteristics that control the 'force' of an utterance (i.e. **absolute politeness**, defined by Leech, 1983) and its appropriateness according to the context (i.e. **relative politeness**, defined by Leech, *ibid.*). More specifically, I will make comparisons between four age and gender groups with respect to 'linguistic' politeness strategies. In this sense Spencer-Oatey's *rapport management* is insufficient: it is more effective in sketching out more general socio-psychological backgrounds to social interactions than in investigating what lexicogrammatical strategies control the scale of **politeness** and **appropriateness** in language. In the next section I will describe what **linguistic politeness** represents in this study.

2.1.2 'Politeness' as defined by the GSP in Leech (2001, 2003) and the PP

In this cross-generation and cross-gender study of linguistic politeness strategies in contemporary Japanese, the *PP* (Politeness Principle – originally presented in Leech, 1983; revised and developed in Leech, 2001 and 2003) – will serve as the main framework. Among all the maxims, constraints and their associated qualities in the original and revised *PP*, the *GSP* (Grand Strategy of Politeness: lowering the value of what relates to self as a speaker (s) and raising the value of what relates to the hearer (h) and others (o)) will operate as the key indicator for the scale of **linguistic politeness.** This is because the *GSP* has several strong points over other approaches in explaining the nature of polite linguistic behaviour in such a language as Japanese, in which the humbleness of s and the exaltation of h and o are recognised as fundamental components of **linguistic politeness**. Its versatility can also provide a useful framework to examine the function of Japanese honorifics in an utterance, in which they serve as an integral part of the lexicogrammatical politeness strategies that express s's modesty and exaltation of h and o. It is expected that the *GSP* can encompass Japanese honorifics, one of the controversial issues in discussing Japanese politeness, in the domain of a general study of polite linguistic behaviour in pragmatics.

In the following sections I will present what the original and revised *PP* are, and how they have been devised and developed so that I can clarify what **politeness** and its associated concepts mean and which direction this study will be taking.

2.1.2.1 The original PP

Leech's pioneering work, Principles of Pragmatics (henceforth *POP*) (1983: 104–151), presented a comprehensive framework of politeness, in terms of a Politeness Principle (or *PP*), based on speech act types and their illocutionary forces. The *PP*, described in terms of its component *maxims*, is consequently directed towards the illocutionary goals of speech acts. Leech classifies illocutionary functions into four categories as follows:

(a) COMPETITIVE: The illocutionary goal competes with the social goal; *eg* ordering, asking, demanding, begging.
(b) CONVIVIAL: The illocutionary goal coincides with the social goal; *eg* offering, inviting, greeting, thanking, congratulating.
(c) COLLABORATIVE: The illocutionary goal is indifferent to the social goal; *eg* asserting, reporting, announcing, instructing.
(d) CONFLICTIVE: The illocutionary goal conflicts with the social goal; *eg* threatening, accusing, cursing, reprimanding. (Leech, *ibid*.: 104)

Of these four speech act categories, politeness mainly concerns the COMPETITIVE and CONVIVIAL. As the descriptions above show, politeness strategies arise where the illocutionary goal 'competes with' or 'coincides with' the social goal of establishing and maintaining good rapport with others. There are two different directions of politeness strategies: (a) mitigation of the discourteous nature of COMPETITIVE speech acts; (b) intensification or clarification of the courteous nature of CONVIVIAL speech acts. The COLLABORATIVE category does not require politeness in most cases[7], and 'politeness is out of the question' in the CONFLICTIVE category because 'conflictive illocutions are, by their nature, designed to cause offence' (Leech, *ibid*.: 105).

It should be noted that the ways in which these speech acts are performed are deeply affected by *s*'s intention – whether it is oriented towards (1) *rapport-enhancement*, (2) *rapport-maintenance*, (3) *rapport-neglect* or (4) *rapport-challenge* (Spencer-Oatey, 2000c: 29–30). The performance of the speech acts classified in the CONVIVIAL category is designed to achieve (1) *rapport-enhancement* or (2) *rapport-maintenance* in general, thanks to their intrinsically polite or face-enhancing nature[8]. On the other hand, the performance of COMPETITIVE speech acts can be any of (2) *rapport-maintenance*, (3) *rapport-neglect* or (4) *rapport-*

challenge, according to *s*'s intention: the mitigation will take place if *s* wants to make his/her request or demand less offensive in order to maintain rapport; no mitigation will be carried out if *s* neglects or wants to challenge the harmonious relationship with *o*. This motivational aspect applies to COLLABORATIVE and CONFLICTIVE utterances as well in a limited sense (e.g. in the choice of adjectives describing what relates to *h* and *o*). After presenting these observations, notwithstanding, I would like to point out that speech act performance in real life situations is more complex. It consists of a combination of these four categories according to *s*'s design for the achievement of his/her intention. In this sense these four categories are 'rough-and-ready' and somewhat oversimplified, but they are a good starting point for classifying the directions of speech act types. The examination of real data in this study will demonstrate how people perform these speech acts in real life.

The *PP* consists of six main maxims (Tact, Generosity, Approbation, Modesty, Agreement, Sympathy) and other sub-maxims, which are designed to perform the illocutionary functions listed above. Here are the original orientations of the six main maxims:

TACT – (a) Minimize cost to *o* (b) Maximize benefit to *o*;
GENEROSITY – (a) Minimize benefit to *s* (= self, speaker) (b) Maximize cost to *s*;
APPROBATION – (a) Minimize dispraise of *o* (b) Maximize praise of *o*;
MODESTY – (a) Minimize praise of *s* (b) Maximize dispraise of *s*;
AGREEMENT – (a) Minimize disagreement between *s* and *o* (b) Maximize agreement between *s* and *o*;
SYMPATHY – (a) Minimize antipathy between *s* and *o* (b) Maximize sympathy between *s* and *o*.   (Leech, *ibid*.: 132)

It should be noted, however, as Leech has always insisted, that these maxims apply only with 'all other things being equal': viz. they have to be applied up to the point where they do not cause problems with other pragmatic principles/maxims.

Politeness scales and the distinction between **absolute** and **relative politeness** are other characteristics of Leech's framework. For example, the following three **politeness scales** are employed to measure how someone has succeeded in showing his/her 'tact' to make a request polite. They are:

1. The COST-BENEFIT SCALE
   (on which is estimated the cost or benefit of the proposed action A to s or h)
2. The OPTIONALITY SCALE
   (on which illocutions are ordered according to the amount of choice which s allows to h)
3. The INDIRECTNESS SCALE
   (on which, from s's point of view, illocutions are ordered with respect to the length of the path (in terms of means-ends analysis) connecting the illocutionary act to its illocutionary goal)   (adapted from Leech, *ibid.*: 123)

These scales are designed for the TACT MAXIM, but it is possible to explain a wide range of linguistic phenomena concerning politeness by applying them to other maxims.

Regarding Leech's distinction between **absolute** and **relative politeness**, **absolute politeness** is assessed with respect to *pragmalinguistic* qualities and **relative politeness** with respect to 'socio-pragmatic' qualities. *Pragmalinguistics* is mainly concerned with the lexical and grammatical features of illocutions. Therefore the scale of **politeness** of this category is estimated by means of an 'absolute' scale. As mentioned earlier, Leech states that an illocution 'can be taken as "overpolite" or "underpolite" under some circumstances', for the scale of **politeness** 'is related to the category of "relative politeness" and to "socio-pragmatics"' (Leech, *ibid.*: 102). This means that **relative politeness**, viz. *socio-pragmatics*, is related to **situational appropriateness**, a matter of social psychology, and that polite linguistic features such as the use of honorifics or indirectness (as measured in terms of **absolute politeness**) do not necessarily give a good impression to the hearer.

2.1.2.2 The renewed PP

After examining such qualities of the original *PP* stated above, Leech restated the treatment of politeness in it, explaining the motivation for this as follows.

> As nearly 20 years have passed since I wrote *POP*, it is appropriate for me to attempt a restatement, taking account of the large amount of research on politeness which has taken place in the mean time.   (Leech, 2001: 109)

He put forward the *GSP* (Grand Strategy of Politeness), subsuming all maxims, which goes as follows:

<u>Grand Strategy of Politeness</u>: In order to be polite, *s* communicates meanings which
    place a high value on what pertains to *o*
    place a low value on what pertains to *s*

(adapted from Leech, 2003: 108)

In stating the above, Leech clearly presented two directions of politeness: a **positive direction** (= **positive politeness**) and a **negative direction** (= **negative politeness**)[9]. According to my interpretation, the **positive direction** can be understood as the performance of *FEA*s (face-enhancing acts) to present or intensify good qualities expressed in some speech acts, whereas the **negative direction** can be comprehended as a performance of *FSA*s (face-saving acts) to mitigate the intrinsically face-threatening qualities of the speech acts called *FTA*s (face-threatening acts) by B&L. These concepts, however, should be clearly distinguished from positive and negative politeness as used by B&L (1987 [1978]), which are used to suggest other aspects of politeness. The differences between these concepts will be discussed later in Sections 2.1.4 and 2.2.3.1.

In the second version of the revised *PP* (Leech, 2003), Leech replaced the word 'maxim' by 'constraint' in order to talk in a less confusing way of how people follow the *GSP* (Leech, *ibid*.: 108), for 'maxim' has a normative implication and can be misunderstood as if some externally-imposed rules are to be obeyed or followed. The term 'maxim', originally used by the philosopher Grice in presenting his Cooperative Principle, has often been disfavoured or misunderstood by linguists or social scientists. It should also be noted here that Leech's motivation for subsuming all his maxims under a 'Grand Strategy of Politeness' was to show that all the maxims were part of a single generalisation; and therefore to combat a criticism made by B&L and others, that his maxims were unconstrained, and that he was inclined to set up new maxims whenever needed. The table below summarises the newly categorised 'constraints' in the revised *PP*:

Table 2.1.2.2 Summary of constraints to pursue the *GSP*

Constraint	part of related pair of constraints	label for this constraint	typical speech act type(s)
1. place a high value on *o*'s wants	*Generosity/Tact*	Generosity	commissives
2. place a low value on *s*'s wants	*Generosity/Tact*	Tact	directives
3. place a high value on *o*'s qualities	*Approbation/Modesty*	Approbation	compliments
4. place a low value on *s*'s qualities	*Approbation/Modesty*	Modesty	self-evaluation
5. place a high value on *s*'s obligation to *o*		Obligation (of *s* to *o*)	apology, thanks
6. place a low value on *o*'s obligation to *s*		Obligation (of *o* to *s*)	response to thanks and apologies
7. place a high value on *o*'s opinions		Agreement	agreeing, disagreeing
8. place a low value on *s*'s opinions		Opinion-reticence	giving opinions
9. place a high value on *o*'s feelings		Sympathy	expressing feelings
10. place a low value on *s*'s feelings		Feeling-reticence	suppressing feelings

(adapted from Leech, 2003: 109–112)

By looking at the list above, we can see how the *GSP* is pursued in different speech acts. I would like to note that these strategies consist of either the **negative direction** (*s*'s humbleness) or the **positive direction** (*h*'s and *o*'s exaltation).

2.1.2.3 The definition of 'politeness' in this study: 'politeness', 'deference', 'camaraderie', 'appropriateness' and 'the scale of politeness'

As mentioned earlier, the definition of the term 'politeness' varies very widely. The problem of terminology was described in Watts *et al.* (1992b: 1) as this: 'Questions about how politeness should be defined, the ways in which it is realised in different cultural frameworks and the validity of a universal theory of politeness are of interest to a wide range of social science researchers…'. As Spencer-Oatey uses the term *rapport-management* to avoid the problem how to manage the definition of politeness, other researchers have used other terms to describe linguistic politeness. Watts classifies such alternative terminology in the past as 'emotive communication' (Arndt and Janney, 1985), 'tact' (Janney and Arndt, 1992; Leech, 1983) or 'politic behaviour' (Watts, 1989; 1992), 'but', he maintains, ' "politeness" always seem to creep back in' (Watts, 2003: 13).

In this study I will use the term politeness, rather than other terms, in order to describe linguistic features that are employed to represent linguistic politeness. Instead of expanding the range of its definition, I would like to concentrate on the fundamental characteristics of politeness so that the framework can explain what is happening in various contexts. After examining the *GSP* as above, I would like to define 'politeness' in this study as 'the linguistic behaviour represented by the two directions of the strategies of the *GSP* by Leech (2001; 2003): **negative direction** (low *s*-values) and **positive direction** (high *h*/*o*-values)'. This definition of politeness is illustrated by Figure 2.1.2.3-1 below.

Figure 2.1.2.3-1 The definition of 'politeness': positive and negative directions

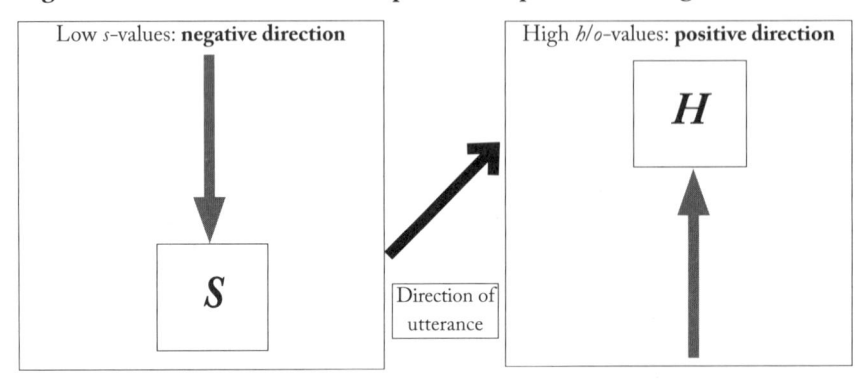

Low *s*-values: **negative direction**	High *h*/*o*-values: **positive direction**
↓ *S*	*H* ↑
	Direction of utterance

The two directions of linguistic politeness above are also supposed to be connected with the desire on the part of *s* for *rapport-management* defined by Spencer-Oatey, mainly for (1) *rapport-enhancement orientation* and (2) *rapport-maintenance orientation* (Spencer-Oatey, 2000c: 29).

I would like to turn to the issue of other 'kindred' notions associated with politeness – 'deference' and 'camaraderie' – these have often been regarded as part of what constitutes politeness and have frequently caused difficulties regarding how to deal with them in the same framework. Here are two descriptions of such difficulties or problems in treating these two notions in the study of politeness, the first being Thomas' on 'deference' and the second Leech's on 'camaraderie':

> Deference is frequently equated with politeness, particularly in discussions of Japanese. ... It refers to the respect we show to other people by virtue of their higher status, greater age, etc. Politeness is a more general matter of showing (or rather, of giving the appearance of showing) consideration to others. ...

> As Ide (1989: 229–30) discussing Matsumoto (1987) notes, the choice of the honorific or plain form of the copula is not a matter of individual choice, it is 'an **obligatory** choice among variants' (my emphasis), reflecting the speaker's 'sense of place or role in a given situation according to social conventions'. The reason why I say that deference has little to do with pragmatics is that generally, unless the speaker deliberately wishes to flout the behavioural norms of a given society (and is prepared to accept the consequences of so doing), the speaker has no *choice* as to whether to use the deferent form or not – usage is dictated by sociolinguistic norms. ... If the use of a particular form is obligatory in a particular situation, ... it is of no significance pragmatically; it is only when there is a choice, or when a speaker attempts to bring about change by challenging the current norms, that the use of deferent or non-deferent forms becomes of interest to the pragmaticist. ... It is also worth noting that the use of a deferent form does not *in and of itself* convey respect.
> (Thomas, 1995: 150–153)

> Here I disagree with B&L (1978: 107–118), who define positive politeness so broadly as to include claims of common ground or in-group membership. I would say such strategies, such as the use of familiar forms of address, have the effect to reducing social distance, so that P [*i.e. relative power*] and D [*i.e. social distance*] are so small that the *PP* applies minimally if at all. This assertion of camaraderie or in-groupness with *h* may have one effect which resembles positive politeness: it promotes concord or conviviality. But the reasoning behind it is different: instead of showing high evaluation or deference to *h*, *s* claims solidarity with *h*, making deference unnecessary but expressing attitudinal warmth. Hence I am defining 'politeness' more narrowly than B&L to exclude this.   (Leech, 2003: 113, annotation mine)

The claims above state that it can be problematic to include 'deference' and 'camaraderie' in the definition and the study of politeness.

The involvement of 'deference' in the framework of politeness can be traced back to R. Lakoff (1975, 1979) or B&L (1978, 1987), according to Matsumoto (1988: 408). Since then the concept of 'deference', when discussed in the framework of politeness, has often been related to the Japanese concept of '*wakimae*' – i.e. 'one's sense of place or role in a given situation according to social conventions' and 'the practice of polite behavior according to social conventions' (Ide, 1989: 230) – translated as 'discernment' in English.

The concepts *wakimae/discernment* and *volition* are the keys to understanding the borders of politeness in the Japanese and the western context. Ide (1989) states that the western politeness frameworks are *volition* based, in that the strategies to perform linguistic politeness are volitional. On the other hand, in Japanese one is supposed to express one's place in the social context using appropriate honorifics in order to show *s*'s polite intention. Therefore even a statement in the TV weather forecast, such as '*Asu-wa hare-desu*' <It will be fine tomorrow>, contains an element of politeness in the use of the formal or polite form of a copula, **desu**[10]. This type of speech act is categorised as COLLABORATIVE as described above, and the polite realisation of this category in Japanese has few or no counterparts in English.

Languages that contain honorifics, such as Japanese, involve a sense of politeness when their speakers perform speech acts of this category by the use of deferential/formal lexical items, and this is where a cross-cultural difference arises. For example, Matsumoto demonstrates three levels of politeness in sentences that report the same content, 'Today is Saturday' as follows:

(a) *Kyoo*   *wa*   *doyoobi*   **da.**
    today   TOP   Saturday   COP-PLAIN
(b) *Kyoo*   *wa*   *doyoobi*   **desu.**
    today   TOP   Saturday   COP-POLITE
(c) *Kyoo*   *wa*   *doyoobi*   **degozai masu.**
    today   TOP   Saturday   COP-SUPER POLITE

(adapted from Matsumoto, 1988: 415)

Japanese speakers can or must show politeness/formality when they report something in a formal situation or to a person of higher status, employing 'relation-acknowledging devices' (Matsumoto, *ibid.*: 414) such as **desu** or **masu**.

'Camaraderie' has been introduced mainly by R. Lakoff, who includes *distance*, *deference* and *camaraderie* in the strategies of politeness (R. Lakoff, 1990). She describes the characteristics of 'camaraderie' and its origin as in the following:

Modern camaraderie probably began in California as an outgrowth of the human potential movement of the 1960s and 1970s. For a while it was a bane to visiting Easterners, who were confounded by the Californian's appearance of good fellowship and deep caring: the immediate first-naming, touching, looking deep into the eyes, and asking *truly caring* questions: "Are you really happy with your life?" (R. Lakoff, *ibid.*: 38)

The attitudes described in the above statement have been included in the strategies in B&L's 'positive politeness' (1987): 'Notice, attend to H', 'use in-group identity markers – address forms, use of in-group language or dialect…'.

Daly *et al.* (2004) present a rather radical view on what could be included in the politeness framework in their article, <u>Expletives as solidarity signals in FTAs on the factory floor</u>. According to their claim, an expletive *fuck*, used by the members of a male factory working team in New Zealand, can function as a solidarity marker and therefore it can be recognised as one form of 'positive politeness' (defined by B&L, 1987). It seems likely that offensive or vulgar expressions connote solidarity and friendliness in a certain 'activity type' (Levinson, 1992), as long as it does not give offence to the hearer. This phenomenon seems to relate to Watts' (2003) and Eelen's (2001) arguments on *politeness1* – the lay notion of politeness – discussed in Section 2.1.3. (Watts states that *politeness1* is not necessarily polite.) Even so, and as a further example of the discrepancy that Ide *et al.* (1992) proved between what Japanese and American informants related to the word politeness, a claim that taboo expletives can contribute to politeness would be distasteful to many Japanese. Japanese people usually relate 'respect' or 'courtesy' to politeness. On the other hand, Americans may think this is acceptable as they tend to associate politeness with 'friendliness'.

One thing these two concepts, 'deference' and 'camaraderie', have in common is that their lexical/morphological features are related to sociolinguistic parameters of distance and solidarity, not to pragmatic values (i.e. illocutionary goal achievement). Following Ide's distinction between 'discernment' and 'volition' (1989), I would like to include the qualities of 'deference' and 'camaraderie' in the former ('discernment'), for they are employed to express the speaker's position in relation to the hearer (*wakimae*); and 'pragmatic' values or strategies in the latter ('volition' – the pursuit of illocutionary goals, which are part of the intentional use of politeness strategies). Table 2.1.2.3 below is my tentative summary of the relationship between 'politeness' represented by the *GSP*, 'deference', and 'camaraderie'. I employ the concepts 'pragmatic value' to indicate 'illocutionary goal achievement' and 'sociolinguistic value' to specify 'deference/camaraderie markers' based on *discernment* in this summary[11].

My standpoint concerning 'camaraderie' and 'politeness' is expressed in my earlier work as follows:

> Development of a sense of 'camaraderie' in liberalised and democratised society seems to be serving as a drive towards such linguistic change. Camaraderie, in my sense, is something different from politeness represented by the *GSP*. This notion or attitude is quite popular among friends or in closed groups: 'We are close friends without distance. So we don't need politeness'. Consequently this leads to the emphasis of in-group membership and the warmth of close relationship. (Suzuki, 2004: 299)

Consequently, this kind of politeness in this study can be recognised as *illocutionary* or *pragmatic politeness*, which can include deferential elements of some lexical and grammatical devices such as honorific prefixes, suffixes and expressions in Japanese; but it generally excludes 'solidarity markers' such as first-naming or the use of expletives as they are supposed to promote 'friendliness', not politeness. However, remembering that **relative politeness** concerns the 'holistic impression' of a speech act, I think it is possible to use an utterance which is 'polite' in a holistic sense while containing solidarity markers, which to some degree contribute to **relative politeness** – e.g. *Could you tell me the time, love?/You look gorgeous, darling!*

At the *politeness2* level[12], I use the *GSP* as a 'pragmatic theory of politeness'. I also acknowledge that there are volitional (i.e. pragmatic) components and sociolinguistic factors ('honorifics' and also 'camaraderie'), which have to be recognized at the *politeness2* level. But at the *politeness1* level, where we deal with the lay person's notions of politeness, these three strands may contribute to the overall 'holistic' impression of politeness that I investigate when I conduct my informant investigations. (The informants and raters, of course, have to deal with *politeness1*.)

The *GSP* can only account for part of the *politeness1* data, even if it may be a major part. This is acknowledged even by Leech, who argues that other principles

Table 2.1.2.3 'Politeness', 'deference' and 'camaraderie'

showing consideration towards *o*: POLITENESS/DEFERENCE/CAMARADERIE		
Leech's *GSP* (Politeness) applies to both columns below (*politeness2* – to be explicated in 2.1.3): (1) *'Place a high value on what relates to o'* (2) *'Place a low value on what relates to s'*		
	Pragmatic value (Politeness in general) [Volition/Strategy based]	
Sociolinguistic value 1 (Politeness in the hierarchy-sensitive situation) [Discernment markers – lexicogrammatical devices] **Deference/Honorific orientation** <Distance increasing in nature> Oriented towards - formality - larger horizontal / vertical social distance - language elaboration with the use of 'deference markers' such as *"Mr Suzuki, …"*	Illocutionary goal achievement 1) Intensification orientation [Performance of FEAs (*face-enhancing acts*)] Oriented towards - emphasis on good values / BENEFITS - language clarification (Directness – Imperative etc.) 2) Mitigation orientation [Performance of FSAs (*face-saving acts*)] Oriented towards - minimisation of face-threatening values / COSTS - language elaboration (Indirectness - Interrogative etc.)	*Sociolinguistic value 2* (Rapport-managing behaviour in the sense of solidarity, friendliness) [Discernment markers – lexicogrammatical devices] **Camaraderie/Solidarity orientation** <Distance diminishing in nature> Oriented towards - informality - smaller horizontal / vertical social distance - language simplification with the use of 'camaraderie markers' such as *"Hey, buddy, …"* Note: 'Banter' is one aspect of this.
Politeness1 (to be explained in 2.1.3) is a holistic interpretation taking account of all 3 factors above, and possibly other factors (e.g. prosody) as well.		
*Honorifics, when used merely to show the relationship between *s* and *h* or *o* and do no not convey any sense of respect, should be treated rather as **social index markers**, not as **politeness markers** according to Ide (1989). I will include honorifics of other kinds in this study of politeness.	← LEXICAL & MORPHOLOGICAL DEVICES INDEPENDENT OF POLITENESS →	*Camaraderie/solidarity markers cannot be explained by the *GSP*, for they usually convey intrinsic politeness-absent implication (especially 'expletives'). They should be treated as **social index markers**, not as **politeness markers** ('We're friends, so we can be impolite this much' – Daly *et al.*'s (2004) view on expletives and 'positive politeness'.)

– Banter ('mock impoliteness') – which is a manifestation of camaraderie – and Irony ('mock politeness') are in play. These principles, on the face of it, interfere with our impressions of politeness, although they are 'higher order principles' which build up the *GSP* (Leech, 1983: 142–144). Quite a lot of my discussion of the results of this research will reveal that these other 'interfering factors' come between the theory of the *GSP* and the actual way people behave and judge others' behaviour in terms of politeness.

A broad study of politeness, in my view, is that which deals with (1) pragmatic values such as 'illocutionary goals' and 'volitional strategies' and (2) sociolinguistic values such as deferential lexical devices such as honorifics in Japanese and other languages (i.e. '*wakimae/discernment* markers'). Both the 'volitional' and '*wakimae*' aspects of politeness (in my definition) tend to maintain or increase social distance between *s* and *h* or *o*. I think '*wakimae/discernment* markers' of 'camaraderie' could be involved in the study of politeness as a related issue in a broader sense (especially in the context of American society), but I will treat them separately in this study in order to distinguish them from politeness as it is indicated by the *GSP*. In this sense, it is necessary to classify these interrelated issues into suitable categories as I did in the Table 2.1.2.3 above.

These concepts are interrelated because all of them have a function in promoting *rapport-enhancement* and *rapport-maintenance* in the larger framework of individual-social interaction under the common value, 'consideration towards others'. 'Deference' shows consideration towards *h/o* by lowering *s*'s position and elevating *h*'s/*o*'s; 'camaraderie' does so by minimising the distance between *s* and *h/o* and so creating solidarity; and 'pragmatic values' intensify the good qualities and mitigate the face-threatening aspects of an utterance to achieve an 'illocutionary goal' by showing consideration. The reason why there has been confusion over treating these concepts in the same framework of politeness seems to lie here. But if they are classified into proper categories and a larger framework of *rapport management* is applied, their relationship seems more straightforward and manageable.

This framework of 'consideration' for *rapport management* also leads to **the scale of politeness**, which relates the degree of politeness (**absolute politeness**) to that of appropriateness (**relative politeness**)[13]. The following Figure 2.1.2.3-2 is my tentative overview of **the scale of politeness**.

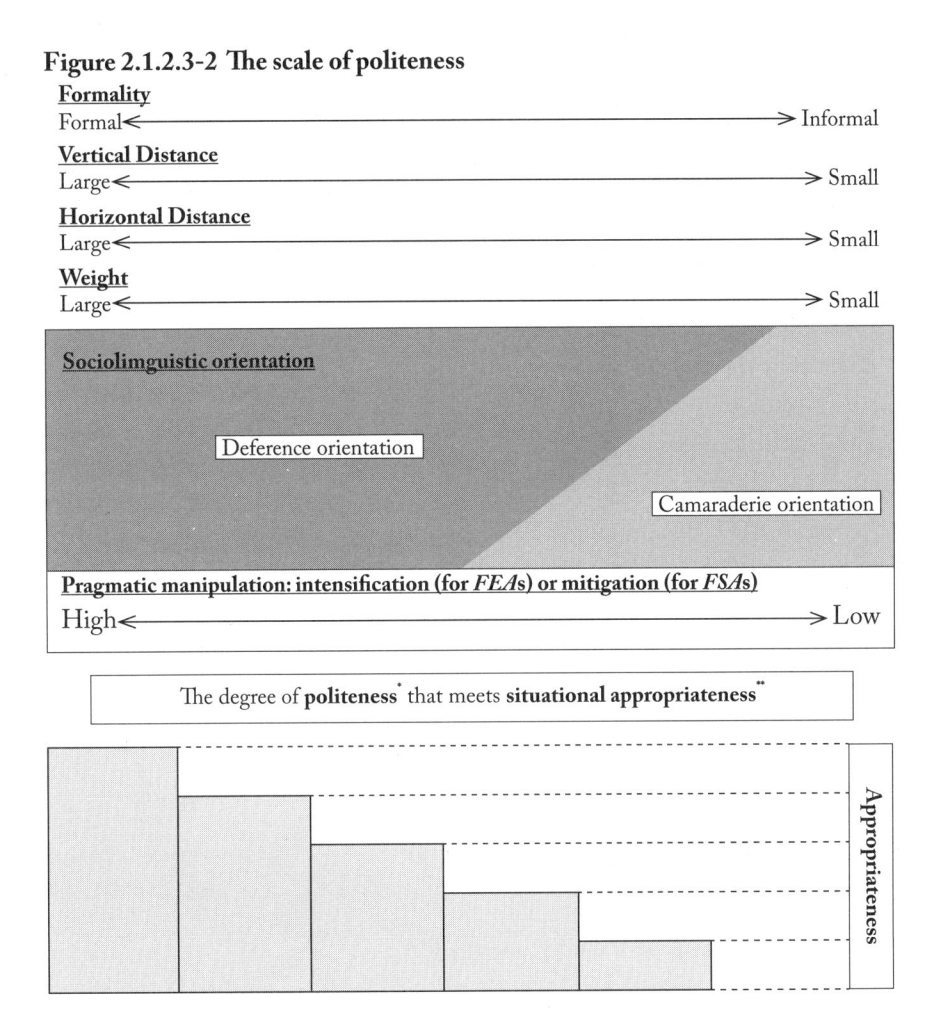

Figure 2.1.2.3-2 The scale of politeness

Formality
Formal ←————————————————————→ Informal

Vertical Distance
Large ←————————————————————→ Small

Horizontal Distance
Large ←————————————————————→ Small

Weight
Large ←————————————————————→ Small

| **Sociolinguistic orientation** |
| Deference orientation |
| Camaraderie orientation |
| **Pragmatic manipulation: intensification (for *FEA*s) or mitigation (for *FSA*s)** |
| High ←————————————————————→ Low |

The degree of **politeness*** that meets **situational appropriateness****

(bar chart showing decreasing Appropriateness)

* **Politeness** corresponds to **absolute politeness** (vertical scale in the diagram)
** **Situational appropriateness** corresponds to **relative politeness** (horizontal scale in the diagram)

This figure is designed to demonstrate in a limited sense that an optimal level of **absolute politeness**, which is represented by lexicogrammatical strategies including the use of deference or camaraderie markers, is decided by the scale of **relative politeness**, which correlates with such factors as 'formality', 'vertical/horizontal distance between *s* and *h/o*' and 'weight' of the issue at stake. 'Formality' means how formal/informal the situation of the conversation is. 'Vertical distance' is an indicator of the asymmetrical relationship between *s* and *h* (in terms of status, power, role, age etc. – cf. B&L's *P*). 'Horizontal distance' is a scale of intimacy and familiarity *s* and *h* feels towards each other (cf. B&L's *D*)[14]. 'Weight' suggests 'how large is the benefit, the cost, the favour, the obligation, etc.' (Leech, 2003: 115) of the issue at stake (cf. B&L's *R*). It should be noted that the suitable degree of politeness is not straightforwardly calculated as the figure above may suggest. For example, a small 'horizontal distance' between *s* and *h* may override other factors such as 'formality' or 'weight' and it can make utterances in this context less polite.

I mean by **the scale of politeness** that the norm of **relative politeness** changes in accordance with the framework of the 'activity type' (Levinson, 1992)[15], which controls situational appropriateness: e.g. students are supposed to take on a formal and deferential attitude towards their teachers in formal settings, but it may not be the case when they are engaging in informal and friendly conversation with the same teachers. It appears that the degree of **absolute politeness** is subject to this change in the norm of **relative politeness**. People seem to choose the suitable level of **absolute politeness** (i.e. lexicogrammatical features of an utterance) that will be regarded as appropriate by the participants in a linguistic interaction. Just as people do 'code-switching' when talking to a person from a different region or social-network, they 'code-switch' politeness criteria, taking into consideration such variables as the formality/informality of the situation, horizontal or vertical distance from *h* (their friends/superiors), or the issue at stake in the conversation – not only these variables themselves but also the position on them.

2.1.2.4 The advantage of the GSP and the PP

In this section, the strong points of the *GSP* and the *PP* (original and revised) will be presented to justify their application as the theoretical framework of this study. Firstly I will look at the strong points of the original *PP*.

Gu (1990) has pointed out the following three advantages of the *PP*: (a) the provision of the missing link between the CP (*The Cooperative Principle* – Grice, 1975) and the problem of how to relate sense to force; (b) the distinction between relative politeness and absolute politeness; (c) the emphasis on the normative aspects of politeness (Gu, *ibid*.: 242–43).

Chen (1993) also supports the *PP* after examining data concerning the politeness strategies American English speakers and Chinese speakers employed to respond to compliments as follows:

> To summarize, I have applied three theories, Brown and Levinson's, Gu's, and Leech's, to the analysis of the AES's [American English speakers'] and the CS's [Chinese speakers'] strategies of responding to compliments and found that neither Brown and Levinson nor Gu can account for all strategies of the two groups. Leech, on the other hand, offers a framework in which all strategies can be explained. (Chen, *ibid.*: 64, annotation mine)

Thomas (1995) also supports the original *PP* as in the following, while pointing out some weaknesses about it as discussed below:

> ... it allows us, better than any of the other approaches discussed here, to make specific cross-cultural comparisons and (more importantly) to **explain** cross-cultural differences in the perception of politeness and the use of politeness strategies. (Thomas, *ibid.*: 167–68)

There have been several weak points about the original *PP*, however. B&L (1987), Fraser (1990) and Thomas (1995) criticise the way the number of maxims in the original *PP* was expanded. Thomas maintains that 'there appears to be no motivated way of restricting the number of maxims' and '[t]his makes the theory inelegant, at worst virtually unfalsifiable' (Thomas, *ibid.*: 167). Ide also claims the *PP* 'could not avoid an ethnocentric bias toward Western languages and the Western perspective' (Ide, 1989: 224), having examined Leech's (1983), B&L's (1978, 1987) and Lakoff's (1973, 1975) frameworks and their claims about 'universality'. Spencer-Oatey (2000c,) and Spencer-Oatey & Jiang (2003) also maintain that 'the politeness maxims all seem to have "universal valences"', presenting their statement as follows:

> ... with regard to *modesty-pride*, Leech implies 'the more modest the better', and with regard to *agreement-disagreement*, he implies 'the more agreement the better". Yet in different cultures, and in different speech contexts within the same culture, we contend that different options or points on the continuum could be favoured. (Spencer-Oatey & Jiang, 2003: 1635)

While introducing these weaknesses claimed by other researchers, I would like to state that they can be overcome by the detailed analysis of the original and the revised *PP*. As for the first claim made by B&L, Fraser and Thomas, Leech has subsumed all the maxims under the *GSP* – therefore such claims can be combated. The second by Ide can be rebutted by the fact that the *GSP* can include Japanese honorifics or '*wakimae*' markers in its framework (mentioned in Suzuki, 2006). As for the third by Spencer-Oatey and Spencer-Oatey & Jiang, this claim can be 'a misunderstanding of the notion of a maxim' (maintained by Geoffrey Leech in personal communication). He has insisted, as mentioned in Section 2.1.2.1, that his maxims operate *ceteris paribus* i.e. other things permitting: they are understood to be applied up to the point where they do not cause problems with other pragmatic principles/maxims.

Leech (2001, 2003), taking into consideration such criticisms and the datedness of employing a 'maxim-base approach' following Grice's CP, reformulated the *PP*, setting the *GSP* at the centre of the framework and modifying the maxims in the previous structure into 'constraints' in performing the *GSP* in social linguistic interactions[16]. Leech states the background of substituting the term 'maxim' with the concept 'constraint' as follows:

> ... it is probably safer to talk of **constraints** which will be observed by people following the GSP. I label and define these constraints below, using such terms as 'Tact' and 'Modesty'. But I avoid using terms like 'the Tact Constraint' as much as possible, as these are not a set of distinct constraints or maxims, but rather variant manifestations of the same super-constraint, the GSP. (Leech, 2003: 108)

With this modification it has become possible to explore the background, motivational factors and other elements that function as 'constraints' in illocutions in relation to the *GSP*. The constraints may vary from one context to another (or from one culture to another) as Spencer-Oatey asserts, but what types of constraints emerge in a certain situation can be examined within the framework of the *GSP* of the revised *PP*.

As for the failure of applicability to the cross-cultural contexts, claimed by Ide (1989), a survey of such constraints will reveal the intercultural variations of politeness strategies under the *GSP*. My findings about the applicability of the *GSP* in the study of cross-cultural linguistic politeness strategies in Japanese and British English in my pilot study data (Suzuki, 2006) have supported the *GSP* for such a purpose. Indeed, Leech's *GSP* is more suitable for the study of Japanese politeness than B&L's or other theories. The two directions of the *GSP* (i.e. **negative** and **positive**) have turned out to be especially effective in explaining the function of Japanese honorifics. (However the *GSP* may not be applicable to a study of politeness where camaraderie is thought to be included in the category of 'politeness'.)

2.1.3 'Politeness1', 'politeness2' and 'politic behaviour'

In this section I will discuss three newly introduced and prevailing concepts related to politeness, viz. *politeness1*, *politeness2*, and *politic behaviour*, mentioning both Watts' framework and Eelen's explication of them. They are the terms designed to differentiate the common notion of politeness among ordinary people (e.g. as a social-norm for polite behaviour) – *politeness1* – and politeness as defined and developed in the theoretical frameworks of pragmaticians up to the present – *politeness2*. The term *politic behaviour* was devised by Watts: 'politeness' is defined as a salient or marked linguistic feature, whereas *politic behaviour* is labelled as the ongoing negotiation between *s* and *h* for the appropriate linguistic attitude, non-salient or unmarked, for social equilibrium.

The distinction between *politeness1* and *politeness2* originates in Watts *et al.* (1992b), in which they are called 'first-order politeness' and 'second-order politeness'. Eelen then applied the terms *politeness1* and *politeness2* to these two concepts in his work on recent politeness theories (Eelen, 2001). Watts *et al.*, in the introduction to their work Politeness in Language: Studies in its History, Theory and Practice (Watts *et al.*, 1992b), state that 'first-order politeness' is 'the various ways in which polite behaviour is perceived and talked about by members of socio-cultural groups'. In other words, it 'encompasses commonsense notions of politeness'. In contrast, 'second-order politeness' can be taken as 'a theoretical construct, a term within a theory of social behaviour and language usage' (Watts *et al. ibid.*: 3). In short, *politeness1* is a 'folk' or 'lay' interpretation of politeness among people, and *politeness2* is a 'sociolinguistic theory of politeness' (Watts, 2003: 4).

Watts discusses the relationship between *politeness1* and *politeness2*, especially in terms of how *politeness2* should incorporate *politeness1* in its framework as follows:

> ... investigating first-order politeness is the only valid means of developing a social theory of politeness. Does this then mean that a second-order theory of politeness, a theory of politeness2, should only concern itself with lay notions of politeness? The answer to this question is equivocal: yes and no. Yes, in the sense that a scientific theory of a lay term must take that lay term in lay usage as its central focus, but no, in the sense that a theory of politeness should not attempt to 'create' a superordinate, universal term that can then be applied universally to any socio-cultural group at any point in time. ...
>
> (Watts, 2003: 9)

From the above, Watts' standpoint can be summarised as follows: (1) theoretical frameworks for politeness should be available to examine and investigate what is going on in people's everyday verbal interaction in any context; (2) yet, their creators should not claim 'universality' for them, as has been done by previous pragmatic researchers such as B&L. Following this same line, Eelen maintains that '... although politeness2 should no doubt be *about* politeness1, the concepts developed in a theory of politeness should be able to *explain* the phenomena observed as politeness1' and 'should provide a view of politeness1 "at one remove", grasping the phenomenon in its totality, revealing its inner workings and its functionality' (Eelen, *ibid.*: 44).

It is difficult, if not impossible, to claim the 'universality' of one theoretical framework in relation to the different notions and embodiments of politeness in different cultural contexts. As evident from the criticisms of the 'universality' of previous politeness theories by Matsumoto (1988) or Ide (1989), there are different notions or criteria about what is recognised as politeness in different cultures. Watts (2003: 14–16) also argues this, mentioning previous works that have focused on cross-cultural perceptions at *politeness1* level – for example, Sifianou (1992): different conceptualisations of *politeness1* between Greek and English informants; Nwoye (1992): absence of a term in Igbo, equivalent to politeness in European cultures; Rathmayr (1996a; 1996b; 1999): Russian perception of *politeness1*; Gu (1990): the different notion of *FTA*s (as defined by B&L) in the Chinese context; Lee-Wong (1999): *limao* in Chinese as the nearest concept to politeness; Blum-Kulka (1992): two first order terms, *nimus* and *adivut*, in Modern Hebrew as equivalent to politeness and the different codes for politeness in the public and the private sphere; Ide *et al.* (1992): different conceptualisations of politeness in Japanese and American society. These reports on the different 'lay' notions of politeness suggest that only observation can shed light on them and that it is difficult for these phenomena to be covered by the 'universality' of one theoretical framework.

However, there is a danger that the theories (i.e. *politeness2*) can end up with 'a lay first-order concept which has been elevated to the status of a second order concept within the framework of some more or less adequate theory of language usage' (Watts *et al.*, *ibid.*: 4). *Politeness1* concepts should not be used 'unquestioningly' (Eelen, *ibid.*: 30). In order to avoid this problem, it is necessary that 'the theoretical second order concept is clearly defined and given some other name'; otherwise 'we shall constantly vacillate between the way in which politeness is understood as a commonsense term that we all use and think we understand in everyday social interaction and a more technical notion that can only have a value within an overall theory of social interaction' (Watts *et al.*, *ibid.*: 4–5). Eelen (*ibid.*: 31) supposes that it is from this motivation that Watts has invented the term *politic behaviour* to define and give a new name to his original theoretical framework, taking into account the concepts *politeness1* and *politeness2* delineated above.

The term *politic behaviour* was introduced and developed in Watts' recent work (e.g. 1989, 1992, 2003) to define 'non-salient' or 'unmarked' linguistic behaviour in discourse oriented towards social harmony. He describes his motivation to revise the term politeness and to introduce a new concept as follows:

> … research in pragmalinguistics and sociolinguistics over the past fifteen years has offered us definitions which do not always correspond with native English speakers' perceptions of the term "politeness", which is often evaluated negatively. I contend that negative evaluations within the framework of British-English culture can be traced back to eighteenth-century definitions and the social application of the term throughout at least the eighteenth and nineteenth centuries. The various realisations of linguistic politeness in language usage which have been discussed in the literature may more profitably be viewed as forms of a more general form of linguistic behaviour geared towards maintaining the equilibrium of interpersonal relationships within the social group, which I have elsewhere termed "politic verbal behaviour" (Watts 1989).

(Watts, 1992: 43)

The above statement suggests that Watts has emphasised the 'positive side' of politeness for social equilibrium, having noticed the shortcomings of that term due to its negative connotations. Watts' position is similar to Spencer-Oatey's (2000b), who had found difficulty in defining politeness and replaced it with *rapport-management* while developing her own framework to explain individual-social motivational factors for (or against) social harmony.

With regard to the negative evaluation of the term politeness, Watts refers to Sell's observations and says, 'If we scratch the surface of polite behaviour in the eighteenth century, we frequently encounter not only "inconsideration and irreligion" but also "positive selfishness, malevolence, evil" (Sell, 1991b: 210)' (Watts, 1992: 44). Sell gives the following description about how politeness was perceived by people at that time:

> ... probably the best thing most people would say about politeness is that it is a social lubricant less nocuous than alcohol, probably useful, like free alcohol, for the *corps diplomatique*. Or, still more likely, that it is a velvet glove within which to hide one or another kind of iron fist. (Sell, *ibid.*: 211)

Having observed the gap between the definition of politeness presented by modern researchers such as Lakoff (1974), Leech (1983), Fraser & Nolen (1981) and B&L (1987) and its connotation in the eighteenth century as mentioned above, Watts claimed the necessity of introducing a 'more comprehensive notion – politic behaviour' (Watts, 1992: 50).

Here are three examples of Watts' explanations of *politic behaviour*:

> [S]ocioculturally determined behaviour directed towards the goal of establishing and/or maintaining in a state of equilibrium the personal relationships between the individuals of a social group (Watts, 1989: 135);

> [L]inguistic behaviour which is perceived to be appropriate to the social constraints of the on-going interaction, i.e. as non-salient, should be called *politic behaviour* (Watts, 2003: 19);

> [T]hat behaviour, linguistic and non-linguistic, which the participants construct as being appropriate to the ongoing social interaction
> (Watts, 2003: 276 – 'Glossary');

From the above definitions, the concept of *politic behaviour* emerges as behaviour, both 'linguistic' and 'non-linguistic', both 'non-salient', and 'appropriate to the ongoing social interaction', and 'directed towards the goal of maintaining in a state of equilibrium the personal relationships between the individuals of a social group'. On the other hand, Watts gives the following description of politeness (and impoliteness) in his framework:

> Polite behaviour will therefore be behaviour beyond what is perceived to be appropriate to the ongoing social interaction, which says nothing about how members evaluate it. At the same time, however, the definition implies that linguistic structures are not, *per definitionem*, inherently polite. Impolite behaviour will be behaviour that is perceived by participants to be inappropriate behaviour, which again says nothing about how individual members evaluate it. (Watts, 2003: 21)

The following is another account of the characteristics of politeness in his definition:

> … an explicitly marked, conventionally interpretable subset of politic verbal behavior responsible for the smooth functioning of socio-communicative interaction and the consequent production of well-formed discourse within open social groups characterized by elaborated speech codes.
> (Watts, 1989: 136)

Although there exists a distinction between politeness and *politic behaviour* in Watts' framework as above, 'the differentiation between politeness and politic behaviour does not really imply a fundamental difference in the strict sense of the word, as politeness is also essentially (a form of) politic behaviour' (Eelen, 2001: 19). I agree with Eelen that there are certainly cases where the distinction between these two concepts is difficult to draw, for Watts has not suggested any way to scale 'salience' and 'non-salience' of words/phrases/sentences in discourse.

My standpoint in this study concerning the notions of *politeness1*, *politeness2* and *politic behaviour* is summarised in the following: (1) as for the concepts *politeness1* and *politeness2*, I agree that it is important to incorporate 'lay' notions of politeness in the theoretical framework to enable it to explain what is happening in human language; (2) still, I do not think that the theoretical framework should be designed only to explain them; (3) with regard to *politic behaviour*, I maintain that this can be subsumed under **relative politeness**, as it is a concept mainly associated with **appropriateness** in relation to some norm of 'polite enough' behaviour; and that Watts' framework concerning *politic behaviour* does not possess effective scales to measure to what degree an utterance is 'salient' or 'non-salient', whereas it can be measured with respect to the scales of **absolute** and **relative politeness** in Leech's framework.[17]

Firstly, concerning the distinction between *politeness1* and *politeness2*, I agree that observation of what is recognised as linguistic politeness by ordinary people (*politeness1*) is important in improving a theoretical framework (*politeness2*). This seems the safest way to construct a theoretical framework of politeness that can be applied to various cultural contexts, by observing relevant linguistic behaviour and the judgements made about it in the relevant linguistic community. The purpose of this study is indeed along these lines: to examine the 'lay' notion of politeness through theoretical hypotheses – the *GSP* and its constraints in speech act performance. Thus in this research the levels of politeness (i.e. both **absolute** and **relative**) of utterances produced by the informants are judged by **raters**, lay persons who are non-experts in pragmatics or linguistics. Therefore the results of this study will (a) reveal the contemporary 'folk' concept of politeness in Japanese society; and (b) shed a new light on the relationship between the 'lay' notion and a particular theoretical framework, viz. Leech's revised *PP*. How theory and practice accord and differ will be examined in Chapter 5, where I will undertake an examination of the Japanese spoken data.

Secondly, I do not agree with Watts' claim in that too much emphasis has been put on the first-order politeness. It seems that he is concerned about the 'dictatorial' orientation of the prescriptive or evaluative aspects of previous politeness theories that originate in the study of speech act performance and conversation maxims in pragmatics (i.e. the 'Gricean approach'). My impression is that he appears to regard such theories as if they were claiming unreasonable 'dominance' over the lay use of language. But this may be only a matter of where a researcher starts from and on which issue s/he puts emphasis: a pragmatic researcher will focus on how *s* represents 'illocutionary force' in speech act performance, and a sociolinguistic specialist will carry out a more descriptive analysis of how language is used in relation to social parameters. Therefore I do not see any serious problem in applying the existing theoretical framework in a study of linguistic politeness analysing the speech act performance of ordinary people.

Thirdly, as for Watts' definition of *politic behaviour*, I relate it to **relative politeness** in Leech's theory. The concept of *politic behaviour*, whose definitions by Watts are mentioned earlier, can be subsumed into the framework of **relative politeness**: **relative politeness** is a more general notion concerning **situational appropriateness**, which involves both salient and non-salient linguistic features: features that are separate in Watts' framework (the former described as '(im)politeness' and the latter *politic behaviour*). I will apply the notion of politeness and its associated concepts as defined earlier to this study – the two directions (i.e. **positive** and **negative**) of politeness are of crucial importance in examining how *s* shows his/her consideration in an utterance and how it is taken by *h*. The degrees of salience and non-salience of words/phrases/sentences can be assessed by the scales of **absolute** and **relative politeness** – these two axes of politeness let us know how linguistic features and situational appropriateness interact for the purpose of maintaining social equilibrium. As mentioned above, Watts' *politic behaviour* does not have such scales to measure how salient or non-salient a phrase or a sentence is in discourse. Salience in language is not a static variable in conversation – its quality changes according to on-going negotiations of contextual factors in verbal transaction[18]. E.g. if an utterance is evaluated as 'optimally appropriate' by lay persons, the linguistic features contained in it can be taken as non-salient. If it is assessed as 'a little inappropriate' or 'very inappropriate', it means that it contains something salient, viz. *overpolite* or *underpolite*. Salience and non-salience are deeply connected with situational factors and thus can be handled within the framework of **relative politeness** (the scale of **appropriateness**).

In addition, the terminological problem of 'politeness', pointed out by Watts and Sell above, is rather subtle and can be ignored. It has been an established notion in many previous studies without its original negative connotation as claimed by Watts. Linguistic behaviour for the orientations of *rapport-enhancement* and *rapport-maintenance* has generally been recognised as 'politeness' and its terminological equivalent in many different cultures. Watts himself observes that 'modern definitions (of politeness) agree on the basic substance of the notion, i.e. that it consists of mutually shared forms of consideration for others' (Watts, 2003: 50, annotation mine).

Watts' standpoint can be recognised as sociolinguistically-oriented rather than pragmatically-oriented, if Thomas's observation on the difference between pragmatics and sociolinguistics is applied. The notion of *politic behaviour* appears to match her statement that '[s]ociolinguistics is static, offering a "snapshot" of the language of a particular community at a particular moment in time' (Thomas, 1995: 185). It seems as if Watts attempted to separate dynamic 'volition' (politeness in Watts' definition & pragmatic values) from static 'discernment' (*politic behaviour* & sociolinguistic values) along the same lines as Ide (1989). His sociolinguistically-oriented approach seems fine in its own right, but other pragmatic-oriented approaches will make a fuller contribution to a study of politeness with their own focal points and with their own agenda.

2.1.4 Speech acts and politeness: 'face', 'constraints' and 'semantic formulae'

In this study of **linguistic politeness**, the main focus will be more on the linguistic features of utterances produced by the informants than the socio-psychological aspects as stated earlier. This means that my approach in this study corresponds to what Leech calls 'a pragmatic approach to politeness' (Leech, 2003: 104). Leech (*ibid*.: 105–6) says this approach can explain 'certain pragmatic phenomena', viz., (a) indirectness, (b) asymmetries of politeness, (c) implicit interpretations of elliptical constructions relying on the Politeness Principle, (d) pragmatic quasi-paradoxes, and (e) gradations of politeness. This approach enables us to 'keep our feet firmly on the ground, and avoid getting lost too easily in abstractions such as "face" or "culture"' (Leech, *ibid*.: 104). Ide emphasises the necessity of distinguishing between 'behaviour strategies' and 'linguistic strategies' as follows, criticising B&L's theory:

> … their list of four specific strategies shows a mixture of categories. The crucial error is mixing behavior strategies and linguistic strategies. They put behavior strategies such as 'Notice, attend to H', 'Seek agreement', 'Offer, promise', 'Be pessimistic', 'Minimize the imposition' and 'Give deference' in parallel with linguistic strategies such as 'Use in-group identity markers', 'Question, hedge', 'Impersonalize S and H', or 'Nominalize'. The result is

confusion in the categorization of expressions. Some linguistic expressions, like plural personal pronouns 'we' and 'vous', are categories under the linguistic strategy 'Impersonalize S and H', while they could also be examples for the behavior strategy 'Give deference'.

The confusion could be resolved if they distinguished consistently between behavioural and linguistic strategies ... (Ide, 1989: 239)

It is true that both linguistic devices such as *please* or *thank you* and the attitudes 'being helpful' or 'men opening doors for the ladies' can be included in the same category, 'polite behaviour' in a broad sense (Watts, 2003: 1). Still, they should be differentiated in order to prevent confusion and to avoid getting lost between the two areas. In order to concentrate on **linguistic politeness**, it is essential to incorporate the study of 'speech acts' into the framework of this study. In this section I will discuss 'speech act performance' and politeness, with the notion *constraints* as the key factor in deciding politeness strategy and *semantic formulae* as the components of the whole strategy embodying *s*'s intention.

Such value scales as 'cost-benefit' or 'modesty-approbation' arise when the 'illocutionary goal' of speech act performance includes a 'value transaction'[19] between *s* and *o*. Leech states that 'illocutionary goals may either support or compete with social goals – especially the goal of being polite' (Leech, 2003: 104). As demonstrated before, he classified speech acts into four general categories – COMPETITIVE, CONVIVIAL, COLLABORATIVE, and CONFLICTIVE – in his earlier work (1983) to group them according to their natures relative to politeness. This means that speech acts have their own directions, orientations or 'facets' that support or compete with social goals (helping to achieve 'social equilibrium').

Prior to Leech, several linguists invented their own speech acts classifications (e.g. Austin, 1962; Searle, 1979; Bach and Harnish, 1979). Among them, Leech (1983: 105–7) relates Searle's classes of 'illocutionary acts' (1979) to his goal-oriented 'illocutionary functions' as follows:

1. Assertives:
   An illocutionary act that commits *s* (= a speaker) to the truth of the expressed proposition: *eg* 'stating', 'suggesting', 'boasting', 'complaining', 'claiming', 'reporting'.

(These belong to the *collaborative* category, except for boasting.)
2. Directives :
An illocutionary act that is intended to produce some effect through action by the hearer: 'ordering', 'commanding', 'requesting', 'advising', 'recommending'.
(These frequently belong to the *competitive* category.)
3. Commissives:
An illocutionary act that commits *s* (to a greater or lesser degree) to some future action; *eg* 'promising', 'vowing', 'offering'.
(These tend to be in the *convivial*.)
4. Expressives:
An illocutionary act that have the function of expressing, or making known, the speaker's psychological attitude towards a state of affairs which the illocution presupposes; *eg* 'thanking', 'congratulating', 'pardoning', 'blaming', 'praising', 'condoling'.
(They tend to be *convivial*.)
5. Declarations[20]:
An illocutionary act that brings about the correspondence between the propositional content and reality in its successful performance: *eg* 'resigning', 'dismissing', 'christening', 'naming', 'excommunicating', 'appointing', 'sentencing'.

(adapted from Searle, *ibid.*: 12–16; Leech, *ibid.*: 105–106, annotation(*) mine)

Here he mentions the relationship between these illocutionary acts and the nature of politeness as follows:

> Although there are some cases not covered by the generalizations above, it is worth making the point that, as far as Searle's categories go, **negative politeness belongs pre-eminently to the directive class,** while **positive politeness is found pre-eminently in the commissive and expressive classes.**
> (*ibid.*: 107, emphasis mine)

The above statement suggests that Leech sees the two directions of expressing politeness according to the natures of their respective illocutionary functions: one for 'face-saving' (**negative direction**) and the other for 'face-enhancement' (**positive** direction). While avoiding 'getting lost too easily in abstractions' (Leech, 2003: 104), I would like to relate the natures of illocutionary acts to the notion of 'face' – in order to relate them to the concepts, *FEA*s (*face-enhancing acts*), *FSA*s (*face-saving acts*) and *FTA*s (*face-threatening acts*), for they can be applied to describe such natures of speech acts.

The notion of *face* was developed by Goffman (1967), taking inspiration from the Chinese conception. Goffman defined *face* as 'the positive social value a person effectively claims for himself by the line others assume he has taken during a particular contact' (Goffman, *ibid*.: 5). B&L divided this notion into two subcategories of *negative face* and *positive face*. They first redefined *face* as 'the public self-image that every member wants to claim for himself [*sic*], and state that *negative face* is 'the basic claim to territories, personal preserves, rights to non-distraction – i.e. to freedom of action and freedom from imposition' and that *positive face* is 'the positive consistent self-image or "personality" (crucially including the desire that this self-image be appreciated and approved of) claimed by interactants' (B&L, *ibid*.:61). In summary, *negative face-wants* is 'the want of every "competent adult member" that his [*sic*] actions be unimpeded by others' and *positive face-wants* is 'the want of every member that his wants be desirable to at least some others' (B&L, *ibid*.:62). These concepts lead to *negative politeness* and *positive politeness*, which are employed to satisfy such face wants[21].

*FTA*s, a widely known concept derived from B&L's work, are the linguistic acts that can cause damage to negative and positive face-wants. B&L divide *FTA*s into seven categories according to their natures (e.g. 'Those acts that predicate some future act A of H, and in so doing put some pressure on H to do (or refrain from doing) the act of A') (B&L, *ibid*.: 65–68). It seems that they attempted to focus mainly on the face-threatening aspects of speech acts and did not include a notion of a *face-enhancing act* in the key part of their theory (their *positive politeness* has been devised to mitigate *FTA*s, in contrast with Leech's **positive direction**, which enhances *h*'s or *o*'s face). It is indeed at this point that B&L's framework shows one of its own weak sides, for the nature of speech acts is multi-dimensional and cannot be judged just by only one aspect. *Negative politeness* and *positive politeness* in their definition are both designed as strategies 'to minimize the threat' (B&L, 1987: 68). Therefore these strategies are employed to mitigate *FTA*s (i.e. are strategies to achieve *FSA*s) as demonstrated in Figure 2.2.3.2 in Section 2.2.3.2[22], and the strategies to perform *FEA*s are virtually ignored.

As for B&L's one-dimensional treatment of the nature of speech acts, Koutlaki (2002) criticises its deficit in her work, 'Offers and expressions of thanks as face enhancing acts: *tæ'arof* in Persian', as follows:

> ... the concept of FTAs is an aspect of Brown and Levinson's model that has received criticism mainly because, according to Brown and Levinson, "some acts are <u>intrinsically</u> threatening to face and thus require 'softening'" (Brown and Levinson, 1987: 24, my emphasis). Communication is, therefore, seen as a minefield full of acts potentially dangerous to face and as "a fundamentally dangerous and antagonistic endeavor" (Kasper, 1990: 195). Schmidt characterises the model as "an overtly pessimistic, rather paranoid view of human social interaction" (1980: 104), while Nwoye (1992: 311) concludes that if the view of constant potential threat to the interlocuters' faces is always true, "[it] could rob social interaction of all elements of pleasure".
>
> (Koutlaki, 2002: 1737–8)

The *GSP*, on the other hand, is intended to match the two aspects of speech acts that relate to linguistic politeness and *rapport-management*. **Negative direction** corresponds to the achievement of *FSA*s (mitigation of *FTA*s) and **positive direction** accords with the performance of *FEA*s: the former redresses the face-threatening aspect of some speech acts mainly categorised as COMPETITIVE and the latter clarifies or intensifies the face-enhancing dimension of the speech acts categorised as CONVIVIAL.

The term *constraints* is a new concept to describe the 'factors' that control the performance of a speech act and politeness strategies. I would like to make a distinction between the concept developed by Leech (2003) and that of Kim (1992, 1993, 1994) and Kim *et al.* (1994). Roughly speaking, Leech's *constraints* reinterpret 'maxims' as 'directions' or 'orientations' of speech acts. Therefore they are *constraints* directed towards or governed by **positive/negative direction**. In contrast, Kim's *constraints* can be recognised as motivational 'factors' that influence (politeness) strategies in performing speech acts, although they share some of the same sphere as Leech's[23].

In Leech's framework, *constraints* are supposed to function as 'variant manifestations of the same super-constraint, the *GSP*' (Leech, *ibid.*: 108). As can be seen in Table 2.1.2.2, they mainly indicate directions for polite speech act performance: 'place a high value on *o*'s wants', 'place a low value on *s*'s wants', 'place a high value on *o*'s qualities' etc. They are assumed to operate in the speech acts/speech act types such as 'commissives', 'directives' or 'expressives' in either a **positive** or a **negative direction.**

Kim's *constraints* are defined as 'fundamental concerns influencing the choice of conversational strategies' (Kim, 1994: 128)[24]. In her study, examining the cross-cultural differences in such *constraints* that affect conversational strategies, she identified the following five constraints in the performance of *requesting*: (a) concern for clarity, (b) concern for avoiding hurting the hearer's feelings, (c) concern for nonimposition, (d) concern for avoiding negative evaluation by the hearer, and (e) concern for effectiveness (Kim, *ibid.*: 131–33). Kim investigated the relationship between cultural orientations, viz. 'individualism' and 'collectivism', and these *constraints*, collecting data from 892 participants from Korea, Hawaii and the mainland United States[25]. These are 'motivational factors' that the speaker is concerned about in performing certain speech acts. Therefore the *constraints* defined by Leech and those by Kim are somewhat different in their functions (although it is also likely that Leech's and Kim's constraints interact and influence each other in many areas).

In order to distinguish these two types of *constraint*, I will use the term *constraints* in Leech's sense, relating it to the *GSP* in his framework. I will regard Kim's constraints (those that do not belong to Leech's concept) as (motivational) factors, considering their nature and function in speech act performance. Another thing that should be noted is that only one dimension, viz. 'concerns', has been presented in Kim's framework. These are supposed to be *constraints* in performing *FTA*s, but another term or concept will be needed to describe *constraints* in the *FEA* performance: e.g. the speaker is likely to have the 'incentive' to make *h* happy and to achieve clarity and/or intensity of good value associated with *h/o* when performing *a compliment*. This dimension, or the **positive direction** of some speech acts, has not been explored yet in the previous studies of *constraints* by Kim and her colleagues.

The 'in-depth guided interview' of informants in this study, carried out to investigate the motivational background of the responses, is designed to reveal these factors and *constraints* behind speech act performance. I would like to point out that this research method allowed the informants to talk freely about such factors based on their 'lay' notions regarding the use of language or conversation strategies. In contrast, Kim used a rating scale and asked the informants to evaluate the *constraints* that had been previously determined by the researcher. Kim's approach appears to be based on a conventional method of testing out particular theoretical hypotheses. I think my approach is more effective in finding the factors that affect people's strategies and in relating them to a theoretical framework than Kim's.

As the final issue in this section, I would like to mention the concept of *semantic formulae*[26], the term designed to explore the linguistic conventions and strategies for speech act performance. Fraser (1981) used this term in arguing a variety of *semantic formulae* as primary strategies for apologising; e.g. 'I'm sorry', 'I apologise for …'. He demonstrates nine primary strategies and seventeen *semantic formulae* in those strategies such as 'Strategy 1: Announcing that you are apologising – "I (hereby) apologise for…"'; 'Strategy 9: Offering redress – "Please let me pay for the damage I've done"' (Fraser, *ibid.*: 263). Olshtain and Cohen, citing this work of Fraser's, explain *semantic formulae* as follows:

> Each semantic formula consists of a word, phrase or sentence which meets a particular semantic criterion or strategy, and any one or more of these can be used to perform the act in question. We would like to suggest that our goal be the description of the maximal potential set of semantic formulas for each act. Therefore, a "speech act set" would consist of the major semantic formulas, any one of which could suffice as an "emic" minimal element to represent the particular speech act. A combination of some of the formulas or all of them is also possible.
> (Olshtain and Cohen, 1983: 20–21)

Blum-Kulka *et al.*'s pioneering work as leader of CCSARP (The Cross-Cultural Speech Act Realization Project)[27], is based on such a study of 'a particular semantic criterion or strategy' for the speech act performance of requesting and apologising, although the term *semantic formulae* does not appear in the description of their project (Blum-Kulka *et al.*, 1989a). The goals of the CCSARP are presented as follows:

1. To investigate the similarities and differences in the realization patterns of given speech acts across different languages, relative to the same social constraints (cross-cultural variation).

2. To investigate the effect of social variables on the realization patterns of given speech acts within specific communities (sociopragmatic variation).
3. To investigate the similarities and differences in the realization patterns of given speech acts between native and non-native speakers of a given language, relative to the same social constraints (interlanguage variation).

(Blum-Kulka *et al.*, 1989b : 12–13)

They categorised strategies into several categories (requesting – *Alerters, Supportive moves, Head acts*; apologising – *IFID* (illocutionary force indicating device – Searle, 1969) and other variations) and attempted to identify *semantic formulae* for them, viz. their linguistic realisation patterns (for details see 'The CCSARP Coding Manual' in Blum-Kulka *et al.*, 1989a: 273ff.).

Among recent work applying the concept of *semantic formulae*, Byon (2004) carried out a study of strategies to perform requesting with American learners of Korean as a foreign language (KFL), comparing their performances with those of Korean native speakers. By Byon's definition, 'semantic formulae represent the means by which a particular speech act is accomplished, such as a reason, an explanation, or an alternative (e.g. Fraser, *ibid*.; Olshtain and Cohen, *ibid*.; Beebe *et al.*, 1990)' (Byon, *ibid*.: 1678). In his study, Byon adopted Hudson *et al.*'s (1995) criteria that divide the strategies for requesting into two overall categories: 'request head act strategies', which are further subdivided into (1) Preparatory, (2) Strong hint, (3) Want statement, (4) Hedged Performative, (5) Statement of facts; and 'request supportive strategies' comprising (1) Grounder, (2) Disarmer, (3) Imposition, (4) Preparatory, (5) Getting a pre-commitment, (6) Apology, (7) Gratitude. (These categories apparently derive from Blum-Kulka *et al.*'s CCSARP, 1989.) By analysing *semantic formulae*, he obtained the following three results: a) support was found for a stereotypical description of Koreans as being more hierarchical, collectivistic, roundabout and formulistic in comparison to American KFL learners; b) KFL learners' performance indicated 'L1 transfer'; c) KFL learners were more verbose and varied in their use of forms than those of the Korean native speakers.

In this study, the concept *semantic formulae* will be employed to analyse the strategies for the eight different speech acts in question (see Section 1.6). The methodologies for encoding the strategies and *semantic formulae* in the previous studies will be employed and tested out wherever they are applicable. In some cases, new criteria will be devised so that it is possible to categorise strategies or *semantic formulae* in Japanese for the performance of certain speech acts, which have not been studied previously.

2.2 An overview of related recent politeness theories

In this section, I will introduce other theoretical frameworks for linguistic politeness. As it is impossible to cover all the academic claims on politeness, I will concentrate on such theories that have a direct or indirect link to this particular study. Eelen maintains '[i]n order to reduce this mass of theoretical claims and innovations to manageable proportions, a selection has to be made' (Eelen, 2001: 1). Firstly, I would like to present Fraser's taxonomy (1990) as it gives a convenient overview of politeness theories according to their types. Then I will present Eelen's treatment of recent major politeness theories. Finally, I will examine B&L's framework, which has been recognised as the most influential in the study of politeness. Since I employ Leech's framework in this study as stated earlier, I will discuss other theories critically, mainly considering in what ways they compare or contrast with both Leech's original and revised *PP*, and this particular study.

2.2.1 Fraser's taxonomy

Fraser (1990) presents a comprehensive overview of politeness theories based on their types, which he lists as *the social norm view, the conversational-maxim view, the face saving view*, and *the conversational-contract view*. To begin with, I follow this taxonomy, as the classification of politeness theories presented by Fraser is a useful starting point, with full descriptions of the attributes and theoretical positions of researchers in the whole politeness paradigm. It should be noted, however, that these different *views* are not mutually exclusive – they can be combined as components of the same theory. E.g. Leech's approach incorporates the notions of social norm, conversational maxims, face saving/threatening, rights & obligations, etc. Fraser is, in this sense, misleading in presenting them as if they were incompatible views.

2.2.1.1 The social norm view

The first approach mentioned by Fraser is *the social norm view*. The notion of linguistic politeness is often deeply related to the 'social codes' or 'socially appropriate behaviour'. *The social norm view* thus puts the focus on such social regulations or codes of human language behaviour. Fraser accounts for this view as follows:

> The social-norm view of politeness reflects the historical understanding of politeness generally embraced by the public within the English-speaking world. Briefly stated, it assumes that each society has a particular set of social norms consisting of more or less explicit rules that prescribe a certain behavior, a state of affairs, or a way of thinking in a context. A positive evaluation (politeness) arises when an action is in congruence with the norm, a negative evaluation (impoliteness = rudeness) when action is to the contrary. (Fraser, *ibid*.: 220)

We can observe that manuals of etiquette often contain what are supposed to be linguistic politeness rules. Those rules are intended to represent a social norm that affects people's recognition of linguistic politeness. Kasher (1986) introduces the following examples from Ladies' Book of Etiquette and Manual of Politeness (1872), which describes the etiquette and polite behaviour ladies were supposed to follow and display in American society in that period:

> '… avoid topics which may be supposed to have any direct reference to events or circumstances which may be painful" (p.12)
> [in the event a lady unintentionally raises a troublesome subject, she is instructed not to] 'stop abruptly, when you perceive that it causes pain, and above all, do not make the matter worse by apologizing; turn to another subject as soon as possible, and pay no attention to the agitation your unfortunate remark may have excited.' (p.12)
> 'Never question the veracity of any statement made in general conversation' (p.16)
> '… if you are certain a statement is false, and it is injurious to another person, who may be absent, you may quietly and courteously inform the speaker that he is mistaken, but if the falsehood is of no consequence, let it pass.' (p.16)
> (From Locke, 1872 Ladies' Book of Etiquette and Manual of Politeness)

In Japan nowadays, there are supposedly many more of such manuals than in any Western countries, promoting such public codes of linguistic politeness. Behaviour in keeping with social norms of this kind is often regarded as required or compulsory for Japanese adults when they speak in public and to a person of a higher status, and to a stranger. Here are some headings in the list of contents of such a manual:

- One's nobility of character is shown by not telling others what they do not desire to be told.
- It is good manners to create an atmosphere in which your partner can speak comfortably.
- '*Shite-**itadake**-mas-en-ka?*' <Would you mind…?> is a refined way of making a request.
- A polished speaker never makes partners feel uncomfortable.
- A customer's dignity (i.e. character and social class) is soon judged in a verbal interaction for a reservation on the phone.
- A clear rejection will not give offence to others as long as it contains the speaker's dignity.

(Table of contents from Shiotsuki, 1995; translation mine)

Another example is a description in a book also published in Japan, which is concerned with good manners in business. It is widely recognised that misbehaviour in the use of language is taken immensely seriously when interacting with others on business issues. The contents of the book include how to engage politely in the following situations (the situations 5-16) that can be taken as 'activity types' as defined by Levinson (1979, 1002):

1) speaking with others, being aware of one's own and their positions/statuses; 2) referring to oneself and others; 3) using honorifics; 4) showing humility properly; 5) making a phone call; 6) making an appointment; 7) speaking in another's company; 8) apologising for a mistake; 9) making a request; 10) thanking others; 11) making a compliment; 12) having a chat; 13) giving a report; 14) stating an opinion; 15) debating; 16) speaking on a ceremonial occasion (e.g., a wedding, party, an event, a funeral).

(Selected from the table of contents of Nakakawaji, 1999; translation mine)

The topics above indicate that a wide-ranging, detailed and highly conventionalised framework of politeness patterns has to be applied properly on various occasions in Japanese society, especially in the world of business. The consequences of failing to meet such social demands can be serious: a person may have his/her reputation damaged, may lose the trust of others, or may even lose his/her position in a company. It is consequently necessary for Japanese office workers to fulfil these social requirements in order to receive a good evaluation in their workplaces.

One noticeable feature of this book is that it contains wide-ranging descriptions about the norms for politeness[28]. In this sense it is a good example of how politeness is recognised by ordinary people in Japanese society. It covers 'one's relative position (*discernment*)' (how to realise one's position in relation to his/her superiors/colleagues/subordinates/people from other companies/clients etc.), 'the correct use of address terms', 'the correct use of honorifics', 'formulaic phrases' in greetings or apologies, 'behavioural politeness' including the proper angles of bowing according to the situation, and the way to express 'consideration towards *h*' with the proper propositional content. It is also interesting that this book emphasises the importance of the distinction between an inner circle and an outer circle of personal contacts, and of the need to understand the hierarchical order in them[29]. This means that the kind of politeness treated in this book is based on the sense of one's relative position, or *discernment* (*wakimae*), as Ide (1989) claims. Honorifics or *deferential* expressions used by Japanese employees in many cases function as social index markers rather than lexical devices that show intentional (volitional) politeness.

Learning such a comprehensive system of expressing politeness as good manners is a requirement for Japanese company employees and thus a book like this is felt to be necessary and is in demand. Knowledge of the rules of good manners (or what can be conceptualised as politeness) is essential in business interactions in Japanese society. This suggests that there still exist highly influential social norms for expressing politeness in Japanese society, despite an assumption that the norm has been changing under the influence of Western individual/liberal culture. This normative view, therefore, is of importance and often necessary when discussing linguistic politeness in Japanese society.

However, this view of linguistic norms is conventional rather than theoretical. The root of such norms lies in social life and the activities of human beings, and thus this *social-norm view* requires combination with relevant theories that can supplement an organised theoretical framework and explain more about the linguistic aspects of politeness strategies. Furthermore, in Leech's approach, 'the notion of "norm" is relative not to society as a whole, as in the Japanese politeness guides, but to particular situations (who is speaking to whom, and what is the "weight" of the transaction, etc) – the notion of **relative politeness** implies a norm against which *s* and *h* judge appropriateness of politeness' (suggested by Geoffrey Leech in personal communication).

2.2.1.2 The conversational-maxim view

Fraser defines this view as that which originates from Grice's theory (1975), the Cooperative Principle (CP), which consists of four maxims: 'Quantity', 'Quality', 'Relation', and 'Manner'. Lakoff's theory (1973 and 1979) and Leech's (1983) Politeness Principles (*PP*) are recognised as belonging to this category.

Lakoff's view is based on her claim, 'We should like to have some kind of pragmatic rules, dictating whether an utterance is pragmatically well-formed or not, and the extent to which it deviates if it does' (Lakoff, 1973: 296). She suggests two rules of Pragmatic Competence:

(1) Be clear;
(2) Be polite.

Besides these two rules, she states sub-maxims of rule (2) (sub-rules), adapted as follows:

> *Rule 1*: Don't Impose
>   (used when Formal/Impersonal Politeness is required)
> *Rule 2*: Give Options
>   (used when Informal Politeness is required)
> *Rule 3*: Make A Feel Good
>   (used when Intimate Politeness is required)

In later works, she extends her original description of politeness and its functions and refers to it as 'a device used in order to reduce friction in personal interaction' (Lakoff, 1979: 64).

It should be noted here that the conversational maxim model supplements, rather than conflicts with, the social norm model of politeness. This is seen in Leech's distinction between **absolute** and **relative politeness**, and his noting that **relative politeness** is politeness 'relative to some norm of behaviour' (Leech, 1983: 83–4).

Another point is that in characterising *the conversational-maxim* approach, we should be aware that terms like 'maxim', 'rule', 'principle', 'constraint' and 'strategy' are often used in ways that cannot easily be explicitly separated. Fraser's recognition of a separate *conversational-maxim* approach is perhaps too much influenced by the fact that Lakoff and Leech (1983), like Grice, express their constraints or rules of politeness in the imperative mood.

2.2.1.3 The face saving view

Fraser places B&L's theory (1987 [1978]) in the 'face saving' category, since their theory is mainly founded on the notion of preserving each individual's 'face'. Based on Goffman's claim (1967), their theory focuses on the notion of *face* in the sense of the 'public self-image that every member [of a society] wants to claim for himself' (B&L, 1987: 61). Fraser asserts that this is 'certainly the best known of the recent approaches to an account of politeness' (Fraser, 1990: 228).

Because of its predominant role in politeness research since the 1980s, I will discuss B&L's theory in more detail later, in a following section. It is important to note here, too, that *the face-saving view* is not necessarily in conflict with *the social-norm view*. On the face of it, B&L's theory is focused more on individuals than on societies, and they actually claim (B&L, 1978: 288) that norms do not play an important role in their view of politeness. On the other hand, elsewhere they make large generalizations about the different tendencies among different societies: 'negative-politeness cultures are those lands of stand-offish creatures like the British (in the eyes of the Americans), the Japanese (in the eyes of the British)'... (B&L, *ibid.*: 250). This kind of statement must surely imply that different societies have different norms of polite behaviour.

2.2.1.4 The conversational-contract view

This view is that adopted in Fraser's own works (1975, 1990; with Nolen, 1981), which are influenced by Grice's CP in its general sense and Goffman's notion of face (1967). Fraser explains this view as follows:

> We can begin with the recognition that upon entering into a given conversation, each party brings an understanding of some initial set of **rights**

and **obligations** that will determine, at least for the preliminary stages, what the participants can expect from the other(s). During the course of time, or because of a change in the context, there is always the possibility for a renegotiation of **the conversational contract**: the two parties may readjust just what rights and what obligations they hold towards each other. (Fraser, 1990: 232, emphases mine)

According to Fraser's explanation, both s and h assume their own *rights* and *obligations* in their illocutions from the beginning. These terms, *rights* and *obligations*, constitute his notion of the *conversational-contract* (henceforth CC). The following are examples of these *rights* and *obligations* in conversation:

- to take turns;
- to use a mutually intelligible language;
- to speak sufficiently loudly for the other to hear clearly;
- to speak seriously.

The above are negotiable and can be replaced by other *rights* and *obligations* according to the circumstances speakers and hearers are in. In the sense that the CC clarifies what conditions are necessary to maintain a harmonious conversation, it resembles Grice's CP. Still, as can be seen from the above *rights* and *obligations*, Fraser's CC focuses on the behavioural aspects rather than on linguistic features, which are the main concern of the CP.

In terms of the relevance of his framework to politeness (and to the CP), Fraser gives the following explanation:

…Within this framework, being polite constitutes operating within the then-current terms and conditions of the CC.

Politeness, on this view, is not a sometime thing. Rational participants are aware that they are to act within the negotiated constraints and generally do so. When they do not, however, they are then perceived as being impolite or rude. Politeness is a state that one expects to exist in every conversation; participants note not that someone is being polite – this is the norm – but rather that the speaker is violating the CC. Being polite does not involve making the hearer 'feel good', à la Lakoff or Leech, nor with making the hearer not 'feel bad', à la B&L. It simply involves getting on with the task at hand in light of the terms and conditions of the CC.

The intention to be polite is not signaled, it is not implicated by some deviation(s) from the most 'efficient' bald-on record way of using the languages. Being polite is taken to be a hallmark of abiding by the CP – being cooperative involves abiding by the CC [*sic*]. Sentences are not *ipso facto* polite, nor are languages more or less polite. It is only speakers who are polite, and then only if their utterances reflect an adherence to the obligations they carry in that particular conversation.

(Fraser, 1990: 233, annotation mine)

Fraser's notion of politeness explained above is similar to Watt's *politic behaviour* in that Fraser recognises politeness as a non-salient ambience around on-going interaction. This is the reason why he says his concept of politeness differs from those of Lakoff, Leech and B&L. It is likely that Fraser thinks that politeness by their definitions is equal to something beyond the CC (or a 'salient linguistic feature' beyond *politic behaviour* in Watts' term).

While appreciating the meaningfulness of the concept *rights* and *obligations* that *s* and *h* share in conversation, I still maintain that *the conversation-contract view* does not supply a sufficient framework for a detailed linguistic analysis, which is to be carried out in this study. It will certainly provide a significant insight into the factors beyond linguistic features contributing to politeness, but it cannot explain why some linguistic strategies (e.g. indirectness, honorifics, deferential expressions) are connected with an assessment of the degree of politeness. (For Fraser, only *impoliteness* seems to be a 'salient' linguistic feature that goes beyond 'unmarkedness'.) It also seems that Fraser makes the notion of politeness very general – covering the CP as well as the *PP*.

2.2.2 Eelen's treatment of politeness theories

An innovative work by Eelen (2000), <u>A Critique of Politeness Theories</u>, provides a critical review of recent politeness theories. He discusses their characteristics, strong and weak points from various aspects (e.g. the epistemological concerns raised by first- and second-order politeness, conceptual bias, normativity, social and psychological issues). The main theoretical frameworks reviewed in this work are as follows: Lakoff, B&L, Leech, Gu, Ide, Blum-Kulka, Fraser & Nolen,

Arndt & Janney, and Watts. In the selection of these theoretical frameworks for discussion, Eelen combined the 'Anglo-Saxon research tradition' in the last quarter of the twentieth century – begun by Lakoff (1973) – with other non-Anglo-Saxon works such as Gu, Ide, and Blum-Kulka (Eelen, *ibid.*: iii). Eelen's selection is reasonable as these theories have formed turning points and have thus been regarded as the most influential. It is meaningful as well because it examines 'how the different perspectives are mutually related by theoretical similarities and points of overlap' (Eelen, *ibid.* ii). Prior to Eelen's work, there were a number of excellent overviews of the field such as Fraser (1990) or Kasper (1990; 1996), but they constituted 'in essence topographical efforts to chart the terrain'. This statement is true, considering Fraser's attempt (1990) discussed in an earlier section, to classify politeness theories into several 'views' as if they were separate and isolated frameworks.[30]

However, as these frameworks are discussed for different purposes from mine (e.g. for the argument of *politeness1* and *politeness2* issues) and are not necessarily integral to the discussions of this particular study, I will choose not to create independent sections to discuss those frameworks (except that of B&L, as stated earlier). Also, as most of the frameworks have already been mentioned and discussed earlier, separate sections dealing with them will be redundant. These theories will appear wherever they have meaningful relations within my later discussions.

2.2.3 Brown & Levinson

B&L's theory on politeness, which many pragmatic researchers have adopted or mentioned in their studies, has been regarded as one of the principal schemes in pragmatics. It is therefore essential to recognize its predominance, particularly in discussing individual speakers' motivations to use specific politeness strategies in response to or in consideration of the production and stimuli of *FTA*s. It is also necessary to recognize its shortcomings in analysing socially appropriate politeness codes or modes, mainly due to its focus on *s*'s or *h*'s individual wants, and the insufficiency of B&L's formula for computing the size of an *FTA* using a limited set of social variables.

2.2.3.1 Politeness and the management of face

B&L argue for politeness in terms of conflict avoidance. The central themes consist of *rationality* and *face*. *Rationality* is a means-ends reasoning or 'logic', while *face* consists of two different 'wants': *negative face* – the want that one's actions be unhindered by others, and *positive face* – the want that one's wants be desirable to others[31]. Their theory claims that some speech acts naturally 'threaten' face-wants, and that politeness is involved in 'redressing' those face-threats. On this basis, three main strategies are distinguished: *positive politeness* (using expressions of solidarity, attending to *h*'s positive face-wants), *negative politeness* (the expression of restraint, attending to *h*'s negative face-wants), and *off-record politeness* (the avoidance of explicit impositions – e.g. hinting instead of making a direct request). *Off-record politeness* is one of the politeness strategies defined by B&L that presents us with an account of a motivation for the use of *conversational implicature*, a sort of violation of the Gricean CP maxims:

> If a speaker wants to do an FTA, and chooses to do it indirectly, he must give H some hints and hope that H picks up on them and thereby interprets what S really means (intends) to say. The basic way to do this is to invite conversational implicatures by violating, in some way, the Gricean Maxims of efficient communication. H is left to ask himself 'Why did S say that that way?' and to hit upon an interpretation that makes the violation understandable. (B&L, 1987: 213)

Whereas the Gricean CP maxims are designed to focus on the cooperative aspects of *s*–*h* interactions for efficient communication (observing the maxims of quality, quantity, manner and relevance in an illocution for *h*'s correct inference without much labour), politeness theories like B&L's, which focus on indirectness in particular, shed light on the tactical aspects of communication strategies for conflict avoidance. Indirectness requires effort on the *h*'s side to make an accurate inference of the *s*'s intention so that an *FTA* is not directly conveyed to him/her, causing offence. B&L's application of the notion of *face* gives a rationale to the employment of some politeness strategies that appear to deviate from the observation of cooperative attitudes in conversation. Their hypothesis regarding *FTA*s also justifies the use of such politeness strategies in their framework, as argued in the next section.

However, I would like to argue here that, compared with **positive** and **negative directions** by Leech's definitions, B&L's *positive* and *negative politeness* have the following two major weak points: (1) they are based mostly on *s*'s/*h*'s individual face-wants; (2) they are based chiefly on only one dimension of speech act performance (i.e. the *face-threatening* aspect). As for (1), B&L's two kinds of politeness are supposed to serve only to satisfy *s*'s/*h*'s face-wants. However, politeness is a composite of individual, social and contextual factors. B&L's concepts do not contain what is thought to be socially or contextually appropriate linguistic behaviour, which is also an important factor in the notion of politeness (i.e. Leech's **relative politeness**: recall that, because of this socio-pragmatic concept, Leech's *GSP* can be applied at the (a) individual, (b) social, and (c) contextual levels). With regard to (2), the two kinds of politeness are strategies devised only to mitigate *FTA*s, as can be seen in the next section, although some of the strategies for *positive politeness* in their definitions resemble *face-enhancement* of *h/o* i.e. Leech's **positive direction** (e.g. 'Notice, attend to H', 'Intensify interest to H', 'Seek agreement'). In B&L's framework, even such quasi-*face-enhancing* strategies are compensations for *h*'s face-loss and not genuine *face-enhancing* strategies. This ignores the multi-dimensional aspects of speech act performance stated in 2.1.4 (i.e. the *face-enhancing or maintaining*, *face-threatening*, and 'non-face-concern' natures of speech acts). In contrast, Leech's **positive** and **negative directions** address the two dimensions of speech acts that relate to politeness.

2.2.3.2 Face-threatening acts and strategies for doing FTAs

As described above, politeness strategies are employed in a conversation in order to redress the size of imposition of face-threats. According to B&L, certain illocutionary acts can threaten or damage *s*'s/*h*'s face. These kinds of illocutionary acts are described as 'face-threatening acts' (*FTA*s). B&L have shown the types of strategies to perform them. In this section I will sketch out the nature of *FTA*s as explained by B&L (1987 [1978])[32]. There are two kinds of (intrinsic) *FTA*s: a) threats to *h*'s face; and b) threats to *s*'s face. It is necessary to distinguish *FTA*s for *h* and those for *s*, as one is likely to employ different politeness strategies according to the nature of an *FTA*. These also embrace different speech act verbs that can affect the strategies[33].

B&L's five main strategies to perform FTAs are as follows– the riskiest one being 'without redressive action, baldly' and the safest 'avoidance':

(1) Without redressive action, baldly:

the most direct, clear, unambiguous and concise way of conveying the communicative act.
(2) Positive politeness:
strategies that orient towards the hearer's positive face needs.
(3) Negative politeness:
strategies that orient towards the hearer's negative face needs.
(4) Off-record:
off-record strategies that allow more than one justifiable interpretation of the act.
(5) Avoidance:
the act is not performed.

(adapted from B&L, 1987: 68–74)

The numbers in the figure below show the order of the size of threats: the number increases in direct proportion to the size of face-threat. The greater the speaker estimates the degree of threat, the higher the numbers of strategies to be selected in this model, as illustrated by Figure 2.2.3.2 below.

Figure 2.2.3.2 Brown & Levinson's (1987) 'Strategies for doing Face-Threatening Acts

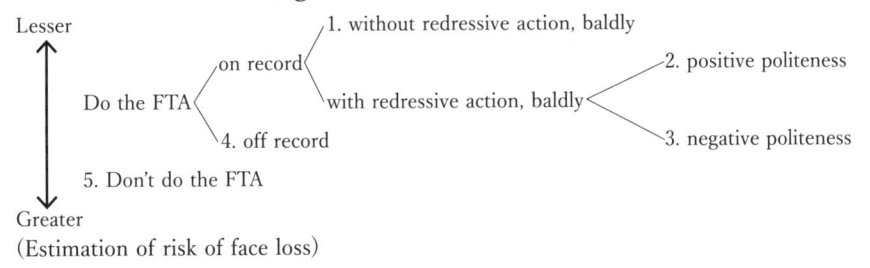

```
Lesser                      1. without redressive action, baldly
  ↑               on record                                  2. positive politeness
        Do the FTA          with redressive action, baldly
                  4. off record                              3. negative politeness
  ↓     5. Don't do the FTA
Greater
(Estimation of risk of face loss)
```

(adapted from B&L, ibid.: 60)

B&L have defined another strategy, *conventional indirectness* (CI), as a compromise between (a) the desire to go on record as a prerequisite to being seen to pay face, and (b) the desire to go off record to avoid imposing. This strategy is a hybrid of on and off record because 'many indirect requests, for example, are fully conventionalised in English so that they are on record (e.g., 'Can you pass the salt?' would be read as a request by all participants; there is no longer a viable alternative interpretation of the utterance except in very special circumstances)' (B&L, 1987: 70).

Another important thing that their model presents is 'the calculation of the weightiness of an *FTA* (W*x*)', using the social variables *D* (the social distance), *P* (the power) and *R* (ranking of imposition) as below:

$$Wx = D(S,H) + P(H,S) + Rx$$

(B&L, *ibid.*: 76)

The formula above suggests that 'the three dimensions *P*, *D*, and *R* contribute to the seriousness of an *FTA*, and thus to the determination of the level of politeness with which, other things being equal, an *FTA* will be communicated' (B&L, *ibid.*: 76). They intend the variables *D* and *P* to be very general pan-cultural social dimensions, which fluctuate with culturally specific sub-variables such as social status for *P* and the dialects or languages interlocutors use for *D*.

An argument here is whether the variables in B&L's formula are sufficient to determine the size of impositions as they claim. There are more social variables that could affect the determination of a certain politeness strategy that I think need to be separately treated from the variables defined by B&L: e.g. the age of *s/h*, sex/gender of *s/h*, although these could be considered as being subsumed under *D* and *P*. In my pilot study for this research I included mention of these two variables in my interview and asked the informants if they affected the ways they responded, as it had turned out that 'gender' was a very important factor to be considered in my previous study (Suzuki, 2000; 2002). The result indeed suggested that there existed differences in politeness strategies based on gender. Concerning the variable 'age', this is also an influential factor in deciding the level of politeness of an illocution in societies where 'seniority' means 'a higher social status', for example, in such countries as Japan or Korea. For example, the notions of *senpai*, a member of a senior year, and *kohai*, a member of a junior year, are significant in signalling superior/inferior status in a Japanese educational institution.

A study of Cypriot Greek by Terkourafi (2002: 198) claims that these variables along with others (e.g. 'social class'), which B&L did not include in their formula, play an important role in the choice of politeness strategy. It seems therefore more accurate to incorporate these other variables that could possibly influence the selection of the politeness level in a certain context within the study of politeness.

All the factors might be (variably) included under 'vertical distance' or 'horizontal difference' (i.e. difference of status in some hierarchy or social nexus) in Leech's framework. Therefore the terminology in Leech (1983) is more appropriate than B&L's term 'power'.

2.2.3.3 Cross-cultural differences in the framework of 'face'

B&L claim universality for their theory and introduce its application to a cross-cultural pragmatic study: 'We wish to emphasize here that our quite specific universal principles can provide the basis for an account of diverse cultural differences in interaction' (B&L, 1987: 242). To justify this claim, they refer to two different kinds of variability: (i) parameters and variables within the scheme itself; (ii) differential distribution of the various strategies across a social population. The first dimension of variation is rather social or group-oriented (*ethos*) and the second more individual-oriented (*ego*) (B&L, *ibid.*: 242).

They define the meaning of *ethos* as 'the affective quality of interaction characteristic of members of a society': it refers, according to their explanation, specifically to 'interactional quality' (B&L, *ibid.*: 243). Here are some examples of such an *ethos* in specific cultures:

> In some societies interactional ethos is generally warm, easy-going, friendly; in others it is stiff, formal, deferential and showing off…; in still others it is distant, hostile, suspicious…. (B&L, *ibid.*: 243)

In order to provide in their theory for the observable cultural differences in *ethos*, B&L create an apparatus to measure and describe cross-cultural variations as follows:

(i) The general level of W_x in a culture, as determined by the sum of P, D, and R values.
(ii) The extent to which all acts are FTAs, and the particular kinds of acts that are FTAs in a culture.
(iii) The cultural composition of W_x: the varying values (and thus importance) attached to P, D, and R_x, and the different sources for their assessment.
(iv) Different modes of assignment of members to the sets of persons whom an actor wants to pay him positive face, and the extent to which those sets are extended: are the relevant persons a highly limited and restricted class, or are they (or some of them) an extensive set?

(v) The nature and distribution of strategies over the most prominent dyadic relations in a particular society: are they distributed symmetrically? asymmetrically? In particular configurations?

(B&L, *ibid*.: 244–45)

They hypothesise that there exist 'positive-politeness cultures' (the western USA, some New Guinea cultures, the Mbuti pygmies, for example) and 'negative-politeness cultures' (the British [in the eyes of the Americans], the Japanese [in the eye of the British], the Malagasy and the Brahmans of India), according to differences in the general level of Wx, as summed up by culturally determined *P*, *D*, and *R* values as (i) above demonstrates (B&L, *ibid*.: 245).

Another dimension, or another set of dimensions, of the cross-cultural grid of their theory is the assessment of the size of an *FTA*. Within this, B&L make a subdivision incorporating the distinction between 'debt-sensitive cultures' and 'non-debt-sensitive cultures':

> In England and the U.S.A., for example, offers are not very threatening FTAs, but in Japan an offer as small as a glass of ice-water can occasion a tremendous debt, and may be accepted as heavily as a mortgage in a Western society (Benedict 1946)[34]. In India, Indians are often taken aback by the way in which Westerners accept offers as tokens of unrequitable metaphysical friendship instead of as coins to be punctiliously repaid. It is only in such cultures that one can express thanks by saying, in effect, 'I am humiliated, so awful is my debt.'
>
> (B&L, *ibid*.: 247)

The social trend, or *ethos*, determines each variable *P*, *D*, and *R* and thus affects the assessment of the Wx of an *FTA*[35]. A different notion of debt in one culture can produce different verbal and pragmatic behaviour. Such different attitudes towards an *FTA* can create 'sociopragmatic failure' (Thomas, 1993) and consequent misunderstandings between interlocutors from different cultural backgrounds. For example, this can happen when an American pays a compliment and a Japanese tries to respond to it in a culturally traditional way by refusing to accept the complement and denying its truth.

Unfortunately B&L's argument about the relationship between *ethos* and *ego* stops here. The criticisms of B&L's theory as biased towards an individualistic

Western culture (e.g. Ide, 1989; Matsumoto, 1988) might have been countered if these concepts had been related to their strategies for performing *FTA*s more deeply. Moreover, it is still unclear how *ethos* by their definition affects their formula or leads to its reformulation. Pragmatic researchers do need to investigate how cultural qualities and tendencies determine the significance/triviality of each social variable for cross-cultural pragmatic studies. It should also be noted that B&L's description about the relationship between *ethos* and the choice of politeness strategies is again based only on the one-dimensional recognition of speech acts. Performance of *FEA*s cannot be explained by their specification above.

2.2.3.4 Criticisms on B&L's theory[36]

While B&L have offered a very influential and widely-used theory for pragmatic research, some researchers have pointed out problems with their theory, especially with their claim as to the universality of their notion of *face*.

Thomas has pointed out three general failures in this theory as follows:

1) …Many acts can be seen to threaten the face of both S and H simultaneously (e.g., apology).
2) …a single utterance can be oriented to both positive and negative face simultaneously (not mutually exclusively, as they claim).
3) Many counter-examples are available for their prediction that the greater the degree of face-threat, the greater will be the degree of indirectness.

(Thomas, 1995: 176)

There are not a few criticisms, from a cross-cultural viewpoint, of B&L's claim of 'universality' for their theory. These are especially important when discussing Japanese politeness, which I am dealing with in this thesis.

First, Matsumoto (1988) has pointed out the discrepancy between B&L's assumption and the Japanese notion of *face*, by looking at Japanese social structure and focusing on formulaic expressions, honorifics and the verbs of giving and receiving. She explains, 'A Japanese generally must understand where s/he stands in relation to other members of the group or society, and must acknowledge his/her dependence on the others' (Matsumoto, *ibid*.: 405), and therefore B&L's concept of *negative face-wants* is most alien to a Japanese. The notion of *negative face*, the desire to be unimpeded in one's action, according to her explanation, is based on the presupposition that the basic unit of society is the individual. She also claims the invalidity of B&L's assertion that Japanese belongs to a 'negative-politeness culture', a category in which they think British and Indians are also included, in that it has been demonstrated by sociological/anthropological studies that they (Japanese, British and Indians) 'hold quite different concepts of "individuals" and of the composition of "face"'(Matsumoto, *ibid.*: 408–9).

Ide (1989) also criticises B&L from a Japanese sociological point of view, mainly focusing on 'formal forms' and *discernment* (*wakimae*), which are conspicuous elements in Japanese, as 'two neglected aspects of linguistic politeness' (Ide, *ibid.*: 223). She states, 'Brown and Levinson's framework fails to give a proper account of formal linguistic forms such as honorifics, which are among the major means of expressing linguistic politeness in some languages' (Ide, *ibid.*: 225–6). With regard to *discernment* or *wakimae*, she explains this as 'one's sense of place or role in a given situation according to social conventions' and as 'the practice of polite behavior according to social conventions' (Ide, *ibid.*: 230). One (a Japanese) is expected to show *wakimae* verbally or non-verbally by sensing his/her social position in a context. She claims that to observe *wakimae* by means of language use is an integral part of linguistic politeness (Ide, *ibid.*: 230). Therefore, she asserts, the discernment aspect of linguistic politeness, which is mainly based on social context, is one of two things that were not included in B&L's theory, which mainly concerns individual face-wants.

Chinese pragmatic researchers have also cast a doubt on the claim of 'universality'. Gu (1990) criticises B&L's theory for its Western bias when it is applied to the study of politeness phenomena in modern Chinese as follows:

1) The Chinese notion of negative face seems to differ from that defined by Brown and Levinson. For example, offering, inviting, and promising in Chinese, under ordinary circumstances, will not be considered as threatening H's negative face, i.e. impeding H's freedom.
2) It may be preferable to treat face as wants rather than as norms or values as Brown and Levinson have done, but it would be a serious oversight not to see the normative aspect of politeness. Failure to observe politeness will incur social sanctions. ... Politeness is a phenomenon belonging to the level of society, which endorses its normative constraints on each individual.

(Gu, *ibid.*: 241–42)

Chen (1993) also shows mistrust in B&L's theory, especially in their description of 'Super Strategy 3, Deflecting'[37]:

> … However, Super Strategy 3, Deflecting, poses a problem for this theory. In other words, Brown and Levinson do not seem able to explain why the responder should do anything to deflect the compliment. … None of their forty strategies bear any resemblance to this strategy, and their theoretical framework does not seem to allow an addition of this strategy either. (Chen, *ibid*.: 58–59)

Terkourafi (2002), in her study of *formulaicity* in interlocutions using corpus data of spoken requests in Cypriot Greek, claims the invalidity of B&L's *FTA* strategies and of the formula to estimate the weightiness of an *FTA*. Among the two findings she made in this study, I would like to take the following as an important proof of the deficiency of B&L's theory:

> B&L's approach places the emphasis on the relationship between interlocutors, i.e. on the dyad, which is clear in their association of politeness strategies with particular pay-offs that the speaker seeks to secure *on the part of the addressee*. Their predictions fall short of accounting for the fact that, in speaking politely, speakers position themselves not only in relation to their addressees, but also in relation to the whole of the culture, with which they seek to identify themselves to a greater or lesser extent. Consequently, the 'pay-offs' sought may transcend the dyad, and as such they may not always be possible to secure via the medium of the addressee. (adapted from Terkourafi, *ibid*.: 194–95)

This finding is in accordance with Ide's claim regarding *wakimae*, or *discernment*. She also found this existing within the western point of view, which suggests that B&L failed to include such cultural frameworks in their theory, even in the western context.

Terkourafi also criticises B&L for the lack of contextual and social factors in their formula for computing *W*. She states 'speakers cannot be operating using Brown and Levinson's formula for computing W and their proposed hierarchy of strategies *in vacuo*' because '[t]he notions of D and P and of indirectness are adequate to account for what goes on synchronically only after they have been "contextualised" taking into account the particularities of the society and of the language at hand' (Terkourafi, *ibid*.: 195). The concepts of the formula and the formula itself are 'theoretical tools a lay person cannot be assumed to master, much less have time to resort to during online processing' (Terkourafi, *ibid*.: 196). She suggests 'formulaicity', which corresponds to Coulmas's 'routine formulae' (1981b, 1994), enables lay persons to make solutions during online processing as follows:

> This is where formulaicity comes in. The combination of linguistic features … provide ready-made solutions to the complex and pertinent problem of constituting one's own and one's addressee's face while simultaneously ensuring that one's immediate goals in interaction are achieved.
> (Terkourafi, *ibid*.: 196)

I would also like to point out that P, D and R are not so stable as to produce the same W even in one particular context: they are greatly affected by the ongoing negotiation between s and h. The following quotation is from Leech & Thomas (1990), who made the same claim about the instability of these constructs:

> Pragmatic force, like 'social distance', 'size of imposition', etc., could no longer be thought of as *given*, but as something to be negotiated through interaction.
> (Leech & Thomas, *ibid*.: 195)

Moreover, there are other factors (i.e. *constraints* in Kim 1992, 1993, 1994 and Kim *et al*.'s definition 1994) that influence the choice of strategies in performing speech acts.

As a final remark in this section, I would like to state that Leech's *GSP* and the concepts of **absolute** and **relative politeness** provide more efficient devices to analyse linguistic politeness strategies than B&L's framework. This is because they are based chiefly on linguistic features (such as lexicogrammatical strategy and propositional content) and their relative force in the context – therefore they can 'avoid getting lost too easily in abstractions such as "face" or "culture"' (Leech, 2003: 104). For analyses of politeness strategies at the individual motivation level, I will incorporate B&L's general concepts *face* or *face-wants* into Spencer-Oatey's newly designed four constructs, *quality face, identity face, equity rights* and *association rights* (described in Section 2.1.1), which can explain the relation between personal wants and social expectations better.

Notes

1. I use bold font sets for the terms that are crucially important and that should be especially emphasised in some contexts, e.g. **politeness, appropriateness, absolute politeness** and **relative politeness.** They will not be accentuated when it is unnecessary to do so, however.
2. The personal qualities include our *competence, abilities, appearance* etc. *Quality face* is closely associated with our sense of personal self-esteem. (Spencer-Oatey 2000c: 14)
3. The social identities or roles include *group leader, valued customer*, or *close friend*. Identity face is closely associated with our sense of public worth. (Spencer-Oatey 2000c: 14)
4. *Equity rights* include 'that we are not unduly imposed upon', 'that we are not unfairly ordered about', and 'that we are not taken advantage of or exploited'. They are related to the notions of *cost–benefit* and *autonomy–imposition*. (Spencer-Oatey 2000c: 14)
5. *Association rights relate to interactional association–dissociation* (the type and extent of our involvement with others) and to *affective association–dissociation* (the extent to which we share concerns, feelings and interests). (Spencer-Oatey 2000c: 15)
6. For the comprehensive study of impoliteness and its framework, refer to Culpeper (1996, 1998, 2005), Culpeper, Bousfield and Wichmann (2003).
7. However, if the contents of 'asserting', 'reporting' or 'announcing' include what relates to the qualities of *s* or (especially) *h* and *o*, the performance of these speech acts can involve the aspects of **politeness** and **impoliteness** – e.g. 'I'm dying to see you' (an example taken from Levinson, 1983: 166); 'I don't respect you and I could never marry a man I don't respect' (an example taken from Thomas, 1995: 135).
8. However, a compliment can misfire and cause offence – so it is the INTENTION or DESIGN that is important here (pointed out by Geoffrey Leech in personal communication).
9. I will use the terms **positive** and **negative directions** in this thesis, instead of 'positive politeness' and 'negative politeness', in order to make a distinction between the terms used by Leech and B&L.
10. In Japanese *formality* and *politeness* are often interchangeable or understood to mean the same, but actually it is necessary to distinguish between them in a strict sense. The reason for this distinction is that the former is based on the sense of '*wakimae/discernment*' and the latter is concerned with '*volition*', or choices of politeness strategies for illocutionary goals. I will attempt to make such a distinction in this thesis wherever necessary.
11. As for the distinction and interaction between pragmatics and sociolinguistics, Thomas (1995) has an insightful observation (185–186). She states: '[s]ociolinguistics is static, offering a "snapshot" of the language of a particular community at a particular moment in time. Pragmatics is dynamic, describing what a speaker from that community does with those resources, how he or she uses them to change the way things are or in order

to maintain the status quo' (Thomas, *ibid.*: 185). My distinction between the two values (sociolinguistic and pragmatic) in Table 2.1.2.3-2 is based on this description.

12 The concepts *politeness1* and *politeness2* will be explained and discussed in detail in Section 2.1.3. Briefly, the former means the notion of politeness at the level of ordinary people, and the latter that in the theoretical frameworks.

13 **Appropriateness** in the context related to speech acts/politeness has been explored in such previous works as Ferrara (1980a, 1980b), Kreuz *et al.* (1999), and Pizziconi (2003).

14 These two concepts regarding 'distance' are devised by Leech, 2003: 115. One strong point of this conceptualisation is that *power* in B&L's term can also be included in the category of 'distance' between s and h/o.

15 Levinson (1979) defines 'activity type' as '… a fuzzy category whose focal members are goal-defined, socially constituted, bounded, events with *constraints* on participants, setting, and so on, but above all on the kinds of allowable contributions. Paradigm examples would be teaching, a job interview, a jural interrogation, a football game, a task in a workshop, a dinner party and so on' (Levinson, *ibid.*: 368). Culpeper (2005) employs the notion of 'activity type' to explain the background context of the impoliteness of the host's utterances in a TV programme.

16 The same line of including 'constraints' in the politeness framework has been pursued by Kim (1994) and Kim *et al.* (1994). Spencer-Oatey and her colleagues are working with a new concept - 'sociopragmatic interactional principles (SIPs)' (e.g. Spencer-Oatey & Jiang, 2003) – to overcome the problem of 'universal valences', which is discussed (against) in Section 2.1.2.4.

17 While saying this, it is necessary to mention that Watts has applied 'Relevance Theory' (RT) (Sperber & Wilson, 1995[1981]) to his explanation of the process of distinguishing between *politic behaviour* (non-salience) and (im)politeness (salience). According to his explication, 'RT provides an excellent means to assess how potential violations of politic behaviour can be recognised and inference processes can be postulated that result in the interpretation of (im)polite behaviour' (Watts, 2003: 203). Although Watts clarifies how an utterance can be assessed as 'salient' or 'non-salient' using RT, it is still presented as a dichotomous choice between the two. This means that RT is used as an apparatus to distinguish between *politic behaviour* and (im)politeness, rather than as a scale to measure the 'degree' of salience in the 'very salient—somewhat salient—non-salient' gradation. In my view, polite/impolite behaviour (including what Watts calls 'politic behaviour') is a continuum and necessarily involves its scale.

18 E.g. formulaic or conventional expressions are usually thought to be non-salient, but they can sometimes become a marked linguistic element: 'How are you?' – 'Fine, thank you' are supposed to be a conventional greeting formula and non-salient, but if the question is asked by the captain of the school rugby team showing unusual consideration to a member of

the team who has been injured and the answer is uttered by this member, this conventional greeting exchange can be a salient one.

19 With regard to 'value transaction', Leech maintains the following: '[U]nlike honorifics, which have to be used appropriately even in transactionally neutral situations such as weather reporting, this concept of politeness is relevant only to certain speech acts, those which involve a <u>value transaction</u>. E.g. a request seeks a <u>transaction of value</u> from *h* to *s*. A compliment is a <u>transaction of value</u> from *s* to *h*' (Leech, 2003: 118).

20 For declaratives, no equivalent is shown in the categories of 'illocutionary functions'. Concerning this, Geoffrey Leech observes as follows (in personal communication):

> I think Declarations are not regarded as competitive, convivial, etc. because they are fundamentally different from the other speech-act categories. No addressee is implied, no reply is expected, no communication takes place except in the sense that the speaker may make the declaration in public so that others listening can take note of the act performed.

21 N.B. These are – by B&L's own definitions – different from the two directions of the *GSP* defined by Leech, 2001; 2003 as described later in this section.

22 For a detailed description about B&L's five main strategies to perform *FTA*s, see Section 2.2.3.3.2.

23 The term *constraints* has also been used by some pragmatic researchers in a wider sense, e.g. 'social constraints (Blum-Kulka *et al.*, 1989b), to describe 'situational factors' such as P, D, age, gender, etc.

24 As mentioned earlier, Spencer-Oatey & Jiang (2003) study Kim's 'constraints', renaming them as 'sociopragmatic interactional principles (SIPs)'.

25 The results are: the importance of 'clarity' was higher in the more individualistic countries whereas the importance of 'avoiding hurting the hearer's feelings' and of 'minimizing imposition' was higher in the more collectivistic cultures (Kim, *ibid.*).

26 *Semantic formulae* were studied by Fraser (1981) under the larger concept, 'Conversational routine' (Coulmas, 1981a). Coulmas maintains that 'routine formulae' are 'highly conventionalized prepatterned expressions whose occurrence is tied to more or less standardized communication situations' (Coulmas, 1981b: 2–3). Other types of 'conversational routine' in speech act performance and for politeness were explored in works such as Ferguson's (1981) "politeness formula", Tannen & Öztek's (1981) "formulaic expressions in Turkish and Greek", Coulmas' (1981c) "thanks and apologies", Keller's "gambits", Manes & Wolfson's (1981) "compliment formula", House & Kasper's (1981) "politeness markers in English and German", Rehbein's (1981) "announcing", Fraser (*ibid.*) "apologising", and Edmondson's (1981) "apologising" in Coulmas (1981a). Aijmer (1996) also studied 'conversational routines' in thanking, apologies, requests, offers and discourse markers, drawing upon the <u>London-Lund Corpus of Spoken English.</u>

27 In this project, comprehensive studies on cross-cultural and interlanguage speech act performance patterns regarding the two speech acts were carried out: 'indirectness' (Blum-

Kulka); 'requestive hints' (Weizman); 'functions of *please* and *bitte*' (House); 'requesting behaviour' (Blum-Kulka & House); 'apologies across languages' (Olshtain); 'problems in the comparative study of speech acts' (Wolfson, Marmor & Jones); 'apologies in German' (Vollmer & Olshtain); 'interlanguage request realisation' (Faerch & Kasper); 'methodological issues' (Rintell & Mitchell).

28 It should be noted, however, that the author used the term *manaa* <manners> instead of the translation of 'polite' or 'politeness' (*teinei-na, teine-sa*). Therefore the type of politeness described here is mainly concerned with 'demeanour' as defined by Ide (1982: 370) – originally Goffman's term, meaning 'good manners'.

29 Regarding the Oriental collectivistic notion of 'ingroup–outgroup relationships', Scollon & Scollon (1995: 134–35) have given Chinese and Japanese anecdotal descriptions.

30 Turner (1996) also gives an excellent comprehensive overview on politeness (and impoliteness) theories, mainly discussing B&L, Lakoff and Leech (and Lachenicht (1980) for the 'dark side' – impoliteness – of human communication).

31 For another discussion of the concept *face* and its associated notions, see Section 2.1.4.

32 For a discussion about the necessity to employ the three concepts of *FTA*s, *FEA*s and *FSA*s in a study of speech acts, see Section 2.1.4.

33 For the comprehensive account of the natures of 'threats to H's face' and 'threats to S's face', as defined by B&L, see B&L, 1987: 65–68.

34 This description does not seem to apply in present day Japanese society. It may still be a big issue when the glass of water is offered by a person of a very high social status, though.

35 Regarding the universality of the variables in the formula by B&L, Tanaka *et al.* (2000: 75) introduce an example where the notions of the customer-clerk relationship differ in Australia and in Japan: an idea of 'customer responsibility' in the choice of goods is prevalent in the former; an idea that 'customers are gods' is dominant in the latter. This example suggests that the *P* factor is differently construed by Australians and Japanese.

36 For the criticisms on B&L for their bias towards *face-threatening* aspects of speech acts, see Section 2.1.4.

37 Chen states that Leech's 'Agreement' and 'Modesty' maxims are more applicable to Chen's contrastive study of compliments by American English and Chinese speakers.

Chapter 3

An overview of linguistic politeness in Japanese

As discussed in the previous chapter, the social-norm or normative aspect of linguistic politeness plays an important role in Japanese society. The Japanese language has a highly developed system of honorifics (*keigo*), morphological or lexical devices for expressing *deference* – respect towards h/o and modesty on the part of s. *Deference* can be summarised as 'behaviour that shows one's respect for someone and therefore shows that one is willing to accept their opinions or judgement' (adapted from *LDOCE*, 1995: 356). These two fundamental directions of Japanese politeness, showing respect and modesty, accord with Leech's **positive** and **negative directions** in terms of the *GSP*. As a consequence, these two concepts are applicable to the study of Japanese politeness. The Japanese honorific system functions according to the situation or the context, requiring interlocutors to take account of their relative social positions; a process, described as *wakimae* or *discernment*, which involves calculating the horizontal and vertical distances between s and h (and any third party, as discussed later).

The use of honorifics has been a matter of 'social concern' in Japanese society. Politeness in Japanese is almost equated with the proper use of honorifics: there are even cases where this is regarded as more important than the propositional content of an utterance[1].

Mizutani & Mizutani (henceforth M&M) (1987) present the following three main themes concerning Japanese politeness in their introduction: (a) Present-day polite language in Japan; (b) Factors deciding the level of politeness; (c) Verbal and nonverbal politeness.

In (a), they equate *keigo* (honorifics) with 'the polite language in Japanese' and explain its current status in Japanese society. They mainly focus on 'changes' in *keigo*, making a comparison between the pre- and post-World War II uses, which will be mentioned and discussed in Section 3.3. As for (b), M&M's discussion of the factors that decide the level of politeness in the Japanese context are presented in Section 3.4. With regard to (c), M&M offer the following four observations, suggesting some verbal and nonverbal means 'to be polite':

> 'apologizing for rudeness'
> To be fully polite one is expected to always reflect on one's actions and ask oneself if one has not been rude unintentionally. Thus the Japanese frequently use apologetic expressions such as *Sumimasen* (I'm sorry), *Shitsuree-shimashita* (Excuse me – I have been rude) and *Gomen-kudasai* (Excuse me);
> 'following the appropriate steps'
> In addition to verbally asking for forgiveness for one's rudeness, one must go through the appropriate steps when starting a conversation and developing it. One should first attract the other person's attention and then in due course indicate the purpose of one's conversation;
> 'tone'
> In Japanese conversation a hesitant tone indicates reserve while sounding too definite when giving one's opinion can seem aggressive;
> 'body language'
> Nonverbal behavior such as bowing, handing things over to others, and keeping an appropriate distance from the listener is also important in conveying a polite attitude. (summary of M&M, *ibid.*: 14–15)

The above can be taken as a good summary of the 'lay' notions of what is supposed to be the 'social norms' of the Japanese linguistic politeness system. Tsuruta (1998), from her experience in teaching Japanese to foreign students, states that '[i]t is widely accepted that the appropriate use of honorific forms is a very important element of linguistic politeness in Japanese as a second/foreign language … to master' (Tsuruta, 1998: 1). She cites Niyekawa's following claim to emphasise the importance of mastering the proper use of honorifics: '[a]n ordinary grammatical error made by a foreigner may simply seem cute to the Japanese, but an error in *keigo* tends to arouse an instantaneous emotional reaction (Niyekawa, 1991: 14) (cf. 'pragmalinguistic failure' in Thomas, 1983). Niyekawa goes on to say, 'The Japanese are an extremely status-conscious people' and 'Despite the postwar democratization, rank hierarchy is strictly observed, in some cases more strictly than in prewar days' (Niyekawa, *ibid.*: 18).

As for the normative (or prescriptive)[2] aspect of Japanese politeness, Coulmas (1992) gives the following explanation:

...correct language use is a matter of keen public interest in Japan, and those who are able to make informed judgments about it enjoy much more prestige than their colleagues in Western countries. There is not only wide agreement that questions of correctness can be decided, but also that this is desirable. Thus, notwithstanding its apparent openness to rapid inadvertent language change, the speech community can be said to possess a highly developed norm consciousness and the willingness to adhere to normative directives. This holds in particular for honorific usage. (Coulmas, *ibid.*: 306)

Because of Japanese people's commitment to social norms of politeness as described above, it is necessary to incorporate this prescriptiveness into the framework of this study. This study will examine the prevailing notions of socially appropriate verbal behaviour in present-day Japanese society, as well as what are considered to be personally motivated politeness strategies.

3.1 Wakimae/Discernment

In discussing Japanese politeness, *discernment* (*wakimae* in Japanese, Hill et al. 1986: 347–48) is one of the keywords. Ide observes that the practice of polite behaviour in Japan is known as *wakimae* (Ide, 1989: 230). According to her definition, *wakimae*, or *discernment*, gives one the idea of how to show verbally and non-verbally one's sense of place or role in a given situation according to social conventions.

This sense of place, role or relationship between interlocutors, which plays a significant role in choosing the proper lexical items in conversation, is especially significant even in present-day Japanese business practices. Table 3.1 (adapted from Nakakawaji, 1999) demonstrates the relational factors Japanese office workers need to take into consideration in choosing appropriate address terms.

In this table, in addition to two things to be taken into account ('to whom to speak' and 'about whom to speak'), two social variables are involved: *horizontal distance* (inside or outside the company) and *vertical distance* (superior, equal and inferior status) as elements to decide which address terms to apply. Employing sociolinguistic indicators, terms of address, the contents of the table above certainly represent Ide's definition of *wakimae*, 'one's sense of place or role in a given situation' (Ide, *ibid.*).

Table 3.1 The guideline for address terms in business practices

Speaking to whom	Speaking about whom	How to call a person – including an addresser him/herself
Regardless of which partner	Self	*watakushi, watashi*
To those inside the company	Colleague	… *san*
	Junior/Subordinate	… *san*, … *kun*
	Direct superior	*ka-choo* (chief), *bu-choo* (director) … *ka-choo*, … *bu-choo*
	President	*sha-choo* (president)
	One's own company	*too-sha, waga-sha, uchino-kaisha*
To those outside the company	Employees at one's own company	… *(without any honorific title) ka-choo-no …, bu-choo-no …* (Chief …, Director …)
	Employees at the other company	… *san*, … *sama*
	Managerial class at the other company	… *ka-choo*, … *bu-choo ka-choo-san/sama, bu-choo-san/sama*
	President at the addressee's company	*sha-choo*, … *sha-choo, sha-choo-san(sama)*
	One's own company	*too-sha, watakushi-domo, hei-sha, shoo-sha*
	The addressee's company	*on-sha, ki-sha, sochira-sama*
	Other companies of the same trade etc.	… *sha-san*
To family members/relatives of an employee	Employee	… *san*, … *kachoo*, …*buchoo*

(adapted from Nakakawaji 1999: 15; translation mine)

The sophisticated and complicated system of honorifics described above is a proof that the Japanese are very sensitive to their relative positions in interactions. For example, when Japanese people meet for the first time at a party, they tend to start conversations with highly polite linguistic forms as the 'safest' strategy. At some point they ask their interactants' age (seniors are supposed to have a higher social status) or their social status so that they can identify which are in the higher/lower position. They then change, if necessary, the degree of politeness of their remarks, in accordance with their *vertical* (and *horizontal*) *distance*(s)[3]. Ide claims, 'to acknowledge the delicate status and/or the role differences of the speaker, the addressee and the referent in communication it is essential to keep communication smooth and without friction', and thus 'to observe *wakimae* by means of language use is an integral part of linguistic politeness' (Ide, 1989: 230).

Matsumoto (1988) also has the following to say about how Japanese speakers' sense of *s*'s and *o*'s positions in an interaction is at the centre of their communication strategies, although she did not use the term *wakimae* or *discernment*:

> A Japanese generally must understand where s/he stands in relation to other members of the group or society, and must acknowledge his/her dependence on the others. Acknowledgement and maintenance of the relative position of others, rather than preservation of an individual's proper territory, governs all social interaction. (Matsumoto, *ibid.*: 405)

These claims illustrate that the Japanese have a keen sense of *vertical* and *horizontal distances* in conversation. Japanese people need to monitor these factors all the time in interaction, to position themselves in relation to others, for these factors are quite influential in deciding the level of linguistic politeness.

Moreover, these variables are important not only in relation to addressees, but also in relation to third parties: this is why Japanese has 'referent honorifics', which denote respect for the third party. They need to show *deference* not only towards *h* but also towards the third person (*o*) in order to show *s*'s good sense of *wakimae*. For example, look at the example below:

A: *Sensei*   *ga*   *kita*   *yo*.
   teacher   NOM1   come-PAST   FP
   'The teacher has come'.

B: *Sensei*   *ga*   **irasshatta**   *yo*.
   teacher   NOM1   come-**EXAL**-PAST   FP
   'The teacher has come'.

Suppose these two sentences were uttered by two different students to the rest of the class. The propositional contents are the same, but the impression the class get will be somewhat different. Student A said this using a plain form '*kuru*' ('come') to express the teacher's action. Therefore s/he did not show any respect for him/her. In contrast Student B used a referent honorific 'irassharu' (an exalted form (sonkeigo) of 'come') and demonstrated his/her *wakimae* as a student to the teacher. Example A entails all or any of the following possibilities: 1) the teacher is regarded as a very familiar person by the students (e.g. a young, friendly class teacher); 2) the teacher is not respected by Student A (and the class); 3) this is an informal setting. The possible interpretation of the setting of the example B is as follows: 1) the teacher is regarded as someone who is not close to the students; 2) the teacher is regarded as a person who deserves respect from the students (e.g. the Principal); 2) this is a formal setting. In this way we can interpret the relationship between the student(s) and the teacher and the formality of the situation by looking at the presence/absence/type of the honorifics, even when the teacher is mentioned as a third person, not as an addressee. These examples explain the Japanese people's awareness of their relative positions in the whole social framework: speaker–hearer –referent. The detailed types and the functions of honorifics are to be discussed in the next section.

3.2 Honorifics

The sense of *wakimae/discernment* illustrated above governs the use of honorific words and expressions, as one is required to show his/her polite intentions in interlocution particularly when s/he is in a lower position than the addressee. The use of honorifics is one of the distinctive features of the Japanese language, as well as some other languages. Takeuchi (1999) explains the relationship between such a sense of one's relative position and the use of Japanese *keigo* (polite language) as follows:

> Japanese, it is well known, anchors any linguistic interaction in social relationships: i.e. the *social deixis* of Japanese speech styles (*keigo*) encodes social significances. This means that in order for the speaker to decide on an appropriate linguistic coding, e.g. to refer to himself, he must assess the status of the referents of the grammatical participants of his utterances, above all the subject and object, their mutual status, their status in relation to himself, and to his interlocutor(s). [*sic*]   (Takeuchi, *ibid.*: 57)

Coulmas (1992) mentions the characteristics and the complexity of the Japanese honorific system as follows:

> Like Javanese, Madurese, Korean, Thai, and many other Asian languages, Japanese is a language in which social meaning is codified in an intricate manner by morphological means largely reserved for this purpose rather than grammatical forms serving other functions (Neustupný 1974). The system of Japanese honorifics is elaborate and not easy to master. ...it is an object of considerable concern to many members of the speech community, and for those trying to become proficient in the language it is one of the biggest stumbling blocks. ... It should be noted that honorific expressions in Japanese are not stylistic frills which, for the sake of efficiency or any other reason, could easily be left out. Many aspects of honorific speech are encoded in the grammar and would be hard to avoid. (Coulmas, *ibid.*: 302)

How and when to show a sense of 'respect' or 'modesty' by the use of honorifics is always under consideration in speaking Japanese in a social context, and this is a considerable barrier for foreigners attempting to master Japanese, as mentioned above. Here is a classification of Japanese honorifics provided by Coulmas:

Figure 3.2-1 The basic model of the Japanese honorific system

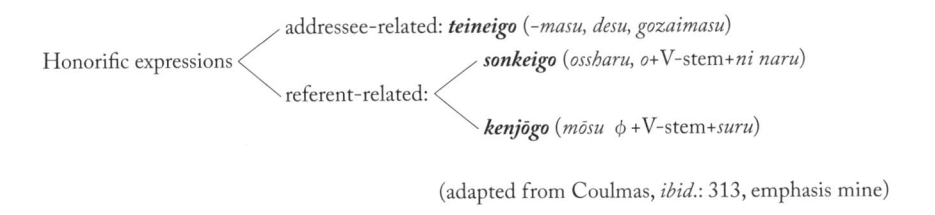

Honorific expressions
- addressee-related: ***teineigo*** (*-masu, desu, gozaimasu*)
- referent-related:
  - ***sonkeigo*** (*ossharu, o*+V-stem+*ni naru*)
  - ***kenjōgo*** (*mōsu* φ +V-stem+*suru*)

(adapted from Coulmas, *ibid.*: 313, emphasis mine)

'Addressee-related' expressions are 'used irrespective of the subject matter referred to and allow speakers to differentiate their speech on a scale of formality and familiarity, that is, to indicate the kind of relationship they wish to maintain with their interlocutors' (Coulmas, *ibid.*: 313). On the other hand, 'referent-related' expressions 'enable the speaker to refer to objects, events and actions in different ways' (Coulmas, *ibid.*: 314).[4]

According to Coulmas, the three main components of the honorific system can be summarised as follows:

> Traditionally, the Japanese honorific system is taught as consisting of the trichotomy of **teineigo** (polite forms), **sonkeigo** (respectful or exalting forms), and **kenjōgo** (modest or humble forms), with *bikago* (beautifying or soft terms) sometimes subsumed under **teineigo** and sometimes treated as a separate, fourth category. (Coulmas, *ibid*.: 313, emphasis mine)

Teineigo, or 'polite forms' are Japanese morphemes that can be applied to all types of 'illocutionary functions' (Leech, 1983: 104) to express *s*'s polite intention and attitude. This is also a distinctive quality of Japanese, as even a weather report, which normally does not have any relationship with politeness in English, requires a sense of politeness. Matsumoto demonstrates three levels of politeness in sentences that report the same propositional content, 'Today is Saturday' as follows:

(a) *Kyoo   wa   doyoobi   **da**.*
    today   TOP   Saturday   COP-PLAIN
(b) *Kyoo   wa   doyoobi   **desu**.*
    today   TOP   Saturday   COP-POLITE
(c) *Kyoo   wa   doyoobi   **degozai masu**.*
    today   TOP   Saturday   COP-SUPER POLITE

(adapted from Matsumoto, 1988: 415)

Japanese speakers can/should show politeness even when they report something in a formal situation or to a person at a higher status, employing 'relation-acknowledging devices' (Matsumoto, *ibid*.: 414) such as **desu** or **masu**.[5]

The studies of politeness in western contexts have chiefly been based on the study of illocutionary acts and goals, viz. 'pragmatic values', as Thomas stated (see Section 2.1.2.3). As discussed earlier in Section 2.1.2.3 and demonstrated in Table 2.1.2.3, honorific politeness (also recognised as *deference*) is mainly concerned with 'sociolinguistic values' in my recognition. This is where a discrepancy arises when applying existing (pragmatic) politeness theories to the framework of Japanese honorific politeness, as discussed in Section 2.2.3.4.

Geoffrey Leech (in personal communication) points out that there are overlapping and separate areas in the western and the Japanese (and some other cultures') notions of politeness. He describes the key factor as a 'value transaction' (cf. B&L's *R*), which mainly concerns the two illocutionary functions, COMPETITIVE and CONVIVIAL. The division between *sociolinguistic politeness* (i.e. the use of honorifics) and *pragmatic politeness* (i.e. illocutionary goal achievement) lies in the absence/presence of a 'value transaction' as demonstrated by Figure 3.2-2.

Figure 3.2-2 Pragmatic and sociolinguistic politeness: their values

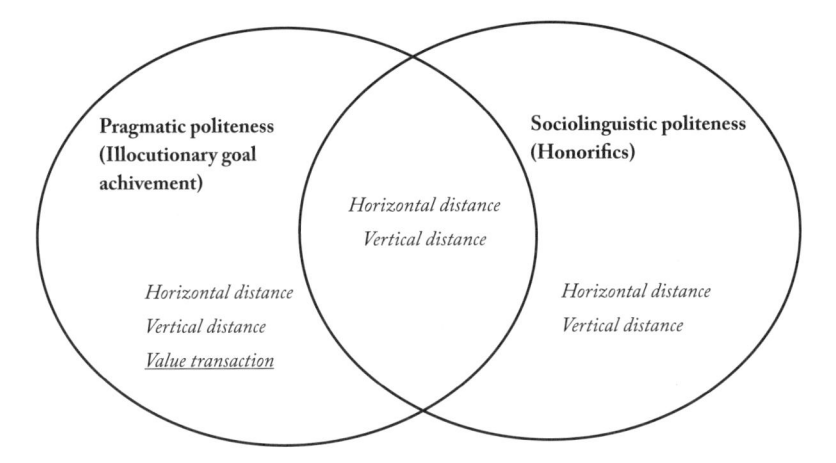

[Venn diagram with two overlapping circles]

Left circle: **Pragmatic politeness (Illocutionary goal achivement)**
- *Horizontal distance*
- *Vertical distance*
- <u>*Value transaction*</u>

Overlap: *Horizontal distance / Vertical distance*

Right circle: **Sociolinguistic politeness (Honorifics)**
- *Horizontal distance*
- *Vertical distance*

Pragmatic politeness includes 'values' from *s* to *h/o*, e.g. 'place a high value on *o*'s qualities' in approbation or 'place a low value on *s*'s wants' in request. Honorifics are independent of such values attached to certain speech act types, on the other hand, and apply to most kinds of illocutionary functions (including COLLABORATIVE and CONFLICTIVE ones) to show 'respect to the addressee/referent' or 'modesty of the speaker'.

I assume the study of politeness necessarily involves these two kinds of values, especially in a cross-cultural context. I would claim that politeness should be seen as the composite of pragmatic and sociolinguistic values (see Section 2.1.2.3 and the footnote referring to Thomas, 1995: 185–186). Conflating these two kinds of values has blurred the definition of politeness offered in earlier works. These values should be clearly distinguished from each other but combined as two related aspects. It is particularly important to incorporate 'sociolinguistic values' (or *sociolinguistic politeness*) when observing Japanese linguistic politeness, for they are often thought to be its integral part. Still, it is also necessary to study Japanese politeness through adopting the 'pragmatic values' as well, viz. how 'consideration towards h/o' is expressed in the 'value transaction' in the forms of 'tact', 'cost-benefit', 'optionality' or 'indirectness', aside from normative/sociolinguistic aspects of the Japanese linguistic situation.

3.3 Changes in honorifics and politeness strategies

Like many other languages, Japanese has undergone changes in its politeness system in recent years. A more 'liberal' and 'gender-free' use of words and expressions has been prevailing in Japanese society. M&M observed such changes in Japanese honorifics in 1987 as follows:

1) Special polite terms used for referring to the emperor and his family members have been abolished.
2) Terms referring to oneself and terms of respect referring to others have been tremendously simplified.
3) Wide discrepancies have disappeared. There used to be great classes such as between bosses and workers, customers and salesmen; but now the former talk more politely, and the latter less politely, than before.
4) Gender differences in language usage have been minimized.
5) However age differences have not undergone as much change.

(M&M, *ibid*.: 1–2)

The first point of the above is one of the characteristics that mark the more liberalised society of present-day Japan. M&M state that some of the polite wordings applied to the activities of the Japanese Royal family now are 'not different from those commonly used in daily conversation when referring to one's acquaintances politely' (M&M, *ibid*.: 1). What is mentioned in point 2 seems to be a piece of evidence that the Japanese now have a simplified social structure, which requires less consciousness of *wakimae* and less variety of 'relation-acknowledging devices'. Point 3 is another piece of evidence of a more liberalised Japanese society as described in point 1. Point 4 can be taken as a world-wide phenomenon concerning gender issues and 'politically correct' linguistic behaviour. This issue will be discussed separately in Section 3.4 and 3.5, for it is important to look at gender issues in politeness strategies in the Japanese context. (The gender-related factors will be included in most of the scenarios of this study.) With regard to point 5, 'age issues', M&M state as follows:

> Older people are still referred to and spoken to politely even in present-day society. Probably this aspect has undergone the least amount of change.
> And generation differences are very strong even now. Young students speak politely to students a year or two ahead of them... (M&M, *ibid*.: 2)

This age factor mentioned above will be investigated in most scenarios in this study: 'conversation with a female teacher' in Item 02 (Section 5.2.2), 'conversation with *senpai* (a senior student)' in Item 03 (Section 5.2.3), 04 (Section 5.2.4); 'conversation with an old lady' in Item 05 (Section 5.2.5). On the other hand, *senpai*-s are supposed to have the right to speak to *kohai*-s (juniors) without polite forms. This issue will be explored in Item 06 (Section 5.2.6) and 07 (Section 5.2.7).

The changes in *keigo* have been recently widely discussed elsewhere recently as well. Very recently there was a report that the National Institute for the Japanese Language (NIJL) will conduct a survey on Japanese-language competency as the following article shows:

> **'Govt to check citizens' Japanese-language ability'**
> A government research institute announced Thursday that it will conduct a nationwide survey in 2006 to assess the decline in Japanese-language competency.
> The National Institute for Japanese Language (NIJL), an independent administrative institution operating under the umbrella of the Education, Science and Technology Ministry, will conduct the survey, the first of its kind since 1955.
> The survey comes amid rising worries over the decline in Japanese language competency, especially among younger people, which usually is blamed on increases in words of foreign origin and deteriorating reading habits, NIJL said.
> Details of how the survey will be carried out will be completed by autumn as part of NIJL's five-year program to help people enhance their Japanese abilities.

Ability to use honorific speech and capability to express oneself in daily situations, as well as standard assessments of kanji and sentence comprehension, will be included in the survey, according to NIJL officials.

Several thousand people from all age groups will be surveyed. The aim will be to clarify gaps in abilities among age groups, it said.

(adapted from Daily Yomiuri On-Line,<http://www.yomiuri.co.jp/newse/ 20050107wo61.htm>, accessible on 2005/01/08, emphasis mine)

This newspaper article demonstrates that competence in honorifics is still regarded as one of integral abilities in Japanese language competency, which is assumed to be declining or changing.

Taishukan, one of Japanese major publishing companies of linguistic literature, conducted a survey on 'Japanese youth speech' from Oct. 2003 to Feb. 2004 collecting data from 495 high school teacher respondents. This study focused on '*kotoba-no midare*' <confusion in language> as a characteristic of 'Japanese youth speech nowadays'. In total the following quantitative findings were presented:

(1) the proportion of high school teachers who think there is confusion in language – approx. 91%;
(2) the confusion is mainly seen among 'junior high school students and younger – 34.3%, among high school students – 81.1%, among 18-30 – 65.0%, among 40-50 – 16.1%, and among 60 and older – 3.8%
(3) the confusion results from 'the lack of vocabulary' – 63.8% is over 'the use of honorifics' – 60.6%, 'the use of Chinese characters' – 41.9%, and 'the way of speaking' – 63.3%

(translated and summarised from Taishukan Shoten, <http://www.taishukan.co.jp/meikyo/0403/0403_top.html>, <http://www.taishukan.co.jp/meikyo/0403/0403_1.html>, accessible on 2005/01/18)

This survey shows that the use of honorifics is one of the major concerns in the assessment of 'youth speech' as well as the newspaper article above does. To this variety, 'youth speech', is also attributed some outstanding linguistic features including the wrong use of *keigo* and vogue words[6].

In this study, however, such changes in *keigo* or other sociolinguistic features will be treated as only partial evidence for the generation gap: politeness strategies concerning **absolute** and **relative politeness**, *constraints, motivational factors* or *semantic formulae*, viz. politeness in the more general sense will be explored and examined. This study is unique in that the Japanese politeness strategies are studied with a pragmatic approach, while they tend to be treated only with a sociolinguistic approach in the Japanese context.

Dr Noriko Tanaka at Meikai University in Japan reports her research on such change in politeness strategies for apologies in 1986 and 1999 in an article in Hashimoto (2003). In the survey of 1986 with about 40 university students, the majority chose to apologise even in the case where they had not committed any fault, prioritising the hierarchical relationship[7]. In contrast, the informants' attitudes had changed in the 1999 survey, which was based on about 130 informants: (1) they would apologise to their friends more often than to their seniors or people of higher social status; (2) they would not apologise to their partners if their partners were angry in the case where they had not committed any fault, even if they were seniors or people of higher social status; (3) they would try to justify their deeds under certain circumstances (translated and summarised from Hashimoto, *ibid.*: 71). She also presents the following anecdote as the motivation for those surveys: 'when I was having lunch in my office a student came in. I said "I'm sorry, as I'm having lunch…", but the student said "It's no problem" and did not seem to understand my point at all. It was not an issue of rough or rude use of language, but it was a strange interaction. The ones who should say "I'm sorry" and "It's no problem" should have been the opposite' (Hashimoto, *ibid.*: 70, translation mine). Behavioural changes of this kind among younger Japanese demonstrate their more liberal or rather inconsiderate attitudes towards seniors or people of higher social status. In this study, such observations concerning different attitudes among younger people as Tanaka's may not be investigated, but differences in linguistic politeness strategies could possibly be explained by examination of such attitudinal changes.

3.4 Variables that determine the level of politeness

There are a number of variables to be taken into account in Japanese society, as may also be the case in western countries. M&M (*ibid.*) discuss this issue under the heading 'Factors deciding the level of politeness,' listing: (1) Familiarity; (2) Age; (3) Social relations; (4) Social status; (5) Gender; (6) Group membership; and (7) Situation (M&M, *ibid.*: 3–14). The list below is a summary of these.

Table 3.4 Variables that determine the level of politeness

Variables mainly related to horizontal distance	Familiarity
	Gender
	Group membership
Variables mainly related to vertical distance	Age
	Social relations[8]
	Social status
Variable independent from both above	Situation

(adapted from M&M *ibid.*:3–14, under my classification)

Ide (1982), in line with the above classification, states that 'the major factors' among numerous others are (1) social position, (2) power, (3) age, and (4) formality; and describes Japanese politeness strategies under the title of 'social rules of politeness' as follows:

Rule 1. 'Be polite to a person of a higher social position'
Rule 2. 'Be polite to a person with power'
Rule 3. 'Be polite to an older person'
Overriding rule. 'Be polite in a formal setting'   (Ide, *ibid.*: 366–78)

It is meaningful that she has set a rule concerning 'formality' as an overriding one presumably because it would apply whatever the social position, the power relation, or the age of the other person are. She distinguishes 'formality' from politeness in the following statement:

… We need to touch here upon the relation of formality to politeness, formality being fundamental in governing the overriding rule.

Formality is expressed by the distance maintained between participants, while politeness is expressed by the speaker's deferential attitude toward the other participants. However, their occurrences are partially overlapping, as formality is partly expressed by politeness and vice versa.

Though formality and politeness are closely correlated in their nature, they are distinct when expressed in linguistic forms. We assume three linguistic levels on the axis of formality, i.e. formal, neutral, and informal. Formal speech is characterized by a high-level lexicon which includes honorifics, technical terms, and Sino-Japanese forms. Careful pronunciation and such syntactic forms as passive are among the other ways of rendering speech formal. Informal speech, which is colloquial speech, is characterized by sentence final particles, contraction, slang and local dialects. Rapid or slurred pronunciation also characterizes informal speech. Neutral speech is characterized by the absence of formal or informal speech. As to the axis of politeness, we assume two levels, i.e. polite and plain. (We could assume a deprecatory level at the opposite end of politeness, but this is outside the scope of the present paper.) Polite speech is characterized chiefly by honorifics, though the high-level lexicon, which characterizes formal speech, also contributes to make speech polite. Plain speech is characterized by the absence of honorifics.   (Ide, *ibid*.: 371–72)

The distinction between 'formality' and politeness above is not very clear because there are many overlapping areas, as Ide stated, and the distinction (or regarding them as one thing) depends on one's understanding of, and approach to them. Also, there are other means to express politeness than the use of honorifics, e.g. positioning oneself on the scales of 'cost-benefit', 'optionality' or 'indirectness' as Leech suggests (1983, 2000, 2003). Still, it is assumed that this is an attempt to distinguish 'situational factors' (independent from *horizontal* and *vertical distances*) from 'addressee factors' (related to *horizontal* and *vertical distances*) and also to explain their overlapping areas. I assume that Ide's discussion of formality can be linked to the point I made earlier about a 'sociolinguistic' approach to politeness: formality/informality can be placed in that category.

B&L also mention the relationship between situational 'formality' and politeness. Their description also agrees with the classifications by the Japanese researchers presented above, in noting the overlapping relation between these factors:

> In our view, P, D, and R ... can be seen to subsume most of the culturally specific social determinants of FTA expression, but we must concede that there may be a residue of other factors which are not captured within the P, D, and R dimensions. In addition to the liking factor, the presence of an audience is another, as we mentioned above, which operates in part to affect definitions of situational 'formality', and so enters into the context-variability of P, D, and R assessments. It seems likely that formality (and other sorts of situation and setting classifications – see e.g. Levinson 1979; Brown and Fraser 1979) will have a principled effect on assessments of FTA danger, and there may well be cross-culturally valid generalizations as to the direction of this effect. (B&L, 1987: 16)

I would now like to focus on two other variables, 'age' and 'gender', which also play significant roles in Japanese politeness, and will be investigated in this thesis.

'Age' is in many cases associated with 'power' in Japan and it is unavoidable for a younger person to use polite forms of words and expressions when addressing an older person in a normal situation. The concept of the terms *senpai* (a senior) and *kohai* (a junior) is the key to understanding the *vertical distance* between seniors and juniors in educational/working settings. M&M states, 'If persons are even one year senior to you, you have to use the polite form to them' (M&M, *ibid.*: 5). This rule is dominant in secondary and tertiary schools and workplaces in Japan.

The variable 'gender' connotes a sense of 'group differences based on gender', and is therefore connected with social distance. Japanese women use distinctive forms of words or expressions that may well be regarded as a sort of 'register' (*onna-kotoba*, or 'women's language'). Ide notes, 'In a discussion of polite language, women's language cannot be ignored, for one of the fairly wide-spread features of women's language is its politeness. Japanese women's speech, which has features distinct from men's speech, is no exception' (Ide, 1982: 357). My observation is that the variable 'gender' relates mainly to *horizontal distance* in the present-day situation. I have observed in my daily life that the Japanese often change the way they speak when they talk to a person of the different gender. This is partly a reflection of the in-group/out-group differences felt between men and women.

However, it is traditionally associated with *vertical distance*. As for such a traditional view on 'gender' as a variable of *vertical distance*, Ide comments as follows:

> The high frequency of the use of honorifics by women partly results from the women obeying social Rule 1, i.e., 'be polite to a person of a higher social position'. Men's dominance over women in social positions, a legacy of feudalism, is still maintained as a basic social norm, despite the improvement of women's status in the last few decades. Women, therefore, are supposed to be more polite than men. (Ide, *ibid.*: 378)

I assume the situation described here as 'a legacy of feudalism' has undergone further changes in recent years. There is much less social pressure on Japanese women to show their obedience by using more polite forms than men, but it is true that Japanese women's more polite language derives from such historical power-related reasons. The issue of Japanese women's language will also be discussed in the next section as well, for it has often played a key role in previous studies discussing Japanese politeness.

3.5 Supplementary discussions on Japanese politeness

This section presents some other discussions about Japanese linguistic politeness, particularly the ones that are relevant and significant to this study. Firstly, issues concerning 'gender' will be presented in more depth, for there are various characteristics and different tendencies that are supposed to be based on gender identity in Japanese linguistic politeness.

Secondly, some discussions of the relationship between social and individual orientations of polite linguistic behaviour will be introduced. This has been the main area where Western and Japanese paradigms have been in conflict with each other. Traditionally the study of Japanese politeness has been equated with that of honorifics: consequently it has belonged to a large extent to the sociolinguistic domain. Since this study applies a pragmatic approach to the exploration of Japanese linguistic behaviour, it is necessary to look at it from the side of pragmatics. The focus of this thesis is on Japanese speech act performance strategies both at an utterance and at a discourse level. Therefore this study is in one sense on the same lines as previous pragmatic studies of Japanese (e.g.

Takahashi & Beebe, 1993; Fukushima, 2000; Tanaka, 2001; Usami, 2002). However, I will attempt both to integrate and keep separate the two approaches, pursuing a new direction in studying Japanese politeness as Pizziconi (2003) suggests. For this purpose I will present how the pragmatic and sociolinguistic values function separately yet in cooperation in speech act performance in Japanese.

3.5.1 Gender issues[9]

In the study of Japanese politeness, it seems essential to mention some gender issues. Japanese women's language, as described earlier, has been treated in many publications (e.g. Mochizuki, 1980; Loveday, 1981; Shibamoto, 1982; 1987; Sakata, 1991; Takahara, 1991; Takano, in press). Different characteristics of men's and women's language have been widely recognised and studied with reference to Japanese. Although the differences have been diminishing under the influence of recent more liberal and democratic trends, Japanese men and women still have different tendencies in language use, and employ somewhat different politeness strategies, as will be discussed later in the data analysis sections.

Gender issues have attracted linguistic researchers' interests worldwide since about 1975, when the *International Women's Year* was proclaimed by the United Nations (Preisler, 1986: 5). Characteristics of women's language have been treated or mentioned in such works as Trudgill (1975), Lakoff (1975), Chambers (1992), Holmes (1995) and Christie (2000). For example, Trudgill states the following with regard to gender and linguistic social norms:

> ...women, allowing for other variables such as age, education and social class, consistently produce linguistic forms which more closely approach those of the standard language or have higher prestige than those produced by men, or, they produce forms of this type more frequently. (Trudgill, *ibid.*: 89)

Lakoff also points out some characteristics of women's language such as the frequent use of '"empty adjectives" – *divine, charming, cute...*', 'tag questions', 'rising intonation', 'hedges', 'intensive *so*', 'hypercorrect grammar', 'superpolite forms' and less frequent use of 'jokes' (Lakoff, *ibid.*: 53–56).

In the pragmatics context, Holmes (1995) carried out a survey on gender differences in the performance of the following speech acts in English: *apologies, compliments*, *greetings* and *expressions of gratitude*. She confirmed gender differences in the performance of these speech acts and found that women on the whole had achieved higher degrees of politeness than men[10].

Gender differences in the Japanese context have been discussed in quite a few publications. Peng & Hori report that they observed more frequent use of honorifics in women's speech than in men's (Peng & Hori, 1981). Ide, discussing this finding, explains that such a difference can be attributed to women's different sense of 'demeanour'. She gives the following description about Japanese women's 'demeanour' and their more frequent use of honorifics:

> As noted earlier, honorifics are not always used as the expression of the speaker's deferential attitude, but can also be used as an expression of the speaker's demeanor. The elaborate use of honorifics is considered as a manifestation of good upbringing, a higher social class, just as careful pronunciation is a marker of a higher social class in English. Therefore, the elaborate use of honorifics is considered as well mannered behavior. Women, who attach much importance to demeanor, tend to use honorifics frequently as a manifestation of their propriety. Sometimes they use them as a means to impress others. ...   (Ide, 1982: 378)

Miyake (1996), in line with Ide's description above, claims that the Japanese prefix *o-* and its allomorph *go-*, defined as an 'honorific particle' (Martin 1964; Seward 1968) or 'honorific prefix' (Ide 1982; Shibatani 1990), are strongly associated with women's language. She states, 'the frequency of *o* is ... related to status consciousness among Japanese women; they use it because it has traditionally symbolized the language of high-class ladies' (Miyake, *ibid.*: 540).

Ide, working with McGloin, illustrates some aspects of Japanese women's language (Ide & McGloin, 1991)[11]. In this work Ide claims that Japanese women use more polite language than Japanese men, especially in their (1) use of different personal pronouns, (2) avoidance of vulgar expressions, (3) use of beautification/hypercorrect honorifics, and (4) use of feminine sentence-final particles (Ide, 1991b: 73–76).

In my previous studies of Japanese university students' pragmatic competence in English as a foreign language (Suzuki, 2000; 2002), I conducted a quantitative analysis of gender differences in the responses to rapport-challenging remarks.

The factors surveyed are as follows: (1) the choice of politeness strategies – i.e. 'Impolitely', 'Normally/Less politely', 'Politely', 'Extremely politely'; (2) the percentages of responses in each DCT (discourse completion test/task) item; (3) the average number of words; (4) the use of sentence forms – i.e. 'Declarative', 'Hypothetical', 'Imperative' and 'Interrogative'; and (5) the use of 'politeness markers' – i.e. *please, could, would* (Suzuki, 2002). The results can be summarised as below:

1) There is no significant gender difference in the choice of politeness strategies;
2) There is no significant difference in the percentages of responses;
3) There are some significant gender differences in the average number of words;
4) There is one significant gender difference in the use of sentence forms;
5) There are some significant gender differences in the use of 'politeness markers'.

(Suzuki, *ibid.*: 53–54)

These quantitative results on gender differences illustrate some characteristics and tendencies of Japanese learners' use of English as a foreign language. The first finding means that both groups chose the safest strategy, 'Politely', in most cases. The second means that both groups showed the same ability to respond to an utterance. The third shows that female informants used more words in the categories 'Politely' and 'Extremely politely' and the differences were significant. In terms of the fourth, female respondents used more interrogative forms than males in the 'Extremely politely' category. As for the fifth result, female speakers used more *please* than males in 'Impolitely' and *could* in 'Extremely politely'. These findings suggest that there are some significant gender differences in the use of English as a foreign language, and also that female informants have their own techniques in conversation for achieving politeness – as shown in the third, the fourth and the fifth findings.

In this study of politeness strategies in Japanese as a native language, however, some different observations will be presented. This study will demonstrate gender-related differences in politeness strategies both in accord and in contrast with the results described above. The differences seem to lie partly in the speakers' different attitudes in their use of native and foreign languages: they tend to employ a rather uniform strategy in the second/foreign languages but they tend to express their 'identity' – i.e. their regional background, generation, gender etc. – more clearly in their native languages. It also appears that Japanese speakers have more gender-related lexical and grammatical devices than English speakers for showing their own and group identities.

3.5.2 Interaction of 'wakimae' and 'individual intention' in polite linguistic behaviour

In this section, I would like to discuss the relationship between 'social politeness' (also described as 'discernment politeness' that originates in the sense of *s*'s and *h*'s positions – *wakimae*) and 'intentional/volitional politeness' (i.e. individual intentional strategies for politeness). Traditionally polite linguistic behaviour in Japanese has been related to social norms and the use of sociolinguistic values (i.e. *keigo*/honorifics) because of an emphasis on the relative positions of *s*, *h* and *o* described as *wakimae* (or 'discernment' as its English translation). On the other hand, the western approach to politeness has focused on the individual's 'intentional' values in achieving illocutionary goals (pointed out by Geoffrey Leech, in personal communication). There have been discussions of these two approaches to politeness, treating them as if they are two incompatible paradigms (e.g. Matsumoto, 1988; Ide, 1989).

However, I take the two approaches to politeness as two essential scales of polite linguistic behaviour. They are not incompatible with each other; they function on a 'more or less' basis. It is the situational framework represented as an 'activity type' that decides which kind of politeness the speakers tend to be sensitive about. For example, people (especially Japanese) engaging in business are expected to follow social-norm politeness for business practices but the same people will use individually motivated politeness strategies when they are with their family or friends. Similar to the road traffic, there are 'regulations' and 'personal choices' in politeness strategies. If the traffic signal is red, a car should stop: otherwise the driver will be punished – this is a 'social norm'. If a driver sees another car coming from a side road and waiting for a chance to join the main traffic, it is his/her choice whether or not to let it move in before his/her car – this is a 'personal choice'. There is no punishment if the driver does not yield to the other car, but this kind of considerate behaviour will make the other driver feel good and will contribute to keeping the traffic smooth and harmonious. These are 'regulative' and 'intentional' aspects of the choices to make driving on roads safe and harmonious. There are similar 'regulative' and 'intentional' aspects of language use: there are normative/prescriptive and individual aspects serving to make verbal interaction smooth and harmonious.

The interrelatedness of 'social' and 'individual' aspects of politeness is of great importance in the study of polite linguistic behaviour. Leech, although not mentioning this relationship directly, employs the terms *pragmalinguistics* and *socio-pragmatics* in order to make a distinction between the language-specific and culture-specific areas in 'general pragmatics' (Leech, 1983: 10-11). Leech states that 'socio-pragmatics is the sociological interface of pragmatics' (Leech, *ibid*.: 10) and *pragmalinguistics* 'can be applied to the study of the more linguistic end of pragmatics – where we consider the particular resources which a given language provides for conveying particular illocutions' (Leech, *ibid*.: 11). Both concepts can incorporate the speaker's individual and intentional manipulation of language, and of the social norms and appropriateness of language use in certain contexts, including sociolinguistic values – because they are subsumed under 'lexicogrammatical strategies'. 'General pragmatics' therefore consists of both social and individual language management.

B&L have a similar description of this relationship in discussing their 'strategies'. They refer to 'norms or rules' as 'possible alternatives' to their model (strategy), but reject the use of these terms for the following reason.

> However, this possibility has no attraction in a cross-cultural perspective. For norms, being specific to particular social populations, have a severely limited explanatory role in comparative (cross-cultural) research. Moreover, as has been persuasively argued by Lewis (1969), **conventions – and therefore also norms – may have rational origins**. This suggests that the notion 'norm' may not have the utility as a sociological primitive that it has usually been accorded.
>
> (B&L, *ibid*.: 86, emphasis mine)

After examining Japanese honorifics, they conclude that 'honorifics, which are perhaps the most obvious and pervasive intrusion of social factors into grammar, are not in origin arbitrary markers of social status, but rather are – at least in many cases – frozen outputs of face-oriented strategies' (B&L, *ibid*.: 279). I interpret this as B&L's effort to apply 'individual intentional politeness' to 'social-norm politeness' and to include a sociological domain as a component of their 'strategy' based framework. According to their claim, even language use regulated (or imposed) by social norms (i.e. honorifics) has its own face-attending and strategic aspects.

Fukuda & Asato (2004) can be taken as an example of attempts to escape from the 'spell' of *wakimae* cast by Matsumoto and Ide. They support B&L's theory and argue against Matsumoto's (1988, 1989) and Ide's (1989) 'discernment theory' in a rather radical way. They contend that 'discernment politeness' is a part of 'negative politeness' defined by B&L. Contrary to the assertions of Matsumoto and Ide, they claim that the use of honorifics to show deference to a person of higher status in non-FTA situations can still be included in B&L's theoretical framework.

> When a person of higher status is involved, distance and power are given markedly high values, which in turn, elevates the value of W(x), the weightiness of the FTA. Thus, any act, whether intrinsically face-threatening or not (meaning, regardless of the value of imposition), will be counted as face-threatening in Brown and Levinson's model.
> (Fukuda & Asato, *ibid.*: 1997)

This is an interesting proposal and I would agree that there is a face-sensitive issue involved in the conversation between people in asymmetrical power relationships. However, it should be noted that this phenomenon has not been 'counted as face-threatening in Brown and Levinson's model'. The same authors go as far as to say the following:

> Hence, even though the degree of imposition is not high in this situation, the assessment of W(x) will become high. This high W(x) value calls for some sort of mitigation, and that accounts for the occurrence of honorifics, which we claim to be a negative politeness strategy. (Fukuda & Asato, *ibid.*: 1997)

This also seems a somewhat extreme claim in defence of B&L's theory. I assume that what is missing in the link between 'discernment theory' and B&L's theory is indeed the absence/presence of 'weightiness'. B&L's claim was founded on the notion of 'face' and how *s* mitigates *FTA*s. It is therefore meaningless to discuss the question of whether a strategy is truly 'negative politeness' (defined by B&L) without examining the nature of the speech act at stake. The discussion above goes a step beyond B&L's framework and, as far as I know, goes beyond all speech act or pragmatic politeness theories up to the present ones.

Furthermore, I wonder if such use of honorifics is basically a personal strategic choice to satisfy *h*'s 'face-wants', which is the main issue in B&L's framework. My earlier description on the 'obligatory' use of honorifics in certain situations, mainly in formal occasions, has clarified that there are some 'activity types' in which the social-norm or *wakimae* precedes individual strategic choices. This is where 'discernment politeness' emerges in the conversational framework, and this is what B&L did not incorporate in their key discussion on their strategies. (They did mention these kinds of variables, such as 'formality', but only as a supplementary issue.) Fukuda & Asato in asserting that the use of honorifics is a 'negative politeness' strategy (as defined by B&L) disregard the fact that B&L's theoretical framework is based on the notion of individual 'face' and related speech act performance strategies.

Fukuda & Asato then demonstrate examples of their own making such as 'The teacher murdered my classmate', 'The teacher raped my classmate' and 'The teacher broke into a bank' using the honorific nominal '*Sensei ga ...*' (Teacher – NOM1 ...) structure. They construe that the use of honorifics in these examples is incorrect/unacceptable and claim that Ide's claim that 'Formal forms are socio-pragmatically obligatory' (Ide, 1989: 227) is wrong. The strangeness of those sentences is caused mainly by the 'disgraceful' nature of the predicates: it is contradictory for the subjects of these verbs to receive respect. It is also unlikely that deferential address terms and these kinds of 'dishonourable' speech acts would be combined in one sentence. In this sense it is an issue of illocutionary act types and not an issue of socio-pragmatics. For these reasons I do not agree that these marginal examples are able to falsify Ide's claim that the use of honorifics is socio-pragmatically obligatory[12].

However, I would like to contend that Ide's claim is fairly excessive, as I suggested above. In my view the use of honorifics is 'obligatory' under some circumstances but not always. Therefore the motives and factors for polite linguistic behaviour in Japanese (and in other languages) seem to lie somewhere between *wakimae* and personal intentional strategies.

Pizziconi's work (2002) gives some insightful observations on the distinction and interaction between 'discernment' and 'volition', in many ways agreeing with my points presented above. She re-examines Matsumoto's and Ide's views on

Japanese politeness through an 'exhaustive exploration' of their work, trying out B&L's paradigm in the analysis of the examples Matsumoto and Ide used to reject its claim of universality[13]. She contends that '[t]he borderline between behaviour that simply abides by norms, and behaviour that originates in an individual's expressive intention can be extremely difficult to pinpoint' (Pizziconi, *ibid.*: 1480). As I stated earlier, human communication is determined by both social norms and personal motivations: there is certainly interaction between these two aspects and they function jointly or separately according to the situation. In a re-examination of the Japanese greeting formula *doozo yoroshiku onegai shimasu* [*lit.* Please treat me favourably/take care of me], Pizziconi makes the following observation:

> ... the distributional characteristics of *doozo* indicate a case of begging (if not an invitation), the humble form *o/go*-V-*suru* indexes status differential, but most of all denotes an act done for the hearer; if anything, both facts provide support to the view that the main function of the formula is a prevalently 'positive', face-giving one. (Pizziconi, *ibid.*: 1484)

On this ground she maintains that this kind of Japanese greeting formulae are 'instances of positive politeness' and not 'a straight forward imposition' as Matsumoto (1988) claimed (Pizziconi, *ibid.*: 1485).

However, she is aware of the strangeness of the definition of 'positive politeness' by B&L as a strategy designed to redress *FTA*s as the following description shows.

> According to the alternative analysis proposed here, all devices in this particular expression – modal adverb, humble forms, the begging – converge to construe what Geis (1995: 102) would call a face *respecting* act (FRA), and Kerbat-Orecchioni (1997: 14) a face *enhancing* act (FEA). Geis argues that there are no reasons to think that displays of positive politeness need to be construed as a redress for threats. We need not be constrained to view politeness within a theory of speech acts, but the important point is that to envisage positive politeness as redressive action (albeit "less redressive", Brown & Levinson, 1987: 17ff.) that is typical of intimate behaviour, is an extremely reductive position, with two major consequences. The first is a counterintuitive – if not counterfactual – implication that behaviour in non-intimate encounters can do without positive politeness, and the second is the

> onus of explaining any non-intimate behaviour marked by politeness-related devices as instances of redressed FTAs, in this way triggering a proliferation of FTAs – the problem exemplified by (but not limited to) Japanese, and a rather misanthropic view of human interaction (or at least an 'overtly pessimistic view, as in Schmidt, 1980: 104). (Pizziconi, *ibid.*: 1486)

She supports Ide's and Matsumoto's claim and rejects B&L's politeness framework designed to redress *FTAs*: 'B&L's categorizations of polite strategies as redressive work, oriented to negative or positive aspects of the speaker's or the hearer's face, has been shown to be inadequate by Matsumoto and Ide's emphasis on the significance of face-work, even and especially in the absence of threats to face' (Pizziconi, *ibid.*: 1494).

At the same time, she criticises Ide's claim to separate 'discernment' and 'volition' as follows.

> Ide's clear-cut categorization of devices as either instances of 'Discernment' or 'Volition' suffers from the same flaws as B&L's criticized attempt to link linguistic strategies on the one hand directly to types of face-work on the other. ... Volition does not just take place in a vacuum, but is constrained by social norms of appropriateness (themselves dictated by culturally determined notions of ranks and roles), and Discernment devices can have a strategic use. Discernment and Volition do not neatly discriminate sets of linguistic devices; they cut across them. (Pizziconi, *ibid.*: 1494)

I would emphasise that 'discernment' and 'volition' function jointly and separately on a 'more or less' basis. It is impossible to ignore the normative aspects of any language. There also exists 'discernment politeness' in English under some circumstances – in British and American schools pupils/students are normally supposed to call their teachers with their titles and the last names. Pizziconi contends the following in line with this.

> Jary's [1998], Meier's [1995] and Watt's [e.g. 1989; 1992; with Ide & Ehlich, 1992b] work suggests that notions of social role do have a crucial bearing on English as well, in that it is these macro-factors that constitute the background against which micro-factors can make a speaker's intentions (and

local, contextual uses of honorific devices) interpretable at all... In this sense, the need of *wakimae* (discernment) is vital in communication, regardless of language.   (Pizziconi, *ibid.*: 1500, annotation with [ ] mine)

What is important is (1) to make distinctions between the 'sociolinguistic values' and 'pragmatic values', (2) to distinguish *wakimae* (or 'discernment') and *s*'s individual intention, and (3) to observe the balance between these two types of constituents of politeness. I would also claim, again, that the balance depends on the 'activity type', for it is the key factor that decides whether *s* places him/herself in the framework of society or of individuality. How an utterance or a unit of speech act performance is polite should be estimated with the scales of **absolute** and **relative politeness**. They are the measures of individual manipulation of language and its appropriateness in society. The former treats linguistic features (including such sociolinguistic values as honorifics) and propositional contents, whereas the latter deals with the total impression or impact of the speech act performance. The issues of individual strategies/social-norm in a certain context can all be included in the scale of **relative politeness**. Besides, the concepts of the *GSP*, and of **absolute** and **relative politeness** can cover both 'social-norm' and 'individual face-wants'. These concepts have wide versatility in the study of linguistic politeness. Neither B&L nor Ide has offered such a comprehensive framework to study Japanese politeness: they have offered frameworks to portray only part of polite linguistic behaviour from an individual or a social point of view.

In another up-to-date study of politeness in Japanese at a discourse level, Usami (2002) makes the following observation to explain how honorifics have been treated in the study of Japanese politeness.

> Few researchers, within the circle of traditional Japanese linguistics, have attempted to extend the scope of study of honorifics to that of pragmatic politeness[14], which would make it possible to contrast languages with differing grammatical structures. Thus, traditional Japanese researchers have shown little interest in constructing a universal theory of politeness.
>
> (Usami, *ibid.*: 8)

She also claims that '[t]he elaborate nature of the Japanese honorific system ... may have diverted attention from other equally important areas: alternative expressions of politeness, non-normative functions of honorifics, and ways to capture politeness beyond the use of honorifics as linguistic forms' (Usami, *ibid.*: 7). She concludes her discussion of the theoretical framework for her study of Japanese politeness at a discourse level as follows:

> In both honorific and non-honorific languages, the discussion needs to deal with politeness at the discourse level that considers both "language use that conforms to social norms and conventions" and "the individual speaker's strategic language use," as well as the interaction between the two...
>
> (Usami, 2002: 28)

I would maintain that Usami's approach described above is quite reasonable in the present-day or 'post-honorific' study of Japanese politeness. I assume that a study of linguistic politeness necessarily includes the interaction between the regulative and autonomous dimensions. The balance between the two is greatly affected by the activity type ('formal' or 'informal' setting, types of participants, etc.).

Notes

1. Coulmas introduces an incident in 1975 where a Japanese man was killed by a social superior he had inappropriately addressed using the intimate –kun form (Coulmas, 1992: 299).
2. I use 'prescriptive' as well as 'normative' here, because 'normative' could cause a little confusion: I have previously discussed an approach to pragmatics based on norms (especially described in Fraser, 1990), and this can mean a different notion of norm from the one that I am talking about here which is 'normative' in the sense that some kind of judgement of the 'best' behaviour is set up for others to follow.
3. Iwamoto (1998: 51) also mentions this phenomenon as follows:
   > For example, the Japanese often change their way of talking to a person whom they do not know well after finding out in the course of the conversation that the person is older than they are.
4. According to Tsuruta (1998: 14–15), these two categories originate in Tsujimura's (1963) terms, *Sozai-Keigo* (*lit.* 'honorific forms in which respect for the designated is encoded') and *Taisha-Keigo* (*lit.* 'honorific forms in which respect for the addressee is encoded'). They were translated as 'referent honorifics' and 'addressee honorifics' respectively by Comrie (1976) and have been in common usage in the study of honorifics (e.g. B&L, 1978; 1987; Levinson,

1983; Ide, 1989). However, Tsuruta states she would use two alternative terms according to the semantic criterion of whether or not they have a referent: Referent's Social Rank Connoters (RSRCs) – referring to those which connote a fictitious relative social rank of the person related to the action/state referred to by the forms; Situation Markers (SMs) – referring to those which mark the formality of the situation (Tsuruta, *ibid*.: 15, 92).

5 B&L mention the unique nature of Japanese *teineigo* (taking 'masu' as an example) as follows:

> The Japanese honorific morpheme *mas* provides a possible case of a further kind of transition from a signal of the speaker-addressee relation to the speaker-setting relation, for now it is a marker of formal speech independent of S and H status, as well as a relative-status marker (Uyeno 1971: 14–15; Makino 1970: 186)
>
> (B&L, 1987: 277)

They describe that *teineigo*, courteous words/expressions, are used to indicate 'the speaker-setting relation' or 'formality of the setting', which are independent of the social goals that some speech acts aim at, but they do not clarify the relationship between the honorific functions and illocutionary functions so that this can be incorporated into their main politeness framework. Consequently, I assume, their recognition of 'Japanese culture as that of negative politeness' (B&L, *ibid*.: 245) has been criticised since the socially required use of honorifics does not match the definition of personally motivated negative face-wants or negative politeness by their definition.

6 A research project on English 'teenage talk', which can be compared with those on Japanese, was carried out by a research team at the University of Bergen using the corpus data called COLT (The Bergen Corpus of London Teenage Language). Their work is summarised in Stenström, Andersen & Hasund (2002): e.g. 'slanguage', 'variation in the use of reported speech', 'non-standard grammar and the trendy use of intensifiers', 'teenage use of tags'. Their works are also available on the following web sites (accessible on 2005/01/18).
<http://www.hf.uib.no/i/Engelsk/colt/COLTinfo.html#MTTT>
<http://www.ach.org/ACH_Posters/colt.html>

7 The traditional response in Japanese is to apologise even in circumstances where no blame should attach to one's behaviour.

8 M&M define 'social relations' as follows:

> Social relations here refer to such relationships as those between employers and employees, customers and salesmen, and teachers and students. This might also be called "professional relations"   (M&M, *ibid*.:6)

9 An earlier version of what is described in this section was in Suzuki (2002: 34–37). I have adapted my earlier description to make it suitable for this study.

10 Gender issues (excluding those in Japanese) in pragmatics, pragmatic politeness strategies or speech act performance have been discussed in other works such as Rundquist (1992);

Johnstone, Ferrara & Bean (1992); Kotthoff (2000) and Macaulay (2001) .

11 Their work includes the following themes except for Ide (1991b) mentioned earlier: 'overview' (Jorden, 1991); 'a phonological difference' (Haig, 1991); 'sentence-final particles' (McGloin, 1991); 'person references of Japanese and American children' (Ide, 1991a); 'the ellipsis of *wa* and *ga*' (Shibamoto, 1991); 'empathy in written Japanese discourse' (Makino, 1991); 'communication strategies' (Wetzel, 1991); 'female speakers of Japanese in transition' (Reynolds, 1991); 'female terms' (Nakamura, 1991).

12 Pizziconi (2003), mentioned next, also points out the invalidity of the same example ('*?Sensei ga dookyuusei o o-koroshi ni natta*' – 'My teacher killed my classmate') presented in their earlier work (1997:5), but uses it to rebut Ide as follows.

> The oddness ... is caused by conflicting interactional effects. ...[G]lobal dimensions of status, rank etc. work as 'framing' devices which determine what sort of acts are allowed at all (e.g. a mention of a higher-ranked subject which is calibrated politely, rules out inherently impolite propositions, and vice versa). If even referent honorifics are sensitive to the type of propositions they predicate, they are not just a static "socio-pragmatic equivalent of grammatical concord" as claimed by Ide (1989: 227).
>
> (Pizziconi, *ibid.*: 1495)

13 As the background of this work, she points out that their line of work 'has gained relatively unquestioned acceptance by politeness theorists (Kasper, 1990; Janney and Arndt, 1993; Agha, 1994; Meier, 1995), as well as regular mention in works on Japanese and other languages (Nwoye, 1992; Ikeda, 1993; Mao, 1994; de Kadt, 1998; Ji, 2000)' and those questioning several aspects of Ide's and Matsumoto's claims have been just two – Fukuda and Asato, 1997 and Usami, 1997. (Pizziconi, *ibid.*: 1472).

14 Usami defines 'pragmatic politeness' as 'functions of language manipulation that work to maintain smooth human relationships'. She distinguishes it from 'politeness' in a broader sense and 'discourse politeness' – 'the dynamic whole of functions of various elements in both linguistic forms and discourse-level phenomena that play a part within the pragmatic politeness of a discourse' (Usami, *ibid.*: 4).

Chapter 4

Methodology

In this chapter, I will specify how this study of eight different speech acts has been organised – using 24 Japanese informants, consisting of 12 university undergraduates (6 male & 6 female) and 12 higher age informants (6 male & 6 female) in the first stage, and two younger age raters (male and female university undergraduates: 18-22 years old) and two higher age raters (male and female: 40–55 years old) in the second stage. First, I will introduce recently developed research methodologies for pragmatic studies and related discussions, which are relevant to the research techniques employed in this study.

In carrying out pragmatic research, it is of crucial importance to choose a suitable research methodology for effective data elicitation and for data analysis. The balance between the degree of authenticity of responses made by informants (especially in a qualitative study) and the efficiency of collection of a large amount of data (as required by a quantitative study) should be taken into consideration.

The following is a summary of the main topics investigated in pragmatic research in general, suggested by Kasper & Rose (1999):

1) The perception and comprehension of illocutionary force and politeness;
2) The production of linguistic action;
3) The impact of context variables on choices of conventions of means (semantic formulae or realization strategies) and form (linguistic material used to implement strategic options);
4) Discourse sequencing and conversational management;
5) The joint negotiation of illocutionary, referential, and relational goals in interpersonal encounters and institutional settings.

(Kasper & Rose, *ibid*.: 81)

For the purpose of exploring the above issues, various kinds of methodologies have been applied in studies mainly concerning cross-cultural and interlanguage pragmatics (e.g. the CCSARP by Blum-Kulka *et al.*, 1989). Each research methodology has its own strong and weak points: there has never existed a 'perfect' research method. Consequently, pragmatic researchers nowadays employ a combination of different methods that supplement each other in order to obtain data of good quality and in good quantity (see the discussion of 'triangulation' later in 4.1.3). This study needs to answer the following question: 'What combination would be the best to investigate the realisation strategies of certain speech acts?' In order to find a solution to this, I would like to examine the methodologies previously used in pragmatic studies and attempt to clarify what type of methodology is best for the exploration of the eight different speech acts in this thesis.

4.1 An overview of methodological issues in pragmatic research

4.1.1 Classification of methodologies

Kasper (2000) made a comprehensive study of methodology and gave a definitive description of the contemporary 'state of the art' in pragmatic research methodology. She classifies methodologies into the following categories:

1) Spoken interaction
    a) Authentic discourse
    b) Elicited conversation
    c) Role-play
2) Questionnaires
    a) Production questionnaires
    b) Multiple choice
    c) Rating scales
3) Interviews
4) Diaries
5) Think-aloud protocols

The characteristics of the methodologies, viz. what they focus on and what procedures they follow, are summarised in Table 4.1.1 below:

Table 4.1.1 Focus and procedure in some data collection formats

	Focus				Procedure	
	Interaction	Comprehension	Production	Metapragmatics	Online/offline	Interaction with researcher
Authentic discourse	+	+	+	−	on	−/+
Elicited conversation	+	+	+	−	on	+/−
Role-play	−	+	+	−	on	−
Production questionnaire	−	−	+	−	off	−
Multiple choice	−	+	+	+	off/on	−
Scales	−	−	−	+	off	−
Interview	−	−	−	+	off	+
Diary	−	−	−	+	off	−
Think-aloud protocols	−	+	+	+	on	−

(Kasper, *ibid.*: 317)

According to Kasper's definition, 'Focus' is the term that specifies the aspects of language in use (interaction, comprehension or production) and whether the data is about the informants' metapragmatic knowledge or subjective theories. 'Online/offline' under 'Procedure' explains whether subjects are engaged in a language use activity during the data collection (online) or else are required to report pragmatic information from memory without using it (offline). 'Interaction with researcher' describes 'whether or not researcher-participant interaction is an inherent part of the procedure, as in interviews', because 'even in the data types marked minus interaction, researcher and participant will have some form of contact prior to and sometimes during the data collection, and this interaction may well influence the data' (Kasper, *ibid*: 317).

The classification above is useful in discussing the strong and weak points of each method and which combination could be ideal for triangulation or supplementation. An important distinction made in the table above is between 'interaction' and 'production'. One may well regard these as the same action, for example one may think of a 'role-play' as a task that includes an interactional activity (between an examiner and an examinee). And this view seems reasonable when it is designed to focus on their interaction itself. But the nature of a role-play, according to Kasper's definition, is an activity that elicits a response (the production of an utterance) from an examinee. Therefore, a role-play that is interaction-oriented can be included in 'elicited conversation'.

In my proposed study, I will make use of the following range of methodologies: [1] for the first-stage data collection, data concerning speech act performance and related politeness strategies will be gathered via (a) a 'spoken DCT' (discourse completion test) with video prompts, (b) an 'in-depth guided interview' to access the informants' own reflection on their responses in order to investigate what factors or constraints were functioning; [2] for the second-stage data collection, assessment of the levels of **absolute** and **relative politeness** by the 'raters' with their 'lay' or 'folk' notions on politeness will be gathered via (c) a 'rating scale' to rate the level of two types of politeness, (d) an 'in-depth guided interview' of the raters to explore the backgrounds of their judgements of the levels of politeness of the remarks. Hence, I will focus on the characteristics of the 'questionnaire' and 'interview' types of data-collection methodology in the following sections.

4.1.2 Types of questionnaires

There are three main types of questionnaire: 1) MCQ (multiple-choice questionnaire), 2) rating scales and 3) DCT (discourse completion test). These types of questionnaires have been commonly used in pragmatic researches because of their convenience in data collection, especially for quantitative studies. In this section I will focus on 'rating scales' and 'DCT', for these are the two types of questionnaires that will be employed in this study.

4.1.2.1 Rating scales

Rating scales have been used as a means to study respondents' pragmatic assessment of utterances, especially in relation to other utterances. Researchers nowadays tend to combine this method with another, especially with a productive one, to assess both the *pragmalinguistic* and *socio-pragmatic* qualities of semantic formulae for speech act performance. This study will employ a rating scale in the second-stage data collection to investigate the 'lay' or 'folk' notions of politeness that have been applied to assess the level of **absolute** and **relative politeness**.

Tanaka & Kawabe (1982) asked ten native speakers of American English and ten Japanese advanced ESL learners to rank expressions of requests according to the degree of politeness. The expressions used in the research and the results are summarised in the following Table 4.1.2.1:

Table 4.1.2.1 Tanaka & Kawabe's list of politeness rank orders

	Requests	Rank Orders	
		Americans	Japanese
1.	I'd appreciate…	1	1
2.	Could you…?	2	2
3.	Would you…?	3	2
4.	Can you…?	4	5
5.	I'd like you to…	5	6
6.	Will you…?	6	4
7.	Turn down X, won't you?	7	8
8.	Why don't you…?	8	9
9.	Turn down X, will you?	9	10
10.	I want you to…	10	7
11.	Turn down X.	11	11
12.	X (The Radio)?	12	12

Rating scales of this kind have been criticised, however, for their lack of context and the effects of the incompleteness of the sentence structures used. In a pragmatic study of politeness, it is essential to include background information in the context descriptions provided, such as the *horizontal* and *vertical distances* or the weightiness of the value transacted between *s* and *h*. Recent studies have included such background information in rating scales so that respondents can make judgements taking social variables into their consideration. In this study, in accordance with this trend, the raters' assessments of **absolute politeness** (i.e. *pragmalinguistic* features) of the responses are made with the full context of the scenarios provided.

Tanaka, Spencer-Oatey & Cray (2000) used a *socio-pragmatics* oriented rating scale in their study of 'Japanese and English responses to unfounded accusations'. The following is one of the scenarios in the questionnaire and the attached rating scale (English version):

> This morning your father went to a clinic for his annual medical health check (which his company provides for their employees). About a week ago, you overheard your father telling his boss about the date and time of the health check on the phone. However, mid-morning today, the telephone rings and it

is your father's boss. He says in an annoyed tone:

Father's boss: *I'm phoning to ask where your father is. He's supposed to be here for our team meeting, and we've all been waiting for him for about 30 minutes. What's happened to him?*

[Please write the EXACT words you think you would say in response.]

You:_ _

For each scenario, respondents had to provide the following contextual ratings on Likert-type 5-point scales:

When [your father's boss] says to you, '...', at this point (i.e. before you reply)
- How annoying do you think the problem is for [your father's boss]? (Not at all – Very annoying)
- How far do you feel responsible for the problem occurring? (Not at all – Very responsible)
- How important do you think it is to try and make [your father's boss] less annoyed? (Not at all important – Very important)

(adapted from Tanaka, Spencer-Oatey & Cray; 2000: 92–94)

Their research was carried out with a combined questionnaire consisting of a productive part (written responses) and a rating-scale as demonstrated above. The rating-scale in this research is an example of a '*socio-pragmatic* (or rather *socio-psychology*) oriented' rating scale, designed to investigate respondents' notions of the impacts of (1) situational and motivational factors and (2) constraints involved in speech act implementation.

Spencer-Oatey, Ng & Li (2000) conducted a preliminary comparative study of evaluative judgements of compliment responses with British, Mainland Chinese and Hong Kong Chinese informants, using another type of *socio-pragmatic* rating scale, focusing on the degrees of **relative politeness** of the responses. The following is one of five English scenarios used in their study:

1) John has just found out that he came top in an examination, after working really hard for it. After class, his teacher calls him over:
    Teacher: Congratulations, John! You did very well.

John: (1) No, no, I did badly.
John: (2) I was lucky with the questions, I guess.
John: (3) Yes, I'm really pleased with the mark.
John: (4) Thank you.
John: (5) No, you're flattering me!

(Spencer-Oatey, Ng & Li; 2000: 117)

The procedure of the research using this rating scale is described as follows:

> **Respondents were asked to evaluate each of the responses in terms of appropriateness, conceit, and impression conveyed (favourable/bad).** Three 5-point Likert-type rating scales were listed under each compliment response, and respondents were asked to circle the numbers on these scales that corresponded to their reactions to that response. For each scenario, **respondents were also asked to add some explanatory comments**, if they had rated any of the responses negatively (circling numbers 1 or 2) in terms of the impression it conveyed.
>
> <div style="text-align: right">(Spencer-Oatey, Ng & Dong, <i>ibid</i>.: 103; emphases mine)</div>

'Appropriateness', 'conceit' and 'impression' all relate to **relative politeness**. Therefore the data collected with this rating scale is thought to be in the *socio-pragmatic* category. It is also worth noting that these researchers combined the rating task with a type of 'retrospective interview' in written form, to have the informants comment about the background of their judgements. This combination allows researchers to explore the process: **relative politeness** is evaluated at a deeper level.

The second-stage data collection of this study employs rating scales to assess the levels of both **absolute politeness** (represented as *teineisa*, an equivalent of 'politeness' in Japanese) and **relative politeness** (represented as *tekisetsusa*, an equivalent of 'appropriateness' in Japanese); hence they will cover both *pragmalinguistic* and *socio-pragmatic* aspects. The in-depth guided interview, in which the raters reflect on the backgrounds of their assessments, is intended to elucidate the relationship or interaction between the two types of politeness.

4.1.2.2 DCT (Discourse completion test)

DCTs have been widely used in large-scale pragmatic research studies such as the CCSARP (Cross Cultural Speech Act Realization Project, reported in Blum-Kulka *et al.* 1989). The merits in using a DCT can be summarised as follows: 1) it elicits data from a large sample of subjects relatively easily; 2) it can be designed to effectively control the contextual variables important to the study; 3) it has been especially effective for the comparison of strategies from different languages; and 4) it is also effective for the comparison of strategies used by native speakers and learners of the same language (Rintell & Mitchell, 1989: 250).

According to Kasper (2000: 326ff.), DCTs can roughly be divided into four types: (1) a 'classic discourse completion' type with rejoinders, (2) a 'dialogue construction' type without rejoinders, (3) an 'open item, verbal response only' type, and (4) an 'open item, free response' type. The following are samples of such types provided by Kasper (*ibid.*: 326–28).

(1) 'classic' discourse completion
   After a meeting
   Walter and Leslie live in the same neighbourhood, but they only know each other by sight. One day, they both attended a meeting held on the other side of town. Walter does not have a car but he knows that Leslie has come in her car.
   Walter: _____
   Leslie: I'm sorry but I'm not going home right away.
   (Blum-Kulka *et al.*, 1989)

(2) dialogue construction
   Your advisor suggests that you take a course during the summer. You prefer not to take classes during the summer.
   Adviser: What about taking Testing in the summer?
   You say: _____
   (Bardovi-Harlig and Hartford, 1993)

(3) open item, verbal response only
   It is not the first time that loud rock music is heard from your neighbour's apartment quite late at night.
   You pick up the phone and say: _____

(Olshtain and Weinbach, 1993)

(4) open item, free response
It's your birthday, and you're having a few friends over for dinner. A friend brings you a present. You unwrap it and find a blue sweater.
You would: _____

(Eisenstein and Bodman, 1993)

As the number of the DCT examples increases, the item becomes more 'open-ended'. E.g. the second type can be considered more 'open-ended' than the first in that it allows respondents to write their responses without being influenced by the constraints of the rejoinders. In this study, the second and the third types are employed – considering the only difference between the two to be the presence/absence of the prompt. (I excluded the fourth type, as it allows both linguistic and other responses – e.g. respondents are able to write/say 'I would keep quiet' or 'I would smile to *h*. This study is designed to focus on linguistic politeness strategies.)

I added an audio-visual prompt to each scenario in the main study (described in more detail later) so that the informants can produce their responses more naturally. Some prompts are just formulaic greeting expressions like '*Yaa, genki?*' ('Hi. How are you?'), so they do not convey any specific illocutionary force other than that of a greeting. Others are designed to elicit responses to specific speech acts: e.g. I added a prompt in the form of a specific apology to get the informants to perform 'response to apologies' – otherwise it is impossible to elicit this speech act (see Appendix 3 for the scenarios).

Whereas a DCT is an effective tool for large-scale data collection, it has been pointed out that the 'authenticity' of DCT data is questionable when compared with that derived from more naturalistic methods (e.g. ethnography), which are based on natural oral interactions. Kasper mentions such weak points and how they have been covered by the DCT's strong points, introducing two examples in previous studies:

> A serious concern is how production questionnaires compare to authentic data. Beebe and Cummings (1996, originally presented in 1985) compared refusals elicited through a single-item questionnaire with refusals performed in telephone conversations in response to the same request. Interlocutors

> in these interchanges were native speakers of American English. The questionnaire responses did *not* represent natural speech with respect to the actual wording, range of refusal strategies, and response length, but they modelled the 'canonical shape' of refusals, shed light on the social and psychological factors that are likely to affect speech act performance, and helped establish an initial classification of refusal strategies.
>
> Hartford and Bardovi-Harlig (1992) examined the rejections by native and non-native graduate students of their academic advisers' suggestions for the students' course schedules. The production questionnaire elicited a narrower range of semantic formulae and fewer status-preserving strategies than the authentic data, yet it proved an adequate instrument to test hypotheses derived from the authentic interactions. The questionnaire data confirmed Hartford and Bardovi-Harlig's (1992) hypothesis that the non-native speakers were more likely to use unacceptable content to reject advice than the native speakers.
>
> (Kasper, 2000: 329)

Finally, she concludes by emphasising the strong points of the DCT as follows.

> When carefully designed, production questionnaires are useful to inform about speakers' pragmalinguistic knowledge of the strategies and linguistic forms by which communicative acts can be implemented, and about their sociopragmatic knowledge of the context factors under which particular strategic and linguistic choices are appropriate. Whether or not speakers use exactly the same strategies and forms in actual discourse is a different matter, but the questionnaire responses indicate what strategic and linguistic options are consonant with pragmatic norms and what contextual factors influence their choices (although recent studies suggest some qualification …). In interlanguage pragmatic research, we may be interested in finding out what L2 learners *know* as opposed to what they can *do* under the much more demanding conditions of conversational encounters. For such research purposes, production questionnaires are an effective option.
>
> (Kasper, *ibid.*: 329–30).

This study of cross-cultural and cross-gender differences in linguistic politeness strategies also focuses on such 'pragmalinguistic knowledge of the strategies and linguistic forms' (**absolute politeness**) and 'socio-pragmatic knowledge of the context factors' (**relative politeness**) and their performance by Japanese informants. As will be discussed in the later chapter on data analysis, some informants are careful about the metapragmatic aspect of language and conventions of linguistic politeness – the remarks of such informants tend to be more polite in the **absolute politeness** scale. On the other hand, others do not care much about such traditional or prescriptive use of language – the utterances of such informants tend to be less polite in the **absolute politeness** scale.

'Authentic discourse' or 'elicited conversation' may elicit 'more authentic' responses, but these methodologies are not suitable for quantitative studies – it is difficult to get different informants to perform the same speech acts in the same context without overt control. Kasper points out that 'authentic data may just not be a viable option when an essential component of the research goal is to compare the use of specific pragmatic features by different groups of speakers in a given context'. This is because authentic data 'may take an unreasonable amount of data to obtain sufficient quantities of the pragmatic feature under study – for instance, of a particular speech act' (Kasper, 2000: 320). As for 'elicited conversation', while clarifying its capacity to 'shed light on such discourse aspects as conversational organization and management', she states that 'they (elicited conversations) are also limited in that participant roles cannot be manipulated, and they allow investigation of only a restricted set of communicative acts and activities' (Kasper, *ibid*. 322). Therefore the DCT remains a useful research tool in studies of certain speech acts if designed carefully to diminish its weak points.

The spoken DCT with video prompts, devised for this study, can be recognised as a hybrid between a DCT and a role-play[1]. While preserving the convenience of the DCT for large-scale data collection, it has some advantages that a role-play possesses: it enables an informant to interact with the addressee visually and verbally. Although the response interaction was limited to just one turn, there were some informants who performed 'mock turn-takings' and produced a more extended response at a discourse level. It should also be noted that the addressees who appeared on the video could be presented as the stereotypical images of (e.g.) their friends, their teacher, or female restaurant managers. This would not have been possible with a traditional role-play: it is impossible under normal circumstances to ask the informants to bring in their friends, teachers or restaurant managers; also it is impossible for a researcher to have such a variety of people at hand for research. The handiness of the data collected by the DCT made the second-stage data collection possible and efficient: as there were eight different speech acts to perform, each remark needed to be confined to a reasonable length.

Jonathan Culpeper (in personal communication) points out the following grave concerns about the use of the DCT: (1) the impoverishment of the context; (2) restriction of the discoursal context to a single exchange; and (3) a danger that the experimental context may cause people to gravitate towards prescriptive politeness. As for the first point, the spoken DCT with video prompts designed for this study preserves a considerable amount of context, although it is not perfect in projecting reality (the effectiveness of the video prompts will be discussed in more detail later). Moreover, I talked to the informants before they made their responses so that I could confirm that they had a sufficient grasp of the situation. Regarding the second point, since this study investigates 'speech act performance for politeness strategies', one exchange in conversation is assumed to be good enough: the informants provided a sufficient range of semantic formulae – some indeed tended to produce lengthy responses. The third point seems to be one of the main issues in this study: this research on linguistic politeness focuses on *rapport management* – especially, *rapport-enhancing* and *rapport-maintenance* acts. In this sense the informants' notion of 'politeness' plays an important role. Group differences indeed appear in their different notions of 'politeness', whether prescriptive or individual. Different attitudes towards 'prescriptive politeness' can be one of the main issues that mark group differences – e.g. in the survey mentioned earlier, the older generation showed more competence in the use of *keigo*. In the context of Japanese, 'prescriptive politeness' is indeed one of key issues to discuss. Interestingly, however, in the data collected with my spoken DCT a few responses were rated as 'impolite'– it seems that the impact of this disadvantage (i.e. 'gravitation towards prescriptive politeness') was reduced by the immediacy of the real images of the video prompts. Some informants seemed to be too absorbed in the scenarios to keep to the norms of politeness.

4.1.2.3 Interviews

In this study, the 'in-depth guided interview' is employed as a complementary methodology in order to explore the factors and constraints that have affected the informants' speech act performance. The type of interview used in this study belongs to the class of 'retrospective interview' and partly the 'think-aloud protocol' as Kasper defines these. The normal type of interview is an 'off-line' one (i.e. an interview not related to a specific immediately preceding activity – Kasper, *ibid.*: 333), while the interviews in this study include some 'on-line' aspects in that they allowed examination of the process of response production retrospectively. Kasper states the following, explaining such 'retrospective interviews'.

> ... another interview genre, often referred to as the retrospective interview, informs about participants' thoughts while they are engaged in a specific activity. This interview genre is usually categorized as a form of think-aloud protocol...
>
> (Kasper, *ibid.*: 334)

One thing that should be noted is that 'think-aloud protocols' normally refer to an activity that is carried out during the data collection process: 'think-aloud protocols (TAP) are verbalizations of thought processes during engagement in a task' (Kasper, *ibid*: 336). As this study is based on spoken responses, it is not possible to employ an 'on-going' think-aloud protocol: the retrospective interview in this study is both 'on-line' and a type of 'think-aloud protocol' in that it is carried out right after the response production stage.

Robinson (1992) (quoted in Kasper *ibid.*: 337–338) carried out a 'think-aloud protocol' and a 'retrospective interview' in the same research project. Robinson asked six intermediate and six advanced Japanese learners of English to think aloud while completing a production questionnaire on refusals. Immediately after they finished the task, the tape-recorded think-aloud protocol was played back to subjects in a retrospective interview. In this research 'the concurrent report sheds light on the response alternatives that the learner considered, whereas the retrospective report informs about the learner's views of social relationships that guided her decision-making' (Kasper, *ibid.*: 337). In my view these two tasks, viz. thinking of alternative responses and talking about social relationships, can be done at the same time after the response production stage, probably in the same or even in a better way. I think the informants will concentrate better if the two stages (i.e. 'response production' and 'reflection on the production strategy') are separate. Furthermore, they can produce more 'authentic' data if they are allowed to talk freely in the 'response production stage', instead of writing something and speaking about another thing at the same time. For these reasons I am going to employ a 'retrospective interview' to analyse situational or motivational factors and the 'constraints' of the speech act performance.

4.1.3 Triangulation[2]: combination of research methodologies

In the past, pragmatic research studies were carried out using a single methodology. For example, the biggest cross-cultural pragmatic research project ever undertaken, the Cross-Cultural Speech Act Realisation Project (CCSARP), the results of which were revealed in 1989, employed DCTs in order to facilitate a large-scale worldwide study. Whereas the results obtained by the project brought about great benefits to cross-cultural pragmatic study, some researchers have cast doubts on the validity and credibility of data obtained only through DCTs, as mentioned earlier.

After examining the strong and weak points of each pragmatic research method, researchers have started to consider the importance and necessity of triangulation: application of more than one methodology. This allows a researcher to investigate pragmatic phenomena from various perspectives and increases the reliability of the result. This concept is beneficial since different methodologies are likely to compensate for each other's weaknesses.

Kasper (2000: 340) emphasizes the importance of triangulation and, after examining various methodologies used in previous pragmatic studies, comes to the following conclusion:

> In fact, researchers in different disciplinary traditions advocate the use of multiple data collection procedures as a means to offset the instrument or observer bias that is necessarily involved in each technique. Material collected by means of complementary techniques and from different sources allows triangulation, which may be necessary or desirable in order to increase the validity/credibility of a study.

In this study, as stated earlier, a combination of different methodologies will be employed. The first stage of data collection is conducted with (1) a spoken DCT with video prompts, and (2) an in-depth guided interview. 'A spoken DCT' means that the informants are requested to make oral responses, instead of making written ones. This is an attempt to elicit more authentic spoken data in verbal interaction. The use of 'video prompts' is an effort to make a DCT closer to the 'role-play'. The contextual factors (e.g. the addressee's age, gender, appearance, the setting) are more transparent and give the informants more similar background information than the traditional DCT. An in-depth guided interview is designed to investigate situational and motivational factors that might have affected speech act performance orientations/directions.

The second-stage data collection consists of (3) a rating scale, and (4) an in-depth guided interview. The raters evaluate the remarks selected from the first-stage data using this scale. After the rating stage, an in-depth guided interview is organised to find out what affected the rater's judgement on the scales of **politeness** and **appropriateness**. This interview is devised to explore the 'lay' or 'folk' notion concerning these two constructs. The details of the research design in this study will be presented in Section 4.3.

4.2 Pilot study

As this study was originally planned to explore cross-cultural differences between Japanese and British English, I carried out a pilot study with Japanese and British informants. In this pilot stage I examined the theoretical framework and the research methodologies to be employed in this study. The data was collected from four university undergraduates and four higher age informants aged between 44 and 55 (Japanese) and between 40 and 51 (British), each group consisting of two male and two female informants: this is a perfect match in terms of the number of informants and their gender. More background information on the informants is in Appendix 1.

In the pilot study, I used a 'spoken DCT' and an 'in-depth guided interview' to examine their advantages and disadvantages, and to improve the research methodologies for the main study. A 'spoken DCT' can be recognised as a hybrid of a 'written DCT' and a 'role-play' as mentioned earlier. Informants in this study were asked to read the scenarios and the prompts on the DCT to imagine the situations and the conversation partners. After that they heard the prompts (provided by the researcher in the pilot study) and were asked to say, not write, their response(s) immediately. This method was applied in order to overcome at least part of the problem of the lack of 'authenticity' of DCTs – the traditional written type of DCT is assumed to elicit 'written language' rather than natural responses in spoken form. An 'in-depth guided interview' was designed to elicit such information as (1) the social variables, (2) the evaluation of the level of politeness of the responses, and (3) the process in which the informants produced their responses.

The research procedure of the pilot study consisted of two stages: (1) the spoken DCT; (2) the interview. Regarding the spoken DCT, the respondents were reguested to read eight scenarios, and to imagine they were in the situations and make a response to the most likely person they could have in mind (e.g. a friend, a senior or a junior person who they know/do not know well). I did this in order to investigate whether each informant recognised social variables in the same or different ways, in order to improve the design of the main study. As I needed consistency in the informants' notions of social variables, it was important to clarify what the 'general' images of the conversation partners in the scenarios were like for the sake of the main study. They were also requested to make verbal responses, as natural as possible. I then asked them to write them down on the sheet provided so that they could evaluate how polite their own responses were after this stage.

In the interview, after going through the DCT for the first time, the informants were requested to think of alternatives to their first response, and to put a number against each option in relation to each scenario in accordance with their notions of politeness in a general sense (1= most polite, 2= less polite…). This was to investigate how many options they had and to study their notions of linguistic politeness.

After the completion of the spoken DCT as described above, I carried out an interview to investigate the background to their responses. The guidelines for the questions to be asked in the interview were as follows:

1. What situation and what sort of person did you have on your mind, reading the description?
2. How did you evaluate the impact of the elements below in your answer?
    a) Social distance with the hearer (D)
    b) Relative power between you and the hearer (P)
    c) The size of imposition/ The seriousness of the topic (R)
3. How did you evaluate the impact of the elements below in your answer?
    a) The gender of the hearer (G)
    b) The age of the hearer (A)

4. Please point out other variables that seem to have affected your response, if there are any.
5. Please describe the naturalness/unnaturalness of each situation (N).
6. Please describe anything you felt about this research, as a suggestion for future improvement.

I changed the way I asked the above questions so that informants could understand my intention in the question more clearly (e.g. 'Did you think this person was close to you?' for 2-a, 'Do you think this person has power over you, or do you have power over him/her?' for 2-b), and I asked more detailed questions when I found something interesting (e.g. the reason for choosing certain expressions).

After examining the strong and weak points of the 'spoken DCT' in the pilot study, I devised 'video prompts' so that the informants had equivalent images of who their interlocutor was, and in what situation. In the first-stage data collection of the main study, the 'spoken DCT' along with 'video prompts' and the 'in-depth guided interviews' were applied – primarily to elicit responses and the associated background information, e.g. the situational/motivational factors and constraints that might have affected the production of the illocutions. For the second-stage data collection, the 'rating scale' and the 'in-depth guided interview' were implemented, so that the raters could evaluate the levels of **politeness** and **appropriateness** of the responses collected in the first-stage, and so that I could investigate the backgrounds of their assessments.

4.3 Methodology for this study: research procedure

4.3.1 Summary of the data collection procedure

I carried out two kinds of data collection in the main study, viz. 'the first-stage' – collecting responses from the informants, and 'the second-stage' – evaluation of the level of politeness and appropriateness of the responses collected in the first-stage.

In the first-stage, I employed the 'spoken DCT' with 'video prompts'. After the completion of the DCT, an 'in-depth guided interview' was implemented in the second part of the first-stage, just as in the pilot study. In the main study, however, the questions were only on the backgrounds of the responses. I transcribed the data collected at this stage and eight randomly chosen responses from each item were used in the second stage (details are specified in Section 4.3.6)[3]. In the second-stage, the raters judged the levels of politeness and appropriateness of the responses using the 'rating scale', supplying background information relating to their assessments in the 'in-depth guided interview'.

4.3.2 First-stage data collection: classification of informants

In the initial stage of data collection I acquired spoken data from 24 Japanese informants, consisting of 12 university undergraduates (JYA – 6 male & 6 female) and 12 higher age informants (JHA – 6 male & 6 female). The classification of the respondents is as follows.

<u>Higher Age Group – Male (JHAM) (6)</u>
(40-55, with a university/college degree or diploma)
    2 from business, service occupations or the civil service
    2 from an academic field (concerning education or research)
    2 from a scientific field

<u>Higher Age Group – Female (JHAF) (6)</u>
(40-55, with university/college degree or diploma)
    2 from business, service occupations, civil service or a scientific field
    2 from an academic field (concerning education or research)
    2 from those with household responsibilities (with/without a part-time occupation)

<u>Younger Age Group – Male & Female (JYAM – 6 & JYAF – 6)</u>
(18-22)
    2 from the humanities
    2 from social science
    2 from science and technology

I designed this categorisation so that the collected data would represent as far as possible general tendencies of the four Japanese age and gender groups' linguistic politeness strategies in performing the eight designated speech acts. The difference in the classification of the 'higher age male' and the 'higher age female' is based on the fact that taking household responsibilities (with or without a part-time job), rather than pursuing full-time responsibilities outside the home, is still common for Japanese middle-aged women who graduated from college/university. The details of the backgrounds of the first-stage informants are listed in the Appendix 2.

4.3.3 First-stage data collection: scenarios

The eight scenarios used in this study were designed to examine how the *GSP* is realised in the performance of speech acts with *constraints* under the *GSP* described in Section 2.1.2.2. The following is the summary of the items, constraints and speech acts to be elicited by the eight scenarios:

Item 01: GENEROSITY (*Place a high value on o's wants*) – offers/invitations;
Item 02: TACT (*Place a low value on s's wants*) – directives (requests);
Item 03: APPROBATION (*Place a high value on o's qualities*) – compliments;
Item 04: MODESTY (*Place a low value on s's qualities*) – self-evaluation (self-depreciation);
Item 05: AGREEMENT (*Place a high value on o's opinions*) / OPINION RETICENCE (*Place a low value on s's opinions*) – agreeing/disagreeing / giving opinions;
Item 06: SYMPATHY (*Place a high value on o's feelings*) – expressing feelings;
Item 07: FEELING-RETICENCE (*Place a low value on s's feelings*) / OBLIGATION (of *o* to *s*) (*Place a low value on o's obligation to s*) – suppressing feelings / response to thanks and apologies;
Item 08: OBLIGATION (of *s* to *o*) (*Place a high value on s's obligation to o*) – apologies/thanks.

The ten *constraints* under the *GSP* are incorporated in the above eight items – Item 05 and Item 07 include two types of *constraints* in one scenario. The details of these scenarios will be presented in Section 5.2 (individually in 5.2.1–5.2.8), which discuss the results of the research carried out utilising these scenarios. All the scenarios with some pictures from the video prompts are in Appendix 3.

4.3.4 First-stage data collection: the spoken DCT with video prompts

Prior to the specification of the procedure I employed to implement the spoken DCT with video prompts, I would like to sketch out the history of the application of 'video prompts' in pragmatic studies first.

Whereas DCTs and the role-play have widely been used to elicit data in pragmatic research, one of the common disadvantages of these two methods is a lack of contextual authenticity. While 'ethnography' has been recognised as the 'ultimate naturalistic method', it is difficult to combine an ethnographic style of research with a quantitative study – for example, in an investigation of the tendencies in the politeness strategies of a specific group or comparisons between groups from different backgrounds. For this reason, quantitative research methods (i.e. DCTs or role-plays) have been invented to allow a researcher to investigate cross-cultural/interlanguage politeness strategies (e.g. CCSARP).

One of the common characteristics DCTs and the role-plays share is that both require an informant to take an imaginary role in an imaginary situation. For example, in previous DCT studies, respondents were requested to become 'Tom' or 'Mary' or a part-time worker at a restaurant. In the case of role-plays, they were required to talk to an experimenter or someone else taking an imaginary role – e.g. a 'parking maid' (Fraser & Nolen, 1981). Puppets were sometimes used when the research involved children. While these 'alternatives' – the use of a disguised experimenter or puppets – helped informants understand the context of the scenarios, they were still a step away from reality. In addition, traditional DCTs and role-plays have supplied respondents with information in written form and required them to interpret the situations only on the basis of their previous experiences. As a consequence, it has been difficult for the informants to have identical real images of the situation and the addressee.

Koike (1992) used videotaped dialogue prompts in scenarios to elicit 'suggestions', 'apologies' etc. In the video, native speakers of different varieties of Spanish spoke directly to the addressee. The informants, Anglo learners of Spanish and bilingual Spanish-English Chicano students, were required to make a response to the speaker on the video. Koike explains the reason for the employment of this prompt as follows: '[a] videotape was used instead of an audio-cassette tape because it was believed that the communication of speech acts is much more effective with "holistic" information, including not only the actual utterance but also body movements and facial expressions' (Koike, *ibid.*: 264). Bardovi-Harlig & Dornyei (1998) similarly adopted videotaped scenarios in a study of pragmatic and grammatical awareness in different EFL and ESL populations. They decided to use videotaped scenarios following a discussion at the 1994 annual meeting of the AAAL (American Association for Applied Linguistics) in Baltimore, in which participants agreed that the videotape had the potential to make situations clearer than written scenarios could. These two recent studies have shown that the video medium is applicable to pragmatic research. It is effective in giving informants clearer and more identical images of the situations and the addressees.

'Video prompts' in this study give audiovisual cues to informants. They provide them with real images of the persons in the scenarios to whom they are supposed to talk. With 'video prompts' informants see people who appear to be their friends, seniors, juniors, an old lady or a restaurant manager. This new method made my DCT a step closer to an authentic task with a real image, not an imaginary one, in the minds of the informants. (For the details of the spoken DCTs and the video prompts, see Appendix 3.)

The performers on the video were members of my family and colleagues at my previous workplace in Tokyo. I recruited those who could act as the persons designated in the scenarios, taking into consideration their characteristics such as their age, gender, and ability to represent their age group. Some of the performers took more than one role: (1) a female friend for JYAF informants also acted as a younger female worker for JHA informants and a younger female student for JYA informants, (2) a male friend for JYAM informants also acted as a younger male student for JYA informants, (3) a senior male student for JYA informants also performed as a young male worker for JHA informants, as can be seen in Appendix 3. I consider that these multi-roles of some performers can be justified by the fact that no informant in the following interview expressed any feeling of strangeness about one person taking different roles; informants talked to the video figures as if they were a real 'friend' or a true 'younger worker/student'. In the post-research interview most of the informants were positive about this type of DCT and said that the aid of the video image was helpful to them.

The spoken DCT with video prompts in this study elicited spoken responses from the informants. The data collected by this methodology enabled an investigation into the colloquial and prosodic aspects of the politeness strategies, e.g. the use of interjections, loudness or pitch of voice. The informants were not requested to transcribe their spoken responses, contrary to the procedure in the pilot study. The written data collected in the pilot study was much more 'tidy' than the spoken recording, as the informants were given a chance to trim their utterances by cutting off unnecessary things such as interjections, hesitations, redundant words or errors[4]. Although written data transcribed by informants was convenient for initial analysis, spoken data is thought to be less manipulated and more authentic than its written counterpart.

Informants were first requested to read through all eight items and to understand the research procedure. Then they were shown the video prompts and made responses to them (1st part). After completing all eight items of the DCT, they were requested to go back to Item 01 and to make second responses, if they could think of them. Then the 'in-depth guided interview' was carried out to learn what factors and constraints affected their utterance(s) (2nd part). After the interview, some informants were asked about the video prompts in order to investigate the effect of them, as mentioned above.

4.3.5 Some noticeable characteristics of the spoken DCT in this study

In addition to the previous account of advantages of the DCT in the pilot study section, I would like to describe some other aspects of this methodology, especially in comparison with a role-play.

Beebe & Cummings (1996) explored this issue by comparing written data obtained by the DCT with more 'natural' data acquired by a role-play on the phone and drew the following conclusion:

> Returning to our original research questions, we asked whether questionnaire data were an accurate reflection of spoken data or a useful research method in other respects. In this chapter we argue that Discourse Completion Tests are a highly effective research tool as a means of:
> 1) Gathering a large amount of data quickly;
> 2) Creating an initial classification of semantic formulas and strategies that will likely occur in natural speech;
> 3) Studying the stereotypical, perceived requirements for a socially appropriate response;
> 4) Gaining insight into social and psychological factors that are likely to affect speech and performances; and
> 5) Ascertaining the canonical shape of speech acts in the minds of speakers of that language.   (Beebe and Cummings, *ibid.*:80)

Indeed, a complex study of several speech acts at the same time, like in the present study, benefits from these strengths of the DCT, especially when there are as many as eight items to be examined. As for the first observation above, although I had no more than twenty-four informants in this study, there were eight items to be investigated and the research sessions had to be held one by one. Furthermore, I asked for informants' second responses, if they had any, and organised an interview to explore various factors behind their responses – consequently I collected a large amount of data. The second characteristic above makes the task of data analysis more straightforward: it is easier to focus on the patterns of 'semantic formulae' of speech act performance with large-scale data collected with the DCT. The third, the fourth and the fifth strengths perfectly match the purpose of this study: an investigation into intra-cultural differences in speech act performance. Above all, the consistency of the data collected through the DCTs is suitable for the aims and features of this research.

On the other hand, a role-play, if it invites the respondent to interact freely with the person they are talking to, allows the conversation to extend in directions that do not serve the purposes of the research. Regarding such shortcomings, Beebe and Cummings (*ibid*.) state a possible bias that was included in the spoken data obtained by a role-play as follows, citing other researchers' previous descriptions on the effect of "mm hm", and "uh-huh".

> Finally, we feel that the telephone conversation data may have inadvertently been biased by us. At the outset of the study we decided to remain neutral by interacting as little as possible with the telephone respondents, giving only the minimal responses of "mm hm," "uh-huh," etc. However, this was not the expected response in a remedial exchange. Owen (1983: 57) found that "if one speaker merely acknowledges that remedial work has been performed, rather than accepting it, it…has the effect of 'eliciting' further remedial work," which he refers to as "elaborations" or "recyclings."
>
> (Beebe & Cummings, *ibid*.:70; annotation mine)

The description above suggests that there are both qualitative and quantitative differences in the data collected by a DCT and that collected by a role-play. A role-play may well elicit a response as some 'by-product' incidental to the main direction of the exchange, and consequently it may also elicit more than the core part of the speech act. This kind of 'turn-taking' is observed in one kind of role-play. Kasper (2000) describes the differences between two types of role-play by using the terms 'open' and 'closed'.

> Role-plays also differ in the extent of the interaction. In interlanguage pragmatics, a distinction has been suggested between closed and open role-plays (Kasper and Dahl 1991). In closed role-plays, the actor responds to the description of a situation and, depending on the communicative act under study, to an interlocutor's standardized initiation. They are thus organized as single-turn speech acts. ... Open role-plays, on the other hand, specify the initial situation and each actor's role and goal(s) on individual role cards, but the course and outcome of the interaction are in no way predetermined. ... Unlike closed role-plays, an open role-play ... will evolve over many turns and different discourse phases. Communicative acts will be organized over multiple turns and their sequencing will be strongly influenced by the interlocutor's uptake. The conversational activity will address interpersonal functions, such as politeness, and interactional functions, such as coordinating speaker and listener contributions through turn-taking and backchannelling.
> ...
> (Kasper, 2000:322–23)

Interestingly, my spoken DCTs also elicited a wider array of speech act performance, such as those mentioned by Beebe & Cummings above. As I mentioned in Section 4.1.2.2, some informants talked to the video performers and created imaginary turns: therefore their responses were considerably longer and contained elements other than the speech acts themselves, e.g. a 'warm-up' for conversation, backchannel actions, or talks on casual topics such as going to the latest film. In this sense there was an element of an 'open' role-play, as described by Kasper above. This is a unique quality of my spoken DCT, as the conventional questionnaire, with limited writing space for the informant's response, has not elicited such 'discourse style responses' so far. In conclusion, the spoken DCT in this study is a hybrid of a productive questionnaire and a role-play, both 'closed' and 'open', in that (1) its main purpose was to elicit condensed information on speech act strategies (mainly achieved by DCTs and a 'closed' role-play), (2) it allowed informants to interact with figures in a video (mainly achieved by a 'closed' and 'open' role-play), and (3) it also encouraged some informants to perform responses to imaginary turn-taking (analogous to the 'open' role-play).

4.3.6 The second-stage data collection

In the latter phase of research, I employed 'rating scales' and asked the raters to evaluate the degree of politeness (on a five-point scale) and appropriateness (on a three-point scale) of the responses that the first-stage informants made. I had two younger age raters (university undergraduates: 18–22 years old) and two higher age raters (40-55 years old), both pairs consisting of one male and one female person (classified as HFR, HMR, YFR and YMR respectively). The details of the raters' backgrounds are given in Appendix 4.

The eight responses used in the second-stage were chosen basically randomly as follows.

	1	2	3	4	5	6	7	8
Item01	JHAF01	JHAM01	JYAF01	JYAM01	JHAF02	JHAM02	JYAF02	JYAM02
Item02	JHAF02	JHAM02	JYAF02	JYAM02	JHAF03	JHAM03	JYAF03	JYAM03
Item03	JHAF03	JHAM03	JYAF03	JYAM03	JHAF04	JHAM04	JYAF04	JYAM04
Item04	JHAF04	JHAM04	JYAF04	JYAM04	JHAF05	JHAM05	JYAF05	JYAM05
Item05	JHAF05	JHAM05	JYAF05	JYAM05	JHAF06	JHAM06	JYAF06	JYAM06
Item06	JHAF06	JHAM06	JYAF06	JYAM06	JHAF03	JHAM01	JYAF01	JYAM01
Item07	JHAF01	JHAM02	JYAF03	JYAM05	JHAF02	JHAM03	JYAF04	JYAM04
Item08	JHAF06	JHAM05	JYAF04	JYAM03	JHAF05	JHAM04	JYAF03	JYAM02

These are all first responses, as they were assumed to be impromptu and more natural than the second ones. Also, as many informants did not produce second responses, it was inevitable to focus on the first ones. I had intended to have responses with orderly patterns, but I must report that it was not perfectly done because of some technical reasons (e.g. 'JHAF03' in Item06 – I had taken this as JHAF01 first). However, I made corrections wherever necessary so that these imperfections would not cause any serious problem.

'Politeness' in this stage is related to *pragmalinguistic* features of responses and therefore to **absolute politeness**, whereas 'appropriateness' is connected with *socio-pragmatics* and consequently **relative politeness** (cf. Leech, 1983). This study will focus on how these two types of politeness function jointly and separately. The relationship between *pragmalinguistics, socio-pragmatics*, 'grammar' and 'socio-psychology' is demonstrated in the figure below.

Figure 4.3.6 The relationship between General pragmatics, Pragmalinguistics and Socio-pragmatics

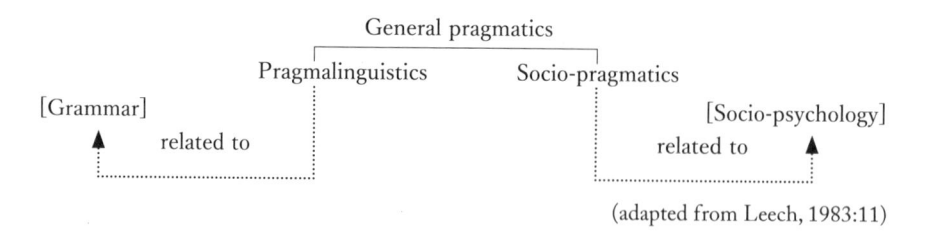

```
                    General pragmatics
              ┌────────────┴────────────┐
          Pragmalinguistics       Socio-pragmatics
[Grammar]                                              [Socio-psychology]
   ▲       related to              related to           ▲
```

(adapted from Leech, 1983:11)

I asked the raters to judge the degree of politeness (i.e. **absolute politeness**) not just by looking at the use of honorifics, as what is important is to examine the propositional content of an utterance and the 'lexicogrammatical strategies' used to express it – honorifics are just morphological and lexical devices that function as 'linguistic ornaments'. Too much emphasis on the correct use of honorifics could blur the illocutionary force of an utterance created by its 'propositional content' and 'lexicogrammatical strategies'. Then I requested them to judge the degree of appropriateness (i.e. **relative politeness**) of the responses in relation to the situation. I hypothesised that the scale of appropriateness could be assessed by comparing the *pragmalinguistic* dimensions with the social variables, viz. vertical and horizontal social distance, the weightness of 'value transaction', and the formality of the situation (to name a few).

The five-point scale for the level of politeness I used is as follows: [1] '*Totemo teinie / Totemo kizukai ga mieru*' (Very polite / Showing high consideration), [2] '*Teinei / Kizukai ga mieru*' (Polite / Showing consideration), [3] '*Futsuu*' (Neutral), [4] '*Sukoshi kudakete iru / Sukoshi kizukai ga mie nai*' (A little informal / A little lack of consideration), and [5] '*Totemo kudakete iru / Shitsurei*' (Very informal / Impolite). I set these definitions in order to allow the raters to understand the basis of judging the *pragmalinguistic* quality of the response without difficulty or confusion. I explained these using a very simple example to show different levels of politeness – four ways of saying 'I'm Toshihiko Suzuki' in Japanese. I controlled the level of politeness of the example by manipulating the first person pronoun (*watakushi – watashi – boku – ore*) and honorific and non-honorific verb forms (*gozaimasu – moushi-masu – desu – da yo – da*). The characteristic of Japanese of controlling the level of politeness by the use of lexically embedded honorifics worked well to show those differences, for the content was the same in all five examples. As I mentioned above, however, I asked the raters not to judge the degree of politeness only by looking at honorifics but also by considering the propositional contents, demonstrating with the following supplementary example:

(1) *Ato juppun,*   *juu-ji*   *choodo*   *made*
    another ten minutes, ten o'clock   just   until

*o-machi-shite-**orimasu**.*
waiting(**EXAL**)-will be(**HUM**)

[I will be waiting for another ten minutes, until just ten o'clock.]

(2) *Juu-ji*   *sugite-mo*   *kamawa-nai*   *yo,*
    ten o'clock   passed-even if   doesn't matter   FP

kuru-made   *matteru*   *yo.*
come-until   will be waiting   FP

[It doesn't matter if it's after ten o'clock. I'll be waiting until you come.]

The first example contains honorifics whereas the second includes none, but the propositional content in the second remark can be taken as 'more polite' or 'showing more consideration'. Although the judgement cannot be made in a straightforward way, I asked the raters to assess the level of **absolute politeness** considering all these features.

In terms of 'appropriateness', the three levels were defined as follows: [1] '*Tekisetsu*' (Appropriate), [2] '*Sukoshi fu-tekisetsu – Sukoshi teinei sugiru / Sukoshi shitsurei*' (A little inappropriate – a little too polite / a little impolite), and [3] '*Totemo fu-tekisetsu – Totemo teinei sugiru / Totemo shitsurei*' (Very inappropriate – too polite / very impolite). Unlike politeness, 'appropriateness' does not possess the category of 'neutral' (i.e. 'polite' – 'neutral' – 'impolite' vs. 'appropriate' – 'inappropriate'). Therefore I set a three-point scale for the level of appropriateness in this research. I illustrated the degrees of appropriateness by using the following sample utterances for making a request in a queue at crowded popular and rather casual places such as Tokyo Disneyland or a famous Japanese noodle-shop (I explained this verbally to the raters). The common propositional content of the requests was 'move a little forward'.

(1) 'appropriate'
    Suimasen,   *sukoshi*   *tsumete-morae-**masu**-ka.*
    I'm sorry(**POL**)   a little   move forward-receive(**POL**)-Q

    [I'm sorry. Can you move a little forward?]

(2) 'a little inappropriate – a) a little *overpolite* or b) a little *underpolite*'
    a) *Moushiwake-ari-**masen**-ga   o-tsume-itadaku-koto-wa*
        I'm sorry, but(**POL**)   move forward(**EXAL**)-receive(**HUM**)-NOM2-TOP

        *deki-**masu-deshoo**-ka.*
        is possible(**POL**)-Q

        [I'm sorry, but is it possible for you to move forward?]

    b) *Chotto*   *tsumete-yo.*
        a little   move forward-FP

        [Move a little forward, man.]

(3) 'very inappropriate – a) very much *overpolite* or b) very much *underpolite*'
    a) *Taihen kyooshuku-de-**gozaimasu**-ga,*
        terribly obliged-COP(**SUPERPOL**)-but

        *o-tsume-**itadakeru**-to*
        move forward(**EXAL**)-receive(**HUM**)-COMP

        hijooni   *ureshuu-**gozaimasu**.*
        very much   glad-COP(**SUPERPOL**)

        [I'm terribly sorry, but if you could move forward I would be very glad.]

b) *Nani yatten-da-yo.*   *Tsumero-yo.*
   what   doinf-COP(PLAIN)-FP   move forward(IMPERATIVE)-FP

[What-ya doin'? I'm telling you to move forward.]

This time I used indirectness and lexical devices that express the speaker's modesty to indicate a higher degree of politeness; and showed impoliteness with the absence of such tact or with the use of rude expressions. I presented these examples to demonstrate the continuum of *overpoliteness* and *underpoliteness*. This experimental research on the distinction and correlation between 'politeness' (i.e. **absolute politeness**) and 'appropriateness' (i.e. **relative politeness**) had some very interesting results, which are to be presented and discussed later.

I would also like to mention that the video performers and I had worked together to modify the wording of the prompts. We designed the prompts so that they sound most suitable in the contexts of the scenarios, but we planned the modified versions to keep the same illocutionary force as the originals. (For the details see Appendix 5.) This modification was carried out because of the fact that younger people and older people – say, young female university undergraduates and middle-aged male office workers – speak differently. If they had said precisely the same as the original prompts they might have sounded unnatural to the informants. For example, female Japanese generally do not use the 'male' interjection form, '*yoo*', instead they use '*ara*' or '*a'*/'*aa*' when addressing their friends. Therefore it is usually strange if they say '*yoo*' to their friends (although recently much younger girls might do it, for such gender differences are disappearing in Japanese society).

I have so far reviewed the methodology and the procedure of this research, referring to and examining methodologies employed in previous pragmatic studies. In summary, the spoken DCT with video prompts and the in-depth guided interview are employed in the first-stage data collection with 24 Japanese informants. The rating scale and the in-depth guided interview are applied in the second-stage with four raters to assess the scales of politeness and appropriateness of the responses collected in the first-stage. In the next chapter (Chapter 5), I will present the results of the quantitative and qualitative data analyses and discuss their implications for this pragmatic study of politeness strategies. The strong and weak points of the methodologies applied in this study will be summarised and discussed in relation to future studies in Section 7.2.

Notes

1. Kasper states the strong and weak points of the 'role-play' as follows: 'Obviously, when conversational interaction and the sequencing of communicative action in conjunction with turn-taking is the research focus, an interactive procedure such as role-play needs to be chosen. On the other hand, if the purpose of an investigation is to inform about the types of strategies by which a communicative act can be implemented, written production questionnaires are an effective means of data collection… (Kasper, 2000: 325).
2. 'Triangulation' in a pragmatic research means the application of more than one methodologies to investigate a research interest from different angles. This is effective in overcoming weak points in the methodologies and in achieving a more comprehensive observation by looking at a phenomenon from different angles.
3. I did this for a practical reason: if the number of responses had not been limited to a manageable number in one research session, the second stage informants (i.e. 'raters') would have needed to handle more than three hundred responses. This is certainly impractical, if not impossible. The reduction of the number to eight for each item made the research task possible. In order to obtain statistical significance in the results, I chose two responses from each group (i.e. 'higher age male', 'higher age female', 'younger age male' and 'younger age female') for each item. In total, the second-stage 'rating scale' questionnaire contained sixty-four utterances (eight responses for each item).
4. However, I would claim this does not render the pilot study data invalid as it still provides condensed information about speech act performance – the pilot study data has been used in my other studies (e.g. Suzuki, 2004).

Chapter 5

Results

5.1 Summary of findings based on quantitative analysis

5.1.1 Overall observations

In summary, the overall quantitative analysis of the data, using *SPSS (Statistical Package for Social Science) ver. 11.5.0*, shows the following statistical evidence[1].

(1) The statistics show that there is a very significant difference in the mean scores of the level of **politeness** between JHA and JYA ($p<.001$). JHA showed a much higher level of **politeness** than JYA. (Means: JHA – 2.59; JYA – 3.07 ($n=128$ each)) (See Appendix 6 for details.)

(2) There is no significant statistical difference concerning the level of **appropriateness** between JHA and JYA ($p>.05$). (Means: JHA – 1.49; JYA – 1.54 ($n=128$ each)) (See Appendix 6 for details.)

(3) One-way ANOVA (Analysis of Variance) shows that there are significant differences among the four sub-groups in **politeness** ($p<.001$). As for appropriateness, as unequal variance was confirmed, Kruskal-Wallis test was applied alternatively. Through this examination, significant mean differences among the four groups were confirmed ($p<.05$). JHAF showed higher standards of **politeness** and **appropriateness** than the rest of the groups. As for the level of politeness, JHAF (Mean = 2.39) was followed by JHAM (Mean = 2.64), JYAF (Mean = 2.98), JYAM (Mean = 3.16) in order (n = 64 each). In terms of the level of **appropriateness**, the JHAF group (Mean=1.30) was followed by JYAF (Mean = 1.47), JYAM (Mean = 1.61), JHAM (Mean = 1.69) in order (n = 64 each). In terms of **politeness**, the post hoc test (Bonferroni test) has confirmed significant mean differences between JHAF–JYAF ($p<.05$) and between JHAF–JYAM's ($p<.001$). The result of the Dunnet test demonstrated significant differences in **appropriatentess** between JHAF–JHAM ($p<.05$) and between JHAF–JYAM ($p<.05$). (See Appendix 8 for details.)

(4) As for correlation between **politeness** and **appropriateness**, the statistics demonstrated a very significant link between the two ($p<.001$). However, this was not the case in JHA's (i.e. combined JHAF and JHAM), JHAF's and JHAM's data. Their data did not exhibit a meaningful link between them. On the other hand, JYA's (i.e. combined JYAF and JYAM), JYAF's and JYAM's data presented a significant correlation between the two (in all cases $.p<.001$). (See Appendix 9 for details.)

(5) Concerning the raters in the second stage data collection, the statistics showed no significant difference in rating the levels of **politeness** and **appropriateness** between HARs (higher age raters) (Means: **politeness** = 2.69, **appropriateness** = 1.50, n = 128) and YARs (younger age raters) (Means: **politeness** = 2.90, **appropriateness** = 1.53, n = 128). One-way ANOVA shows significant mean differences among the raters in **politeness** ($p<.05$). YFR (younger age female rater) tended to assign higher points to the level of **politeness** (i.e. gave a lower rating of politeness) (Mean = 3.16) than the rest. According to the post hoc test (Bonferroni test), significant differences were confirmed between YFR–HMR (higher age male rater – Mean = 2.55) ($p<.005$), and YFR–YMR (younger age rater – Mean = 2.64) ($p<.05$), but not between YFR–HFR (higher age female rater – Mean = 2.83). Although no significant group mean differences were found in **appropriateness**, YFR's average score was lower (Mean = 1.41) than the rest: HFR (Mean = 1.52), HMR (Mean = 1.48), YMR (Mean = 1.66). This means that her evaluation in **appropriateness** tended to be higher than the other raters. (See Appendix 10 for details.)

In the following sections I would like to discuss the implications of the above results for this study's objective of investigating the generation gap in linguistic politeness strategies in contemporary Japanese society.

5.1.2 The generation gap in politeness from the quantitative perspective

Firstly, (1) clearly shows that there is a generation gap between the higher age group and the younger age group, with a much higher level of **politeness** being achieved by the former. JHA has a higher *pragmalinguistic* competence, viz. the ability to control lexicogrammatical politeness devices (including the propositional content of an utterance), than JYA does. This supports the hypothesis of this study: the Japanese higher age group has higher competence in linguistic politeness than the younger age group does.

Charts (1) and (2) of Appendix 7 demonstrate the proportions of the levels of **politeness** used by the two groups. According to the pie charts, the combination of level 1 (very polite / showing high consideration) (15.6%) and 2 (polite / showing consideration) (38.3%) surpasses fifty percent in JHA's data, while this is not the case in JYA's. In the case of JYA, the combination of level 3 (neutral) (33.6%) and 4 (a little informal / a little lack of consideration) (31.3%) constitutes the majority of the total. These results show that JHA's proportion epicentre is skewed towards higher level politeness and JYA's towards lower level politeness, as the means (JHA – 2.59, JYA – 3.07) demonstrate.

5.1.3 The generation gap in appropriateness from the quantitative perspective

Secondly, (2) indicates that a higher level of linguistic politeness does not necessarily mean a higher level of **situational appropriateness** and vice versa. Too much sophistication in **absolute politeness** (i.e. *pragmalinguistic* features) can lead to *overpoliteness* in the scale of **relative politeness** (i.e. in the *sociopragmatic* domain), while little sophistication in the former does not necessarily result in *underpoliteness* in certain contexts and when all the factors (such as horizontal/vertical distance between *s* and *h* or 'weightiness' of the issue) are taken into consideration. The absence of any significant difference concerning **appropriateness** shows that the JYA informants were successful in making their responses appropriate in spite of their less polite features in **absolute politeness**. It can also imply that some JHA responses were regarded as *overpolite* and consequently this led to their being evaluated lower in **relative politeness**. Individual item analysis in the following sections will demonstrate how **politeness** and **appropriateness** were associated or dissociated with each other in the assessment of informants' responses.

Charts (3) and (4) of Appendix 7 illustrate the similarity of the proportions of the levels of **appropriateness** shown by the two age groups. About 60% of the responses were rated as 'appropriate', around 25% as 'a little inappropriate – a little too polite / a little impolite', and the rest (approximately 15%) were ranked as 'very inappropriate – too polite / very impolite'. From this result it can be safely said that the majority of the responses created by both age groups were recognised as 'appropriate' and that 'very inappropriate' responses were rather marginal in this study.

5.1.4 Group differences from the quantitative perspective

Thirdly, (3) demonstrates that JHAF achieved the best performance in both **politeness** and **appropriateness**. Japanese women are traditionally known as performers of sophisticated politeness, and this common assumption was confirmed statistically. On the other hand, JHAM showed the lowest mean score in appropriateness, while they accomplished second best performance in **politeness**. This implies that they might have performed *overpoliteness* as well as *underpoliteness*, as defined by Leech (1983). I will conduct an analysis of each individual item to find out where and how JHAM made such inappropriate responses in the following sections.

Charts (1) and (2) of Appendix 8 Section (B) demonstrate the proportion of the levels of **politeness** and **appropriateness** achieved by each group. Chart (1) clearly indicates the declining trend in level 1 and 2 politeness in relation to the order of the age–gender groups (JHAF: 32%, JHAM: 27%, JYAF: 12%, JYAM: 9%). This rank order suggests that JHAF demonstrated the highest competence in terms of *pragmalinguistics*, while JYAM showed the lowest achievement there.

Chart (2) presents some noticeable features. JHAM's data shows the lowest percentage of level 1 **appropriateness** (23%) of all the groups. In contrast, the proportion of JHAF's level 1 **appropriateness** exceeds half the responses that were assessed by the raters (52%). The most striking feature is probably JHAM's highest proportion of level 3 **appropriateness** (44%). Even though JHAM achieved the second highest achievement in **absolute politeness** as mentioned in the previous section, nearly half of their utterances were rated as 'very inappropriate'. The implication of this result is that they did not relate **absolute politeness** to **relative politeness**. This failure of JHAM to connect **absolute politeness** to **relative politeness** will be investigated in the following qualitative analysis section.

5.1.5 Correlation between politeness and appropriateness

Fourthly, (4) indicates that the level of **appropriateness** increases in accordance with the increase in the level of **politeness**. (For figures, see Appendix 9 (A)-(1).) This indicates that **absolute** and **relative politeness** are interrelated. This finding creates one piece of new evidence concerning the relation between these two concepts of politeness: in order to achieve a satisfactory level of **appropriateness**, one needs to have command of the strategies in **absolute politeness**, viz. the lexical and grammatical competence to manage the propositional content of an utterance.

A generation gap and group differences emerge in this area as well, when the two main groups and four subgroups are examined and compared with each other. As for the main groups (JHA and JYA), whereas correlation between the two variables were proven to be significant in the JYA data, it was not the case in the JHA data (for figures, see Appendix 9 (A)-(2)&(3).) Graphs (8) and (9) in Appendix 9 (B) illustrate this discrepancy. It should be noted that more than half of level 1 politeness responses (57%) were rated as 'very inappropriate' in JHA's case. This means that their most polite utterances were judged as displaying *overpoliteness*. By looking at the graphs (10) and (11) (Appendix 9 (B)), we can spot where this phenomenon comes from: whereas JHAF's level 1 politeness does not possess level 3 appropriateness, 66% of JHAM's level 1 politeness was rated as level 3 appropriateness. Therefore JHAM was the key group in controlling the balance between **absolute** and **relative politeness**. However, as Figure (4) and Graph (10) of Appendix 9 illustrate, JHAF showed a hint of discrepancy between the two kinds: 64% of their level 1 politeness scores were rated as level 2 appropriateness while over 50% of their level 2, 3, and 4 politeness scores were rated as level 1 appropriateness . This is another piece of evidence of *overpoliteness* on the higher age group's side.

On the other hand, the results of the data analysis of the two JYA groups showed highly significant correlations between the two politeness varieties. (See Appendix 9 (A)-(6)&(7).) The graphs (Appendix 9 (B)-(12)&(13)) demonstrate this as well. While JYAF has a slight tendency towards *overpoliteness* in level 1 politeness, JYAM achieved a perfect correlation. Their level 1 politeness was rated as level 1 appropriateness by 100%, whereas their level 5 politeness was entirely rated as 'very inappropriate' (level 3). Moreover, the percentages of the level of appropriateness increase and decrease in accordance with the level of politeness. This evidence indicates that the JYAM informants were perfect in linking absolute and relative politeness and their performance did not result in any *overpoliteness*. This is interesting considering that their group performance in **politeness** was rated the lowest, as mentioned in the earlier summary (5.1.1. (3)). Despite this, their responses' levels of **politeness** matched perfectly with the scale of **appropriateness**.

5.1.6 Raters' performance

Lastly, (5) means that there was no significant difference in rating between the two groups of raters, viz. the higher age ones and the younger ones (see Appendix 10 (a)). It should be noted, however, that YFR tended to give a response higher scores (i.e. lower levels) of **politeness** than the rest did, and lower scores (i.e. higher levels) of **appropriateness** than the rest (see Appendix 10 (B), and refer to 5.1.1-(5) above for significant differences between YFR and other raters). This seems to be because she tended to take some 'salient' linguistic features as 'non-salient' and on the whole to regard responses as 'non-salient' in the context. The reason for this tendency of the YFR will be discussed and investigated in more detail in the following sections.

5.2 Individual item analyses

In this section, I will look at each item from both qualitative and quantitative perspectives to examine the group differences concerning politeness strategies. In discussing the linguistic qualities of responses, I would like to employ some analytical techniques using designated terms to explain the scales of **politeness** and **appropriateness** of illocutions performing speech acts, developed by researchers in previous studies of Japanese politeness. Here is an overview of the concepts and definitions of the terms that are to be utilised in this chapter.

Firstly, in order to classify the levels of formality of Japanese pronouns I will adopt the categories 'very formal', 'formal', 'average' and 'colloquial'[2]. Takeuchi shows the following table to demonstrate how the Japanese pronouns that correspond to English 'I' can be categorised according to the level of formality[3].

Table 5.2-1 Classification of Japanese 1st person pronoun

speaker:	male	female
very formal	*watakushi*	*watakushi*
formal	*jibun, watashi*	*watakushi*
average	*boku*	*watashi*
colloquial	*ore, washi*	*atashi*

(adapted from Takeuchi, 1999: 64)

As for the honorific forms of predicatives and other parts of speech, I will use the terms 'exalted' (showing respect towards *o* or *h*), 'humble' (showing *s*'s modesty), 'plain', and 'colloquial' to describe the concepts expressed by the terms, using the same conventions some researchers have previously adopted. The following table shows how categorisation is to be done with these terms.

Table 5.2-2 Classification of Japanese verb honorification

exalted	humble	denotation	plain	colloquial
irassharu	*mairu*	'come' 'go'	*kuru, iku*	---
	oru	'be/exist'	*iru*	
kudasaru	*sashiageru*	'give, bestow'	*ageru*	*yaru*
ossharu	*mooshiageru*	'say'	*i(w)u*	---
meshiagaru	*itadaku*	'eat' 'drink'	*taberu, nomu*	*kuu*, ---
nasaru	*itasu*	'do'	*suru*	*yaru*

(adapted from Takeuchi, 1999: 60)

The original list demonstrated by Takeuchi does not include a category of 'colloquial', but I will use this term to classify such words as *kuu* (eat) or *yaru* (do). (I will call *yaru*, meaning 'give' as shown above, 'colloquial' as well, for from my observation *ageru* is the plain form of its English denotation.) I will also include *desu*, a polite form of a copula *da*, and a morpheme *-masu* as formal/polite markers in the 'exalted' category.

Secondly, wherever applicable, I will use the four main classifications of speech act moves employed in the CCSARP (The Cross-Cultural Speech Act Realization Project) conducted by Blum-Kulka *et al.* (1989): *alerters, supportive moves, head acts*, and *IFIDs* (Illocutionary force indicating devices; Searle, 1969: 64) (Blum-Kulka *et al.*, 1989: 17 onwards) in my own way for the particular purpose of analysing the (sub-)strategies of the utterances presented in this study effectively. *Alerters* are 'attention-getters', which are usually put at the beginning of speech act performance, e.g. 'address terms' (Blum-Kulka *et.al, ibid.*: 17). I will include Japanese interjections such as *aa* (hey/hi) or *anoo* (excuse me/well) in this category, for they also function as such 'attention getters'.

Supportive moves are the phrases used to 'persuade the hearer to do x' (*ibid.*: 17)[4]. Elements either preceding or following core parts (*head acts* or *IFIDs*), which function to support them, are recognised as such moves. The functions of *head acts* and *IFIDs* are quite similar: they serve as the 'core parts' in speech act performance.

An *IFID* 'selects a routinized, formulaic expression of a speech act'. Therefore 'I'm sorry' or 'I regret...' etc. in apologies are examples of *IFIDs* (*ibid.*: 17–18). In a similar way, *head acts* 'might serve to realize the act independently of other elements' (*ibid.*: 17). I will use this term, *head acts*, where the core part of speech act performance is demonstrated by other means than an *IFID* (the core part that is without such verbs that directly represent the speech act itself – e.g. 'apologise'. 'request', 'sympathise'). These moves are useful in an investigation of the *semantic formulae* being applied in speech act performance.

Blum-Kulka *et al.* (*ibid.*) used more detailed classifications in their study of 'requests' and 'apologies'. However, since most of the speech acts to be studied in this thesis are unrelated to most of such moves, I will concentrate on the most relevant four major moves. Although this research also contains the two speech acts above, I will continue to apply these four categories in order to simplify and clarify the procedure of analysing sentence and discourse structures.

While applying the four major moves to investigate *semantic formulae* for the general purpose, it is necessary to describe many other linguistic features and many other factors behind speech act performance. I will conduct a descriptive analysis of these features and the issues they raise, for they cannot be explained or summarised by the moves classified by Blum-Kulka *et al.* My audiovisual DCTs have let informants make freer/more extensive responses than the conventional written DCTs used in the CCSARP. In this sense, the types of responses used to perform the same speech act in this study are not uniform: thus it is necessary to go beyond previous studies to probe the 'stereotype' in speech act performance. Indeed the new technique of audiovisual DCTs has encouraged people to elaborate on their responses.

5.2.1 Item 01
Constraint: Generosity – '*Place a high value on o's wants*'
Speech act(s): offers / invitations
Activity type: Conversation with a friend
Social variables: vertical distance = no, horizontal distance = no
Formality: informal
(For more details of the scenario, see Appendix 3.)

In this section I will investigate how Japanese informants performed speech acts of 'offers' and 'invitations'. Leech (1983: 106), citing Searle (1979[1975]), classifies 'offer' as a 'commissive verb', which 'commits *s* (to a greater or lesser degree) to some future action', and as an act 'performed in the interests of someone other than the speaker'. 'Invitations' can be included in the 'commissive' category as well, for they share the same quality as 'offers' (a special kind of offer – an offer of hospitality). Consequently it is assumed that people will 'place a high value on *o*'s wants' in performing these speech acts in a polite and harmonious way. Analysis of this item hence focuses on how Japanese informants realised the *GSP* and satisfied the constraint through the observation of raters' assessments.

As for the video prompts for this item, I made four different types of video clips because the stereotype of a 'close friend' varies according to the age and the gender of *s*. As mentioned in Section 4.3.6, I asked the performers to work with me to modify the wording of the prompt so that it would sound as natural to *h* as possible. I carefully negotiated with the performers on what to say and how to say it in order to make the modified version mean the same thing as the original does – in other words these different prompts were designed to have the same illocutionary force. As the original prompt was just a simple greeting 'Hi. How are you?', we had to think of quite a few alternatives. The modified prompts used by the four different performers are as follows.

<u>The prompt for JHAM:</u>
   Yaa, genki?
   hi   alright
   <Hi. How are you?>

<u>The prompt for JHAF:</u>
   Ara, doo   shita   no?
   hey what   do-PAST   FP
   <Hey. What's up?>

<u>The prompt for JYAM:</u>
   Yoo, doo   shita   no?
   hey what   do-PAST   FP
   <Hey. What's up?>

The prompt for JYAF:
A, genki?
ah alright
<Hi. How are you?>

All these prompts consist of *alerters* (<hi> and <hey>) and *head acts* (<How are you?> and <What's happened?>) to perform a 'greeting' formula. One notable difference among these variations is the use of interjections at the beginning. They are the most typical hails among people in each age and gender group: Japanese middle-aged women will never use *yoo* and male Japanese university students never use *ara*. If they did, they would sound quite strange and it would give the hearer a very funny impression (or s/he could think of the performer as a very unique person). Sociolinguistic distinctions of this kind are important in order to make the prompts sound appropriate. If measured by the formality scale described above, all these illocutions are classified somewhere between 'average' and 'colloquial'.

Another difference is that two performers (JHAM and JYAF) used *genki* <alright> and the other two (JHAF and JYAM) used *doo shita no* <what's up>. They made a choice from these because they thought they would normally use either of the two expressions. Both of them are common formulaic expressions for greetings and are usually synonymous and interchangeable in this context.

Now I will move on to the results of the data analysis. The following table is a summary of the statistical data of Item 01.

Table 5.2.1 Summary of statistical data: Item 01

	Average scores in politeness		Average scores in appropriateness		Average scores in politeness		Average scores in appropriateness
1	JHA (2.88)	1	JHA (1.38)	1	JHAF (2.75)	1	JHAF (1.38)
				2	JHAM (3.00)		JHAM (1.38)
2	JYA (3.56)	2	JYA (1.81)	3	JYAF (3.25)	3	JYAF (1.50)
				4	JYAM (3.88)	4	JYAM (2.13)

The data obtained in the second stage shows that JHA showed a higher level of **politeness** (Mean = 2.88, n = 16) than JYA (Mean = 3.56, n = 16) and the difference is statistically very significant ($p<.005$). As for **appropriateness**, the data did not show a significant difference between the two age groups, although JHA's average score was lower (i.e. 'more appropriate') (Mean = 1.38, n = 16) than JYA's (Mean = 1.88, n = 16).

In terms of differences among age–gender groups concerning the degree of **politeness**, JHAF (Mean = 2.75, n = 8) comes at the top and is followed by JHAM (Mean = 3.00, n = 8), JYAF (Mean = 3.25, n = 8) and JYAM (Mean = 3.87, n = 8) in order. Kruskal Wallis test has confirmed significant mean differences among the four age–gender groups ($p<.05$). Through the post hoc test (Bonferroni test), significant diference was observed between JHAF and JYAM ($p<.05$).

As for **appropriateness**, JHAF and JHAM are at the top with the same mean scores (1.38, n = 8 each), with JYAF (Mean = 1.50, n = 8) and JYAM (Mean = 2.13, n = 8) following them. No significant mean differences were found among the four groups and between any paired groups, however.

I would like to move on to the qualitative analysis of the data collected in the second stage in order to look for particular reasons why some responses were rated as 'more polite' or 'more appropriate' and vice versa. I will adopt for this purpose the analytic techniques described above for this purpose. Expressions that have almost the same illocutionary force as 'Let's go to the concert together' (a suggestion or offer) are recognised as *head acts* and all the others, except for the replies to the video performers' greetings, are put into the categories of *alerters* and *supportive moves*.

Firstly I will search for the reasons why JYAM's responses were rated lower than all the rest in **politeness** and than JHAF and JHAM in **appropriateness**. The following are the two responses from JYAM.

MJ130 – JYAM01

Ano-saa,	*tomodachi-kara*	*konsaato-no-tiketto*
do you know what	friend-ABL	concert-GEN-ticket

moratta-n'-dakedo,	*kyoo*	*hima?*
receive-PAST-but	today	free

[Do you know what? <*alerter*> I was given concert tickets by my friend. <*supportive move*> Are you free today? <*supportive move*>]

[Alerter] + [Explanation of the situation] + [Indirect offer / invitation]

MJ131 – JYAM02

Konaida-saa,	*konaida,*	*raion-kingu-no-tiketto*
recently-FP	recently	Lion-King-GEN-ticket

moratta-n'-dakedo,	*dare-ka*	*iku-hito*	*i-nai-ka-naa.*
receive-past-but	who-q	go-person	be- neg-q-FP

Hitori-de	*iku-no-mo-nan-da-shi-sa.*
alone	going would be uncomfortable-FP

Ne,	*chotto*	*sagasiteru-n'-dakedo.*
INTERJEC	somewhat	looking for-but

[I was given tickets for "Lion King" recently. <*supportive move*> I am looking for a person who can go with me. <*supportive move*> I don't like to go alone. <*supportive move*> Say, I'm looking for someone. <*supportive move*>]

[Explanation of the situation 1] + [Explanation of the situation 2] + [Expression of *s*'s desire] + [Very indirect offer / invitation]

The first response by JYAM01 was rated as 3.75 on average for the level of **politeness** (the second lowest) and as 1.50 for the level of **appropriateness** (just above the average of all responses in this item – 1.59). The second one uttered by JYAM02 was rated as 4.00 for **politeness** (the lowest) and as 2.75 (the lowest) for **appropriateness**. A qualitative observation shows that these two responses have one thing in common: they do not contain obvious *head acts*. As can be seen from the data (see Appendix 11), all the other responses contain some sort of recognisable *head acts*, whereas these two are the only cases where they were omitted or were not clearly presented. This evidence suggests that the lack of the most important part in the performance of an *FEA* was evaluated as 'lack of consideration towards *h*'.

The follow-up interviews with these informants give information on the backgrounds of their utterances. Firstly JYAM01 said in the interview, 'I wouldn't say it directly. I wanted it to mean something like, "If you like, if your schedule is OK, please come"'. JYAM02 said, 'I tried to make a casual invitation'. These explanations imply that these informants tried to decrease the weightiness of the invitation and to make it as casual as possible.

The follow-up interviews with the raters in the second stage data collection revealed why these responses were rated as they were. The raters thought the casual expression '*Ano saa*' <Do you know what?> and the part, '*kyoo hima?*' <Are you free today?> were the reasons for a low evaluation of JYAM01's. The raters thought the question, 'Are you free today?' was too abrupt and lacked consideration. As for JYAM02's, they pointed out that the part '*dare-ka iku-hito i-nai-ka-naa. Hitori-de iku-no-mo-nan-da-shi-sa. Ne, chotto sagasiteru-n'-dakedo*' <I am looking for a person who can go with me. I don't like to go alone. I'm looking for someone> sounded impolite and inappropriate. They said that this part did not seem to mean invitation; instead the speaker made it an incidental and an optional matter for his own benefit. HFR even told me that she got 'the worst impression' of all the responses from this response.

The reasons for the low evaluation of these utterances can also be found in relation to the constraint examined here – these informants failed to observe it. Firstly, JYAM01, by saying 'Are you free today?', neglected h's own agenda: it is difficult for a person to make a quick decision without knowing what s is going to propose. So the question 'Are you free today' implies the foreclosure of h's options. In this sense this informant failed to 'place a high value on o's wants'.

The lowest evaluation for both **politeness** and **appropriateness** of JYAM02's response can be explained from the same perspective. He prioritised his own two wants, viz. (1) his want to go to the musical, and (2) his want to go with someone, over h's wants, by saying 'I am looking for a person who can go with me. I don't like to go alone. I'm looking for someone'. He told h merely that he was looking for someone and did not make an actual invitation. This kind of 'too much indirectness' is evaluated negatively, for directness or emphasis on the good quality of something is usually a suitable strategy for performing a face-enhancing act (*FEA* – towards the hearer). This is a piece of evidence that indirectness is a strategy for mitigation of a face-threatening act (*FTA*), and that it can be evaluated as impolite and inappropriate if used for an *FEA*. This finding corresponds with Blum-Kulka's observation that 'indirectness does not necessarily imply politeness' (Blum-Kulka, 1987: 131).

The two phenomena above may have resulted from a general tendency of present-day Japanese young males when they interact with their friends of the same gender and at the same age. The two JYAF's data demonstrated a similar lack of a sophisticated way to show consideration towards *o*. Still, they used *head acts* to invite their friends and were evaluated higher.

The next observation is on the two 'politest' responses to this item. JHAF02's response was rated as the most considerate: 2.00 on average on **politeness** and 1.50 on **appropriateness**. Although the appropriateness score was not the best one (probably evaluated as 'a little overpolite'), an analysis of how she achieved such a high level of **politeness** presents some interesting facts. The second politest response was made by JHAM01. It scored 2.75 on **politeness** and 1.25 on **appropriateness** (one of three best scores in this item).

MJ102 – JHAF02

Ano-ne,	*zenjitsu*	*shiriai-no-hito-kara*
do you know what	yesterday	acquaintance-ABL

ima-hyooban-no-konsaato-no-tiketto		***itadaita**-n'-dakedo,*
now-well-reputed-concert-GEN-ticket		receive-PAST(HUM)-but

tsugi-no-nichiyoobi	***anata***	*aiteru?*	*Moshi*
next-Sunday	you(**POL**)	be free	if

jikan-ga	*aru-n'-dattaraissho-ni*	*ika-nai?*
time-NOM	be-COP-COND together	go-NPST-NEG

[Do you know what? <*alerter*> I was given tickets of a concert that's reputed well now from my acquaintance yesterday. <*supportive move*> Are you free this Sunday? <*supportive move*> Why don't we go to the concert together <*head act*>, if you have time? <*supportive move*>]

[Alerter] + [Explanation of the situation] + [Asking *h*'s convenience] + [Invitation] + [Saying that *h*'s convenience is the condition for going]

MJ112 – JHAM01

A,   genki-da-yo.   *Hisashiburi-da-nee.*
ah   fine-COP-NPST-FP   long absence-COP-NPST-FP

Soo-ie-ba   kondo-no-doyoobi,   jikan-ga
by the way   next Saturday   time-NOM

aite-inai-ka-naa.   Ima-hyooban-no-konsaato-no-tiketto
free-be-NPST-NEG-Q-FP   now-well-reputed-concert-GEN-ticket

moratta-n'-de,   issho-ni   iketara-to
receive-PAST-because   together   go-COND-COMP

omou-n'-dakedo,   doo-ka-na.
think-but   how-Q-FP

[Yes, I'm fine. Long time no see. <u>Come to think of it *<alerter>*, do you have time this Saturday?</u> *<supportive move>* <u>I got tickets for a concert that's well reputed now.</u> *<supportive move>* <u>So I'm hoping to go to it together.</u> *<Head act>* <u>What do you think?</u> *<supportive move>*]

[Response to a greeting] + [Alerter] + [Asking *h*'s convenience] + [Explanation of the situation] + [Invitation] + [Asking for *h*'s opinion]

YFR explained the reason why JHAF02's response was rated as the 'best' response of all for **politeness** as this: 'This person asked if the friend would be free and gave details of the concert'. As for JHAM 01's remark, HMR said that the part 'do you have time' gave a good impression. The raters put priority on how informants gave options to their friends and consequently these two invitations with a query on *o*'s convenience were evaluated highly. I think that what the raters said in the interview is a piece of evidence that they evaluated such consideration for *o* more than linguistic forms such as honorifics, as I had asked them to. Thus it is possible to understand how the informants followed/ignored the *constraint* and how their responses were rated based on the propositional content. (Of course, honorifics are another measure to control the scale of **absolute politeness,** as mentioned earlier.)

Furthermore, concerning linguistic forms, JHAF02's remark includes two honorific expressions, ***itadaita*** (a humble form of 'receive') and ***anata*** (a polite/formal form of 'you'). The formality of these words, as well as the detailed explanation of the concert, created a good impression on the raters. She also succeeded in enhancing *o*'s wants by mentioning the good reputation of the concert. So, here, honorifics do seem to have played a positive role in judgements of **politeness**. On the other hand, although JHAM01 did not use such formal expressions, he showed consideration for *o* by putting one *supportive move* after the *head act* ('What do you think?'). This question is much more open than JYAM01's 'Are you free today?', and seems to genuinely invite *h* to consider his own wishes. All these features are supposed to be related to 'consideration for *o*' and accords with the concept 'place a high value on *o*'s wants'.

However, it should be noted that most of the indications of politeness here seem to be oriented towards **negative direction** – preserving options for *h*, so it's the *constraint* for Tact that seems to have a more important role than that for Generosity in this case. This can be taken as a piece of evidence that Tact is also used in an invitation. This finding may be suggesting a more complex picture than the scheme presented in the original and the revised *PP*.

I would also like to examine remarks from the data gathered in the first stage data collection that bear similarity to the most and the least polite ones. To make a comparison with the most polite response, I sought remarks with 'reference to good quality of the concert/musical', 'a query about *h*'s convenience', and a *head act*. For a comparison with the least polite one, I searched for responses without *head acts*.

[Remarks with 'reference to good quality of the concert/musical', 'queries about *h*'s convenience', and *head acts*]

MJ105 – JHAF03

Ureshi-soo-na-kao	*shiteru-desho?*	*Genki-ni yatteru?*
happy-look-face	doing-CJEC	cheerfully-doing

Jitsu-wa nee,	*tottemo-ii, nee,*	*myuujikaru-no- ken-ga*
to tell the truth-FP	very-good-FP	mujical-GEN-tickets-NOM

haitta-n'-dakedo,   isogashiku-nakattara   issho-ni
receive-PAST-but   be busy-NEG-COND   together

ika-nai?
go-NPST-NEG

[Don't you think I look happy? <*supportive move*> To tell the truth, <*alerter*> I got tickets for a very good musical. <*supportive move*> What do you say to going to it with me, <*head act*> if you aren't busy? <*supportive move*>]

[Implying *s*'s gladness] + [Alerter] + [Explanation of the situation] + [Invitation] + [Saying that *h*'s convenience is the condition for going]

MJ115 – JHAM03[5]

A, genki-yo. Socchi-wa doo? Doo, genki? Genki-soo-da-ne. Ano, jitsu-wa-ne, ano, shiriai-kara ima-hyooban-no-konsaato (-no-tiketto) moratta-n' -dakeredo, shigoto, doo-ka-ne. Imagoro? Isogashii? Naruhodo, nakanaka jikan-ga tore-soo-mo-nai-yo-ne. De, kore-wa ichigatsu-no-tooka nan'-da-kedo, son-toki aitoru-ka-ne? Jikan-wa hachiji-gurai nan'-da-keredo. Ma, muri-shi-naku-temo-ii-n'-dakedo. A, aitoru? Sore-ja son-toki-ni mata, yari-mashoo. Ja, arigatoo. Sayonara.

[I'm fine. How about you? Fine? Yeah you look fine. Do you know what? <*alerter*> I was given (tickets for) a concert that's well thought of. How about your work? Busy at this time? I see. You don't seem to have time to spare. Speaking of the concert, it's held on the 10th January. Are you free then? It will be about eight in the evening. Well, you don't need to change your schedule if it's not possible. <*supportive move*> You're free? OK, let's do it then. <*head act*> Thank you. <*supportive move*> Good-bye.]

[Response to a greeting] + [Alerter] + [Explanation of the situation] + [Enquiry about *h*'s situation] + [Talking about the date of the concert] + [Enquiry about *h*'s convenience] + [Talking about the time of the concert] + [Mentioning the priority of *h*'s convenience] + [Confirming that *h* can go and they will go together] + [Gratitude] + [Farewell]

As can be seen from above, these two responses show consideration in the same way as JHAF02 did. One difference between JHAF02's response and these is that the latter do not contain any formal or honorific expressions. Therefore these are more casual but appropriate remarks to their (close) friends.

In addition to the absence of formality, JHAF03 did not ask about *h*'s convenience in a question form. Instead she used a conditional form 'if you aren't busy'. JHAM03 said, '*Sore-ja son-toki-ni mata, yari-mashoo*', roughly meaning 'let's do it, then'. It is doubtless that this part is meant to serve as a *head act*, but it was presented in a rather ambiguous way, for '*yari-mashoo*' is not a common expression for an invitation in Japanese and '*yaru*' (do) can mean various things. While JHAM03 made a very strenuous effort to confirm that *h*'s schedule allows him to come to the concert, he did not perform the core part in such an elaborated way. This seems to mean that this person's strategy for invitations is almost the same as a strategy of asking about *o*'s convenience. This can be taken as a strategy of showing consideration in the use of a suggestion for joint action (-*mashoo*). S makes it seem as if this is not so much an 'invitation' as a 'suggestion' for both of them to do something jointly. The idea that *s* is making an 'offer' or an 'invitation', viz. doing a favour for *h*, is suppressed, perhaps making it easier for *h* to accept.

It is not certain how these two would be evaluated, but I think, as a native speaker of Japanese, their levels of politeness would still be regarded as high because they are showing a high level of consideration towards *h*. Nevertheless I expect them to be considered as less polite than JHAF02's due to the less elaborated linguistic features of their responses described above.

[The remarks without *head acts*]

<u>MJ116 – JHAM04</u>

Eiga-no-tiketto-ga   tenihaitta-n'-dakedomo,   kondo
cinema-GEN-tickets-NOM   receive-PAST-but   next time

*itsuka   jikan   ari-**masu**-ka.*
some time   time   be(**POL**)-Q

[<u>I obtained cinema tickets. <*supportive move*> Do you have time some time in near future? <*supportive move*></u>]

Chapter 5 Results 149

[Explanation of the situation] + [Asking *h*'s convenience in near future]

MJ127 – JYAF05

Un,	*genki-da-yo.*	*Ano-ne,*	*shiriai-kara*
yes	fine-COP-FP	do you know what	acquaintance-ABL

konsaato-no-tiketto	*moratta-n'-dakedo,*	*kono-konsaato-tte*
concert-GEN-tickets	receive-PAST-but	this concert

kyoomi-aru?
interest-be

[Yeah, I'm fine. Do you know what? <*alerter*> I was given a concert ticket from one of my acquaintances. <*supportive move*> Are you interested in this concert? <*supportive move*>]

[Responding to the greeting] + [Alerter] + [Explanation of the situation] + [Asking *h*'s convenience in near future]

MJ135 – JYAM04

Iyaa, nanka konomae, uun, nanka, senpai-ni-atta-toki-ni iroiro hanashi-shitara, nanka, "Moteshon"-ga sukina, hora, ano-bando iru-jan. Namae wasurechitta-kedo. Maa. Sonoo , tiketto moracchatta-kara-saa. Ano, moshi, shigatsu-nijuugonichi-ka-na. Shigatsu-nijuugonichi-gurai-datta-to omou-kedo, nanika sore-gurai-ni, tte hima-ka-naa.

[When I was talking to my *Senpai* (a senior student) about this and that when I met him just recently, he gave me tickets for, yeah, the band "Moteshon"* (= you) like, I forgot the name though, I was given tickets for that. I wonder if it's 25th April. I think it's about 25th April. Are you free about that time? <*supportive move*>)

[Explanation of the situation] + [Explanation of the ticket, saying it is for a concert of *h*'s favourite band] + [Talking about the date of the concert] + [Enquiry about *h*'s convenience]

*= this is seemingly a friend's nickname

Although these three remarks lack *head acts*, they seem to be more polite than the ones made by two JYAM informants presented above. They show more consideration for *o*, by asking 'Do you have some time in the near future?', by using a formal morpheme **'masu'** (JHAM04), by saying 'Are you interested in this concert?' (JYAF05), by saying 'he gave me tickets for, yeah, the band "Moteshon" (nickname of *h*)' and by asking 'Are you free about that time?' (JYAM04).

The following are what these respondents said in interviews about what they thought when making these responses.

JHAM04: *I will try my best to have my friend go with me.*

JYAF05: *I prioritised my friend's tastes and asked if she liked the content of the concert.*

JYAM04: *I will follow the friend's schedule. I won't impose. It's all right if he can't. I showed care for the addressee.*

Their explanations demonstrate that they hoped to show consideration towards *o* in inviting him/her. Especially the two younger informants clearly stated they had prioritised their friends' taste or convenience over their own wants. Accordingly their strategies resemble JHAM03's mentioned above, in that what was most important for them was to confirm that their friends would like to go to the concert and they had the time to do so. In addition, it seems that they were waiting for *h*'s answer and would continue to complete their invitations afterwards. In this sense, their responses may be partial, but I would like to emphasise that they thought these parts were the 'centre / core part' of an invitation. It is likely that *h* will take these as an invitation and say 'Yes, let's go' or something similar even if the *head act* is not performed, for they have already been told *s* has got two tickets. Since all these are free from such abruptness as JYAM01 showed ('Are you free today') and have shown *s*'s good intention towards *h*, I presume that they are at a higher level of **politeness** than the two least polite responses.

5.2.2 Item 02

Constraint: Tact – '*Place a low value on s's wants*'
Speech act(s): directives (request)
Activity type: Conversation with a teacher/ an instructor / a lecturer
Social variables: vertical distance = yes; horizontal distance = yes
Formality: formal
(For more details of the scenario, see Appendix 3.)

The aim of this item is to probe how the Japanese two age groups operate with a speech act of 'request'. Leech (1983) classifies this speech act in *directives*, using Searle's term (1979 [1975]). *Directives* 'are intended to produce some effect through action by the hearer' and 'therefore comprise a category of illocutions in which negative politeness is important' (Leech, *ibid*.: 106). This means that a strategy to make a request in a harmonious way is based on mitigation, or *s*'s performance of an *FSA* for *h*, rather than an *FEA*. Showing *s*'s modesty or humbleness is expected in making a polite request.

The *head acts* in this item should be something that has the same illocutionary force as 'Please let me ask you some questions', 'Please give me some advice', or 'Please give me some help by answering some questions'.

I had only one type of video prompt for this item, for the setting was a conversation with a female teacher/instructor. The original prompt in English 'Hello. How are you?' was designed to serve as a formulaic greeting. Therefore the Japanese form '*A, konnichiwa*' (Oh. Hello) – a common formulaic expression for greetings – is supposed to have the same illocutionary force as the original.

The following is the summary of the quantitative analysis of the Item 02 data.

Table 5.2.2-1 Summary of statistical data: Item 02

	Average scores in politeness		Average scores in appropriateness		Average scores in politeness		Average scores in appropriateness
1	JHA (2.63)	1	JYA (1.31)	1	JYAF (2.13)	1	JYAF (1.13)
				2	JHAM (2.50)	2	JYAM (1.50)
	JYA (2.63)	2	JHA (2.13)	3	JHAF (2.75)	3	JHAF (1.53)
				4	JYAM (3.13)	4	JHAM (2.63)

The table shows that JHA and JYA demonstrated exactly the same level of **politeness** (Mean = 2.63, n = 16 each) in this item. As for **appropriateness**, the data shows a significant difference between the two age groups ($p<.005$), with JYA's average score being lower (i.e. more appropriate) (Mean = 1.31, n = 16) than JHA's (Mean = 2.13, n = 16).

In more detailed analysis of differences among the smaller age–gender groups concerning the level of **politeness**, JYAF (Mean = 2.13, n = 8) comes out on top and is followed by JHAM (Mean = 2.50, n = 8), JHAF (Mean = 2.75, n = 8) and JYAM (Mean = 3.13, n = 8) in order. No significant mean differences were found here, however.

As for **appropriateness**, JYAF comes out on top again (Mean = 1.13, n = 8 each), with JYAM (Mean = 1.50, n = 8), JHAF (Mean = 1.53, n = 8) and JHAM (Mean = 2.63, n = 8) following them. One-way ANOVA demonstrated very significant mean differences among the four groups ($p<.001$). The post hoc test (Bonferroni test) showed that JHAM's evaluation in this area was significantly lower than those of the rest: JHAF–JHAM ($p<.05$), JYAF–JHAM ($p<.001$), and JYAM–JHAM ($p<.05$).

The above results demonstrate a unique tendency of this item: that JHA informants failed to surpass their younger counterparts in both **politeness** and **appropriateness**, contrary to their performance in Item 01 and in all the items combined. In particular, JYAF's performance was remarkable, for the group came on top in both categories. It should also be noted that the levels of politeness and appropriateness of JHAM responses showed a sharp contrast (politeness > appropriateness) and that JYAM's performance was just the opposite (politeness < appropriateness).

I am moving on to the qualitative analysis to explore the reasons for the above results and other outstanding features of the responses. Firstly, I would like to look at the two JYAF responses. Although they were not assessed as 'the politest' as individual responses, the group performance gained the highest evaluation in **politeness**.

MJ222 – JYAF02

A,	konnichiwaa.	N'- too,	chotto,	anoo,
IJ	hello	IJ	a little	IJ

*o-**kiki**-shi-tai-koto-ga*   *aru-n'-**desu**-keredomo,*   *ano,*
HON-hear-do-DESI-thing-TOP   be-COP(**POLITE**)-but   IJ

raishuu-no-shiken-no-ken-ni-tsuite,   *chotto,*   *anoo,*
next week-GEN-test-GEN-issue-about   a little   IJ

jugyoo-no-naka-de-fumei-na-ten-ga   *ari-**mashi**-te,*   *moshi*
lesson-GEN-in-unclear-point-TOP   be-COP(**POLITE**)-and   if

yoroshi-kereba,   *chotto*
all right(**FOR**)-COND   a little

*shitsumon-**sasete-itadaki**-tai-n'-**desu**-keredomo,*
question-do(**HUM**)-DESI-COP(**POLITE**)-but

go-tsugoo-no-yoi-jikan-ga   *ari-**masu**-deshoo-ka.*
HON-convenience-GEN-good-time-TOP   be(**POL**)-CJEC-Q

[Ah, hello. I have one thing I would like to ask you about. <head act> About the exam next week, I have one small thing in the lesson that is unclear to me. <supportive move> If possible I would like to ask you about it. <head act> Do you have any convenient time? <supportive move>]

[Greeting (formulaic)] + [Request 1 (declarative)] + [Explanation of the reason] + [Request 2 (declarative)] + [Query on *h*'s convenience]

This response was rated as 2.00 for **politeness** and 1.25 for **appropriateness**. Therefore it is 'polite' and close to 'optimal appropriateness'. In terms of lexicogrammatical features, this remark has seven honorific expressions (as represented by bold font). Furthermore, the words such as '*ken*' (issue), '*fumei*' (unclear), '*yoroshi-kerebe*' (all right-COND) are usually used in formal occasions. These features show that this informant demonstrated a considerably formal and respectful attitude in this response. This is certainly a big reason why this response was rated as 'polite'. As for the strategic aspect, this informant used *head act* twice. The first part comes right after the greeting, presented like an initial conclusion or a 'preparatory' request to make the request. Then she moved on to an explanatory part (*supportive move*), repeated the request (*head act*), and asked the teacher's convenience (*supportive move*). This combination seems to have constituted a well-organised way of making a request.

JYAF02 *placed a low value on her own wants* by using a humble form of a verbal expression 'want to do', '***sasete-itadaki-tai***' (do(**HUM**)-DESI) at the lexical level. Furthermore she used such expressions as '*moshi* ***yoroshi****-kereba*' <if possible> or '***go****-tsugoo-no-yoi-jikan-ga ari-****masu****-deshoo-ka*' <Do you have any convenient time?>, and abased herself in making this request. These facts suggest that she satisfied the *constraint* of TACT.

She said in the follow-up interview, 'As I am asking her to spare me time, I tried not to sound impolite to her as much as possible. I talked to her considering her schedule and the fact that I'm the one asking her for her instruction'. This remark represents her modest attitude in her response.

According to an interview with HFR on this response, it sounded polite for two reasons: (i) this informant had given a clear reason in the part 'I have one thing that is unclear to me', and (ii) asked the teacher's convenience in the part 'Do you have any convenient time?'.

Furthermore, this young female informant showed **politeness** by belittling the size of the request by using an expression '*chotto*' <a small thing> [*lit.* a little]. '*Chotto*' is a commonly used lexical device for hedging, which functions to mitigate the size of imposition, seriousness or a face-threatening dimension of an utterance.

MJ223 – JYAF03

A,	*konnichiwa,*	*JYAF03-to*	***mooshi-masu.***
IJ	hello	JYAF03-COMP	say-**HUM-POL**

Anoo,	*kondo,*	*jugyoo-ni-kansuru-shitsumon-o*
IJ	next time	lesson-about-question-ACC

sasete*-itadaki-tai-n'-desu-kedomo*	*raishuu*	***o****-jikan*
do-**HUM**-DESI-COP-**POL**-but	next week	**HON**-time

itadake-masu-deshoo-ka.
receive-**HUM-POL**-CJEC-Q

[Ah, hello. I'm JYAF03. <supportive move> I would like to ask you a question about the lesson next time in the near future and can I ask you to spare me time next week? <head act>]

[Greeting (formulaic)] + [Self-introduction] + [Request (declarative) + Query on *h*'s convenience]

This remark was rated as 2.25 for **politeness** and 1.00 for **appropriateness**. So it is close to 'polite' and 'optimally appropriate'. What is interesting is that this response, although less polite than the above (JYAF02's), was rated as more appropriate. This is probably because JYAF02's response was taken as a little *overpolite* in this context. The raters' expectation of the suitable level of **politeness** for this item was a little lower.

Although this informant used less honorific forms than JYAF02, she still employed five of them (as represented in bold face) in her response, and this certainly created a polite impression. The strategy she used is straightforward: one *supportive move* and the subsequent *head act*. Since the *supportive move* in this response is a self-introduction, this response virtually consists only of a *head act*. Clarity is usually avoided when performing a speech act of an impositive nature like a 'request', but this informant succeeded in achieving it in a polite way with the use of honorific expressions and giving options to *h*. The use of honorifics obviously represented the informant's modest attitude and *placed a low value on s's wants*. This informant said, 'I'll try not to bother the teacher as much as possible, by expressing my willingness to meet her convenience'.

As for the optionality mentioned above, HRF explained in the interview that the parts '*kondo*' <next time> and '*raishuu*' <next week> sounded polite, for they showed the informant's consideration towards the teacher. This comment supports the above description. How much one satisfied the constraint of TACT can be measured in relation to three scales, viz. those of COST-BENEFIT, OPTIONALITY, and INDIRECTNESS (Leech, 1983: 123).

The homogeneity of the above two JYAF informants' responses seems to stand for the common respectful attitude of the JYAF group towards the social role of 'a teacher'. They expressed *deference* towards her and their modesty and humble attitude in making a request. This JYAF's attitude certainly provides a contrast with their older counterparts (JHAM and JHAF).

Now I would like to examine the two responses of JHAM. Both of them were rated as 'close to inappropriate'. Interestingly one of them was rated as 'most polite' and the other as 'least polite'. Therefore they are outstanding examples of *overpoliteness* and *underpoliteness*.

MJ214 – JHAM02

Ano-nee,	*chotto-tanomi-tai-koto*		*aru-n'-da-kedoo,*	*uun,*
IJ	a little-ask-DESI-thing		be-but	IJ

jugyoo-ni-tsuite	*chotto*	*shitsumon-**sasete**-morai-tai-koto-ga*
lesson-about	a little	question-do-**HUM**-DESI-thing-NOM

aru-n'-de,	*nantoka*	*jikan*	*tore-**mas**-en-ka-ne.*
be-as	possibly	time	take-**POL**-NEG-Q-FP

O-negai-**shi-masu.**
HON-wish-do-**POL**

[Do you know what? <*alerter*> I want to ask a little favour of you. <*head act*> I have some small questions about the lesson. <*supportive move*> Can you manage to spare me some time? <*head act*> I beg you. <*IFID*>]

[Alerter (formulaic)] + [Request 1 (declarative)] + [Explanation of the reason] + [Request 2 (interrogative)] + [IFID (formulaic)]

This remark was rated as 4.00 for **politeness**, viz. 'a little informal / a little lacking in consideration' and turned out to be rated 'the least polite' of all the responses to this item. It was also rated as 2.50 for **appropriateness**, viz. just in the middle of 'a little inappropriate' and 'very inappropriate' and was 'the second least appropriate' response. This informant said, 'As I'm the one that's asking, I will consider the teacher's convenience and find a suitable way to ask her', but this modest attitude and consideration towards the teacher was not successfully realised in a linguistic form.

On the surface the strategy this informant used looks fine. The translation does not convey any impolite impression of the utterance at all. It is the lexical and grammatical features that give a rather impolite and inappropriate impression. Three out of four raters gave 4 or 5 to this remark for **politeness** and 3 for **appropriateness**. Two of them (HFR and HMR) said that the part *'nantoka jikan tore-**mas**-en-ka-ne'* (possibly time take(**POL**)-NEG-Q-FP) <Can you manage to spare me some time?> sounded rude and inappropriate towards the teacher. This part contains an honorific form *'**mas**(-en)'*, which is meant to show politeness to the teacher, but there is a reason why this part sounded rude: the subject of the verb *'toru'* (take) is supposed to be the teacher (*h*) not the informant (*s*). The translation to express the same impression in English would be like 'You can't possibly spare time for me, eh?'. In addition, the final particle *'ne'*, which is used to show familiarity, was possibly taken negatively. If a Japanese wanted to use *'toru'* in a polite way in this context, s/he would say *'totte-**itadake**-**mas**-en-ka'* (take(**HUM**)(**POL**)-NEG-Q). By containing *'itadaku'*, which shows humbleness on *s*'s side, this remark would compose a politer illocution that could be translated as 'Is it possible for you to take time for me?' in English.

HMR pointed out that the part *'chotto-tanomi-tai-koto aru-n'-da-kedoo'* (a little-ask-DESI-thing be-but) <I want to ask a little favour of you> was inappropriate to the teacher. The reason for this is quite clear: the copula *'da'* is a plain form and does not show any respect for the teacher. If he had used *'desu'*, a polite form, instead, this part would have sounded more appropriate.

In addition, it is likely that this informant recognised the social parameters of this scenario somewhat differently from the others, especially the JYAF informants mentioned earlier. The lack of a polite form or an honorific in the above seems to show that he did not take the social role of a teacher as seriously as the JYAF informants.

A similar attitude is seen in the response by JHAF02 (see Appendix 13): the lack of consideration in this case was rated as 3.75 (the second least polite). This informant used formal and polite forms, but her response was evaluated negatively by lack of consideration in the part *'jikan-o totte-**itadake**-nai-kashira'* (time-ACC take(**HUM**)-NEG-Q) <I wonder if you can spare me time>. This part again looks fine on the surface, for the humble form *'itadaku'* is included. However, the part *'kashira'* <I wonder> was taken as an impolite phrase because 'it is rude to force a person at a higher status to meet *s*'s demand' (an explanation by HMR in the interview). The English translation 'I wonder' may not connote such a selfish impression in this context, but the expression '*kashira*', usually used by Japanese women and taken as a question marker, also expresses '*s*'s "wish" or "request"' (the word definition translated from *Kooji-en*, fifth ed.). Consequently this expression contains a sense of imposition, rather than consideration towards *h*, and gives a similar expression as '*jikan tore-mas-en-ka-ne*' (time take(**POL**)-NEG-Q-FP) <Can you manage to spare me some time?> mentioned above. This lack of consideration towards the teacher led to the low evaluation of the higher age group's responses.

Next I will make an analysis of the politest but the most inappropriate response of JHAM03.

MJ216 – JHAM03
*A, konnichiwa, sensei-**desu**-ka. Ano, JHAM03-**de-gozai-masu**-ga. Itsumo o-sewa-ni natte-**ori-masu**. Ano, iyoiyo shiken-ga raishuu-ni chikazuite-kita-n'-**desu**-keredomo, Jitsu-wa moo-chotto-**desu**-ne, jishin-no-nai-tokoro-ga aru-n'-**desu**-ga, raishuu dokoka-de jikan-o totte-**itadake-mashitara**-arigatai-n'-**desu**-ga. Ano, **watashi-no go-tsugoo-o mooshi-agete** mooshiwake-nai-n'-**desu**-ga, raishuu deshitara kayoobi-ka suiyoobi-ka kinyoobi-no mikka-de, moshi jikan-ga totte-itadake-mashitara saiwai **de-gozai-masu**-kedomo, ikaga-de **gozai-mashoo**-ka.*

[Ah, hello, is that you, the teacher? It's me, JHAM03. I thank you for your daily care. As we know, the exam is approaching and it will be next week. To tell the truth, I don't have confidence in some parts. <*supportive moves*> I would appreciate it if you could spare me any time during next week. <*head act*> I'm sorry to tell you my schedule, but if you could find some time on any of three days of the week, Tuesday, Wednesday or Friday, I would be grateful. <*head act*> I wonder if it is possible. <*supportive moves*>]

[Self introduction] + [Thanking (for the teacher's care)] + [Explanation of the background] + [Explanation of the reason] + [Request 1 (hypothetical)] + [Request 2 (specification of the date)] + [Query about the teacher's convenience]

As the lexical devices in bold face illustrate, there are quite a few honorofics and formal expressions contained in this remark. There are 18 of them, and this number has definitely created a very formal and very polite impression of this remark. Furthermore, three 'super polite' forms (two '*de-gozai-masu*' and one '*gozai-mashoo(-ka)*') are included. This higher age male informant explained the background of this response in the follow-up interview as follows:

> Although I ask her to spare me some time, I'm also busy. So I'll present two or three possibilities and ask her to choose one from them. (Ask a favour and show consideration for the teacher.).

He achieved his aim very successfully, as this response was rated as 1.00 for **politeness**, which corresponds to 'very polite' or 'showing high consideration'. However, the raters took it as *overpolite* and rated it as 2.75, which corresponds very closely to 'very inappropriate – too polite'. All of the raters pointed out in the interviews that this remark had sounded 'too polite'.

This is a striking example where the sensitive relation between **politeness (absolute politeness)** and **appropriateness (relative politeness)** was demonstrated. As I previously mentioned, these two qualities have a strong correlation ($p<.005$) on the whole in my data, but the JHA's data showed no significant correlation between the two. This phenomenon is well represented in the above example: the higher age informants tended to perform *overpoliteness*. I assume demonstrating too much linguistic politeness than is required is one tendency, if not a strategy, of an experienced language speaker. While saying this, *overpoliteness*, as long as it is based on *s*'s 'good intention', does not cause any threat to social equilibrium and contributes to 'rapport management' (Spencer-Oatey, 2000: 11–46) in general, whereas *underpoliteness* can cause offence to *h* and head towards 'rapport-neglect' or 'rapport-challenge orientation' (Spencer-Oatey, *ibid.*: 29–30). In sum, *overpoliteness* can be taken as a 'safe' approach, while *underpoliteness* is often a 'risky' one. One thing to bear in mind about *overpoliteness* is that it perhaps creates a sense of distance. *Overpoliteness* can also imply that s is trying to manipulate *h*'s behaviour against *h*'s will. In English there are terms like 'ingratiating', 'smarmy', 'obsequious' which implies the unpleasantness of *overpoliteness* (pointed out by Geoffrey Leech in personal communication). I would like to add that the inappropriate impression of this response may have also been caused by the 'awkwardness' of being so humble towards a (seemingly) younger female teacher. Japanese higher age males are generally thought to be at a higher social position than the younger female ones – it appears 'awkward' or 'inappropriate' if they show too much politeness toward younger women.

The above response contains one wrong usage of honorifics: '*watashi-no go-tsugoo*' (I(**FOR**)-GEN **HON**-convenience) is used to show respect to an object that belongs to *s*. The honorific prefix *go-* belongs to *sonkeigo* (respectful or exalting form) and is 'referent-related' (Coulmas, 1992: 313): the word with this prefix shows respect to the person who possesses/possessed the thing. Therefore the above *go-* is used in a wrong way. This kind of wrong use of honorifics is often caused by *overpoliteness*, or an excessive use of polite lexical/grammatical devices. I think this is a unique case of a wrong use of honorifics by higher age informants, who are supposed to have more experience with using them and would therefore be less liable than younger people to make such mistakes.

In order to investigate the comprehensive relation between the strategies and the constraint of TACT in this item, I counted the number of humble forms[6], which *s* uses to show his/her modesty, used in all responses. Humble forms are thought to represent the essence of the constraint. Here is a summary of the kind and the number of humble forms:

The above results show that the humble form ***itadaku*** and its variations were commonly used to show *s*'s modesty and humbleness. The overall frequency of all humble forms is nearly once per response in all the groups. This means all the informants somehow used this form at least on one occasion in their responses and hence the attitude 'showing modesty' was closely related with the strategy of making a request.

However, I would like to mention that there were few examples that satisfied the constraint by controlling the propositional content. This means that there were not many typical expressions that accompany the request proper, meaning 'I'm sorry to bother you, but …' or 'It's my fault that I couldn't understand some points in the lesson, but …' in Japanese equivalents, which clearly express *s*'s attitude to *place a low value on his/her wants*. This fact tells us that the informants did not take the request of asking a question to the teacher as a 'rapport challenging' one that should be mitigated by *semantic formulae*. On the other hand the politeness strategy here was mainly achieved by the use of lexicogrammatical devices. It seems that Japanese people (especially nowadays) assume a teacher should give support to his/her students automatically on demand and it is the teacher's duty[7]. The informants may have also thought that asking a question is a good practice

Table 5.2.2-2 Summary of humble form usage

itadaku	JHAF	10
	JHAM	6
	JYAF	8
	JYAM	6
kudasaru	JHAF	–
	JHAM	–
	JYAF	–
	JYAM	1
moosu	JHAF	–
	JHAM	–
	JYAF	2
	JYAM	–
o-hanashi suru	JHAF	1
	JHAM	–
	JYAF	–
	JYAM	–
o-negai suru	JHAF	1
	JHAM	2
	JYAF	–
	JYAM	–
o-tazune susu	JHAF	1
	JHAM	–
	JYAF	–
	JYAM	–
o-ukagai suru	JHAF	–
	JHAM	1
	JYAF	–
	JYAM	–
ukagau	JHAF	1
	JHAM	2
	JYAF	1
	JYAM	1

	Group	N. of humble forms	N. of responses	Frequency
Overall result	JHAF	14	12	1.17
	JHAM	11	7	1.57
	JYAF	11	10	1.10
	JYAM	8	9	0.89

and hence it is an *FEA* for both the teacher and the student. This explains why JYAM's responses received a higher evaluation in **appropriateness**, regardless of their low assessment in **politeness**. The scenario used for this item does not seem to have required a very high degree of absolute politeness for appropriateness.

This may be a limitation of this scenario in examining strategies to satisfy the constraint of TACT. A similar scenario that requires an informant to borrow a car / a CD player / something else valuable from the addressee might have elicited clearer examples of *placing a low value on s̲'s wants* with the control of propositional content.

5.2.3 Item 03
Constraint: Approbation – '*Place a high value on o̲'s qualities*'
Speech act(s): Compliments
Activity type: Conversation with a senior male person (Senpai in Japanese)
Social variables: vertical distance = yes; horizontal distance = no
Formality: informal
(For more details of the scenario, see Appendix 3.)

For the purpose of testing out the constraint of APPROBATION in this item, I requested the informants to perform the speech act of 'complimenting' towards a senior male person, represented by the term *senpai* in Japanese, in this item. The analysis will focus on how they performed this speech act by controlling the propositional content, and how lexicogrammatical strategies were applied to manage the scale of **politeness** and **appropriateness**.

The speech act of 'compliment' can be classified in Searle's category of EXPRESSIVES (speech acts whose illocutionary point is to express the psychological state of affairs specified in the propositional content, e.g. 'thank', 'congratulate', 'apologise', 'condole', 'deplore' and 'welcome') (Searle, 1979: 15), and in Leech's (1983: 104) CONVIVIAL (an illocutionary function whose goal coincides with the social goal). Leech states that 'politeness here [i.e. in CONVIVIAL functions] takes a more positive form of seeking opportunities for comity' (Leech, *ibid.*: 195). This means that the performance of this speech act in a considerate way takes the **positive direction**. Since this direction is mainly achieved by *FEA*s, the degree of success is measured by how one *places a high value on what relates to o̲*, as indicated by the *GSP*.

As the discussion below shows, the responses in this item contain a lot of 'congratulating', however. This is because the senior male person's achievement is worth 'congratulations'. Consequently many responses exhibit a hybrid character: they contain either one or both of two speech acts, 'complimenting' and 'congratulating'. As these two speech acts are included in the same illocutionary function categories above, they are assumed to take the same **positive direction** in nature. Still, this makes a definition of the *head act* in this item difficult. In order to overcome this difficulty such expressions as follow will be labelled as the *head acts*: (i) genuine compliments – e.g. 'You're/That's great', 'I want to be like you'; (ii) congratulating – i.e. 'Congratulations'.

Senpai and *kohai*, which are taken by seniors and juniors respectively, refer to widely acknowledged social roles in Japanese society. It is necessary for *kohai*-s to use honorifics, 'respect markers', towards *senpai*-s because of the seniority/ superiority of the latter. Japanese people usually start to employ this social convention when they become junior high school students and join in (mainly) sports clubs. Under some circumstances a failure to use proper honorifics towards a *senpai* can lead to serious consequences. Still, closeness or familiarity in relation often establishes an informal and a friendly setting, and invalidates such a rigid relationship between *senpai*-s and *kohai*-s.

I made two kinds of video prompts for this scenario: one for JHA and the other for JYA. I did this because the stereotypical concept of *senpai*, or a senior person at one's workplace or school, differs for different age groups. If I had used the video prompt designed for JHA to elicit responses from JYA, the younger informants would have taken the person on the video as a teacher, not as a *senpai*. This is because *senpai* is usually applied to a student in a higher grade in the university setting. For this reason I created a prompt with a younger male person who could act as a senior student at university for JYA.

Here are the two types of prompts designed for the scenario in this item:

The prompt for JHA:
Yaa,   tenki   yoku-natte   yokatta   ne.
IJ   weather   good-became   be good-PAST   FP
<I'm glad the weather turned out fine.>

The prompt for JYA:
Chiwaa   su.
Hello-COL   COP(**POL**)-COL
<Hi.>

The original prompt, '*Yaa, tenki yoku-natte yokatta ne*' <Hi, nice day, isn't it?>, was devised only to give a cue to the informant to start speaking, so it does not have a special meaning. The modified version for JYA thus has the same illocutionary force of 'greeting'[8]. The higher age performer chose to keep the original, and the younger one preferred to change it into what would sound more natural to him and to Japanese university undergraduates. One thing they have in common is informality. The higher age performer's utterance does not contain any honorific or formal forms. The younger age actor used a polite form copula *su* on the other hand, but this is an abbreviated form of *desu* and is a colloquial expression that young boys prefer to use. The whole utterance '*Chiwaa su*' is a formulaic expression for greetings that is frequently used by young males and is taken as nothing but a salutation (cf. 'Hi' in English as an informal equivalent of 'Hello'). Furthermore, the Japanese younger generation rarely talk of the weather as a gambit for conversation. So the above sounds more authentic to young informants than it would with an expression mentioning good weather. These facts about the two utterances explain why the video performers used them in order to sound natural to informants of the different age groups. These two prompts both functioned as a gambit for conversation as had been expected.

Now I would like to turn to the quantitative analysis of this item. The following table shows the summary of the results of the statistical analysis of the second stage data.

Table 5.2.3 Summary of statistical data: Item 03

	Average scores in politeness		Average scores in appropriateness		Average scores in politeness		Average scores in appropriateness
1	JHA (2.25)	1	JYA (1.25)	1	JHAM (2.00)	1	JHAF (1.00)
				2	JHAF (2.50)	2	JYAM (1.13)
2	JYA (3.25)	2	JHA (1.38)	3	JYAF (3.25)	3	JYAF (1.38)
					JYAM (3.25)	4	JHAM (1.75)

As for the age group differences, JHA showed higher level of **politeness** (Mean = 2.25, n = 16) than JYA (Mean = 3.25, n = 16), but the younger age group (Mean = 1.25, n = 16) surpassed the older one (Mean = 1.38, n = 16) in the level of **appropriateness**. The t-test has proven that the difference in the level of **politeness** is statistically very significant ($p<.001$), whereas that in the level of **appropriateness** is not.

In terms of the age–gender group differences, JHAM came first (Mean = 2.00, n = 8), followed by JHAF (Mean = 2.50, n = 8), then JYAF and JYAM came third with the same mean score (Mean = 1.38, n = 8) in the level of **politeness**. One-way ANOVA has confirmed significant mean differences among the four groups in **politeness** ($p<.05$). Moreover, significant mean difference emerged in pairs JHAM–JYAF ($p<.05$) and JHAM–JYAM ($p<.05$) in the post hoc test (Bonferroni test).

As for the level of **appropriateness**, JHAM was ranked as the fourth (Mean = 1.75, n = 8) – this group fell from the top in **politeness** to the bottom in **appropriateness**. As regards other groups, JHAF came first in **appropriateness** (Mean = 1.00, n = 8), JYAM followed (Mean = 1.13, n = 8), and JYAF came third (Mean = 1.38, n = 8). Significant mean differences among the four groups appeared in the result of Kruskal Wallis test ($p<.05$). Also, a significant mean difference between JHAF–JHAM was found ($p<.05$) by the post hoc test (Tukey HSD).

In this item the statistical analysis did not show a significant correlation between the scale of **politeness** and that of **appropriateness**. This seems mainly due to the performance of JHAM described above. So I will start with a descriptive analysis of two responses of this group.

MJ315 – JHAM03
*Aa, hontooni ii-tenki-**de-gozaimasu**-ne. Tokorode, sakihodo, shokuba-no-mono-ni kiita-n'-**desu**-ga, nodojimantaikai-de shoo-o-**torareta**-to-iu-koto-de, hontooni omedetoo-**gozaimasu**. Ano, fudan **desu**-ne, itsumo uta-o kiite-ite hontooni subarashii-na-to omotte-ita-n'-**desu**-ga, hontooni yokatta-**desu**-ne. Hontooni omedetoo-**gozaimasu** shitsurei-shi-**masu**.*

[Yes, it's indeed a good weather. <u>By the way <*alerter*>, I heard from one of fellow workers a little while ago that you had won a prize at an amateur singing contest. <*supportive move*> I really congratulate your accomplishment. <*head act*> I always thought your singing talent was splendid. <*head act*> That was really a good thing for you. <*head act*> I really congratulate you. <*head act*></u> See you soon.]

[Reply to the greeting] + [Alerter] + [Explanation of *h*'s achievement] + [Congratulation 1 (formulaic)] + [Compliment 1 (Praise of *h*'s talent)] + [Compliment 2 (Celebration of the prize winning as a good thing for *h*)] + [Congratulation 2 (formulaic – repetition of 1)] + [Farewell]

This response was rated as 1.50 for **politeness** (right in the middle of 'polite – showing consideration' and 'very polite – showing high consideration'), and as 2.25 for **appropriateness** (just beyond 'a little inappropriate – a little too polite / a little impolite'). As the other JHAM informant's remark was rated as 2.50 and 1.25 each, this response of JHAM03 had a considerable influence on the performance of JHAM as a group (of two higher age male informants). This informant showed *overpoliteness* in Item 02 as well, and he demonstrated it here again. The remark contains nine polite honorific forms, three of which being 'superpolite' – '***gozaimasu***'. Although the expression '*omedetoo-**gozaimasu***' used twice here is formulaic, his use of honorific/deferential expressions so many times certainly gave an *overpolite* impression.

In the follow-up interview he mentioned the point of his response as follows: 'I wanted to tell him my feeling of congratulation honestly. I wanted to tell him that it was his effort before that was rewarded'. So his intention in this remark is twofold: honest 'congratulation' and a 'compliment' for *h*'s previous effort. In this sense the strategy he took was an ordinary one and there is no uniqueness about it. Still, how he realised this strategy with lexicogrammatical devices made this response rather exceptional.

The raters, while admitting the sophisticated linguistic features (*pragmalinguistic* value) of this response, pointed out its inappropriate impression as follows: 'This is not what and how I'd say this' (YMR); 'This is too much of a compliment' (YFR); and 'This may sound impolite to *h* because of its *overpoliteness*' (HMR). The third remark clearly indicates the negative impact of *overpoliteness*. HMR also mentioned the closeness and informality of the relationship between *senpai* and *kohai* in this context as one reason for his evaluation.

HFR, however, indicated a different point as an origin of inappropriateness: 'The part "See you soon" sounds as if this person wanted to escape from *h* as soon as possible. The sincere feeling of complimenting or congratulating is not conveyed because of this part'. It is a pity that JHAM03's courteous farewell '***shitsurei-shi-masu***' [*lit*. I will carry out rudeness to excuse myself] was taken this way. It is a linguistically modest and very polite expression, but its illocutionary force was recognised in a different way, as a marker of his desire to leave the place.

With regard to conformity to the constraint for APPROBATION, this informant did his best to *place a high value on o's qualities*, '*fudan* **desu**-*ne, itsumo uta-o kiite-ite hontooni subarashii-na-to omotte-ita-n'-**desu**-ga*' <I always thought

your singing talent was splendid>. I would like to state that this substantial aspect, apart from lexicogramamtical features, certainly contributed to increase the level of **absolute politeness**.

The other JHAM informant, on the other hand, received a more 'normal' evaluation (politeness = 2.50, appropriateness = 1.25) as described earlier.

MJ316 – JHAM04

| *A,* | *konnichiwaa.* | *Soo-**desu**-ne,* |
| IJ | hello | true-COP(**POL**)-FP |

| *tenki-yokunatte-yokatta-**desu**-nee.* | | *A,* | *soo soo,* |
| weather-good-become-PAST-COP(**POL**)-FP | | IJ | by the way |

| *soo-ieba,* | *konomae,* | *ee,* | *supootsutaikai-de* |
| come to think of it | recently | IJ | sports competition-LOC |

*yuushoo-**sareta**-soo-**desu**.*
championship-do(**EXAL**)-likely-COP(**POL**)

*Omedetoo-**gozaimasu**.*
congratulation-COP(**SUPERPOL**)

*Yokatta-**desu**-ne.*
good-be-PAST-COP(**POL**)-FP

[Hello. Yes I'm glad the weather has turned out good. <u>Oh, by the way <alerter>, I heard you won a sport tournament recently. <supportive move> Congratulations. <head act></u> That's good. <head act>]

[Greeting (formulaic)] + [Reply to the greeting mentioning weather] + [Alerter] + [Explanation of *h*'s achievement] + [Congratulation (formulaic)] + [Compliment (Celebration of the prize winning as a good thing for *h*)]

The core part here consists of simple two *head acts*, a formulaic congratulation '[*o*]*medetoo-**gozaimasu*' (congratulation-COP(**SUPERPOL**)) <Congratulations>, and a plain compliment '[*y*]*okatta-**desu**-ne*' (good-be-PAST-COP(**POL**)-FP) <That's good>. These seem to be enough for a compliment to a male *senpai*. This informant said in the interview, 'I wanted to tell the senior person my gladness honestly, as he honourably received a prize'. This remark means that his intention was to be 'honest'. This motivation has led to 'simplicity', but the propositional content and the linguistic features of his response were evaluated as very close to 'appropriate'. This makes a contrast with JHAM03's, in that JHAM03's response created a 'flattering' or 'obsequious' impression with too much 'elaboration'.

This informant made one minor mistake in the above. The part '*yuushoo-**sareta**-soo-**desu***' (championship-do(**EXAL**)-likely-COP(**POL**)) should be followed by a final particle '*ne*', if it is to be addressed to *h*. Otherwise this part appears to mention someone else's achievement, for '*sareru*' is a referent-related honorific (*sonkeigo*) and needs another/other function word(s) to identify the referent. Although there is a belief that older people are better at using honorifics than their younger counterparts, there are cases where they make this kind of mistake.

One thing to be noted about this item is the disparity between **politeness** and **appropriateness**. This suggests that **absolute politeness** diverged from **relative politeness** here. This informant did not make reference to *o*'s *good qualities* in his response. It implies that he neglected the constraint of APPROBATION and consequently his remark failed to create a nicer impression. This seems to be one reason for a relatively low evaluation in **absolute politeness**. Still, the total impression created by the propositional content and the linguistic features of this response was judged as 'almost appropriate' by the raters.

I will now look at the JYAF informants' two responses, for the gap between the two categories was the biggest in the performance of this group (**politeness** = 3.25, **appropriateness** = 1.13).

MJ321 – JYAF03

A,	konnichiwaa.	Ano,	konomae,	ee,	nanka
IJ	hello	IJ	recently	IJ	somehow

hyooshoo-saretatte-iu-hanashi-o	kiita-n'-**desu**-kedomo,
honour-receive-PAST-what says-story-ACC	hear-PAST-COP(**POL**)-but

omedetoo-***gozaimasu.***
congratulation-COP(**SUPERPOL**)

[Hello. I heard that you were given a prize for something or other recently. <*supportive move*> Congratulations. <*head act*>]

[Reply to the greeting] + [Explanation of *h*'s achievement] + [Congratulation (formulaic)]

This response was rated as 3.25 for **politeness** (a little less polite than 'neutral') and as 1.50 for **appropriateness** (right between 'appropriate' and 'a little inappropriate'). In terms of lexicogrammatical features, this response could have been rated higher, as the use of honorifics appears correct and sufficient. I think the main reason for the low evaluation in terms of **politeness** is because of the expressions '*konomae*' (recently) and '*nanka*' (somehow). HFR pointed out that the former had sounded 'perfunctory', for it could mean that she had not cared about the detail of *h*'s honour. This seems also the case with the word '*nanka*', although no rater mentioned it. '*Nanka*', translated as 'for something or other', includes ambiguity and vagueness. As *FEA*s or **positive direction** usually requires clarity and intensification of *h*'s/*o*'s good quality, this kind of ambiguity is not highly appreciated. In the second trial, this young female informant specified what *h*'s honour is as can be seen in Appendix 16. I assume she noticed the importance of being clear and consequently modified her first response accordingly.

Still, this response was evaluated as close to 'appropriate'. This appears due to the raters' judgement of the context: this is an informal conversation between *senpai* and *kohai*, so such vagueness can be taken as 'no problem'. It should be noted, however, that HMR rated it as 'very inappropriate' (category 3), while all the others rated it as '(optimally) appropriate' (category 1). This implies that it is likely that there are people who take such ambiguity (and 'insufficiency') as 'very inappropriate' – but such a low assessment was 'neutralised' by the others' ratings in the average score.

MJ323 – JYAF04

A,	—*senpai,*	*kiki-**mashita**-yoo.*	E,	*hora,*	*anoo,*
IJ	(name) ADD	hear-PAST(**POL**)-FP	IJ	IJ	IJ

benrontaikai.	*E,*	*senpai*	*ichii-datta-n'-**desu**-ka?*
oratorical contest	IJ	ADD	first prize-be-PAST-COP(**POL**)-Q

Moo	*bikkuri.*	*Nande*	*itte-**kudasara**-nai-n'-**desu**-ka? (laughter)*
IJ	surprise	why	say-HUM-NEG-COP(**POL**)-Q

[Ah, … (name) senpai (an address term for a senior student), I heard the news. Yeah, about the oratory contest. Really? Did you get the first prize? <supportive move> Surprising. <supportive move / head act> Why did you not say it to me? <supportive move> (laughter)]

[Explanation of *h*'s achievement 1 (introduction)] + [Explanation of *h*'s achievement 2 (the point)] + [Question for confirmation of the truth] + [Showing surprise] + [Question for accusation]

The assessments of this response were 3.25 in **politeness** (a little less polite than 'neutral') and 1.25 in **appropriateness** (very close to 'appropriate'). As for the use of honorifics in it, the amount and the quality look fine. However, this response is quite unique: instead of making a compliment herself, this young female informant elicited what honour *h* had received. She first implied that she had heard about this matter and tried to draw out information from *h*. Then she asked a question to confirm the information and showed surprise. This part is supposed to function as a virtual compliment: having *h* say what achievement he had accomplished, repeating it, and showing surprise as if to praise the honour. Then she performed an apparent 'mock accusation', again, as if to say 'You should have told me this honourable story earlier'. This seems to be an alternative way to perform a compliment and congratulation among friends to show closeness, familiarity and informality. The fact that she used a sufficient amount of honorifics indicates that she still shows respect to *h*'s seniority as a courtesy. Therefore her 'mock accusation' functions like a piece of 'banter', and the hidden intention is to praise *h*'s achievement.

The evaluation in **politeness** is not high because this response lacks clarity and directness in complimenting *h*, but this strategy is still 'acceptable' in this context. YFR indeed said that this remark had looked like one in a friendly conversation and therefore was appropriate. This is a case where 'banter' is judged positively.

This informant's response is contrary to the *GSP* because she expressed 'surprise' and even 'disbelief' that *h* had won the honour. This implies that she did not have a high opinion of *h*. But this is where *camaraderie* seems to be a more appropriate strategy for young people.

The two responses by female university undergraduates above do not contain a part '*place a high value on o's qualities*'. This means they also neglected the constraint of APPROBATION, just like JHAM04 mentioned above. I assume that these responses could have been evaluated higher if the part that satisfies the constraint of APPROBATION had been included.

Lastly, in order to specify what kind of expressions were used to satisfy the constraint of APPROBATION, I chose from the rest of the data (including the responses used in the second stage data collection) phrases that realised '*placing a high value on o's qualities*'. As for the number of an expression '*sugoi(-desu-ne)*' ('You're/That's great') and its variations, I found eighteen out of thirty-eight responses. This means that the frequency of this phrase is 0.47 and that nearly half the responses contain such phrases.

However, with regard to other expressions than '*sugoi*' that directly *place a high value on o's qualities*, I found only eight such face-enhancing comments for *h* (out of thirty-eight responses) in the data, including the one made by JHAM03 mentioned above.

MJ304 – JHAF03
Sasuga-desu-ne
[You deserve it]

MJ305 – JHAF03
ii-o-hanashi-o sareta
[you gave a good speech]

MJ310 – JHAF06
*Konomae-wa nanka **go**-katsuyaku-datta-soo-de*
[I heard you did a good job recently]

MJ311 – JHAF06
*Konomae-wa taikai-de **go**-katsuyaku-datta-soo-de*
[I heard you did a good job at a contest recently]

MJ332 – JYAM03
*Konomae-no-shiai, yokatta-**ssu**-yoo*
[The match you played was good]

MJ333 – JYAM04
*futsuu-ni boku-mo, ano, senpai-mitai-ni naretara-ii-naa-to omoi-**masu***
[I honestly hope I can be like senpai (you)]

MJ334 – JYAM04
*anna-fuu-ni-saishuuteki-ni boku-mo nareta-ra-ii-naa-to omoi-**masu**-ne.*
[I want to be like that after all]

After all, the number of this kind of expressions was rather limited. This suggests that the objective of complimenting was achieved mainly by a formulaic phrase '*sugoi-**desu**-ne*' and its variations, or else by congratulating. This may be implying that the informants needed to know more about the achievement of the male senior and that it is a limitation of the scenario.

Some of the other comments in the Appendix 16 contain matters of interest. Strategies associated with complimenting include (a) expressing surprise; (b) expressing *s*'s delight or pleasure – which is in accordance with the constraint of SYMPATHY, rather than APPROBATION; (c) expressing the wish to imitate *h*'s example; (d) asking for more details about the achievement of *h*. (Perhaps this last is partly a tactic to overcome *h*'s modesty – *h* might feel reluctant to talk about his/her achievement, because it would seem like boasting (= self-approbation)). Again, these characteristics seem due to the fact that the scenario did not specify the nature of the achievement. Some informants invented some achievement – e.g. success in a speech contest or sports contest – but others didn't think of the particular nature of the achievement, and so could not say anything specifically complimentary about it (such as 'I've heard you're an excellent sportsman'). That may be why there wasn't much variation in the use of complimentary expressions, and why so many informants relied on a few formulae like *o-medetoo-**gozaimasu*** or *sugoi-**desu**-ne.*

5.2.4 Item 04
Constraint: Modesty – '*Place a low value on s̲'s qualities*'
Speech act(s): self-evaluation (self-depreciation)
Activity type: Conversation with a senior male person (Senpai in Japanese)
Social variables: vertical distance = yes; horizontal distance = no
Formality: informal
(For more details of the scenario, see Appendix 3.)

The speech act tried out in this item is 'self-depreciation', which is supposed to be performed in a response to a compliment to show politeness by expressing *s*'s modest attitude. There is no direct reference to this speech act in Leech's (1983) or Searle's (1979) classifications, but it can be placed in Searle's category of EXPRESSIVES, for '[t]he illocutionary point of this class is to express the psychological state specified in the sincerity condition about a state of affairs specified in the propositional content' (Searle, *ibid.*: 15). The speech acts that also belong to this category are 'thank', 'congratulate', 'apologise', 'condole', 'deplore', 'welcome' etc. These speech acts 'tend to be CONVIVIAL' (Leech, *ibid.*: 106) in Leech's classification, where the illocutionary goal 'coincides with the social goal' (Leech, *ibid.*: 104).

From another perspective, B&L have described this speech act as 'acceptance of a compliment' and as an act 'that directly damage[s] S's positive face' (B&L, 1987: 68). According to them, 'S may feel constrained to denigrate the object of H's prior compliment, thus damaging his own face; or he may feel constrained to compliment H in turn' when performing this speech act (*ibid.*: 68). I have presented their description to assist further exploration of this speech act, but do not agree with their claim that it is totally in the category of *FTA*s. The reason why their description is worth mentioning here is that the first part of their explanation ('S may feel constrained to denigrate the object of H's prior compliment') corresponds to Leech's *GSP* (**negative direction**). As mentioned above, polite performance of this speech act is expected to show modesty on *s*'s side. Therefore the kind of politeness for the performance of this speech act is oriented towards the **negative direction** of the *GSP*: *Place a low value on s̲'s qualities*.

However, as can be seen in the data and the discussion below, there were not many informants that included 'self-depreciation' in their response to the compliment in a direct way. This leads to the problem of defining the *head act* in the data of this item. For convenience' sake, I will take such self-depreciating expressions as '*watashi-dake-dewa dekinakatta*' <I would not have succeeded if I had been alone> as the *head act1*, although phrases of this kind were rather rare. The more frequent thanksgiving type of phrase, '*arigatoo-**gozaimasu***' (thank you), can also be recognised as a core part of a response to a compliment, therefore will be treated as the *head act2*. The interesting thing is that 'thank you' here is showing gratitude for the speech act uttered by *h* – not for a gift or service in the normal sense. Perhaps the advantage of a thanking in response to a compliment is that *s* doesn't have to commit him/herself either to the truth or the falsehood of the compliment. The compliment is simply accepted as a pleasant act that *h* has performed for *s*.

This scenario has two kinds of prompts as the previous one does, for this is presented as a continued exchange from the preceding conversation with the same male *senpai*. Here are the two prompts differently designed for JHA and JYA, which were modified from the initially designed one, '*Are-wa subarashikatta. Kandoo-shita yo.*' <That was marvellous. I was really impressed>:

The prompt for JHA:

Iyaa,	*are-wa*	*subarashikatta*		*yo.*
IJ	that-TOP	be marvellous-PAST		FP

Kandoo-shita	*yo.*
be impressed-PAST	FP

<Why, that was marvellous. I was impressed.>

The prompt for JYA:

Konaida-no	*are*	*sugokatta*		*ne.*
last time-GEN	that	be marvellous-PAST		FP

Kandoo-shita	*yo.*
be impressed-PAST	FP

<That performance of yours last time was marvellous. I was impressed.>

There are no big differences in meaning between these two types of prompts. This is because a similar pragmalinguistic realisation was required to have the same 'force' in complimenting informants. The prompt for younger informants included lexical items that are frequently used by the younger generation: *'konaida'* is a shortened form of *'konoaida'*, thus more informality and familiarity is included in the former; *'sugoi'* is preferred by young Japanese to describe something wonderful, terrible, serious etc.; the final particle *'ne'* (a sentence-final particle, used for confirmation of a statement – Kamiya, 1997) has a softer impression than *'yo'* (a sentence-final particle that indicates a strong conviction – Kamiya *ibid.*).

The results of the quantitative analysis of the data for this item are summarised in the following table.

Table 5.2.4 Summary of statistical data: Item 04

	Average scores in politeness		Average scores in appropriateness		Average scores in politeness		Average scores in appropriateness
1	JHA (1.88)	1	JHA (1.25)	1	JHAF (1.75)	1	JHAM (1.13)
				2	JHAM (2.00)	2	JYAM (1.25)
2	JYA (3.44)	2	JYA (1.56)	3	JYAM (3.13)	3	JHAF (1.38)
				4	JYAF (3.75)	4	JYAF (1.87)

With regard to the generation differences, JHA demonstrated higher level performances in both **politeness** (Mean = 1.88, n = 16) and **appropriateness** (Mean = 1.25, n = 16) than JYA (**politeness**: Mean = 3.44, n = 16; **appropriateness**: Mean = 1.56, n = 16). The difference in **politeness** was proven to be statistically very significant ($p<.001$) by the t-test, while that in **appropriateness** was not.

In the age–gender classification, JHAF comes first in **politeness** (Mean = 1.75, n = 8), being followed by JHAM (Mean = 2.00, n = 8), JYAM (Mean = 3.13, n = 8), and JYAF (Mean = 3.75, n = 8). Kruskal-Wallis test has confirmed significant mean differences among the four groups. ($p<.005$). Also, significant mean differences were found in the Dunnet test between JHAF–JYAF ($p<.05$), JHAF–JYAM ($p<.05$), JHAM–JYAF ($p<.05$), and JHAM–JYAM ($p<.05$).

As for **appropriateness**, JHAM comes on top (Mean = 1.13, n = 8), and JYAM (Mean = 1.25, n = 8), JHAF (Mean = 1.38, n = 8), JYAF (Mean = 1.87, n = 8) follow in this order. The fact that JHAF came third in **appropriateness** seems to be because this group's performances were judged *overpolite* as JHAM's were in the previous two items. There were no statistically significant group differences in **appropriateness**, however.

I would like to examine JHAF's and JHAM's responses qualitatively in order to evaluate the above results further. The focus will be on (1) the reason why JHAF's evaluation in **appropriateness** came third; (2) the reason why JHAM came first in **appropriateness**. After that I will look at the responses made by one JYAF informant and one JYAM informant to make a comparison: their levels of **politeness** were both low, but the level of **appropriateness** of the former was given a very low rating, and that of the latter was much higher. Firstly, I will analyse JHAF's two responses.

MJ406 – JHAF04
*Arigatoo-**gozaimasu***
thankful-COP(**SUPERPOL**)

*Minasan-no-**o-kage**-de*
everyone(**EXAL**)-GEN-by the grace of(**EXAL**)-CONJ

nantoka	*yaru-koto-ga*	*deki-**mashita***
barely	do-NOM2-NOM1	be able(PAST-**POL**)

*Arigatoo-**gozaimasu**.*
thankful COP(**SUPERPOL**)

[Thank you. <head act2> I just managed it with the help of everyone. <head act1> Thank you. <head act2>]

[Thanking (formulaic)] + [Mentioning the aid from others (showing modesty)] + [Thanking (formulaic)]

This remark was rated as 1.50 (just in-between 'polite' and 'very polite') in **politeness**, the best average score in this item. Its **appropriateness** was 1.25 (close to 'appropriate'), which was the second best among all the responses. It should be noted, however, that there were three responses rated as 1.00 as can be seen from Appendix 17: this perhaps provides evidence of slight *overpoliteness* of this response. YMR said in the interview that the phrase '*Minasan-no-o-kage-de*' <with the help of everyone> had sounded polite but it was not his way to say this. He added that this response was a little long and this may have affected his evaluation in **appropriateness**. YFR and HMR also pointed out the above phrase as the reason for the polite impression of this remark.

As the strategy analysis above suggests, this is a very good example of 'self-depreciation' in a response to a compliment: 'thanking' – 'showing modesty' – 'thanking'. This JHAF informant showed her modesty by mentioning others' help and consequently lowered her own ability in the achievement. This part gave a polite impression on the raters. It is also worth noting that this response totally consists of the two kinds of *head acts* I explained earlier. This is indeed a case where such a performance of two *head acts* together was evaluated highly with regard to politeness. The minimising use of '*nantoka*' also seems to be a strategy of modesty – it means that she barely or only just succeeded: to say that she succeeded without this hedge might have seemed a little boastful.

This informant described the background of her remark as this: 'I emphasised my thankfulness as a courtesy because he is a senior person. I was glad, but I wanted to show modesty by mentioning others' efforts as he is a senior'. She certainly mentioned the modesty involved in the response, but it is interesting that the reason why she did so was because of *h* as a senior person. This suggests that modesty plays an important role in displaying politeness towards a person with seniority/superiority.

MJ408 – JHAF05
*Arigatoo-**gozaimasu**.*   *Tottemo,*   *anoo,*
thankful-COP(**SUPERPOL**)   very much   IJ

*kinchoo-shi-**mashita**-kedo,*
be nervous(PAST-**POL**)-but

taihen-ii-deki-datta-to-wa
very-good-achievement-COP(PAST)-COMP-TOP

       omou-n'-***desu***-kedo   ikaga-***deshita***-deshoo-ka.
       think-NOM2-COP(**POL**)-but   how-COP(**POL**)-CJEC-Q

[Thank you. <u><head act2> I was very nervous, but I think it was a very good performance. <supportive move> What did you think? <supportive move></u>]

[Thanking (formulaic)] + [Mentioning nervousness + self-evaluation of the performance] + [Asking for *h*'s opinion]

This response was rated as 2.00 in **politeness** (i.e. 'polite') and 1.50 in **appropriateness** (just in-between 'appropriate' and 'a little inappropriate'). These evaluations are a little lower than the response by JHAF04 above. The reason for this lies in the part '*taihen-ii-deki-datta-to-wa omou-n'-desu-kedo*' <I think it was a very good performance>. This phrase does not show 'self-depreciation' or *s*'s modest attitude, but the informant's high evaluation on her own achievement – boastfulness. The part '*ikaga-deshita-deshoo-ka*' <What did you think> is controversial: YFR took this as polite and appropriate, whereas HFR thought this polite but a little inappropriate because it was a redundant question seeking further confirmation after the male *senpai*'s compliment 'That was marvellous'. This kind of question has a multiple function, viz. 'a question to show *s*'s modesty by asking for *h*'s opinion (from a high place)' and 'a question to show *s*'s interest to know more about *h*'s (high) evaluation'. Indeed it seems that YFR chose the former possibility and HFR the latter. The latter can be recognised as an indirect request for more compliments; as a result it can lead to a negative assessment by some people. This female informant indeed said in the interview, 'I want to express my willingness to accept the senior person's compliments as much as possible', and explained that her intention was to hear about the *senpai*'s compliment as much as possible. By this observation I think that HFR made a correct judgement.

   Now I would like to examine JHAM responses to explore the reason why this group came on top in **appropriateness**.

   <u>MJ415 – JHAM04</u>
   A,   *arigatoo-**gozaimasu**.*
   IJ   thankful-COP(**SUPERPOL**)

Ee, renshuu-shita-seika-ga-dete-yokatta-to
IJ   practice-do(PAST)-achievement-NOM1-come out-be good(PAST)-COMP

*omoi-**masu**.*
think(**POL**)

[Thank you. <*head act2*> I think it was good that I had a good result after all that practice. <*supportive move*>]

[thanking (formulaic)] + [showing *s*'s gladness about the good result (with the hedge 'I think')]

This response was rated as 2.25 in **politeness** (a little less polite than 'polite'), but was rated as 1.00 in **appropriateness** ('(optimally) appropriate'). This means that it has been judged more appropriate than JHAF's responses in spite of its lower assessment in **politeness**. As can be seen from the strategy analysis, the components of this remark are quite simple. One reason for a lower evaluation in **politeness** seems due to lack of 'self-depreciation' and modesty. Still, it was recognised as '(optimally) appropriate' seemingly because of the use of proper honorifics and sufficient propositional content as a reply to a *senpai*. YMR said in the interview, 'there is no problem about this response' so it was taken as appropriate. JHAM04 explained about the background of this remark in the follow-up interview as follows: 'Although this may be just a superficial compliment, I will express my gratitude honestly because I think he admitted I had made an intense effort'. So the point of his response was 'expression of honest gratitude for *h*'s recognition of *s*'s intense effort'. This is the reason for the lack of 'self-depreciation' or modesty. By saying he achieved what he had hoped to, he succeeded in making his response appropriate in this context, while having failed to heighten the degree of **absolute politeness**.

MJ416 – JHAM05
A,   *arigatoo-**gozaimasu**.*   *Ma,*   *sore-nari-ni,*
IJ   thankful-COP(**SUPERPOL**)   IJ   as such

jibun-nari-ni   doryoku-shita-mono-**desu**-kara,
in my own way   effort-make(PAST)-as-COP(**POL**)-because

ee,   soo-itte-***itadakeru***-to   totemo-ureshii-***desu***.
IJ   so-say-can receive(**HUM**)-COMP   very-glad-COP(**POL**)

*Doomo-arigatoo-**gozaimasu**.*
indeed-thankful-COP(**SUPERPOL**)

[Thank you. <*head act2*> I tried my best in my way. So I'm really glad you said so. <*supportive move*> Thank you very much. <*head act2*>]

[thanking (formulaic)] + [mentioning *s*'s effort in the achievement] + [expressing pleasure in *h*'s compliment] + [thanking (formulaic – emphatic)]

This response was rated as 1.75 for **politeness** (a little higher than 'polite') and 1.25 for **appropriateness** (close to 'appropriate'). It is the second best response in terms of **politeness**, following JHAF04's above. This higher age male informant did not show 'self-depreciation' in the propositional content in a direct way, but demonstrated modesty with the lexical item that expresses humbleness '*itadaku*' <receive>. Indeed, he used five honorific expressions in his remark in total and this seems one reason why it was evaluated highly in **politeness**. As for the propositional content, HMR and YFR pointed out in the interview that the utterance '*soo-itte-**itadakeru**-to totemo-ureshii-**desu***' <I'm really glad you said so> created a polite impression. This implies that expressing one's gladness over a compliment in an honest way is recognised as a polite linguistic practice. It may be one form of realisation of the **positive direction** in performing a reply to a compliment, while 'self-depreciation' is one way to follow the **negative direction** in the same speech act. This response can be taken as a kind of 'counter-compliment' – that is, on receiving a compliment, one can compliment the other person on making the compliment.

What this informant said in the follow-up interview also supports the above hypothesis: 'I honestly express gladness that the senior person praised me. I don't have any secret intention'. This statement clarifies what strategy he took in achieving the illocutionary goal in this context. As for **appropriateness**, YMR took this response as 'a little inappropriate' for its slight *overpoliteness*. But except for that, all the other raters regarded it as '(optimally) appropriate'.

As the third thing to look at, I would like to focus on two responses made by the younger informants, one by a JYAF and the other by a JYAM. Their levels of politeness are low, but there is a sharp difference in their levels of **appropriateness**.

MJ423 – JYAF04

E, (laughter)	sonna	senpai,	kandoo-nante
IJ	as such	ADD	that you were impressed

uso-baakka. (laughter)
lie-only

[Hey, (laughter) senpai (senior student), impressed? <*supportive move*> That's totally a lie. <*Unable to classify – countering a compliment?*>]

[interjection to show surprise with laughter] + [address term] + [repetition of *h*'s word] + [countering *h*'s opinion]

The assessments of this response in both **politeness** (4.75 – very close to 'impolite') and **appropriateness** (2.75 – very close to 'very inappropriate') were the worst throughout the second stage data. Although there were some other responses in other items at the same inappropriateness level, there are no others at an equal level of impoliteness. This young female informant talked of the background of this response (described as 'the first response in the quotation') as follows:

> *The first response is to a very close senior student. The second one is to a senior student with a little social distance. I can have a funny conversation with a close person. I can say 'You're kidding if you say you were impressed' to hide my embarrassment, but I will say 'thank you' first as a courtesy to a senior student with a little social distance.* ***I don't like to be praised by a senior male student. I want to stop this topic as soon as possible.*** (emphasis mine)

As the part emphasised by bold face indicates, she wanted to stop this topic because she did not like to be praised by *h*. This seems to be the main reason why she produced such an impolite response. Moreover, as she pointed out, she showed her emotion honestly because she was addressing a close male *senpai*: this closeness allowed her to behave in a way that can be taken as rather rude. For her this scenario was not an appropriate one, for she could not accept the compliment and refused to perform a proper speech act in response. Her attitude can also be interpreted by the non-existence of honorifics in her remark. Although she used an address term *senpai*, it sounds as if it were used for a deictic marker rather than to bring a respectful connotation. She could have said '*uso **desu** yo ne*' <That is a lie, isn't it> or equivalent instead of '*uso baakka*' <That's totally a lie> if she had intended to show any sense of **politeness**. Indeed the phrase '*uso baakka*' is very colloquial, slangy, and has an insulting implication. From this we can see her determination to reject *h*'s compliment.

This response was judged accordingly. YFR told an interesting observation: she mentioned this informant's response in Item 03, where she awarded 4 for politeness but 1 for appropriateness. Her previous response 'sounded like one in a friendly conversation', thus seemed appropriate. (Her previous response contains sufficient number of honorifics, in contrast with the one in this item.) On the contrary, this response sounded rude, for 'the male *senpai* had kindly complimented but she responded to it in such an impolite way'.

On the face of it, this is an example of banter, in that she is demonstrating she can be impolite to a *senpai* with whom she has a close relationship. However, another interpretation is that she really wanted to be seriously impolite – she 'wanted to stop this topic as soon as possible'. She may have interpreted the compliment as a kind of sexual approach and tried to stop it.

MJ433 – JYAM04
*Aa, soo-**desu-ka**,suimasen. Wazawaza mite-**itadaite** arigatoo-**gozaimasu**. Maa, demo, are-wa soo-**ssu**-nee, nanka, warito jibun-teki-ni-mo yokatta-naa-to omou-shi, maa, soo-**desu-ne**, mite-**itadaite** arigatoo-**gozaimasu**. Tsugi-mo chito, ganbari-tai-to omoi-**masu**.*

[Ah, really, sorry, it was considerate of you to come and see it. <*supportive move*> Thank you. <*head act2*> Well, from my point of view as well, that performance of mine was good. <*supportive move*> Yes, thank you for having seen it. <*head act2*> I hope to do my best next time, too. <*supportive move*>]

[apology for *s*'s causing trouble (troublesome event) to *h* (This is actually thanking.)] + [thanking] + [acceptance and confirmation of *h*'s appreciation] + [thanking] + [expressing hope for another good performance in future]

This response was rated as 3.75 (very close to 'a little informal / a little lack of consideration') in **politeness** but was rated as 1.50 in **appropriateness** (just in-between 'appropriate' and 'a little inappropriate'). It means its level of **appropriateness** is relatively high in spite of its low evaluation in **politeness**. This young male informant used enough honorifics to show respect to *h* and his semantic strategy looks fine, which was not the case with JYAF04's above. The only problem he had in showing **politeness** was in the use of the proper level lexical items. The words '*soo-ssu-nee*' <that's right>, '*jibun-teki-ni-mo*' <from my point of view>, and '*chito*' <a bit> are all colloquial and slangy ones that are mainly used by Japanese young males. HMR said, 'This remark is not polite in terms of the quality of language, but it does not sound strange considering the relation between the two people'. HFR said a similar thing, pointing out that those lexical features are fine as young boys' language. However, these attitudes are in contrast with that of YFR: she took this response as impolite and inappropriate.

This young male informant said in the interview, 'I will try to keep my self-image as a modest person. So, I will say something like "No, it was nothing. Thank you. I will do my best next time, too"'. Although there seems to be some discrepancy between what he meant to say and what he really said (e.g. instead of saying 'it was nothing', he said 'that performance of mine was good'), he seems to have succeeded in conveying his polite intention. This point contributed to a higher evaluation in **appropriateness**.

As a summary of the data analysis of this item, I would like to state that 'self-depreciation' is an important strategy to respond to a compliment, for it is one form of realisation of **negative direction** of the *GSP* (showing self-effacement on the *s*'s side). A number of informants said that they tried to demonstrate self-effacement in replying to the male *senpai*. The below are their accounts of their attitudes in the follow-up interview.

JHAF02
If the person I'm talking to was a friend of mine, I would say, 'Yes, I agree'. But since he is a senior person, I showed modesty in my response.

JHAF04

I emphasised my thankfulness as a courtesy because he is a senior person. I was glad, but I wanted to show modesty by mentioning others' efforts as he is a senior.

JHAM02

I show modesty by saying I was lucky.

JYAF06

This time I was embarrassed by the senior student's compliment. I feel as if I got shrunk and say 'Thank you'. (It's like I'm belittling myself and humbling.)

JYAM02

I showed modesty in the first response…

JYAM03

I usually humble myself even if I think I am great in my mind. This may depend on how satisfied I am.

JYAM04

I will try to keep my self-image as a modest person. So, I will say something like 'No, it was nothing. Thank you. I will do my best next time, too'.

The other main strategies observed were (a) 'thanking for the compliment' and (b) 'expressing *s*'s pleasure in the compliment (honestly)', as mentioned earlier. These belong to the **positive direction** in terms of the *GSP* and enhance *h*'s position by implying 'You said such a nice thing to me and made me glad'. So it is confirmed that both **positive** and **negative directions** are employed in a response to a compliment in the present Japanese context. This may seem a contradictory finding to the traditional notion of Japanese culture, as one where modesty is highly valued. One JYAF informant (JYAF01) indeed said in the interview, 'I don't like a reply, "No, it wasn't". I don't want to reject his praise. I don't want to hear the person I'm talking say "It was nothing", either'. This statement reveals a new trend in Japanese, viz. the younger people have begun to value honesty more than modesty. However, one JHAM informant, while almost all the other informants performed both or either one of the above, responded without either of the

positive direction strategies:

<u>MJ413 – JHAM02</u>
Iyaa,   tamatama-de-saa.
No   by accident-COP(PLAIN)-FP

Umaku-matomatta-tte-kanji-de-nee.
well-organised-COMP-impression-COMP-FP

Maa,   hontooni   tamatama   nan-da-yo.
IJ   really   by accident   COP(PLAIN)-FP

[No, I was just lucky. I seemed to manage things. Yeah, it was really a matter of luck.]

[negation] + [saying it was a luck] + [describing the achievement using 'seem']
+ [emphasising that *s* was lucky]

This uses a significant strategy in the **negative direction** (modestly) to say that one's achievement was a matter of luck. In effect, he is saying that the achievement for which he is being complimented was not due to any of his personal good qualities – he wasn't clever, skilful, etc. – he was just lucky. This kind of traditional strategy to express *s*'s modesty still exists in older people's language. It may be because of the nature of the scenario that responses of this kind were not elicited more.

Another interesting thing about this response is that this informant did not use any honorifics to address the senior person. It seems that the use of honorifics to seniors in his workplace have become unnecessary in the course of time with shrinking vertical and horizontal distances.

5.2.5 Item 05

Constraint: Agreement – '*Place a high value on o's opinions*'
Speech act(s): Agreeing / Disagreeing with mitigation
Activity type: Conversation with an old lady
Social variables: vertical distance = yes; horizontal distance = yes

Formality: informal
(For more details of the scenario, see Appendix 3.)

In this item, the performance of the speech acts of 'agreeing' and 'disagreeing with mitigation' are to be examined in informants' conversation with a Japanese old lady. Although there are few direct references to these speech acts in earlier literature, they can be categorised in Searle's (1979) EXPRESSIVE and Leech's (1983) CONVIVIAL types: they both 'express the psychological state specified in the sincerity condition about a state of affairs specified in the propositional content (Searle, *ibid.*: 15) and their goals 'coincide with the social goal' (Leech, *ibid.*: 104). 'Agreeing' has an aspect of an *FEA* for *h* in nature, and 'disagreeing with mitigation' functions as an *FSA* when performing the *FTA* of disagreeing with *h*. Thus the former takes the **positive direction** and the latter the **negative direction** in the *GSP*. Although they take different directions of politeness, they are both realised by the same attitude, '*placing a high value on o's opinions*'. This means that *s* respects *h*'s opinion or idea whether *s* is for or against it. If *s* agrees with *h*, *s* performs a speech act of 'agreement', sometimes with intensification. On the other hand, if *s* disagrees with *h*, *s* is likely to opt for 'mitigated disagreement' to soften the confrontational aspects of *s*'s counter-opinion and to redress possible face-threats. Such mitigation often takes the form of hedging.

The *head acts*, or the core parts, of these speech acts are expressions such as '*Soo-desu-nee*' <Yes, I agree> and a repetition or reinforcement of *h*'s opinion. In the case of 'mitigated disagreement', expressions beginning 'but...', or other expressions that communicate *s*'s counter-opinion in an indirect way can be taken as the *head act*, as they are the parts in which *s* disagrees with *h*.

I had only one prompt for both age groups in this scenario, for the representation of the notion of 'an old lady' is thought to be common to both age groups, in contrast with the notion *senpai* in the previous two items. Here is the prompt used in this item.

Saikin-no-koto-nanka-de-mo,	*Koizumi-**san**-wa*	*hontooni*
recent-GEN-COMP-LOC-too	Mr Koizumi-TOP	really

yoku-yatteiru	*wa*	*yo*	*ne.*
well-be doing	FP	FP	FP

<Mr Koizumi has been doing a really good job dealing with recent issues, hasn't he?>

The performer, the old lady, said this in an informal and a friendly way, putting in only one respectful expression *–san*, an address term, referring to the Japanese Prime Minister at that time. As we know, this kind of political opinion can invite both agreements and disagreements. It is sometimes dangerous to express one's political position clearly, for some people might be offended and be provoked to show their anger in response. However, I chose an old lady as a performer, for people are supposed to show respect and consideration to such a person in the context of Japanese society. Besides, an old lady is usually thought of as politically 'harmless', which may not be the case with an old gentleman. Therefore an old lady was the best choice to perform this potentially controversial speech act of complimenting a politician[9].

Now I would like to look at the results of the data analysis from a quantitative viewpoint. The following is the summary of the statistical analyses:

Table 5.2.5 Summary of statistical data: Item 05

	Average scores in politeness		Average scores in appropriateness		Average scores in politeness		Average scores in appropriateness
1	JHA (3.13)	1	JHA (1.69)	1	JYAF (2.38)	1	JYAF (1.13)
	JYA (3.13)	2	JYA (1.75)	2	JHAF (3.13)	2	JHAF (1.38)
					JHAM (3.13)	3	JHAM (2.00)
				4	JYAM (3.88)	4	JYAM (2.38)

I have obtained an interesting result here, in that JHA and JYA are at the same **politeness** level (Mean = 3.13, n = 16 each). In **appropriateness** JHA (Mean = 1.69, n = 16) surpassed JYA (Mean = 1.75, n = 16), but there was no statistically significant difference between the two groups' data. This means that the two groups performed in a very similar way on the whole.

However, more detailed analysis of age–gender groups reveals some significant differences. As for the level of **politeness**, JYAF comes first (Mean = 2.38, n = 8), JHAF and JHAM being second with the same average scores (Mean = 3.13, n = 8), and JYAM coming last (Mean = 3.88, n = 8). Significant mean differences among the four age–gender groups were found ($p<.05$) through one-way ANOVA. The post hoc test (Bonferroni test) has also confirmed a significant mean difference between JYAF–JYAM ($p<.05$). With regard to **appropriateness**, JYAF again comes out on top (Mean = 1.13, n = 8), followed by JHAF (Mean = 1.38, n = 8), JHAM (Mean = 2.00, n = 8), and JYAM (Mean = 2.38, n = 8) in order. Significant mean differences among the four groups were confirmed by Kruskal-Wallis test ($p<.05$). The Dunnet test has found significant mean differences between JHAF–JYAM ($p<.05$) and JYAF–JYAM ($p<.05$).

I would like to undertake qualitative analysis in comparing JYAF and JYAM, for the former performed top levels of **politeness** and **appropriateness** and the latter performed just the opposite. First I would like to look at JYAF responses and explore the reasons why they were evaluated highly.

MJ526 – JYAF05

Hontoo	*soo-**desu**-yo-ne.*	*Taihen-soo-**desu**-kedo*
really	true-COP(**POL**)-FP-FP	seem to have much trouble-COP(**POL**)-but

yoku	*ganbatte-**masu**-yo-ne.*
well	doing his best(**POL**)-FP-FP

[I indeed agree with you. <*head act*> It seems to be a tough job, <*supportive move*> but he has been making a good effort. <*head act*>]

[agreeing to *h*'s opinion with an intensifier '*hontoo*'] + [showing care about the PM's job] + [repetition of *h*'s opinion – high evaluation of the PM]

This response was rated as 2.00 in **politeness** (i.e. 'polite') and 1.00 in **appropriateness** (i.e. '(optimally) appropriate'). It is a good example of a 'polite' and 'appropriate' response. As can be seen, this remark is rather short and does not contain many honorifics or any super-polite form. Still, it has received the top average scores by making a good impression on the raters. Strategically, this informant (1) accepted *h*'s opinion with an intensifier '*hontoo*', (2) mentioned a possible tough situation the PM had been possibly encountering, and (3) repeated *h*'s opinion. Indeed she showed total agreement with *h*'s opinion in her response on the surface. However, she admitted in the interview, 'I have some opposite opinions, but I said this to get along with her. I took her age into consideration'. So she hid her opinion and prioritised consideration towards the old lady.

Although this informant did not observe the 'sincerity condition' in her speech act performance, it complies with Searle's classification of EXPRESSIVE (Searle, *ibid.*). This is because Searle allowed that *s* could break the sincerity condition, without failing to perform the relevant speech act (here agreement). In other words, there is sincere agreement and insincere agreement – both are kinds of agreement. Leech's CONVIVIAL category (Leech, *ibid.*) can also incorporate this type of contradictory attitude in speech act realisation, as long as its goal 'coincides with the social goal'.

YMR, who awarded 1 for this response for both **politeness** and **appropriateness**, said, 'the way this informant said this is good. S/he responded conscientiously'. HFR, putting 2 for **politeness** and 1 for **appropriateness**, also said, 'The way s/he said this looks fine. S/he accepted *h*'s opinion without denying it'. These statements suggest that 'conscientiousness' and 'total acceptance' were judged as the source for the high degree of **politeness**.

We move on now to another response by a young female informant:

MJ527 – JYAF06
*Soo-**desu**-nee,*   *yoku*   *yatte-**masu**-yo-nee.*
true-COP(**POL**)-FP   well   doing(**POL**)-FP-FP

Kore-kara-mo   *ganbatte-hoshii-**desu**-yo-nee.*
from now on-too   do his best-want-COP(**POL**)-FP-FP

[Yes, I agree. <*head act*> He has been making a good effort. <*head act*> We want him to continue to try his best, don't we? <*head act*>]

[agreeing to *h*'s opinion] + [repetition of *h*'s opinion – high evaluation of the PM] + [reinforcement of *h*'s opinion – suggestion to hope for his continuation]

The average score of this response on the scale of **politeness** is 2.75 (i.e. a little higher than 'neutral') and that on the scale of **appropriateness** is 1.25 (i.e. a little lower than 'appropriate'). The average score 2.75 does not seem too high, but is the second best for this item. HFR, the only one that gave 2 to this response in **politeness**, said in the interview, 'There is no problem about this remark. This informant showed agreement to *h*'s opinion and consideration towards her'. Basically this remark has almost the same structure as JYAF05's above. It has as many honorifics as JYAF05's and consists only of phrases to show agreement. The difference between the two, viz. the source of the different average scores in **politeness**, seems to lie in the intensifier '*hontoo*' at the beginning of JYAF05's remark. By this she showed 'total agreement' and 'total acceptance' at the beginning. On the other hand, it seems that JYAF06 showed 'moderate agreement' and 'moderate acceptance', although she also reinforced *h*'s opinion at the end. This means that 'total agreement/acceptance' was evaluated higher by the raters.

This informant gave the background to this remark as follows: 'Instead of stating my opinion, I show acceptance of her opinion. I took her age into consideration. If I'm talking to a person of my own age, I would want to discuss this with her'. Again this informant seems to have had a different opinion but concealed it and performed 'mock agreement' in a sense, to show consideration towards the aged lady.

Secondly I would like to observe the responses of JYAM, which came at the bottom in both **politeness** and **appropriateness**.

MJ534 – JYAM05
Soo-da-ne,   *o-baa-chan.*   *Koizumi-**san**-wa*
true-COP(PLAIN)-FP   grandma(ADD)   Mr Koizumi-TOP

jieitai-o   *haken-shitari,*   *iroiro-yatte-kureteru-to-omou-yo.*
Self-Defence Force-ACC   send-or   various-do-granting-COMP-think-FP

Taihenna-koto-da-to   *omou-ne.*
serious-thing-COP(PLAIN)-COMP   think-FP

[Yes, grandma. <head act> I think Mr Koizumi has done various things like sending the Self-Defence Force and so on. They seem to be serious issues. <head act>]

[showing agreement] + [stating *s*'s own counter-opinion in an indirect way]

The average score of this remark in **politeness** was 3.50, viz. just in-between 'neutral' and 'a little informal / somewhat lacking in consideration' (the second lowest), and that in **appropriateness** was 2.00, viz. 'a little inappropriate' (the third lowest). One notable feature of this remark is the lack of honorifics. This young male informant used an address term '-*san*', but it was not for *h* but for the PM. The address term '*o-baa-chan*' is a form that does not contain a sense of respect but that of friendliness, for the suffix '*–chan*' is usually used in address to a familiar person such as a child, a friend, or a family member. HFR especially disliked this address term, saying, 'I can't tolerate this at all. I will never let someone address me like this when I have got old'. She gave a mark of 5 to this response for **politeness** and 3 for **appropriateness**, both of which are the lowest scores in the two categories. She also said that she did not like the part '*to-omou-yo*' ('I think that'). I think the reason for her antipathy to this phrase comes from the lack of a suitable honorific expression and the too friendly impression created by the final particle '*yo*'. This kind of structure is used to show friendliness when a Japanese speaks to a person at an equal or a lower status. For these two reasons HFR took this response as 'very rude' and gave the lowest scores to it.

This younger age male informant said in the follow-up interview, 'I spoke in a way to show consideration for her, as I'm talking to a much older person. I don't agree with her'. It seems that he thought 'speaking in a friendly way' was the manner to 'show consideration' to an old lady, but the way he realised that idea sounded awful to HFR. It is interesting that the HMR gave 2 to this response for **politeness** and 1 for **appropriateness**. This means that this rater thought this response was 'polite' and 'appropriate'. For him this way of 'showing consideration' by 'speaking in a friendly way' was fine. This is a good example of diversity in the recognition of *rapport-management* strategies among people. It consequently suggests the instability of the social variable 'vertical distance'. We have not only cross-cultural differences but also intra-cultural or even inter-personal varieties in acknowledging the relation between *s* and *h/o* and a suitable strategy to cope with it.

The other response of JYAM is the following very short and abrupt one:

MJ536 – JYAM06
A,   hai.
IJ   yes

[Ah, yes. <*head act*>]

[showing agreement by a simple formulaic response]

This response received an average score of 4.25 for the level of **politeness**, viz. a little lower than 'a little informal / a little lack of consideration' (the lowest), and that of 2.75 for the level of **appropriateness**, viz. very close to 'very inappropriate' (the lowest). As a starting point of discussing this response, I would like to present what this informant said in the interview: 'Basically I agree with this person's opinion. Mr Koizumi is better than the previous PMs. If this conversation was right after his visit to North Korea, I may have added that topic. I wait for a reply from the other person, because of my personality'. This indicates that he had had much to talk about and could have shown his agreement by expressing it. But as he said, he 'waited for a reply' after his brief response. This is a case where an informant did not represent his/her intention in a response because of his/her communication strategy, not because of his/her politeness strategy. It is possible that the old lady would not talk any more to him, having seen his lack of interest or unwillingness to talk about this issue; therefore I suspect that this kind of communication strategy can place a politeness strategy at risk. Also, the minimal response 'Yes' strikes other people as abrupt, because if someone expresses his/her opinion to h, there is an impression of abruptness and lack of consideration if s/he does not give his/her opinion sufficient attention.

Here are what the raters said about this response:

HFR: 'Terrible' (5 for politeness, 3 for appropriateness);

HMR: 'A perfunctory response. As he made a response anyway, it is not totally impolite, but he did not reply to the addressee properly'
(4 for politeness, 2 for appropriateness);

YFR: 'As the old lady had kindly talked to him, he should have talked more about his opinion'
(5 for politeness, 3 for appropriateness);

YMR: 'This is not bad for politeness, but is inappropriate'
(3 for politeness, 3 for appropriateness).

As can be seen from this, all four raters found some problems about this response. They could not understand that this informant had had an intention of showing agreement to the old lady's opinion. This is a piece of evidence that an insufficient communication strategy of this type can lead to misunderstanding.

The female raters seem to have taken this response as more 'impolite' and 'inappropriate' than the male counterparts. This seems to suggest that there are differences in the notion of suitable degrees of politeness/appropriateness for certain social roles (in this case for 'an old lady') between men and women. I think YMR had a similar communication strategy to this informant's and could understand why this informant made such a brief response. This kind of minimal response may be one of the prevailing Japanese young men's communication (and politeness) strategies, but more exhaustive research is necessary in order to prove this observation is really the case.

I would now like to present another example where such a difference in judgement apparently based on gender occurred. The following is a response from JHAM06, which was rated as 2.75 (i.e. very close to 'neutral' – second best) for **politeness** and 2.75 for **appropriateness** (very close to 'very inappropriate' – the lowest).

MJ519 – JHAM06
*Ee, soo-**desu**-nee. Un, aa, demo **anata**-ga, uun, manzoku-**sareteiru**-nara kitto, ee, ii-koto-o takusan yatte-kurete-iru-n'-da-to omoi-**masu**-keredomo, demo, maa, seken-niwa, ma, Koizumi-**san**-ni chotto-doo-ka-na-to-omou-hito-mo i-**masu**-yo. Demo, anoo, **o**-genki-soo-de naniyori-**desu**.*

[Yes, I agree. <*head act*> Uhm, but if you feel satisfied, I think he has been doing a lot of good things. <*supportive move*> But there are people in society who don't evaluate Mr Koizumi highly. <*head act*> But it is something that you look well. <*supportive move*>]

[showing agreement] + [showing a hint of disagreement by an interjection, showing mitigated agreement] + [performing mitigated disagreement] + [saying something nice to *h*]

In this response the interjections '*un, aa*' and '*ma(a)*' play an important role to express *s*'s hesitation to demonstrate both agreement and disagreement. Also the use of '*demo*' ('but') three times well represents such hesitation and mitigation. The part '*un, aa, demo*' ('uhm, but') can be interpreted as implying, 'no, I don't think so ..., but...', viz. (1) in saying '*un*', this informant seems to have thought of his own opinion (against *h*'s), and (2) in saying '*aa*' it seems that he considered that he should not say it directly, and (3) in saying '*demo*' he implied that he would respect *h*'s opinion in spite of his different view. In addition, his proper use of honorifics (indicated by the boldface) denotes his respectful attitude or consideration towards the old lady. In the interview he described the background of his remark as this: 'On the whole Japan is in peace as visible things have been going well, but as a doctor I have doubt about Mr Koizumi's policy on the social health service system. Still my attitude is, "if you're happy I am, too". I want to present something that this person doesn't know'. This suggests that there was a mixture of different response strategies in his mind, and it seems that this condition led him to use three 'buts'.

It is interesting that this response contrasted with the JYAM06's minimal response (a) in that it was quite long: *s* could be said to be taking *h*'s remark about Mr Koizumi as worthy of serious attention – which must count as a factor in favour of **politeness**. His sudden change of topic to talking about the old lady's health seems a bit strange, but it is reasonable because *s* is a doctor, and also because he is trying to say something positive, to counteract the negative view of Mr Koizumi. Another interesting thing is the mitigating strategy of 'displacement' of disagreement – he attributes the negative view of the PM to a third person, not to himself.

As can be seen from Appendix 19, there was a wide range of **politeness** assessments among the raters. Two raters gave 4, while one rater gave 1 to this response. Here are the comments from them:

HFR: 'This is an unfavourable remark. I don't think it is necessary to be as unfavourable as this'. (4 for politeness, 2 for appropriateness);

HMR: 'As for the quality of language it is polite, for this informant used such terms as "***anata*-ga**" (you(**EXAL**)-TOP) or "*omoi-**masu** keredomo*" (think(**POL**) but). Still, I would be offended a little if I was addressed with a phrase like "*Ee, soo-**desu**-nee... demo*" (Yes, true-COP(**POL**)-FP... but)'. (1 for politeness, 3 for appropriateness);

YFR: 'I did not like the part "*anata*-*ga*" (you(**EXAL**)-TOP)[10]. This remark sounds as if this person were not interested in this topic. I think s/he should have told his/her opinion. S/he didn't say this in a serious way'. (4 for politeness, 3 for appropriateness);

YMR: 'This response contains criticism'. (2 for politeness, 3 for appropriateness).

As can be seen from the above, the female raters assessed this response's level of politeness very low, whereas the male ones thought of it as high. Apparently this discrepancy arose from their different reasons for the judgements: the assessment from the lexicogrammatical aspect vs. that from the propositional content. The male raters prioritised the lexicogrammatical feature while female counterparts took the propositional content more seriously. There is indeed a balance between lexicogrammatical features and propositional content in making a judgement of the scale of **absolute politeness**, but it is also difficult to judge to assign priority in doing so. This result indicates that only one of them, viz. either one of the lexicogrammatical features or the propositional content, cannot govern the decision of the level of **absolute politeness**. It is also worth noting that their different attitudes in the judgement of **politeness** did not affect their assessment in **appropriateness** for all the raters put 2 or 3 to this response.

Through inspection of the rest of the data, it was confirmed that the phrase '*soo*-***desu***-*ne*(*e*)' (true-COP(**POL**)-FP) was used in twenty-six responses out of thirty-six in total. The responses with this expression constitute 72.22% of all the responses. This means that this phrase served as one of *semantic formulae* to perform the speech acts of 'agreement' and 'mitigated disagreement' in this context. Also, affirmations including this expression amounted to thirty-three responses out of thirty-six (91.67%), with a negation occurring just twice (5.56%) and a neutral expression occurring only once (2.77%). This implies that acceptance of *h*'s opinion is the key strategy for both 'agreement' and 'mitigated disagreement'.

Concluding the data analysis of Item 05, I would like to mention my further observations. It is interesting that the ranking of JYAF was top in this item, while JYAF in Item 04 was at the bottom. This seems to imply that JYAF informants tend to feel more sympathy and show more consideration towards an old lady than towards a senior male student. The level of **politeness** and **appropriateness** they think required to address an old lady is higher than that required for a male *senpai*.

I see a difference in their recognition between the two vertical distance variables (viz. 'an old lady' and 'a male *senpai*'), both of which are traditionally thought to have a similar power over juniors. On the other hand, this does not seem the case with the other groups. JHAF, which was ranked top in **politeness** with an average score of 1.75 in Item 04, has received 3.13, i.e. 'a little less polite than "neutral"', in Item 05. This suggests that there are various views on a certain social role (in this case the old lady's role): some may regard it as one to be highly respected; others may take it as one that has no power over them and therefore may think great respect is unnecessary.

In addition, I have tested out two speech acts at the same time, but it turned out that 'agreement' was evaluated higher than 'mitigated disagreement' no matter how successfully an informant mitigated his/her counter-opinion. This is genuinely because the former is taken as more considerate than the latter, as the interview with JYAF05 above suggests. In addition, JYAF01 emphasised the importance of accepting an old lady's opinion as follows: 'I will never reject her opinion. I respect it and strengthen it. I will not ask for another opinion. It doesn't matter whether I'm for or against it. In order to show my understanding, it is necessary to say "Yes, he has"'. It seems to be the case that Japanese young women are the kindest to the old women; therefore their responses were the politest and the most appropriate.

5.2.6 Item 06

Constraint: Sympathy – '*Place a high value on o's feelings*'
Speech act(s): Expressing feelings – showing sympathy/concern, giving h good wishes
Activity type: Telephone conversation with a junior female person (kohai in Japanese)
Social variables: vertical distance = yes; horizontal distance = no
Formality: informal
(For more details of the scenario, see Appendix 3.)

In this item, the informants were requested to respond to a younger female person (represented as *kohai* in Japanese) after being told that her brother had been involved in a traffic accident and that she needed to go to the hospital to see him, instead of participating in an activity of which they are supposed to serve as a coordinator. The speech act/acts to be examined here is/are 'expressing feelings' –

'showing sympathy/concern' and 'giving good wishes'[11]. The common aspect these three speech acts share is that one is supposed to *'place a high value on o's feelings'* in performing them. Searle (1979: 15) directly mentioned the speech act of 'condolence' and put it in his EXPRESSIVE category, viz. the illocutionary point of which is 'to express the psychological state specified in the sincerity condition about a state of affairs specified in the propositional content'. This category corresponds to Leech's (1983: 104) CONVIVIAL and 'therefore intrinsically polite' (Leech, *ibid*.: 106). As 'showing sympathy/concern' and 'giving good wishes' have the same nature as 'condoling', I assume that they belong to these same categories.

In this scenario, it is assumed that people generally perform (1) showing sympathy to *h*, by saying something like *'taihen-desu-ne'* <that's serious' or 'you must be upset>, (2) showing concern to *h*, by saying something like *'otooto-wa daijoobu?'* <is your younger brother alright?>, and/or (3) giving *h* good wishes by saying something like *'o-daiji-ni'* <I hope he gets better soon>. These are supposed to function as the *head acts* in this item, being supported by the *supportive moves* that show consideration to *h* or express other various things about the incident and the activity that *h* was expected to join. Thus expressions that can be classified in (1) will be recognised as *head act 1*, the ones in (2) as *head act 2*, and the ones in (3) as *head act 3*.

This scenario has two types of prompts, although they were performed by the same person[12].

<u>The prompt for JHA:</u>

*Sum**imas**en-kedo,*	*otooto-ga*	*kinoo-no-yoru,*
I'm sorry(**POL**)-but	younger brother-NOM1	yesterday-GEN-night

kootsuujiko-ni	*atteshimatte,*	*byooin-ni*
traffic accident-DAT	get involved(PAST)-and	hospital-DAT

*ikasete-**itadaki**-tai-no-**desu**-ga.*
let me go(**HUM**)-DESI-NOM2-COP(**POL**)-but

<I'm very sorry, but I have to go to hospital today, because my younger brother had a traffic accident last night. I hope you will allow me to visit him.>

The prompt for JYA:

Sumimasen-kedo,   *otooto-ga*   *kinoo-no-yoru,*
I'm sorry(**POL**)-but   younger brother-NOM1   yesterday-GEN-night

kootsuujiko-ni   *atteshimatte,*   *byooin-ni*
traffic accident-DAT   get involved(PAST)-and   hospital-DAT

*ika-naku-cha-nara-nai-n'-**desu**-ga.*
necessary to go-NOM2-COP(**POL**)-but

<I'm very sorry, but I have to go to hospital today, because my younger brother had a traffic accident last night. You see, I need to visit him.>

There are no major differences in lexicogrammatical aspects and in the propositional content between the two types, the only difference being '*ikasete-itadaki-tai-no-**desu**-ga*' <I hope you will allow me to visit him> and '*ika-naku-cha-nara-nai-n'-**desu**-ga*' <I need to visit him>. The performer and I made this modification because it is common for Japanese undergraduates to speak more casually in their group activities, whereas it is necessary for *s* when addressing a senior person at a workplace to demonstrate formality and make a request more pleadingly. The former prompt (for JHA) contains an honorific to show humility and also contains a polite request expressing her hope, while the latter (for JYA) contains the rather colloquial expressions '*cha*' (a shortened form of '*tewa*') and '*-n'-*' (a shortened form of '*no*') and is a statement of her necessity to go to the hospital, instead of such a plea[13].

The following table shows the results of the quantitative data analysis of this item.

Table 5.2.6-1 Summary of statistical data: Item 06

	Average scores in politeness		Average scores in appropriateness		Average scores in politeness		Average scores in **appropriateness**
1	JHA (2.06)	1	JHA (1.25)	1	JHAF (1.75)	1	JHAM (1.00)
				2	JHAM (2.38)	2	JHAF (1.50)
2	JYA (3.31)	2	JYA (1.94)	3	JYAM (2.75)	3	JYAF (1.88)
				4	JYAF (3.88)	4	JYAM (2.00)

As can be seen from the above, JHA surpassed JYA in both **politeness** and **appropriateness** (n = 16 each). Furthermore there are statistically significant differences between the two groups (**politeness**: $p<.005$; **appropriateness**: $p<.05$).

According to a more detailed analysis on informant subcategories, JHAF came out on top (Mean = 1.75, n = 8), JHAM second (Mean = 2.38, n = 8), JYAM third (Mean = 2.75, n = 8), and JYAF at the bottom (Mean = 3.88, n = 8) with regard to the level of **politeness**. Significant mean differences among the four groups were confirmed by Kruskal-Wallis test ($p<.05$). Furthermore, there were significant mean differences in pairings JHAF–JYAF ($p<.001$) and JHAM–JYAF ($p<.05$), according to the Dunnet test. With regard to **appropriateness**, JHAM came first (Mean = 1.00, n = 8), followed by JHAF (Mean = 1.50, n = 8), JYAF (Mean = 1.88, n = 8), and JYAM (Mean = 2.00, n = 8) in that order. While Kruskal-Wallis test has confirmed significant mean differences among the four groups on the whole, no significant differences were found between any paired groups.

There are several issues to be addressed within the above results: (1) the reason why there were sharp differences between JHA and JYA in both **politeness** and **appropriateness**; (2) the reason for the high performance of JHAF in **politeness**; (3) the reason for the low performance of JYAF in **politeness**; (4) the reason for the high performance of JHAM in **appropriateness**; and (5) the reason for the low performance of JYAM in **appropriateness**. I would like to start with JHAF responses, which received the highest average score in **politeness** and the second highest in **appropriateness**.

MJ610 – JHAF06

*Maa, sore-wa   taihen-**desu**-ne.*   *Kochira-no-koto-wa*
IJ   it-TOP   awful-COP(**POL**)-FP   this place-GEN-thing-TOP

*kininasara-nakute-kekkoo-**desu**-kara,*
worry(**EXAL**)-NEG-alright-COP(**POL**)-as

*suguni   itte-**sashiagete**-kudasai.*
soon   go-offer(**HUM**)-please(**POL**)

[Oh, that's awful. <*head act1*> You don't need to worry about things here. <*supportive move*> I would like you to visit him immediately. <*supportive move>*]

[showing sympathy] + [telling *h* not to worry] + [urging *h* to go to the hospital immediately]

This response received 1.50 for **politeness** (i.e. just in-between 'very polite' and 'polite') and 1.25 for **appropriateness** (i.e. very close to 'appropriate'). The score for **politeness** was the best (one other equal response) and that for **appropriateness** the second best (two other equal responses). The high level of **politeness** of this response is achieved by the lexicogrammatical strategy. Although this is a response to a *kohai* and it is usually unnecessary to use honorifics to her, this higher age female informant used as many as five honorifics, including one exalted (i.e. respectful) form '*nasaru*'. One humble form '*sashiageru*' <offer humbly> is showing respect to *h*'s younger brother, a referent, assuming *h*'s position in the category of 'we' (i.e. *s* and *h*). I do not expect this person to talk to her female *kohai*-s this way in her casual conversation, but it seems that this informant prioritised the seriousness of this issue and judged that a high level of formality is required.

This informant said in the interview, 'I don't know anything about the traffic accident, but I imagined her situation as if it were mine and thought she really wanted to go immediately because her family member was involved. I prioritised, above all, consideration for her necessity to go to the hospital'. Consideration was well represented by the contents of the remark and the formality of the language, as can be seen from above. HMR (1 – **politeness**, 1 – **appropriateness**) and HFR (2 – **politeness**, 1 – **appropriateness**) both evaluated the quality of language highly. YMR assessed the level of politeness highly (1 – politeness), but thought the part '*sashiagete-kudasai*' a little *overpolite* and put 2 for its **appropriateness**. This seems to be a good example of Japanese women's traditional way of showing a high degree of **politeness** in a formal situation, using a high level of polite/formal expressions.

The following is the other response by JHAF.

MJ601 – JHAF03

*A, soo-**desu**-ka. Sore-wa taihen-**desu**-nee. Ano, saki-ni otooto-**san**-no-hoo-ni itte-agete-**kudasai**. Anata-ga-inai-to komaru-n'-da-keredomo, demo-ne, otooto-**san**-no-hoo-ga taisetsu-dakara soko-no-hoo-ni itte-agete-**kudasai**. Ato-wa kichitto* *renraku-shi-**masu**-kara-ne.*

[I see. You must be upset. *<head act1>* I would like you to visit your brother first. It's awkward that you can't come, but please go there because your brother is more important. I will contact you to let you know about what we have done without fail. *<supportive move>*]

[acceptance of *h*'s explanation] + [showing sympathy] + [requesting *h* to visit *h*'s brother] + [showing regret for *h*'s absence] + [urging *h* to visit *h*'s brother] + [offering support for *h*]

This response was rated as 2.00 in **politeness** (i.e. 'polite') and 1.75 in **appropriateness** (i.e. very close to 'a little inappropriate'). This remark is also full of polite/formal expressions that constitute a feature of a high degree of **absolute politeness**. The propositional content seems fine as can be seen from the translation and the strategy analysis above, but the part '*anata-ga-inai-to komaru-n'-da-keredomo*' <It's awkward that you can't come, but> has drawn rather complicated reactions from the raters. HMR, who put 2 for **politeness** and 2 for **appropriateness**, and YMR, who put 1 for **politeness** and 2 for **appropriateness**, evaluated the quality of language of this response highly, but had similar comments: 'this part causes anxiety in *h*'s mind' and said it is the reason for the lower degree of **relative politeness** in their assessments.

This informant gave a rather perplexing explanation about this response as follows:

As she has(?) a big responsibility as an organiser, it is important for her(?) to fulfil it. But if it is a matter of a person's life, I think she should ask others and go. It also depends on how serious the injury is.

As she said this without specifying who had the 'big responsibility' in Japanese by omitting the subject of the sentence, it is possible that she misunderstood that *h* was the organiser of the activity. If this is the case, it is more understandable why she expressed regret for missing *h* in the activity. Besides that, she is also showing her firm attitude on this kind of issue ('It also depends on how serious the injury is'). Consequently, although it seems that she showed enough consideration and politeness to *h*, her remark implied that she also cared about their activity. JHAF's comparatively low degree of **appropriateness** in spite of its high evaluation in **politeness** put this group in the second position in **appropriateness**.

Next, I would like to turn to JYAF responses, to survey the reasons for their lowest evaluation in **politeness**.

MJ627 – JYAF06

Sokkaa,	*taihen-datta-nee.*		*Sokka,*	*sokka,*	*maa,*
I see	serious-COP(PAST)-FP		I see	I see	IJ

kyoo	*kurabukatsudoo*	*aru-kedoo,*	*maa*	*shooga-nai-karaa,*
today	club activities	be-but	IJ	can't be helped-as

byooin	*itte*	*o-mimai-shite-kite-agena-yo.*
hospital	go and	visit (**POL**)-do-go-offer-FP

[I see. You must have been upset. <*head act1*> I see. We have club activities today, but we understand your situation. <*supportive move*> I suggest you to go to the hospital and visit him. <*supportive move*>]

[acceptance of *h*'s explanation 1] + [showing sympathy] + [acceptance of *h*'s explanation 2] + [understanding *h*'s situation] + [suggestion to visit *h*'s younger brother in hospital]

This response received an average score of 4.25 for **politeness** (i.e. a little lower than 'a little informal / a little lacking in consideration) and 2.50 for **appropriateness** (i.e. just in between 'a little inappropriate' and 'very inappropriate'). The reason for the low evaluation in terms of **absolute politeness** is partly due to the lack of honorifics, which is easily recognised when this response is compared with those produced by JHAF above.

However, lack of honorifics is a common feature in all the JYAF responses, as can be seen in Appendix 22. (There are some exceptions: in some cases they used such expressions as '***kudasai***' (please(**POL**)) or '*o-mimai*' ('visit' with a polite prefix) just as this informant did. There is only one JYAF informant that used '*desu*' in one of her responses, but she used plain forms in the other one.) It appears that the Japanese female undergraduates do not use honorifics to their juniors even in a serious situation like this. It seems that they think a friendly and warm attitude is more important than formality, just like an older sister taking care of a younger, or a mother soothing her daughter. It also seems that Japanese young women feel more familiarity and more closeness towards their juniors of the same gender than the rest of the age–gender groups do, judging from this observation. This hypothesis concerning the unique attitude of JYAF is also supported by the further survey summarised in Table 5.2.6-2 and related descriptions about it.

HMR had the strongest opinion against this response, giving 5 for **politeness** and 3 for **appropriateness**. He especially disliked the parts '*shooga-nai-karaa*' [*lit.* as it can't be helped] and '*o-mimai-shite-kite-agena-yo*' [*lit.* why not go and offer him your visit], and said, 'They are inappropriate expressions. I would be offended if I were told this (the latter phrase)'. The former expression, '*shooga-nai-karaa*' ('as it can't be helped'), makes a sharp contrast with the expressions '*Kochira-no-koto-wa kininasara-nakute-kekkoo-desu*' <you don't need to worry about things here> by JHAF06 and '*otooto-san-no-hoo-ga taisetsu*' <your brother is more important> by JHAF03 above. It was taken to be an inconsiderate phrase by HMR, for '*shooga-nai-kara*' is an expression used for general interruptions such as storms, traffic congestion, or even subtle things like train delays. The latter phrase is also quite different from JHAF06's '*itte-sashiagete-kudasai*' <I would like you to visit him immediately.> and JHAF03's '*itte-agete-kudasai.*' <please(**POL**) go there>. These honorific expressions uttered by the higher age female informants show respect for *h* by '*kudasai*' and for her brother by '*sashiagete*', whereas JYAF06's response did not show any respect for either. While higher age female informants made polite requests by the use of politeness markers, this young female informant gave a direct instruction without such lexical items. I think this is why HMR was upset by this particular phrase.

HFR also had a strong opinion against this remark, putting 4 for **politeness** and 2 for **appropriateness**. She gave a low evaluation to the quality of language of this response, and did not like the part, '*kyoo kurabukatsudoo aru-kedoo*' <we have club activities today, but>, saying 'It's outrageous. This phrase puts pressure on *h*. This person is ignoring the fact that *h* is worrying about her brother'.

YMR pointed out that this response focused more on the club activity than on *h*'s serious situation, putting 4 for **politeness** and 3 for **appropriateness**. He also mentioned that the word '*o-mimai*' was the only clue that this informant was concerned about h's brother's traffic accident.

Still, I would like to maintain that this response sounded like a kind and caring one when I heard it. This informant said in the follow-up interview, 'I will show understanding about what happened to her younger brother and show consideration for it. I tell her kindly that her absence is indispensable'. It is a pity that her intention was probably not represented well in the written form. The assessment might have been different if the raters were able to know about the age and the gender of this informant, to hear how she said this, and to imagine she was talking to her female junior. This was not possible because of the purpose of this research: these things had to be concealed to investigate the generation and gender gaps that were to be judged mainly only by the quality of language itself (i.e. lexicogrammatical and semantic features only) and the information on social variables in the scenarios. Otherwise the raters might have set different criteria for different age and gender groups, and this could have affected their evaluation. Her response was in a sense dominated by the informal atmosphere created by the situational factor that this conversation was supposed to be held in a university community and that she was talking to a female junior. In my judgement, after listening to her response, its **politeness** and **appropriateness** levels are a little higher than those that were given by the raters (3 for **politeness** and 2 for **appropriateness**), for I could hear a caring tone in her voice. This seems to be one thing that should be improved in a future study using an audio device. This example demonstrates what is often claimed – that politeness (**absolute** and **relative**) depends considerably on features of speech such as intonation and tone of voice. It is a 'built in' defect of my research method that such factors cannot be taken account of – but qualitative interpretative comment, such as what I add above, does a lot to mend this defect.

The following is the other response of JYAF, uttered by JYAF01.

MJ620 – JYAF01

Aa,   soo-nan-da.   Jaa,   ano,   zenzen-mondai-nai-kara,
IJ   true-COP(PLAIN)   then   IJ   at all-problem-NEG-as

*n'-to,   byooin-ni   itte-agete-**kudasai**.*
IJ   hospital-DAT   go-offer-please(**POL**)

Jaa,	*minna-ni*	*ittoku-kara,*	*chanto.*
then	everyone-DAT	say in advance-as	for sure

Shinpaishi-nai-de-ne.
worry-NEG-be set-FP

[Oh, I see. Then, please go to the hospital because there's no problem at all. I will tell everybody about this for sure. Don't worry. <*supportive move*>]

[acceptance of *h*'s explanation] + [urging *h* to go to the hospital] + [making *h* feel secure] + [offer of support] + [telling *h* not to worry]

This response was given 3.50 (i.e. just in-between 'neutral' and 'a little informal / a little lack of consideration) for **politeness** and 1.25 for **appropriateness** (i.e. a little lower than 'appropriate'). This informant did not use polite/formal expressions except for '*kudasai*' <please(**POL**)>, and again this led to the low evaluation in **politeness**. Still, it received a comparatively higher evaluation in **appropriateness**.

HFR, who put 4 for **politeness** and 1 for **appropriateness**, explained why she evaluated this response as such: 'the way this informant said this does not sound polite, but the content looks appropriate because she said "*shinpaishi-nai-de-ne*" <don't worry> at the end'. The younger age female rater said in a similar way, 'I don't see any particular polite expressions in this response, but I can see consideration in it', after putting 4 for **politeness** and 1 for **appropriateness**. This informant said, 'As this is a serious issue, I want to tell her not to worry about things here and concentrate on her younger brother'. She appears to have succeeded in expressing her idea in the propositional content of her response, as the score in appropriateness suggests.

One interesting aspect of this response is that it consists only of *supportive moves*, as can be seen from the strategy analysis above: this informant did not perform any of 'showing sympathy', 'showing concern', or 'giving *h* good wishes'. She urged *h* to go to the hospital, made her feel secure, offered support, and told her not to worry. This seems to be a quite reasonable alternative method of dealing with this situation using strategies in **positive direction**.

Next, I would like to explore the reason for the high evaluation in **appropriateness** of the two JHAM responses, both of which received 1 (i.e.

'(optimally) appropriate') and surpassed JHAF in this category.

MJ619 – JHAM06

Aa, hai, aa,	*JHAM06-**desu**.*	*Anoo,*	*moo*	*sochira-no-hoo-ga*
IJ yes IJ	JHAM-COP(**POL**)	IJ	IJ	that issue-NOM1

ichiban-daiji-nanode,	*tonikaku*	*hayaku*
most important-as	anyway	soon

*otooto-**san**-no-tokoro-e*	*itte-agete-**kudasai**.*
younger brother(**POL**)-GEN-place-ACC	go-offer-please(**POL**)

Kochira-no-koto-wa	*kinishi-nai-de.*
this place-GEN-thing-TOP	worry-NEG-be set

Doozo	*itte-agete-**kudasai**.*
by all means	go-offer-please(**POL**)

[Hello, JHAM06 speaking. <u>Your concern is the first priority. I would like you to visit your brother immediately. Don't worry about things here. You can go by all means.</u> <*supportive moves*>]

[greeting] + [understanding *h*'s concern] + [urging *h* to visit her brother] + [telling *h* not to worry] + [repetition and intensification of urging]

MJ612 – JHAM01

Ee,	*sore-wa*	*taihen-da-nee.*	*Daijoobu-na-no?*
IJ	that-TOP	serious-COP-FP	alright-Q

Kyoo-no-koto-wa	*shinpai-shi-nakute-ii-kara*
today-GEN-thing-TOP	worry-do-NEG-alright-as

*otooto-**san**,*	*taihenna-koto-ni*
younger brother(**POL**)	serious-situation-DAT

nara-nakereba-ii-ne.
become-NEG(COND)-good-FP

[Oh, that's serious. <*head act1*> Is he alright? <*head act2*> You don't need to worry about today's activities. <*supportive move*> I hope your brother's condition will not become serious. <*head act3*>]

[showing sympathy] + [showing concern] + [telling *h* not to worry] + [giving a good wish]

There is a difference in the evaluation of the level of **politeness** between these two responses: JHAM06 received 2.00 (i.e. 'polite') and JHAM01 got 2.75 (i.e. a little higher than 'neutral'). This can be explained by the fact that the former showed more formality by using more honorifics than the latter. The JHAM06 also showed enough consideration towards *h* as can be seen from the strategy analysis above, although he did not perform any *head acts* like JYAF01. On the other hand, JHAM01's response is one of very few responses in which all three kinds of *head acts* are included. This seems to be the main reason why it was evaluated highly in **appropriateness**, although the lack of honorifics led to a low evaluation in **politeness**. The following are what these higher age male informants said in the follow-up interview:

JHAM06: Above all, this is a serious family issue and she needs to go as soon as possible. She doesn't need to say 'sorry', as she will be given permission as a matter of course. I urge her to go. Showing consideration for *h* is most important.

JHAM01: As it's a serious concern, I wanted to express my consideration for her and to express my hope that her brother will get well as early as possible.

These two persons took this issue as 'serious' and tried to show 'consideration' towards *h*. Although their linguistic realisations were somewhat different, they achieved a high level of **appropriateness**.

YMR said, commenting on both these two responses, 'I would also say "*itte-*

*agete-**kudasai***" <please go to visit him> – in JHAM06's response – and "*kyoo-no-koto-wa shinpai-shi-nakute-ii-kara*" <you don't need to worry about today's activities> – in JHAM01's response, if I were in this situation'. He put 1 for **politeness** and also 1 for **appropriateness** of JHAM06's response, and 2 for **politeness** and 1 for **appropriateness** of JHAM01's. HFR commented that the propositional content and the quality of language of JHAM06's response were good, putting 2 for **politeness** and 1 for **appropriateness**. YFR, who put 4 for politeness and 1 for appropriateness of JHAM01's response, said that she could see consideration in this remark, pointing out the part '*shinpai-shi-nakute-ii-kara*' as well.

I would finally like to look at JYAM responses to investigate the reason for this group's lower performance in **appropriateness** than the rest. The main reason for this phenomenon was found in the response of JYAM06.

MJ637 – JYAM06

A,	otooto-wa		daijoobu?	Konkai-wa
IJ	younger brother-TOP		alright	this time-TOP

shikata-nai-kara,	*mata*	*tsugi-no-toki-ni*
can't be helped-as	again	next-GEN-time-ACC

*sanka-shite-**kudasai**.*
participation-do-please(**POL**)

[Is your brother alright? <*head act2*> We understand your absence this time. Please join us next time. <*supportive move*>]

[showing concern] + [acceptance of *h*'s request] + [invitation to the next occasion]

The translation and the strategy analysis of this response may not demonstrate any sign of impoliteness or inappropriateness, but it was criticized by all raters, receiving 4.00 for **politeness** (i.e. 'a little informal / a little lack of consideration') and 2.75 for **appropriateness** (i.e. close to 'very inappropriate'). This response also lacks polite expressions except for the last part, but the raters all pointed out its inconsiderate impression besides that linguistic aspect.

HMR, who put 4 for **politeness** and 3 for **appropriateness**, pointed out the low level linguistic features of this response, and maintained that there was 'imbalance' between the phrase '*otooto-wa daijoobu?*' <is your brother alright?> and '*shikata-nai-kara*' <as it can't be helped>. HMR presumably meant that the latter phrase did not match the seriousness of the situation, as I described earlier.

HFR did not like the word '*otooto*' <younger brother>. She insisted that this informant should have said '*otooto-san*' instead to show thoughtfulness. She also pointed out that this informant focused too much on the present activities and did not show consideration towards *h*. She gave 4 for **politeness** and 3 for **appropriateness**. YMR also observed the lack of consideration, saying 'this informant focused on the activity'. He awarded 4 for **politeness** and 3 for **appropriateness**. The younger age female rater pointed out its lack of polite expressions, bluntness, and the necessity to say more to show consideration, putting 4 for **politeness** and 2 for **appropriateness**.

This informant said later in the interview, 'I don't know how serious her brother's injury is, but a traffic accident is a big concern. I can't ignore it and tell her to come. I will tell her when we have the next activity'. His remark was mostly motivated by good intentions, but it seems he did not have the linguistic skill to represent such notions effectively. Besides, he appears to have failed to imagine how sad or worried *h* was (e.g. 'I don't know how serious her brother's injury is …') and to have thought more of the activity (e.g. 'I can't ignore it and tell her to come', 'I will tell her when we have a next activity'), judging from what he said in the interview.

The following is the other JYAM response by JYAM01.

MJ629 – JYAM01

A,	*hontooni.*	*A,*	*kinodoku-na-koto-**desu**.*
IJ	really	IJ	pitiful-thing-COP(**POL**)

Etto,	*nara*	*asu-no-katsudoo-ni-tsuite-wa,*
IJ	then	tomorrow-GEN-activity-about

ano,	*minasan-ni-mo*	*itte-oki-**masu**-node,*
IJ	everyone-ACC-too	say in advance(**POL**)-as

otooto-***san***-no-*hoo*-ni   itte-**kudasai**.
younger brother(**POL**)-GEN-place-ACC   go-please(**POL**)

***O**-daiji*-ni.   *Yoroshiku onegaishi*-**masu**.
take care(**POL**)   please give my best wishes (to him) / I leave this entirely to you

[Oh, really? <*supportive move*> I feel sorry. <*head act1*> About tomorrow's activities, I will talk to everybody. So please visit your brother. <*supportive move*> I hope your brother gets better soon. <*head act3*> Please give my best wishes to him. / I leave this entirely to you. <*head act3 / supportive move*>]

[showing surprise] + [showing sympathy] + [offer of support] + [suggesting *h* to visit her brother] + [giving a good wish] + [giving a good wish / asking *h* for her cooperation in near future (I am unable to identify which is the case)]

The response by JYAM01 was highly evaluated in both **politeness** (1.50 – just in between 'very polite' and 'polite') and **appropriateness** (1.25 – a little lower than 'appropriate'). This result was in a sense a little surprising, for Japanese young male university students usually speak to their female *kohai*-s in a casual way without using honorifics. However, as can be seen from above, this informant used as many as six polite expressions in his remark. This certainly contributed to the high evaluation in politeness. This informant gave a simple explanation regarding the background of this response as follows: 'I can't force her to participate as I feel sorry for her. I understand it is necessary for her to go'.

HMR said that he evaluated highly the quality of language and consideration of this informant represented in such parts as '*kinodoku-na-koto-**desu***' <I feel sorry>, '*o-daiji-ni*' <I hope your brother gets well soon>, and '*yoroshiku onegaishi-**masu***' <Please give my best wishes to him / I leave this entirely to you>, putting 1 for both **politeness** and **appropriateness**. YFR, who put 2 for **politeness** and 1 for **appropriateness**, also regarded the phrases '*kinodoku-na-koto-**desu***' and '*o-daiji-ni*' as representing *s*'s consideration.

However, HFR was puzzled by the last phrase, '*yoroshiku onegaishi-**masu***', and this led to the score 2 for **appropriateness**. I have difficulty interpreting this phrase as well because of its ambiguity, as can be seen from my translation. This phrase is a polite formulaic expression that can be used on various occasions, e.g.

when one greets the other person and asks for support (e.g. Matsumoto, 1988: 409ff.), when someone advertises something for sales promotion to the public, or when a candidate meets an examiner when taking a test. Therefore this informant asked some sort of favour of *h*, but there are several possibilities as to what favour he asked for. I put two main possibilities in my translation: (a) *he asked her to give his best wishes to her brother*; (b) *he asked her to sort this issue out herself*. Another possibility can be (c) *he asked for her participation and cooperation on the next occasion*. It is also difficult to judge which possibility HMR took, but he certainly took this phrase as a polite expression. Again it is a phrase to ask *h*'s favour and is a form that represents the **positive direction**, so it is intrinsically polite. This is a case where judgement was divided due to the ambiguity of an expression.

In conclusion, I would like to describe other findings after surveying all the data collected at the first stage data collection. I first investigated group differences in the quality of language by looking at the presence/absence of polite forms (*teineigo*) '*desu*', '*masu*', and '*kudasai*', which serve as 'lexicogrammatical politeness markers'. The summary of the results is as follows:

Table 5.2.6-2 The number of responses with 'lexicogrammatical politeness markers'

	JHAF	JHAM	JYAF	JYAM
Num of res. with politeness markers	11	6	2	3
Num of total res.	11	8	9	10
Percentage	100%	75%	22%	30%

The order of the groups in this survey corresponds to that in the statistical analysis on the level of **politeness**. This suggests that the use of 'politeness markers' has a strong correlation with the level of perceived politeness, viz. in terms of **absolute politeness**. The above result also demonstrates the tendency of each group when talking to their female *kohai*-s in a serious situation. It is worth noting that the higher age and the younger age female groups have different approaches, as pointed out earlier, although they belong to the same gender. The difference in the percentages between these two groups is the sharpest among all. It almost seems as if JYAF were distancing themselves as far as possible from the behaviour of their mothers, in using minimal rather than maximal **politeness**. As I described earlier, JYAF informants have their unique attitude towards juniors of the same gender.

They have shown most familiarity and closeness to the female *kohai*-s.

As for strategies other than the *head acts* defined earlier in this section, I found mainly two other strategies to show *s*'s consideration towards *h*. The first one is [telling *h* not to worry], viz. '*kochira-no-koto-wa kinishi-nai-de*' <please don't worry about things here> and its equivalents. This phrase is supposed to make *h* feel secure about giving up her responsibility in the activity. *H*'s anxiety is two-fold: one aspect is about her younger brother's situation, and the other part is about disrupting the activity. So this strategy attends to the latter part of *h*'s anxiety. The second one is [urging *h* to go to the hospital], viz. '*byooin-ni itte-agete-**kudasai***' <please go to the hospital> and its equivalents. This phrase functions as a total compliance with *h*'s request to let her go or as providing for the total fulfilment of *h*'s needs. Some informants used an intensifier '*suguni*' <immediately> to emphasise such acceptance. As there were various aspects that informants thought about (e.g. the traffic accident, the activities, *h*'s need to go to the hospital), they performed various alternative strategies to show consideration as mentioned earlier. I would maintain that some informants succeeded in achieving high degrees of **absolute** and **relative politeness** even without *head acts* in this particular scenario – this result raises the question about the usefulness of the distinction between *head acts* and *supporting moves*. Particularly in this case, where the prompt involves three different speech acts that to some extent demand different polite responses: (a) the *kohai* apologises for her likely absence, (b) explains the reason: her brother's injury, and (c) asks permission. The variety in the speech act performance strategies can indeed be attributed to such multi-dimensional aspect of the scenario. This implies that different factors in an utterance can be focused on by *h* and can elicit a variety of responses to attend to such different factors. This had been an unpredictable issue, as the prompt was designed to show the young female *kohai*-s shocking and sad situation which should be responded to with the informants' 'sympathy' in a general sense.

5.2.7 Item 07
Constraint: Obligation (of o to s) – '*Place a low value on o's obligation to s*'
Speech act(s): Response to thanks and apologies
Activity type: Conversation with a male junior (kohai in Japanese)
Social variables: vertical distance = yes; horizontal distance = no
Formality: informal

(For more details of the scenario, see Appendix 3.)

In this item the informants are requested to respond to an apology from a male junior, represented as *kohai* in Japanese. In the scenario of this item, this male *kohai* had been asked by the informant to make a reservation at an Italian restaurant for another person's birthday party. It turned out, however, that he had somehow made a mistake and reserved for the wrong date. He consequently apologised for his mistake and the informants were supposed to respond to his apology.

The prompt by h is twofold: (a) h reports the fault, and (b) h apologises. In terms of politeness, s's response is similarly twofold. A natural response to (a) is to blame or criticise h for making the mistake and causing problems. But the **negative direction** on the part of s may lead to a mitigation of this criticism. A frequent response to (b), on the other hand, is to accept the apology (this acceptance is a polite act) – viz. to maintain the position that s does not harbour a (serious) grudge against h – that h is (more or less) forgiven. These aspects of a response may be closely combined, and difficult to distinguish. Both of them are considered to belong to **negative direction** strategies – they both aim at the reduction or removal of an *FTA* (that of (a) blaming or criticising; and that of (b) refusing to exonerate or excuse or forgive – viz. harbouring a grudge.)

This speech act is assumed to be in Searle's EXPRESSIVE category (Searle 1979: 15), because of its second aspect 'showing generosity to pardon h's fault'. In this sense this part can be included in Leech's CONVIVIAL (Leech, 1983: 104). However, the first part 'suppression of s's feeling' is thought to be one strategy of a speech act performance, viz. mitigation of an offensive illocutionary force, rather than a speech act itself. Surely this means that it is a **negative direction** strategy – avoiding impoliteness rather than seeking/maintaining politeness. Both aspects of this speech act are EXPRESSIVE in Searle's sense. However, in terms of Leech's *GSP*, the first half is COMPETITIVE rather than CONVIVIAL: it is a case where the illocutionary goal (of blaming or criticising h) competes with (or is at odds with) the social goal of maintaining good rapport.

B&L (1987) also include this speech act in their politeness framework as one that 'offends s's negative face' (B&L, *ibid.*: 67). In their definition, 's may feel constrained to minimize h's debt or transgression, as in "It was nothing, don't mention it"', when performing either 'acceptance of h's thanks' or 'acceptance of h's apology' (*ibid.*). I do not support their position of treating this speech act as an

FTA (for *s*) that needs mitigation with any of their 'superstrategies' (i.e. 'bald-on-record', 'negative politeness', 'positive politeness', 'off-record' or 'do not perform an *FTA*') in their terms. However, what B&L mentioned is worth noting here because it explains the kind of 'constraint' on *s*'s linguistic attitude that affects his/her politeness strategies.

The *head acts* of this speech act are thought to be expressions that remove or reduce blame for *h*'s fault, such as '*Daijoobu-desu-yo*' <That will be alright>, '*machigai-wa dare-ni-demo aru-kara*' <as everyone makes a mistake>, '*kinishi-nakutte-ii-yo*' <You don't need to worry>, '*ii-yo ii-yo*' <That's okay>, or '*shooga-nai-yo*' <It couldn't be helped>, and their equivalents. These phrases are thought to contain two acts for politeness mentioned above, viz. an *FSA*. On one side these expressions head towards what relates to *h* in nature, but they are also showing *s*'s reservation on the other side in this particular context. As the informants are requested to act as an organiser of the birthday party, this kind of mistake is quite likely to cause damage to their plan, their credibility, their friendship etc. Therefore saying these expressions represents their reservation.

This scenario has two different video prompts, performed by two different persons. This is because the general image of a male *kohai* is different between JHA and JYA. For JHA he must look like a younger male person at a workplace. But JYA will imagine a younger male undergraduate student when they hear the word 'male *kohai*'. The following are the two types of prompts for this scenario, in which the performers apologise for their faults.

The prompt for JHA:

Suimasen,	*tondemonai*	*machigai-o*
I'm sorry(**POL**)	terrible	mistake-ACC

*shite-shimatta-n'-**desu**-keredomo.*	*Tabun*	*raishuu-no-paatyi*-to
done-have-NOM2-COP(**POL**)-but	perhaps	next week-GEN-party-COMP

machigaete	*yoyaku-o*	*irete-shimatta-n'-**desu**.*	*Suimasen.*
mistake and	reservation-ACC	made-have-NOM2-COP(**POL**)	I'm sorry(**POL**)

<I'm sorry. I made a terrible mistake. Perhaps I have mixed it up with another party next week and made a wrong reservation. I'm sorry.>

The prompt for JYA:

Senpai,	*sui**masen.***	*Taihen*	*mooshiwake-nai-n'-**desu**-kedomo,*
ADD	I'm sorry(**POL**)	very	excuse-NEG-NOM2-COP(**POL**)-but

anoo,	raishuu-no-paatyii-to	machigaete-shimai-***mashita***.
IJ	next week-GEN-party-COMP	mistaken-have(**POL**)

*Mooshiwake-**gozaimasen**.*
I have no excuse(**SUPERPOL**)

<*Senpai*, I'm sorry. There's no excuse at all, but I mixed it up with another party next week. I'm awfully sorry.>

These two apologies sound natural and might be commonly uttered by Japanese male *kohai*-s. One difference between them is that the higher age performer's apology was more descriptive of what the cause of the mistake was and the younger age performer's was simpler but more apologetic. The younger age performer omitted the hedge '*tabun*' ('perhaps') and used a super-polite form of an apologetic expression '*moushiwake-**gozaimasen***' [*lit.* no excuse] at the end. This kind of simple and 'no-excuse' apology, viz. without any long explanation or any attempt to defend one's action, has been regarded as 'manly' in Japanese society. This traditional style is especially preferred in athletic clubs where there are stronger attitudinal codes concerning how *kohai*-s are expected to behave in front of *senpai*-s. In the past, and even now, a male *kohai* would receive an accusation 'Don't make excuses' from a male *senpai*, if he tried to give a long explanation and to defend himself. This has also been the case with a teacher (or a father) and a male student (or a son)[14]. This style seems to be part of a social code to realise the **negative direction**, viz. '*Place a low value on what relates to s*', and this social trend can be recognised as part of the ethos of Japan. This performer told me in a private conversation that he had belonged to the tennis club at junior and senior high schools and at university. So he had grown up with this Japanese athletic club tradition and it was quite natural for him to make an apology in this style. Although these remarks were not evaluated by the raters, I would imagine the latter prompt would receive a higher evaluation in **politeness** because of its quality of language and for displaying such a traditional attitude.

A summary of the data analysis results is shown in Table 5.2.7 below.

Table 5.2.7 Summary of statistical data: Item 07

	Average scores in politeness		Average scores in appropriateness		Average scores in politeness		Average scores in appropriateness
1	JHA (2.69)	1	JHA (1.38)	1	JHAM (2.63)	1	JHAF (1.00)
				2	JHAF (2.75)	2	JYAM (1.38)
2	JYA (3.06)	2	JYA (1.63)	3	JYAM (3.00)	3	JHAM (1.75)
				4	JYAF (3.13)	4	JYAF (1.88)

In the major classification (i.e. age groups) JHA (Mean = 2.69 in **politeness**, 1.38 in **appropriateness**, n = 16) bettered JYA (Mean = 3.06 in **politeness**, 1.63 in **appropriateness**, n = 16) in both categories, but there were no statistically significant differences between them in either category, according to the results obtained by the *SPSS* analysis. This means that the two groups performed their reactions to the apologies in a similar way.

In the minor classification (i.e. age and gender groups), JHAM came on top (Mean = 2.63, n = 8), followed by JHAF (Mean = 2.75, n = 8), JYAM (Mean = 3.00, n = 8), and JYAF (Mean = 3.13, n = 8) in **politeness**. Interestingly there were no statistically significant differences among these groups. Again, this means that all the groups responded in a similar way in this category.

As for **appropriateness**, JHAF's performance was outstanding and came first (Mean = 1.00, n = 8). JYAM came second (Mean = 1.38, n = 8), JHAM third (Mean = 1.75, n = 8), and JYAF came at the bottom (Mean = 1.88, n = 8). Significant mean differences were observed among the four groups ($p<.05$) through the Kruskal-Wallis test. The Dunnet test has found significant mean differences between JHAF–JHAM ($p<.05$), and JHAF–JYAF ($p<.05$). It is suspected that JHAM committed *overpoliteness* in this item, considering the fact that this group was first in the **politeness** category.

Consequently, the things that seem worth exploring here are: (1) JHAM's highest ranking in **politeness** and the reason for its lower ranking in **appropriateness**; (2) JHAF's highest performance in **appropriateness**; and (3) JYAF's lowest ranking in both categories.

I would like to begin with the qualitative analysis of JHAM data.

MJ713 – JHAM02

Soo-ka,	shooga-nai-naa.	Moo,	tonikakuu,
true-FP	can't be helped-FP	IJ	anyway

ato-no-koto	junchooni	susumeru-tame-ni,
other/later-GEN-thing	smoothly	let ... go forward-in order to

ima	subeki-koto,	sumiyakani	yaru-shika-nai-ne.
now	should do-thing	swiftly	do-only-FP

Wakari-**mashita**
I understand(PAST-**POL**)

[I see. It's embarrassing. Anyway we just need to do what we have to do immediately to let things go forward. I understand. <*supportive move*>]

[reply to the explanation] + [showing embarrassment] + [suggestion for problem solution] + [showing understanding of the situation]

This response received an average score of 2.75 for **politeness** (i.e. a little higher than 'neutral') and 1.75 for **appropriateness** (i.e. a little higher than 'a little inappropriate'). This means that it is a rather 'normal' response and was unlikely to help explain the high evaluation of the group's degree of **politeness**. As can be seen above there is no *head act* included in this remark. In terms of the quality of the language, this remark includes one polite expression '*wakari-mashita*' <I understand>, and this part seems to have contributed to its slightly higher evaluation than 'neutral' in **politeness**.

The expression '*shooga-nai-naa*' looks similar to the head act, '*shooga-nai-yo*', but it is not affording comfort to *h*, but showing *s*'s embarrassment. The phrase '*shooga-nai*' can be literally translated as 'there's no way to solve it'. The two phrases with different final particles are both formulaic and common expressions but are used in somewhat different ways. The difference in their meanings lies in the final particles '*naa*' and '*yo*'. The former represents *s*'s own emotion, i.e. surprise, anger, joy etc. (*Kooji-en* fifth ed.) so this informant meant to say 'There's no way to go back and prevent this from happening, indeed!' to express his surprise and embarrassment.

On the other hand, the latter is used to address to *h* to 'indicate a strong conviction' (Kamiya, 1997). Therefore the speaker of this phrase means to say 'There **was** no way for you to prevent this from happening, was there?' to express his/her understanding of the unavoidable aspect of what happened, affording comfort to *h* as a result – i.e. taking away the culpability.

This informant said in the interview, 'As everyone makes a mistake, I will guide him in the right direction first, instead of accusing him. I will tell him to be careful later. We'd better not hurt a person when s/he apparently feels his/her responsibility'. Although the good intention behind the actual remark can be observed in this statement, he seems to have prioritised 'guiding *h* in the right direction' and framed his utterance accordingly. This led to YFR's judgement, 'This response sounds blunt. It also sounds cold because this person is saying this as if to deal with a business issue'. This rater awarded 3 for **politeness** and 2 for **appropriateness**.

The following is the other response by JHAM, which received 2.50 for **politeness** (i.e. just in-between 'polite' and 'neutral') and 1.75 for **appropriateness** (i.e. close to 'a little inappropriate').

MJ715 – JHAM03

A, soo-**desu**-ka, jaa, chotto komari-**mashita**-ne. Ma, ima-kara demo, nantoka-nareba-ii-n'-**desu**-kedomo. Ma, yatte-mi-**mashoo**, nantoka. Ma, kongo-wa chanto memoshite-oite-**kudasai**-ne. Ma, kyoo-wa shikata-nai-kara nantoka kore-de, yatte-mi-**mashoo**. Hai, **go**-kuroo-**san**.

[Oh, really. Then I think it's a problem. I hope we can sort this out even from now. Let's try, anyway. Please make sure you take notes for your schedule from now on. Let's try things this way today because it just happened this time. All right, I appreciate your effort. <*supportive move*>]

[reply to the explanation] + [showing worry1] + [showing worry2] + [suggestion for problem solution] + [suggestion for precaution in future] + [acceptance of the situation and stating *s*'s will to sort the problem out] + [appreciating *h*'s effort]

As can be seen from above, this remark is full of polite/formal forms, using a style called '*desu-masu kuchoo*' <*desu-masu* tone>. Still, this feature did not motivate the raters to put higher scores in **politeness**, for this response seems motivated mainly by a negative evaluation of what *h* did. As can be seen from the strategy analysis above, this remark is full of worries and suggestions for improvement. *S*'s 'appreciation' of *h*'s effort for the arrangements (in vain) is shown at the end, but this sounds rather as an additive phrase like a 'story-ending marker'.

While HMR gave 1 to the degree of **politeness** of this response, all the others put 3 for it. This means that the other three raters adjusted the balance between the lexicogrammatical aspect and the propositional content. HMR, while acknowledging its high level lexicogrammatical features, put 2 for **appropriateness** saying, 'My evaluation for the level of appropriateness of this response is lower because of its lack of consideration towards *h*. I was especially concerned with the phrase '*shikata-nai-kara*', for I would feel a little sad to hear this if I had been in *h*'s position and had apologised for my mistake'. '*Shikata-nai*', another linguistic form to mean the same as '*shooga-nai*' discussed above, expresses *s*'s embarrassment or regret, 'There's no way to go back and prevent this from happening'. People may well get a cold impression from this phrase that can directly lead to a negative evaluation of what was done.

YMR, who put 3 for **politeness** and 2 for **appropriateness**, pointed out that the part '*nantoka-nareba-ii-n'-**desu**-kedomo*' [*lit*. I hope we can sort this out, but] could give *h* a shock because it implied *s*'s worries. YFR said she took the utterances '*kongo-wa chanto memoshite-oite-**kudasai**-ne*' <please make sure you take notes for your schedule from now on> and '*kyoo-wa shikata-nai-kara*' (translation discussed above, but this phrase includes the expression 'today') as rather inappropriate expressions, giving 3 for **politeness** and 2 for **appropriateness**.

This informant said, 'I won't blame him for the mistake he made in the past, but it's not good that he didn't take notes to make sure. I said this to teach him how to manage things, thinking of his future'. This means he prioritised education of the *kohai* and gave him an instruction to prevent it from happening again in future. This intention, represented by the propositional content, was not evaluated highly by the raters, but the evaluations of his remark could be changed in the long run (especially that of **appropriateness**), I maintain, after looking at its long-term perlocutionary effect.

As can be seen from the discussion of JHAM responses above, there are some problems preventing them from receiving higher evaluations in both categories.

Still, this group came first in the **politeness** category seemingly because of their more formal impression than others. The lower evaluation in **appropriateness** turned out to be due to the lack of consideration, rather than what I had initially expected them to be (i.e. *overpoliteness*).

Now I would like to turn to JHAF responses to investigate the reason why this group was ranked first on the **appropriateness** scale.

MJ701 – JHAF01

Aa,	*komatta-wa-nee.*		*Demo*	*chotto*
IJ	be in trouble(PAST)-FP-FP		but	a bit

o-mise-no-hito-ni   *tanonde-mi-**mashō**.*
restaurant(**POL**)-GEN-person-DAT   ask-and see(**POL**)

Nantoka-naru-to   *omou-n'-**desu**-kedo.*
in some way-go well-COMP   think-NOM2-COP(**POL**)-but

[Ah, it's a problem. But let's ask the restaurant manager. <*Supportive move*> I think this will be sorted out in some way. <*Head act*>]

[showing worries] + [suggestion of a solution] + [presenting good prospect]

This response received an average score of 3.00 for **politeness** (i.e. 'neutral') and 1.00 for **appropriateness** (i.e. '(optimally) appropriate'). The linguistic features demonstrate that this response is a mixture of polite forms (*desu*, *masu*, and *o-*) and colloquial particles (-*wa* and -*nee*). This must have made it difficult to judge whether this response was polite or not. Therefore an average score of 3.00 represents these two features well, with one rater (YMR) putting 2, another (YFR) 4 and the other two (HFR and HMR) 3 for the **politeness** of this remark.

Still this remark was evaluated as (optimally) appropriate for its propositional content in contrast with JHAM responses. This informant explained the background of her response as this: 'Everyone makes a mistake. I do, too. I think we can always correct it. As it is simply a party and we are close to each other, we can go to another place if the restaurant can't accommodate us. If we can find a solution by asking a restaurant worker, we'd better do so'. Her generous attitude about this kind of mistake can be observed from what she said in the interview, and it seems that she was successful in realising her notion in a linguistic form. HFR and YFR said they both liked the part '*Nantoka-naru-to omou-n'-**desu**-kedo*' <I think this will be sorted out in some way> and it was the main reason for the high evaluation in **appropriateness**. Giving an optimistic prospect can comfort and encourage *h*, for it erases the negative quality of what *h* did in the past. This is what JHAM informants did not include in their remarks, as can be seen from the discussion above.

MJ702 – JHAF02

Aa,	*wakari-**mashita**.*	*Uun,*	*jaa,*	*o-mise-no-hito-ni*
IJ	I see(**POL**)	IJ	then	restaurant(**POL**)-GEN-person-DAT

chotto	*kiite-mi-**mashoo**-ka.*	*Daijoobu-**desu**-yo.*
a bit	ask and-see(**POL**)-FP	alright-COP(**POL**)-FP

*Kiite-mi-**masho**.*
ask and-see(**POL**)

[Oh, I see. Then why don't we ask the restaurant manager? <*supportive move*> That will be alright. <*head act*> Let's ask. <*supportive move*>]

[reply to the explanation] + [suggestion of solution] + [presenting good prospect] + [suggestion to work together for solution]

The average score of this response in **politeness** was 2.50 (i.e. just in-between 'polite' and 'neutral') and that in **appropriateness** was 1.00 (i.e. '(optimally) appropriate'). As for the assessments of the level of **politeness**, the raters put completely different scores to this response (HMR – 3, HFR – 2, YMR – 1, YFR – 4). It is therefore likely that there was confusion in the raters' judgements of the degree of **absolute politeness** of this response. This is interesting because they all agree that this response is quite 'appropriate' (i.e. 'ideal' with regard to **relative politeness**) in this context. YMR said he had correlated the two categories, viz. he thought mostly of the propositional content, rather than the linguistic features. On the other hand YFR regarded this response as 'very informal / impolite', although this remark includes five polite expressions. She said, 'I didn't see any particular polite expressions', as a general impression of the responses in this item – I asked her the reason why she had not given 1 or 2 to any responses for **politeness**. This means that it is quite likely that she ignored, or did not notice, the 'salience' of such polite expressions embedded in the structures of the utterances. This appears to be a general tendency of this rater and it explains why her assessments in **politeness** are significantly higher (i.e. lower degree of **politeness**) than those of other raters'. To her, it is suspected, polite forms do not mean much as long as they are embedded in utterances that sound natural and formulaic – formulaic expressions can affect people's recognition of the scale of **politeness**. It is possible, therefore, that one recognises an utterance with honorifics as a 'non-salient' one especially if it is or contains a commonly used formulaic expression. On the other hand, HFR evaluated highly the quality of language of this response. This suggests that she had focused on polite expressions out of the structures and judged the level of **politeness** accordingly. From this I assume that the HFR took an 'analytical' approach, while YFR employed a 'holistic' approach in the assessments of the scale of **politeness**. I would also like to mention that HFR also pointed out two phrases, '*chotto kiite-mi-mashoo-ka*' <why don't we ask?> and '*Daijoobu-desu-yo. Kiite-mi-masho*' <That will be alright. Let's ask> as semantic features showing a high level of **politeness** and **appropriateness**.

This informant said in the follow-up interview, 'It's not a big public issue. It's not a mistake at an important business meeting, either. I don't care at all about such a small mistake. I make this kind of mistake, too. I will never accuse him, but I want to think of a solution together'. Her good intention described here was represented in her remark and it led to its very high evaluation in **appropriateness**.

Next, I would like to look at JYAF responses to explore the reason for their low evaluations in both **politeness** and **appropriateness**.

<u>MJ721 – JYAF03</u>
 E, ano, raishuu-no-paatyii-to-machigaeta-tte-no-wa
 IJ IJ next week-GEN-party-COMP-mistake(PAST)-say-NOM2-TOP

 *dooiu-koto-**deshoo**.*   *Genjoo-wa*   *doo-natte-iru-no-ka*
 what-thing-COP(**POL**) present situation-TOP how-getting-be-NOM2-Q

*oshiete-morae-**masu**-ka.*
teach-receive(**POL**)-Q

[What do you mean you mistook it for another party next week? Can you tell me the present set-up? <*supportive move*>]

[asking what *h* meant by his explanation] + [asking for more information on the present situation]

MJ723 – JYAF04

E,	*e,*	*do-yu-koto do-yu-koto?*	*E,*	*aa,*	*jaa*	*juunin-de*
IJ	IJ	what do you mean	IJ	IJ	then	ten people-with

yacchatta-tte-koto?	*Aan,*	*maa,*	*un un,*	*hai,*	*wakatta,*
have done-say-COMP	IJ	IJ	yeah	yes	I see(PAST)

e,	*de,*	*mise-no-hoo-wa*	*haire-soo-na-no*
IJ	then	restaurant-GEN-position-TOP	can enter-seem-Q

juugonin-demo?	*Un.*	*E,*	*ja*	*chotto*	*kiite-koyoo-yo*	*iko iko.*
fifteen people-even	Yeah	IJ	then	a bit	ask -go and-FP	let's go

[What do you mean? Oh, then you made a reservation for ten? Uh, okay, I see. Then do you think the restaurant can accommodate even fifteen? Then let's go and ask. Let's go. <*supportive move*>]

[asking for confirmation] + [confirming the present situation] + [showing understanding] + [asking if the problem can be solved] + [suggestion to ask the restaurant] + [urging *h* to go together to ask]

The first response was rated as 2.50 for **politeness** (i.e. just in-between 'polite' and 'neutral') and 2.25 for **appropriateness** (i.e. a little lower than 'a little inappropriate'). The second one received an average score of 3.75 for **politeness** (i.e. close to 'very informal / impolite') and 1.50 for **appropriateness** (i.e. just in-between 'appropriate' and 'a little inappropriate'). These figures suggest that JYAF03's response was rather polite but comparatively inappropriate, while JYAF04's was very informal but relatively appropriate. This implies that the low ranking of this group in **politeness** was caused by JYAF04 and that in **appropriateness** was caused by JYAF03.

JYAF03's response contains two polite forms and one formal word '*genjoo*' (present set-up). She explained the background of her remark as this: 'As I don't know what another party next week is, I want to know how it relates to today's party. I don't understand the situation and it irritates me. The younger student also exasperates me'. She certainly expressed her irritated and exasperated emotion in an honest but a polite and indirect way. In this sense the average scores this response received are quite reasonable. YMR said that this response was polite in terms of the quality of language but was lacking consideration. He added, 'I won't say this myself'. HMR said in a similar way that it had a formal and polite impression in its linguistic features but did not demonstrate consideration towards *h*'s apology. He pointed out two phrases '*dooiu-koto-**deshoo***' <What do you mean?> and '*Genjoo-wa doo-natte-iru-no-ka oshiete-morae-**masu**-ka*' <Can you tell me the present condition?> as such formal expressions. YFR also maintained that it had sounded blunt and cold.

The response of JYAF04 is without any polite or formal forms. On the contrary it is full of very informal expressions such as interjections and colloquial expressions. HFR talked about this response as follows: 'As for politeness, this response sounds too informal. But she did not blame *h* and suggested what they should do to solve the problem. As *h* is in a hard situation, this suggestion can serve as a comfort'. This informant said in the follow-up interview, 'I was affected by the video. It's not such a big mistake. The power relationship is not so tight in the club I belong to. He needn't be worried that much. I want to say it's more important to do the next thing than to say "sorry" or an excuse'. As can be seen from this, her intention was quite different from JYAF03's. This means that an intention for *rapport enhancement/maintenance*, if represented well in a linguistic form, can contribute to a higher evaluation in **appropriateness**, regardless of the degree of **absolute politeness**.

Finally I would like to look at the rest of the data to find out other noteworthy features or tendencies of the responses in this item. Firstly I discovered that there were some informants who did not demonstrate their generosity or offer forgiveness to *h* like JYAF03. I present below the translations of their responses and what they said in the follow-up interviews (For the original Japanese, see Appendix 24).

MJ704	JHAF03	1/2	Oh, really. This is a problem. Although we make a mistake, you need to change the number to fifteen. I ask you.
MJ705		2/2	This is a problem. It's you that made a wrong reservation and it's a problem. Please change the number to fifteen.
	It's the man that made the wrong reservation. So, he is responsible for this.		
MJ708	JHAF05	1/2	Oh, I understand what you mean. But you should be careful next time. This is an important thing.
MJ709		2/2	Yeah, I understand what you mean, but you need to be careful next time to handle such an important thing. I ask you.
	I want him to feel his responsibility for his mistake in an appointment. I asked him to be careful from now on, as it couldn't be helped this time.		
MJ722	JYAF03	2/2	What do you mean by mistaking it for another party next week? I want to understand what's going on now. What's the problem?
	As I don't know what another party next week is, I want to know how it relates to today's party. I don't understand the situation and it irritates me. The younger student also exasperates me.		
MJ730	JYAM02	2/2	Anyway book another restaurant before apologising. Don't you have any alternative?
	In the first response, I prioritised the issue of today's party, taking the fact as it is. (This is the case when I am cool-headed.) In the second one, I told him to try an alternative instead of apologising. (This is the case when I'm feeling impatient.) It doesn't matter who the young student is (close or distant).		
MJ732	JYAM03	2/2	Oh, I see. But don't do this next time. This kind of thing will cause trouble for others.
	In the first response I meant 'I think it's alright'. (When the younger student is not very close.) But if he is a close to me, I will say what I really think.		

These informants, including JYAF03, performed a speech act of '(mitigated) accusation' in all or one of their responses. They chose not to conceal their true unpleasant feelings towards *h* and made responses accordingly. This fact implies that people do not always show generosity and forgive *h*'s fault when they think the fault is too serious to be pardoned easily.

Another interesting thing about this phenomenon is that there are age and gender differences: (1) JHAF and JYAF informants who performed the speech act of accusation did so in both of their two responding opportunities; (2) no JHAM informant performed the speech act of accusation, although JHAM03 suggested a future precaution; (3) the two JYAM informants mentioned above accused *h* in their second responses as their alternative strategies. These observations suggest that JHAM group was the most generous about the male *kohai*'s blunder. They may have made similar mistakes in the past when they were at about *h*'s age and therefore they may be able to understand how *h* was feeling. They may also feel that middle-aged men are supposed to show generosity as a 'manly' attitude. This age and gender characteristic of JHAM seems to correspond to what JYAF demonstrated when talking to a female *kohai* in the previous item. It appears that there are some specific tendencies unique to specific age and gender groups – male solidarity versus female solidarity.

However, the JHAM attitude is also interesting because two British middle-aged male informants showed completely the opposite behaviour in my pilot study (Suzuki, 2004). In a similar scenario where these informants had been requested to respond to a younger male worker's apology, they chose to accuse *h* with rather strong expressions, e.g. '*Look I'm really fed up about this. I did tell you it was 15. This means that 5 of us don't have places and will have to eat somewhere else. This is a mess*' (B704 – BHM01), '*Oh you bloody idiot! This really has messed things up. We are going to have to split up*' (B705 – BHM01). This fact may suggest that there is also a cross-cultural difference in middle-aged men's recognition on how to treat their male juniors.

I would also like to describe what kinds of expressions were used as *head acts* by other informants. The following are the list of such phrases that show sympathy and give comfort to *h*.

MJ710   *Machigai-wa dare-ni-demo aru-kara daijoobu-yo.* <It's alright. Everyone makes a mistake.>

MJ711   *Dare-demo machigai-wa aru-kara kinishi-nakute-ii-yo.*
<Don't worry. Everyone makes a mistake.>

MJ712   *Sonna kinisuru-koto nai-yo.* <Don't worry that much.>

MJ716   *Nantoka naru-to omoi-**masu**.* <I think we can sort this out.>

MJ719   *Zenzen.* <No problem.> / *Tabun doonika-naru-yo.* <We will probably sort out this problem.>

MJ724   *Daijoobu-desho.* <It should be alright.> / *Heiki-da-yo.* <I don't think it's a problem.>

MJ727   *Fueru-bun-ni-wa daijoobu-deshoo.* <I think it's alright as long as we increase the number.> /
Sonna kinishi-nakutte-ii-yo.* <You don't need to worry that much.>

MJ729   *Ii-yo ii-yo.* <That's okay.> / *Moo owacchatta-koto-dakara.* <It's a thing in the past now.>

MJ731   *Ii-yo ii-yo.* <That's okay.> /
Nantoka naru-n'-ja-nai? <I think we will somehow sort this out.> /
Daijoobu. <Don't worry.> / *Kinishi-nai-de.* <Never mind.>

MJ736   *Shooga-nai-yo.* <I understand what you mean.> /
Dare-demo misu aru-shi. <Everyone makes a mistake.>

MJ737   *Shikata-nai-yo.* <I understand what you mean.>

From the above, it is safe to say that there are no stereotypical *semantic formulae* in this item. Showing consideration in 'suppressing *s*'s strong feeling' and 'forgiving *h*'s fault' takes various forms. In this sense individual/volitional strategies are important to show consideration in a situation like this, in addition to the individual/volitional choice of the speech act to be performed.

As for the *constraint* of OBLIGATION, this scenario could not elicit such expression as to express '*place a low value on o̱'s obligation to s̱*'. This is because the scenario emphasised more the performer's apology for his error in the whole plan – rather than his apology to the informant in person. Still, if the phrase 'to s̱' in the constraint rubric is omitted (i.e. '*place a low value on o̱'s obligation*'), those *head acts* above can be included in the strategies to satisfy it.

5.2.8 Item 08

Constraint: Obligation (of s to o) – '*Place a high value on s̲'s obligation to o̲*'
Speech act(s): Apology, thanks
Activity type: Conversation with a female restaurant manager
Social variables: vertical distance = yes; horizontal distance = yes
Formality: formal
(For more details of the scenario, see Appendix 3.)

In this final item, the informants were requested to respond to an offer of special arrangements to accommodate the informant's group from a female restaurant manager. This is a continuation of the scenario from the previous item (Item 07), in which the informant's male *kohai* apologised for making a wrong reservation at the same restaurant. The informants were expected to perform both or either of two speech acts: (1) an apology for the mistake made by his/her *kohai*; (2) thanking for an offer from the female restaurant manager.

Searle directly mentions these two speech acts (i.e. 'thank' and 'apologize') and categorises them within his EXPRESSIVE category, which is defined as this: '[t]he illocutionary point of this class is to express the psychological state specified in the sincerity condition about a state of affairs specified in the propositional content' (Searle, 1979: 15). Leech recognises the speech acts in this category mainly as those in his CONVIVIAL category, whose 'illocutionary goal coincides with the social goal' (Leech, 1983: 104) and as 'intrinsically polite' (*ibid.*: 106). 'Thanking' is supposed to be an *FEA* for *h* because it demonstrates *s*'s gratitude to *h* and therefore belongs to the **positive direction**. 'Apologising', on the other hand, is usually performed to express *s*'s regret for some offence to *h* and consequently *s* needs to lower what relates to him/her as much as possible. Thus it is thought to be one form of the **negative direction**.

B&L also include these speech acts in their framework of *FTAs*, treating 'expressing thanks' as 'that offend S's negative face', and 'apologies' as 'that directly damage S's positive face' (B&L, 1987: 67–68). They claim that 'S accepts a debt, humbles his own face' when performing the former speech act (*ibid.*: 67), and that 'S indicates that he regrets doing a prior FTA, thereby damaging his own face to some degree – especially if the apology is at the same time a confession with H learning about the transgression through it, and the FTA thus conveys bad news' in doing the latter (*ibid.*: 68). In my view 'thanking' is generally an exchange of

*FEA*s between *s* and *h*: *h* does some favourable action to *s* and *s* gives a favourable comment back to *h*. There may be a case where *s* really feels his/her debt and consider it as a threat to his/her face-wants, but I assume this is a rather rare case under normal circumstances, contrary to B&L's generalisation. On the other hand it is true that 'apologising' often has a face-threatening aspect to *s* in many cases. Still, this speech act is not only oriented towards *s* but also towards *h* in order to achieve *rapport enhancement* or *rapport maintenance* (Spencer-Oatey, 2000). In spite of its face-threatening aspect towards *s*, it is more important to appreciate its face-enhancing side oriented towards *h*. For these reasons I recognise these speech acts as an *FEA*, for their primary functions are directed towards achievement of social equilibrium. Furthermore, I would assume that B&L's view on speech acts is based only on one side or aspect of them; they should be considered as to the overall intrinsic polite nature they have under normal circumstances, contributing to *rapport enhancement* or *rapport maintenance* (*ibid.*).

The *head acts* in this item are expected to be the formulaic expressions '*mooshiwake-ari-mas-en*' <I'm sorry> and '*arigatoo-**gozaimasu***' <Thank you (very much)> and their equivalents. I will treat the former as *head act 1* and the latter as *head act 2* in the strategy analysis of this item. Although these *semantic formulae* are assumed to be the core parts of the illocutionary performance, it is also expected that there are various kinds of *supportive moves* to represent informants' feelings and intentions, which sometimes function as the core parts of some responses, in this particular context.

The scenario of this item has only one prompt, for the performer is 'a female restaurant manager' and one performer is enough to act for both JHA and JYA informants. The following is the prompt used in this item:

Soredewa	*suguni*	*tehai-o*	*shite*
then	immediately	arrangement-ACC	do and

nikai-no-koshitsu-ni
upstairs-GEN-separate room-LOC

*juugomei-**sama**-no-yooi-o*
fifteen people(**EXAL**)-GEN-preparation-ACC

> *itashi-masu.*   *Tashoo*   *jikan-ga*   *kakatte-shimai-**masu**-ga,*
> do(**HUM**)   slightly   time-NOM1   will take unfortunately(**POL**)-but
>
> *yoroshii-**deshoo**-ka.*
> alright-COP(**POL**)-Q

<Then we will make an arrangement to accommodate 15 people in a separate room upstairs immediately. But I'm afraid you'll have to wait for a while. Is it alright with you?>

The performer used rather conventionalised phrases that are often employed by workers at restaurants, so that this utterance can be taken as natural by the informants. There are also an appropriate number, level, and type of polite expressions showing respect for the customers and modesty in relation to the worker's contribution. This is a remark full of content: (a) the restaurant manager talks of an immediate arrangement, (b) the necessity to wait for a while, and (c) a query as to whether it is fine with *h*. Consequently it is expected that which part/parts the informants will attend to and focus on will vary; their performances being affected by such variables in the restaurant manager's utterance.

A summary of the results obtained through the quantitative data analysis in this item is as follows.

Table 5.2.8-1 Summary of statistical data: Item 08

	Average scores in politeness		Average scores in appropriateness		Average scores in politeness		Average scores in appropriateness
1	JYA (2.19)	1	JYA (1.06)	1	JHAF (1.75)	1	JYAF (1.00)
				2	JYAF (2.13)	2	JHAF (1.13)
2	JHA (2.63)	2	JHA (1.50)	3	JYAM (2.25)		JYAM (1.13)
				4	JHAM (3.50)	4	JHAM (1.88)

A statistical analysis showed that the JYA performance (**politeness**: Mean = 2.19, *n* = 16; **appropriateness**: Mean = 1.06, *n* = 16) exceeded that of JHA (**politeness**: Mean = 2.63, *n* = 16; **appropriateness**: Mean = 1.50, *n* = 16) in both categories. Although a statistically significant difference between the two age groups was not confirmed with regard to **politeness**, there was a significant difference in **appropriateness** ($p<.05$). These facts suggest that these groups performed their linguistic representations in a similar way in terms of **absolute politeness**, but their performances concerning **relative politeness** were significantly different.

In the age–gender classification, JHAF came first (Mean = 1.75, n = 8), JYAF being the second (Mean = 2.13, n = 8), JYAM the third (Mean = 2.25, n = 8), and JHAM at the bottom (Mean = 3.59, n = 8) in **politeness**. The Kruskal-Wallis test has confirmed significant mean differences among the four groups ($p<.05$). According to the Dunnet test, there is a significant mean difference between JHAF–JHAM ($p<.05$). It is therefore confirmed that JHAM played a key role in JHA's lower rating than JYA in this category.

As for **appropriateness**, JYAF came on top (Mean = 1.00, n = 8), JHAF with JYAM tying in the second position (Mean = 1.13, n = 8 each), and JHAM coming last (Mean = 1.88, n = 8). Significant mean differences were found among the four groups through the Kruscal-Wallis test ($p<.05$), but no significant differences between any paired groups were found by the Dunnet test.

Considering the above results, I will conduct a qualitative analysis to explore (1) the reason(s) for JHAM's lower performance than the rest in both categories; (2) the reason(s) for JHAF's highest performance in **politeness**; and (3) the reason(s) for JYAF's highest performance in **appropriateness**.

I start with observation of JHAM data. The first response by JHAM05 received an average score of 4.50 for **politeness** (i.e. just in-between 'a little informal / a little lack of consideration' and 'very informal / impolite') and 2.50 for **appropriateness** (i.e. just in-between 'a little inappropriate' and 'very inappropriate'). The second response by JHAM04 was rated as 2.50 for **politeness** (i.e. just in-between 'polite' and 'neutral') and as 1.25 for **appropriateness** (i.e. close to 'appropriate'). These figures suggest that the former response by JHAM05 had a greater influence on JHAM's low average scores in both categories.

MJ816 – JHAM05

Oo,	*yokatta.*	*Tasukatta-yoo.*
IJ	be good(PAST)	be relieved(PAST)-FP

Tokorode,	*doregurai*	*mateba-ii-no-ka-naa?*
by the way	how long	waiting will be-enough-Q-FP

[Oh, that's good news. We are relieved. By the way, how long do we need to wait? <u>*<supportive move>*</u>]

[showing gladness1] + [showing gladness2] + [asking how long it will take]

This response was mentioned by all the raters for its lack of consideration, its impoliteness, and its inappropriateness. The following is what they said about this utterance in the follow-up interviews.

HMR (4 for **politeness**, 2 for **appropriateness**):
I was concerned about the part, '*doregurai mateba-ii-no-ka-naa?*' <how long do we need to wait?>. It is not suitable as a response to *h*'s offer. This response may be justifiable considering this informant's position as a customer, but I felt uncomfortable because this person had mentioned this suddenly. I did not put 3 for appropriateness, taking into account *s*'s position as a customer.

HFR (5 for **politeness**, 2 for **appropriateness**):
I don't like the way this person spoke. It's impolite. There's no expression to show gratitude. I did not put 3 to appropriateness because this person honestly expressed his/her gladness in the part '*Oo, yokatta. Tasukatta-yoo*' <Oh, that's good news. We are relieved>.

YMR (4 for **politeness**, 3 for **appropriateness**):
This is an utterance lacking consideration. It does not contain a phrase 'Thank you'.

YFR (5 for **politeness**, 3 for **appropriateness**):
I don't think the part '*Oo, yokatta. Tasukatta-yoo*' <Oh, that's good news. We are relieved> is appropriate as an utterance to a restaurant manager.

As can be seen from the lexicogrammatical analysis of this response above, it does not contain any polite forms. In this sense it has an informal or plain linguistic tone. This means that this informant regarded the restaurant manager as a person whose status was lower than his and did not think formality or politeness was necessary. Furthermore, as the raters pointed out, it does not include any phrases expressing a sense of 'thanking' or 'apologising'. Instead he put a question that seems to originate in his own interest and can be interpreted as an indirect requesting form of 'Will you hurry up?'. The raters were all aware of the inconsiderate aspect of this remark and evaluated its degrees of **politeness** and **appropriateness** rather low.

This informant gave me a rather perplexing comment on the background of his response in the interview: 'As the problem was sorted out, I confirmed how long we needed to wait because it is most important. The manager looked young, so it's no use shouting (at her(?)). I don't get angry (with the manager(?)) about such a thing'. As he omitted 'at/with whom', it is not clear who he would have shouted at or been angry with. Still, it is quite probable that he felt that *h* had not made an appropriate offer to him, judging from the context of his remark. This explains the reason why his linguistic behaviour was rather singular and was taken as quite impolite and inappropriate. It is also possible that he thought it inappropriate that a restaurant manager should say 'it takes a little while' to a customer. He seems to have ignored or forgotten the fact that his group had caused trouble and it was a considerate offer from *h*. He focused more on the length of time they would need to spend during the preparation, instead of appreciating the restaurant's effort. These aspects led to quite exceptional average scores of this remark in comparison with all the rest.

The following is the other response by JHAM04, which received 2.50 for **politeness** (i.e. just in-between 'polite' and 'neutral') and 1.25 for **appropriateness** (i.e. close to 'appropriate'):

MJ815 – JHAM04
*Hai,   kamai-**mas**-en.   Yoroshiku o-negaishi-**masu**.*
yes   no problem(**POL**)   I leave it entirely to you(**POL**)

[Yes, it's no problem. Please make arrangements for us. <*supportive moves*>]

[acceptance of the offer] + [showing dependence on *h*]

In contrast with JHAM05's response above, this is comparatively a 'normal' one as the average scores suggest. Although this remark lacks *head acts*, this informant has shown his polite attitude by employing lexical devices and alternative strategies as can be shown above. The expression '*yoroshiku o-negaishi-**masu***' [*lit*. I leave it entirely on you] and its equivalents are very commonly used by many informants in this item. As discussed in an earlier section (5.2.6) on Item 06, this phrase is a polite formulaic expression to show 'total dependence' on *h*, which can be used on various occasions, e.g. in greetings, in advertising merchandise to customers, or when a candidate in an election asks for voters' support. The informants who used this expression showed their attitude to highly evaluate *h*'s offer and to ask *h* to make arrangement for his group.

YFR, who gave 3 for **politeness** and 2 for **appropriateness**, said that this response was too simple and needed more words and expressions so that it could be awarded a higher score in **appropriateness**. On the other hand, YMR gave this response 1 for **appropriateness** while putting 3 for **politeness**, saying 'This response looks appropriate, for this person showed an intention to apologise for his *kohai*'s mistake, not his/her own'.

This informant explained the background of his remark as follows: 'I only hope she will accommodate all of us and enable us to hold a party. I thought we would manage to sort this out somehow. Yet I really want to ask her to make arrangements although this will cause her trouble'. In my impression he was successful in realising his intention described here in his actual remark, using the phrase '*yoroshiku o-negaishi-masu*'. Still, it seems that he did not notice the importance of 'thanking' and 'apologising' in this kind of situation. Therefore I maintain that this response would have been awarded higher scores if it had contained (either of) the *head acts*.

Now I would like to turn to the responses of JHAF, which was ranked as the best group in terms of **politeness**.

MJ810 – JHAF06
Mochiron   *kekkoo-**desu**.*
of course   fine-COP(**POL**)

***O**-kizukai*   *arigatoo-**gozaimasu**.*
consideration(**EXAL**)   thankful-COP(**SUPERPOL**)

*Yoroshiku **o**-negaishi-**masu**.*
I leave it entirely to you(**POL**)

[Of course that's fine with us. <*supportive move*> I thank you for your consideration. <*head act2*> Please make arrangements for us. <*supportive move*>]

[acceptance of the offer with an intensifier] + [thanking for *h*'s consideration] + [showing dependence on *h*]

This response received an average score of 1.75 for **politeness** (i.e. slightly higher than 'polite') and 1.25 for **appropriateness** (i.e. slightly lower than 'appropriateness'). This remark contains four polite forms, one of which being 'super-polite'. This feature certainly contributed to a high assessment in the degree of **politeness**. This remark also possesses appropriate propositional contents including the *head act*, as shown in the translation and the strategy analysis above. She first showed her willingness to accept *h*'s offer with an intensifier '*mochiron*' <of course>, then expressed her gratitude for *h*'s offer, and finally made a polite and self-effacing request with an expression, '*yoroshiku o-negaishi-masu*', to demonstrate her dependence on *h*.

YMR said, 'this is a perfect manner of speaking in this situation. Yet it sounds a little too polite to me, for I would not speak this way', having put 1 for **politeness** and 2 for **appropriateness**. HFR, who put 2 for **politeness** and 1 for **appropriateness**, pointed out the phrases '*arigatoo-**gozaimasu***' and '*yoroshiku o-negaishi-masu*' as the ground for her high assessment in **politeness**. YFR also mentioned '*yoroshiku o-negaishi-masu*' as a polite expression, giving 2 for **politeness** and 1 for **appropriateness**.

This informant said in the interview, 'As the manager said they will make arrangements immediately and it won't take so long, I won't say something unnecessary like "Can you hurry?" I thought it would be better to ask her politely'. Her attitude makes a sharp contrast with JHAM05 mentioned above, who made an 'unnecessary' question that can be interpreted as an indirect form of 'Will you hurry?'. Her strategy to prioritise politeness towards *h* over her/her group's interest led to a high evaluation in both categories.

MJ808 – JHAF05

Hai,	*yoroshiku **o**-negai-**itashimasu**.*
yes	I leave it entirely to you(**SUPERPOL**)

Anoo,	***o**-heya-o*	*yooi-shite-**itadaketa**-node*
IJ	room(**EXAL**)-ACC	preparation-do-receive(PAST-**HUM**)-as

*tasukari-**masu**.*	*Arigatoo-**gozaimasu**.*
be relieved(**POL**)	thankful-COP(**SUPERPOL**)

[Yes, please make arrangements for us. We are relieved because you will accommodate us in a room. <*supportive move*> I appreciate it. <*head act2*>]

[showing dependence on *h*] + [showing *s*'s relief] + [thanking]

This response was awarded an average score of 1.75 for **politeness** (i.e. slightly higher than 'polite') and 1.00 for **appropriateness** (i.e. '(optimally) appropriate'). This remark includes quite a few polite forms as well, two of which being 'super-polite'. In my view this response is more polite than JHAF06's above because of these two 'super-polite' forms and two polite prefixes '*o-*'. However, it was given the same average score for its level of **politeness** as JHAF06's, mainly because of YFR's comparatively lower assessment (3 for **politeness**). I assume she somehow took this remark as being rather formulaic and judged it as a common or 'neutral' response, as she had done in other items. The average score of 1.00 for **appropriateness** appears quite reasonable, judging also from the propositional content and the politeness strategies described above. This informant first made a polite and modest request to *h* using the same expression as JHAF06, secondly showed her relief that can mean 'you did such a good thing to us', and finally concluded her remark with thanking.

This informant explained the background of her remark as follows: 'We were in trouble and she swiftly arranged a room tactfully. So I showed gratitude and asked her to do so'. HMR, who awarded 1 for **politeness** and also 1 for **appropriateness**, highly evaluated the parts '*yoroshiku o-negai-itashimasu*' and '*o-heya-o yooi-shite-itadaketa-node tasukari-masu*' <we are relieved because you will accommodate us in a room>, saying 'I can see this person's consideration for the restaurant manager in these parts'.

As can be seen from the above discussion, the highest evaluation of JHAF responses in **politeness** was brought from the frequent use of polite and super-polite forms. Still this formal feature also led to a judgement of slight *overpoliteness* in JHAF06's response in the **appropriateness** category.

Now I would like to look at the JYAF responses to investigate the reason why this group's two responses were both awarded an average score of 1.00 in **appropriateness**.

MJ823 – JYAF04

A, hai.	*Ii-n'-**desu**-ka,*		*koshitsu-de?*		
IJ yes	good-NOM2-COP(**POL**)-Q		separate room-COP		

A,	*doomo*	*arigatoo-**gozaimasu**.*	*Hai,*	*a,*	*juppun-gurai?*
IJ	IJ	thankful-COP(**SUPERPOL**)	yes	IJ	ten minutes-about

A,	*daijoobu-**desu**,*	*zenzen.*
IJ	alright-COP(**POL**)	entirely

Hai,	*doomo*	*arigatoo-**gozaimasu**.*
yes	IJ	thankful-COP(**SUPERPOL**)

[Oh, are you sure we can use a separate room? <u><supportive move></u> Thank you very much. <u><head act2></u> About ten minutes? That's absolutely fine. <u><supportive move></u> Thank you very much. <u><head act2></u>]

[showing surprise and reconfirming *h*'s offer] + [thanking1] + [reconfirming the length of time for arrangements] + [stating *h*'s offer is totally alright with *s*'s group] + [thanking2]

MJ821 – JYAF03

A,	*hai,*	*kamai-**mas**-en.*	*Mooshiwake-**gozaimas**-en,*	
IJ	yes	it is fine(**POL**)	I have no excuse(**SUPERPOL**)	

o-tesuu-o		*o-kake-shite-shimatte.*
trouble(**EXAL**)-ACC		cause(**EXAL**)-have

[Oh, it's no problem. <u><supportive move></u> I'm sorry to bother you. <u><head act1></u>]

[stating it is no problem for them to wait] + [apology for the trouble *s*'s group has caused]

The former response by JYAF04 was evaluated as 2.50 for **politeness** (i.e. just in-between 'polite' and 'neutral') and 1.00 for **appropriateness** (i.e. '(optimally) appropriate'). The latter response of JYAF was awarded 1.75 for **politeness** (i.e. slightly higher than 'polite') and 1.00 for **appropriateness** (i.e. '(optimally) appropriate').

Although these two responses contain several polite forms, the former (JYAF04's) also shows some colloquial features such as the frequent use of interjections, the expressions like *'juppun-gurai?'* <about ten minutes?> or *'zenzen'* <entirely>[15]. YFR pointed out such colloquial feature of this response in a similar way, mentioning *'koshitsu-de?'* <in a separate room?>, *'juppun-gurai?'* <ibid.>, and *'daijoobu-desu'* <that's fine>. It is suspected, therefore, that the mixture of polite forms and such colloquial expressions made a less polite impression on the raters although YMR awarded 1 to its level of **politeness**. HFR, who put 3 for **politeness** and 1 for **appropriateness**, said, 'if this remark included "*sumimasen*" <I'm sorry>, I would give 2 for its politeness'. This is an interesting observation, for she still thought this remark was 'optimally appropriate' while being aware of the lack of some propositional content in her judgement of the level of **politeness**. This fact seems to imply that, in lay people's notions, **absolute politeness** is a complex of lexicogrammatical and propositional features, while **relative politeness** is a more comprehensive embodiment of politeness in a specific context (i.e. lexicogrammatical features and the propositional content of a remark with social variables such as horizontal/vertical distance, age, gender or the issue at stake). All the raters agreed to recognise this response as 'appropriate' seemingly because of the consideration *s* showed in her remark. This informant said, 'I'm glad we can find a place here. It's lucky that we can take a room. I will ask her to make arrangements anyway. But, honestly, I think it's not because she made an effort for us but because the room happened to be available. But I thank her anyway'. Her strategy to prioritise consideration towards *h* over her true opinion seems to have succeeded, judging from a high evaluation of her response in **appropriateness**.

On the other hand, the latter (JYAF03's) response was evaluated more highly in terms of the degree of **politeness**, for it does not have such a colloquial tone. HMR, who awarded 1 for both categories, described the part '*Mooshiwake-*

gozaimas-en o-tesuu-o o-kake-shite-shimatte' <I'm sorry to bother you> as a phrase apologising for *s*'s mistake and took it as a polite expression. YFR, who gave this remark 2 for **politeness** and 1 for **appropriateness**, also pointed out the part '*o-tesuu-o o-kake-shite-shimatte*' as the reason for her high evaluation in **politeness**. Still, YMR, when asked the reason for his lower assessment of this response in **politeness**, stated that this response did not include 'thank you'. I asked this because he had awarded 1 to three other responses but had awarded 2 to this response for **politeness**. This informant described the background of her remark as this: 'I will express my gratitude, as the restaurant [manager] offered to accept us'. She indeed included 'thanking' in her second response as can be seen in Appendix 26. In a situation of this kind 'thanking' and 'apologising' are the two sides of the same coin, but this informant unfortunately failed to express one side in her first response and this gave a slight inconsiderate impression on one rater. Still, this response also received 1 from all the raters for its **appropriateness** because of the modest attitude represented above. It seems that the raters thought performing either one of the two types of *head acts* was sufficient in terms of **appropriateness** as long as *s*'s consideration is well represented in responses.

Finally I would like to make observations relating to all the data including the selected responses discussed above in order to explore the general tendency/tendencies of the informants' performance in this item. I conducted further quantitative analysis to determine: (i) the number of occurrences of the commonly used formulaic expression '*yoroshiku o-negaishi-masu*' <I leave it entirely to you> and its equivalents; (ii) the proportion of the responses – (a) with 'thanking', (b) with 'apologising', (c) with both, and (d) without these two *head acts*; (iii) the responses that show some concern about the preparation time.

I would like to start with (i) the number of '*yoroshiku o-negaishi-masu*' and its equivalents, to explore the frequency of this commonly used expression in this item and the reason for its frequent use. I counted the number of '*yoroshiku o-negaishi-masu*', '*yoroshiku o-negai-itashimasu*', '*o-negaishi-masu*', and '*o-negai-itashimasu*'. I excluded '*o-negaishi-masu*' when it was connected with other expressions and made other kinds of specific requests like JHAF03's and JYAF06's first responses. The number of responses that contain '*yoroshiku o-negaishi-masu*' and '*yoroshiku o-negai-itashimasu*' is 16, that of '*o-negaishi-masu*', and '*o-negai-itashimasu*' is 4. There is one response that includes both (JYAM04's second response). The proportion of these responses (= 21) amounts to 56.76% of the total number of responses to this scenario (= 37). This means that more than half the responses contain this formulaic expression for a polite and self-effacing request by showing total dependence on *h*. This appears to be an extreme manifestation of the constraint of TACT and is probably a culturally specific linguistic characteristic of Japanese – while constraining the choices of *h/o*, elevating *h*'s/*o*'s position by expressing 'total dependence' on *h/o* (cf. Matsumoto 1988). Another point is that these phrases, used in various ways as discussed earlier, may well be included in *semantic formulae* in the response to an offer (of help, cooperation etc.) from *h* in the Japanese context. It appears that many informants used this expression because of the necessity to make a polite request to *h* in order to settle the problem.

As for (ii) the proportion of the responses (a) with 'thanking', (b) with 'apologising', (c) with both, (d) without these two *head acts*, I counted the numbers of responses categorising them as one of the above. I carried out this survey to explore the main and alternative strategies employed by the informants in this item. I would regard (d) 'without these two *head acts*' as an alternative strategy to respond to *h*'s offer. The following is the summary of the results obtained through the strategy analysis:

Table 5.2.8-2 **Summary of the results of the strategy analysis**

strategy	thanking	apologising	both	none	Total
num.	12	7	5	13	37
percentage	32.43%	18.92%	13.51%	35.14%	

The number of responses with either or both of the *head acts* amounts to 24 and it means 64.86% of the responses were performed with the *head acts*. The majority of the responses contain both or one of 'thanking' and 'apologising'. I can say that these two speech acts served as the core part and therefore as main politeness strategies in this item. Still, more than one-third of the responses were performed without these speech acts, employing 'alternative strategies'. I conducted a more detailed analysis of the 'none' category to specify what alternative strategies were employed. Here is the summary of this investigation:

Table 5.2.8-3 Summary of alternative strategies

strategy	polite/modest request	Simple query for the preparation time	strong request for immediate preparation
num.	8	3	2
percentage	61.54%	23.08%	15.38%

The majority of the 'alternative strategy' was a polite/humble request represented by '*yoroshiku o-negaishi-**masu***' and other *supportive moves* such as JHAM04 response discussed earlier – this may be implying that '*yoroshiku o-negaishi-**masu***' should be considered a *head act*, rather than a *supportive move*. However, there were five responses in which informants showed their concerns about the length of time for preparation. JHAM05 mentioned earlier, JYAF02 in her first response, and JYAM02 in his second response put a query to ask about the length of time for preparation. JHAF03 surprisingly made a strong request for an immediate preparation in a direct way as follows:

MJ804 – JHAF03
*Ii-**desu**-yo. Anoo, machi-**masu**-keredomo, anoo, watashitachi, ano, yoyaku juugomei-to-shite kite-i-**masu**-node, dekiru-dake hayaku o-negai-**itashimasu**.*
<No problem. We'll wait, but we have a reservation for fifteen people. So please make arrangements as soon as possible.>

MJ805 – JHAF03
*Hayaku-shite-**kudasai**. Anoo, dono-gurai-no-jikan-ga kakaru-ka, hakkiri-to tsutaete-moraereba-ii-n'-**desu**-ga.*
<Please hurry. I want to know how long it will take.>

JHAF03 said, 'I will show my attitude that we will cancel the reservation if it takes long'. This means that she had not had any intention to express gratitude or apology towards the restaurant manager from the beginning. This may be regarded as one example in which an informant showed an attitude to regard service at a restaurant as a matter of course. She had expected it to be as beneficial to the customers as possible. This informant's attitude is quite unique in that she was the only person that demonstrated such strong self-interest or self-centredness[16].

In a sense, JHAF03 was distracted by the phrase '*Tashoo jikan-ga kakatte-*

*shimai-**masu**-ga, yoroshii-**deshoo**-ka*' <I'm afraid you'll have to wait for a while. Is it alright for you?> in the restaurant manager's remark and failed to focus on what other elements she needed to attend to. It is therefore interesting to explore (iii) 'the responses that show some sort of concern about the preparation time' to investigate how many informants were affected by the same part. There were ten responses that mentioned the time issue in total, and they constitute 27.02% of the total responses. This fact suggests that the manager's utterance about the time did affect some informants' strategies. Six of such responses were just queries, but four of them were the request for the restaurant employees to hurry up, including JHAM03's two responses above. The other responses that made a request were the two responses of JYAF06:

MJ826 – JYAF06
*Hai, wakari-**mashita**. Chotto isoideru-n'-dee, jikan narubeku kakan-nai-you-*ni *o-negaishi-tai-n'-**desu**-kedo, ii-**desu**-ka?*

<Oh, I see. We are a little in a hurry, so we would like to ask you to make arrangements as soon as possible. Is that alright?>

MJ827 – JYAF06
*A, hai, wakari-**mashitaa**. Chotto, dekitara sugoi-isoideru-n'-dee, narubeku hayameni o-nega-shi-**maasu**. O-negaishi-**maasu**.*

<Oh, I see. We're in a great hurry, so please make arrangements as soon as possible. We ask you, please.>

These are responses with 'polite/humble' requests, but the main focuses of the remarks are on the length of time for preparation as can be seen from above. This informant explained how she made these two responses as this: 'I want her to hurry as everyone's waiting. But as we made a wrong reservation, I was aware that we couldn't say it in a strong way'. This statement suggests that she was concerned more about her group's convenience. Still, she was aware that it was her group that had caused the trouble, contrary to JHAF03 above. I think this is also the case in which the manager's utterance has caused a concern over *s*'s or *s*'s group's interest. These two informants consequently performed a speech act that is somewhat different from other informants', viz. 'requesting', caring about their present and future situation.

There seems to be some conflict/tension here between consideration towards *h* (the restaurant manager) and that towards the fellow customers, who were going to suffer unless the restaurant staff acted urgently. Also, it could be relevant that in Japanese culture restaurant staff and other service staff (e.g. shop assistants) are expected to show a special degree of deference towards customers. These informants may have felt that the restaurant manager did not show sufficient 'subservience', and so responded in a less polite way themselves.

Notes

1 I conducted t-test to examine statistical significance between two variables, one-way ANOVA (analysis of variance) with related post hoc tests to investigate multiple group differences in mean scores. When unequal variances were confirmed, Kruscal-Wallis test was used instead of one-way ANOVA. Also, 'Bivariate Correlations test' was employed to test for significance of correlations between two variables.

2 Different researchers use different criteria; e.g. Ide (1990) uses the term 'deprecatory' instead of 'colloquial'. However I will use the term 'colloquial', for the word 'deprecatory' may give a negative impression and consequently an impression of 'inappropriateness'.

3 The term 'formality' is often equivalent to 'politeness' in the Japanese context. The degree of the latter increases in accordance with the degree of the former in most cases. I will distinguish between these whenever it is necessary to do so.

4 This definition of *supportive moves* is too narrow for my purposes in this study, however – it seems to apply only to directive speech acts. I will use this term to mean 'the parts that support the *head acts*' in a more general sense.

5 This remark constitutes a whole discourse with some imaginary turn-takings and is therefore fairly long. For this reason I chose not to put lexical and grammatical annotation, which are more suitable for a sentence level analysis. The parts that are related to the scale of politeness and appropriateness will be lexically and grammatically analysed and explained wherever necessary. I will follow this practice in remaining chapters.

6 I referred to *Keigo no i-ro-ha oshie masu* ('I'll teach you ABC of honorifics', translation mine) (Ogino, 2002) for the classification of the humble forms.

7 This can be related to a description of an incident introduced by Spencer-Oatey (2000c: 11), where Chinese students condemned a British teacher saying 'What you're doing is not at all useful for us!'.

8   As for culturally different pragmalinguistic conventions, Spencer-Oatey (2000: 40-41) has given the following statement:

> … in British English, it is common (especially among older people) to greet an acquaintance with a remark about the weather such as 'Hello, a bit colder, isn't it?'… Yet in Chinese, it is more common to ask about meals in such a context and say, for example, 'Hello, have you had lunch?' The functions of the two remarks are virtually identical in the respective languages… In other words, the two languages have different pragmalinguistic conventions for conveying a friendly greeting to an acquaintance.

Modification of the prompt to make it appropriate for a certain age–gender group can be justified by this description.

9   Indeed, this performer at first refused to undertake this task, being afraid of some sort of serious consequences. However, since there were no alternatives as good as this one for inviting agreement and disagreement at the same time, I persuaded her to take part in this DCT, and she finally did so.

10   Although the Japanese pronoun *anata* is an exalted and a formal form, it is sometimes used when a person at a higher position addresses a person at a lower position in a formal occasion, e.g. teacher–student, interviewer–applicant (etc.). The most suitable way to show respect when addressing an old lady is (1) to omit such address terms, (2) to call the person by her last name with an address term -*san* or -*sama* (e.g. '*Suzuki-san*') or (3) to say something like *anata*-**sama** or *obaa*-**sama**, in order to avoid such a rude impression. YFR seems to have taken this dimension of *anata* into her consideration.

11   Although the speech acts of 'showing sympathy/concern' were represented in the forms of 'congratulating' and 'condoling' in Leech's classification (2001), I decided to investigate these in a direct way, using a scenario that makes such exploration possible.

12   As this lady appeared to be able to serve as a *kohai* for both JHA and JYA (see the pictures of the prompts in Appendix 3), she performed for the two types of prompts.

13   Still, the particle *ga* (but) at the end implies that *s* is seeking for *h*'s advice or permission. It corresponds to a more analytical translation 'I need to visit him, but…(what can I do?)' in English. This is also the case with the prompt for JHA.

14   Japanese women also show this kind of attitude sometimes, although it is regarded as *otokorashii taido* (a manly attitude).

15   '*Juppun-gurai*' sounds abrupt and colloquial without a copula '*desu*' and a questioning particle '-*ka*'. The word '*zenzen*' is not a colloquial expression in its original sense, but it is supposed to be used with negative expressions like '-*nai*' and to mean 'not at all'. The application of this word just as an intensifier (i.e. employed to mean 'entirely/absolutely') is thought to be a wrong use, but is getting more and more common in Japanese society, especially among

young people. Still this use gives a colloquial impression because of such a background.
16 However, there may have been another kind of consideration, viz. that towards her fellow-guests. She may have felt responsible for the wellbeing of her colleagues.

Chapter 6

Further survey: comparisons between written and spoken data

In this chapter I will examine the effect of spoken data in the study of linguistic politeness. Some observations will be made to compare the impressions created by spoken and transcribed utterances, and their impact on the judgement of the scales of **politeness** and **appropriateness**. The motivation for this further exploration originates in my earlier observation of the different impressions of the spoken and transcribed data. I found myself disagreeing with the raters' rather low evaluation of a young female informant's response, after listening to it and getting a better impression of it (MJ627 by JYAF06, for details see Section 5.2.6). Also in my pilot study I perceived some discrepancies between what was said and what was written by the same informant (see Section 4.3.4). Since the spoken DCT with video prompts has elicited spoken responses from the informants, it is possible to conduct research on spoken data[1]. I assume it is also meaningful to investigate, as an issue for further research, the impact of prosody in a pragmatic study of politeness.

Traditional DCTs, as widely used in such studies as the CCSARP, elicited informants' written responses. While such conventional DCTs have served as a useful and convenient data collection tool, the authenticity of data collected with the DCT has frequently been questioned. For example, Beebe & Cummings (1996) observed some differences between DCTs and the role-play in their study of refusals, as mentioned in Section 4.3.5. This experimental research is to examine the DCT by focusing on the differences between spoken and written language. What I intend to inspect here is, however, somewhat different from Beebe & Cummings' study – they compared different responses collected by DCT and by the role-play respectively. In this survey the same responses will be used to investigate the possible different impacts of written and spoken entries. This will permit a scrutiny of how prosodic features influence raters' judgements of the scales of **politeness** and **appropriateness** of the same response.

6.1 Previous studies on prosodic features of speech act performance and politeness strategies

Leech & Svartvik (1975: 38–39) illustrate what implications the different tones make in English in a section, 'the meaning of tones'. They describe how *s*'s emotion is conveyed by the use of different types of intonation. According to their observation, a falling tone expresses 'certainty', 'completeness' and 'independence'. A rising tone, on the other hand, expresses 'uncertainty', 'incompleteness' or 'dependence'. As for a fall-rise tone at the end of a sentence, they observe 'it often conveys a feeling of reservation; that is, it asserts something, and at the same time suggests that there is something else to be said' (Leech & Svartvik, *ibid.*: 38–39). These prosodic values serve to clarify *s*'s intention and to make *h*'s inference easier, complementing the syntactic and semantic features of a sentence. While making such general observations on the function of tone, they maintain that '[t]he meanings of the tones are difficult to specify in general terms' (Leech & Svartvik, *ibid.*: 38). This variability should be taken into consideration, I think, in order to learn how the same tone can imply something different with different speech acts, between different interlocutors and in different situations – while applying the general notion of the function of the tone.

Arndt & Janney (1987) incorporated a study of prosody in the whole speech analysis in their work <u>InterGrammar</u>. According to their definition, the term 'prosody' generally refers to 'vocal modulations of the articulatory line caused by shifts in pitch contour, loudness, rhythm, pause patterns, stress, accent, phrasing and so on' (Arndt & Janney, *ibid.*: 226). They maintain the importance of the role of prosody in spoken language as follows:

> The way an utterance is spoken – including the speaker's general voice set, voice quality, accent, intonation, and speech rhythm – simultaneously informs the listener about how the words in the utterance are to be interpreted, and conveys information about the speaker's internal emotional state…
> (Arndt & Janney, *ibid.*: 235)

Analysis of prosody in pragmatic and politeness studies is meaningful (1) in order to explain what sorts of prosodic information speakers rely on in interpreting one another's utterances, and (2) for the purpose of accounting systematically for how prosodic and other types of communicative behaviour interact and convey interpretable impressions (adapted from Arndt & Janney, *ibid*. 236).

B&L (1987: 267–68) have a brief description of the relation between prosody and politeness strategies from their point of view. They examine their and others' observations of prosodic features of politeness strategies in Basque, Japanese, English, Tzeltal, and Tamil. In terms of Japanese, they maintain that 'there seems to be a similar palatalization rule [to that in Basque which they regard as one of the distance-diminishing strategies] in Japanese, which applies in almost identical intimate contexts only' referring to Sansom (1928: 305) and O'Neil (1966: 134) (B&L, *ibid*.: 267, annotation mine). They predict that 'sustained high pitch (maintained over a number of utterances) will be a feature of negative-politeness usage, and creaky voice a feature of positive-politeness usage' and that 'a reversal of these associations will not occur in any culture' (B&L, *ibid*.: 268). I assume this generalisation may well provide pragmatic researchers with a clue in investigating the effect of prosody on politeness strategies to a certain degree.

Knowles (1987: 189–96) makes some observations on the function of intonation in relation to speech act performance and politeness in English[2]. He states that '[i]ntonation is often assumed to **indicate the force of an utterance**, and to do so directly'. Intonation can also be taken as 'one of several factors that together indicate force, and has the special role of hinting at how directly the message should be interpreted' (Knowles, *ibid*.: 189, emphasis mine). With regard to the effect of intonation on the performance of 'social rituals' (i.e. such speech acts as apologising and thanking), he maintains the following:

> … we apologize for some utterly trivial impoliteness in order to avoid giving offence to the other party; or we thank the other party out of politeness for some utterly trivial service. To indicate that these ritual acts are not to be taken seriously, we can give them a final rise.
>
> In such cases, if the speaker uses the fall, the addressee has the job of deciding whether the expression should be taken seriously at face value, or as a mere ritual act. If the rise is used, it must be the latter. Since it is relatively rarely the case that the expressions used in these rituals are to be taken at face value, the use of the rise is very common. (Knowles, *ibid*: 194)

The above description indicates that intonation plays an important role in spotting what *s* means by a certain utterance. The same propositional content can entail different pragmatic meanings if a different intonation is employed. Not having such prosodic features, written language does not convey such nuances and can convey pragmatic meaning only through lexicogrammatical features or propositional content. Therefore people may well get a different impression from a transcribed utterance, as compared with the original spoken utterance.

Aijmer (1996) also carried out a prosodic study of speech act performance, using data from the London-Lund Corpus of Spoken English. She investigated the effect of intonation over three types of speech acts: thanking, apologising and requesting. With regard to the 'prosodic fixedness' of a conversational routine, she maintains the following:

> ... it should be stressed that although intonation is always to some extent fixed, a conversational routine may have several prosodic patterns each with complicated conditions of use. *Sorry* is, for example, used with a rise (fall-rise) tone if the speaker asks the hearer to repeat something, but with a fall tone to signal sincere regret.   (Aijmer, *ibid.*: 15)

Thus the use of spoken data is effective in surveying speech act performance strategies in a real-life situation. The description above also supports Leech & Svartvik's earlier observation (1975: 38) – that it is difficult to specify the meanings of the tones in general terms – and my assumption that the same prosodic pattern can imply something different in various contexts: according to Aijmer's observation *sorry* with a falling tone signals 'sincere regret', while the falling tone is generally thought to express 'certainty', 'completeness' and 'independence' (Leech & Svartvik, *ibid.*: 38). It is important to explore the implication of a tone considering speech act types and other contextual factors.

Prosody in relation to impoliteness has been explored in Culpeper *et al.* (2003) and Culpeper (2005). Concerning incorporation of prosodic analysis in a pragmatic study, Culpeper *et al.* claim that '[n]o utterance can be spoken without prosody, and it is therefore desirable at some point to include this dimension of speech in pragmatic analysis' (Culpeper *et al.*, *ibid.*: 1568). Culpeper (2005) has developed the use of instrumental techniques of analysing prosody in a study of impoliteness strategies in the TV quiz show, The Weakest Link, by the use of spoken data analysing devices[3]. After investigating the strategic use of prosody by Anne Robinson (the host) in conversation, he concludes as follows:

> Looking solely at my orthographic transcriptions, it seems likely that some of the impoliteness would still be interpretable. Just a few verbal clues may be enough in a context where impoliteness is expected. ... However, it is also highly likely that potential instances of impoliteness would be more ambiguous without prosody, and some would be missed. (Culpeper, *ibid.*: 68)

My experimental study in this chapter will provide some observations concerning what is 'missed' in the transcribed data, following the same line as Culpeper above (in a context where politeness or harmonious verbal interaction is expected, however).

Loveday (1982) has studied prosody in relation to politeness in a cross-gender and cross-linguistic context, comparing the spoken data of native Japanese, British English and English read by Japanese. The findings of this study, Loveday observes, 'suggest that there are very clear sex-based intonational differences in the expression of politeness formulae[4] for Japanese speakers that do not hold for English speakers with similar lower phonational limits' (Loveday, *ibid.*: 82). Loveday's study can be taken as an attempt to investigate prosodic differences between Japanese and British men and women. In this sense his study is sociolinguistically-oriented. The experimental study presented hereby, in contrast, focuses on the impact of prosody in speech act performance regardless of gender groups; therefore the focus of the research methodology is pragmatic in orientation, and consequently different from Loveday's.

6.2 Supplementary experiment exposing raters to spoken responses

In this further survey, I asked the same four raters as before to assess the spoken responses and to talk about their observations on the similarities/dissimilarities of the two different (spoken vs. written) data sets. The responses for comment were chosen from the ones with 'highest' and 'lowest' evaluations in both **absolute** and **relative politeness**. These were chosen because they were responses that the raters had recognised as having some salient polite/impolite attributes. They were suitable items to examine, to see whether prosodic features can raise or lower the evaluation of such salient features.

Firstly the raters were asked to read the scenarios again and look at the video prompts in order to remember all the stories and the situational factors included in the scenarios. Secondly they heard each spoken response and rated its degrees of **politeness** and **appropriateness** one by one. Thirdly the researchers made comparisons between their previous evaluation of the transcribed response and the evaluation of the spoken one this time. Fourthly the raters were requested to talk about the different/same impressions they had received from the two types of responses. Finally they reported their general observations on this experiment with spoken responses.

The responses chosen for this experiment are as follows (for details see Appendix 27):

[High evaluation responses]
(1) MJ222 (JYAF02) [#02] <POL= 2.00; APP= 1.25>
(2) MJ406 (JHAF04) [#03] <POL= 1.50; APP= 1.25>
(3) MJ629 (JYAM01) [#06] <POL= 1.50; APP= 1.25>
(4) MJ808 (JHAF05) [#08] <POL= 1.75; APP= 1.00>
(5) MJ810 (JHAF06) [#09] <POL= 1.75; APP= 1.25>

[Low evaluation responses]
(1) MJ131 (JYAM02) [#01] <POL= 4.00; APP= 2.75>
(2) MJ423 (JYAF04) [#04] <POL= 4.75; APP= 2.75>
(3) MJ627 (JYAF06) [#05] <POL= 4.25; APP= 2.50>
(4) MJ637 (JYAM06) [#07] <POL= 4.00; APP= 2.75>
(5) MJ816 (JHAM05) [#10] <POL= 4.50; APP= 2.50>

*[#] indicates the order of the responses in this research: they were arranged according to the item serial numbers (MJ-) so that the raters could not tell whether it was a high evaluation item or a low evaluation one.

The criteria for the selection of the high evaluation responses are as follows: (1) the score of **politeness** is 2.00 or lower; (2) that of **appropriateness** is 1.25 or lower – the smaller the score, the more polite and the more appropriate a response is. Those for the selection of the low evaluation responses are as follows: (1) the score of **politeness** is 4.00 or higher; (2) that of **appropriateness** is 2.50 or higher – the larger the score, the less polite and the less appropriate a response is. With these selection criteria, I chose five responses each for the two categories ('high evaluation responses' and 'low evaluation responses') and made a list of ten responses for this experiment.

6.3 Comparison of raters' evaluation of transcribed and spoken responses

6.3.1 Overall observations through quantitative analysis

The data obtained at this stage was first analysed by *SPSS 11.5* to examine if there were any statistically significant differences in the assessments of the spoken and written responses, using the *t-test* to compare means. The quantitative investigation was carried out on the following scores: (1) general differences in the assessments of the two types of responses; (2) differences in the assessments of high evaluation responses; (3) differences in the assessments of low evaluation responses; (4) differences in the same rater's general assessments of the two types of responses; (5) differences in the same rater's assessments of the two types of high evaluation responses; (6) differences in the same rater's assessments of the two types of low evaluation responses; and (7) differences in the ratings of the same responses. The summary of the results of the quantitative analyses is as follows (for full statistical details see Appendix 28):

(1) general differences in the assessments of the two types of responses (Appendix 28-1):
No significant differences were found in **politeness** (.866, n.s.) or **appropriateness** (.128, n.s.).
(2) differences in the assessments of high evaluation responses (Appendix 28-2):
No significant differences were found in **politeness** (.108, n.s.) or **appropriateness** (.478, n.s.).
(3) differences in the assessments of low evaluation responses (Appendix 28-3):
There was no significant difference found in **politeness** (.052, n.s.), but in **appropriateness** there was (.003, $p<.005$).
(4) differences in the same rater's general assessments of the two types of responses(Appendix 28-4–7):
No significant difference was observed.
(5) differences in the same rater's assessments of the two types of high evaluation responses(Appendix 28-8,10,12,14):
Regarding HMR – the assessments of the two types of responses in **politeness**

were significantly different (.014, *p*<.05). His evaluation was significantly higher (i.e. the levels of **politeness** were lowered) in the evaluation of spoken responses.

(6) differences in the same rater's assessments of the two types of low evaluation responses(Appendix 28-9,11,13,15):
No significant difference was observed.

(7) differences in the ratings of the same responses (Appendix 28-16–25):
MJ131 – the evaluation of its level of **appropriateness** showed a significant rise (.017, *p*<.05).
MJ627 – the evaluation of its level of **politeness** showed a significant rise (.030, *p*<.05).
MJ637 – the evaluation of its level of **appropriateness** showed a significant rise (.005, *p*<.05).

From the observations in the first and the fourth results, reliability of transcribed data for a study of **politeness** and **appropriateness** on the whole has been verified in this particular study: the transcribed stimulus produced a result comparable to the spoken stimulus. However, the other results demonstrate some different tendencies in the two types of data sets. The third finding shows that prosody can give a notably different impression on the judgement of low evaluation responses in terms of **relative politeness**. The fifth outcome reveals that HMR took written linguistic features as more salient than those in a spoken form. The seventh finding – all responses appearing here are 'low evaluation responses' – demonstrates that prosody, or 'vocal information', has neutralised/mitigated an impolite or inappropriate impression created by the syntactic and semantic features of an utterance.

6.3.2 Individual response analysis with instrumental scrutiny

In this section I will survey the similarities and dissimilarities of the two types of data sets at a deeper level. Each response will be examined in terms of what the raters said in the interview or in the 'retrospective think-aloud protocol' in their search for the underlying factors of their assessments. I have employed *Praat 4.2.0.7* for the inspection of the prosodic features of spoken responses as a means of explaining why they had such assessments[5].

Overall, the different impressions of the spoken data seem to stem from (1) prosodic features – intonation, pitch, loudness, tempo and voice quality; (2) information on *s*'s age and gender obtained from the respondent's voice, (3) holistic impressions such as of a 'warm' or 'cold' tone produced by the prosody.

Response 01 (LOW) [MJ131 – JYAM02] POL: 4.00 → 3.50 (n.s.) APP: 2.75 → 1.50 ($p<.05$)

The assessment of **appropriateness** of this response rose with statistical significance. YFR said she had received 'a warm impression' from this young male undergrad's utterance, raising her evaluation in **politeness** from 4 to 3. YMR, who changed his rating in **appropriateness** from 3 to 1, explained why he made such a change as follows:

> When I saw the transcribed response, I tended to grasp it from its grammatical features. But when I heard it, I thought it was good enough as regards appropriateness. I thought the content of the response was appropriate in a conversation between male university undergrads.

This suggests that the information from the audio data on *s*'s age clarified another situational factor that did not appear in the transcription. It contributed to a rise in the evaluation of **appropriateness**.

HMR, who also raised his rating from 3 to 1 in **appropriateness**, said, 'This sounded natural as an utterance of a young person in conversation with a friend'. He had focused on the part '*Hitori-de iku-no-mo-nan-da-shi-sa*' <I don't like to go alone> and '*Ne, chotto sagasiteru-n'-dakedo*' <Say, I'm looking for someone> in his previous reaction to the transcribed response. But he pointed out that these phrases sounded just natural this time.

The following chart is the prosodic record of this response created by *Praat*, focusing on the intensity (the first tier) and the pitch (the second tier)[6].

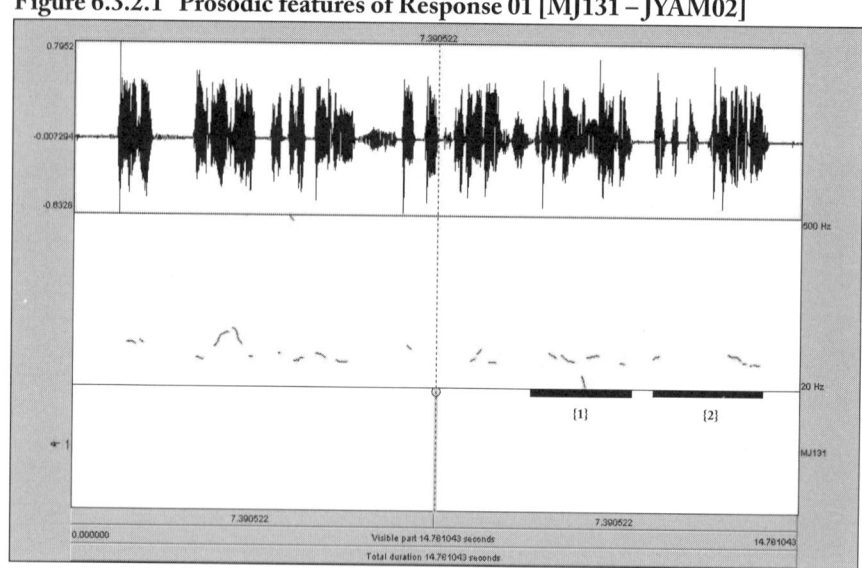

Figure 6.3.2.1 Prosodic features of Response 01 [MJ131 – JYAM02]

The intensity and the pitch of the informant's utterance shown above partly demonstrate the prosodic features of this response, although how the 'warmth' or 'appropriateness' of this utterance was conveyed is not very clear from them. This young male informant's voice is rather low and deep (minimum pitch = 33.93 Hz in the above chart) (actually some parts are too low to be shown in the second tier), and the intonation is rather flat with a downward trend. These features appear to represent some characteristics of 'creaky voice'[7] that expresses *solidarity* or *camaraderie* according to B&L (1987: 268). His voice quality, which does not appear in the above chart, has such characteristics when it is heard. This informant said in the follow-up interview that he had tried to make the invitation casual, and his creaky voice is the evidence of the casualness of a friendly conversation. The flatness of his tone also covered the salience of the last part of his utterance, '*Hitori-de iku-no-mo-nan-da-shi-sa*' <I don't like to go alone> (indicated by the underline {1}) and '*Ne, chotto sagasiteru-n'-dakedo*' <Say, I'm looking for someone> (indicated by the underline {2}) mentioned by HMR above. It thus seems plausible that his voice quality contributed to the rise in the evaluation of **appropriateness**. Indeed HFR, who raised her assessment of **appropriateness** from 3 to 2, said that this utterance did not sound 'polite' but sounded 'natural' (and therefore more 'appropriate').

Chapter 6 Further survey   257

Response 02 (HIGH) [MJ222 – JYAF02] POL: 2.00 → 2.25 (n.s.) APP: 1.25 → 1.50 (n.s.)

This response by a young Japanese female informant was rated a little lower than the last time. The cause of this decline came from HMR. He lowered his assessment of **politeness** from 2 to 4 and that of **appropriateness** from 1 to 2. According to his explanation, he noticed that the part '*go-**tsugou**-no-yoi-jikan-wa ari-**masu**-deshoo-ka*' <Do you have any convenient time?> was not considerate or polite enough when used to address a superior. I assume this impression came from the part '*ari-**masu**-deshoo-ka*'. '[*A*]*ri-**masu***' is a polite expression but it connotes the humbleness of the subject of the verb '*aru*' – this expression usually does not express respect towards *h*. The correct expression to show deference would be '*o-**ari**-deshoo-ka*'. This part was, however, not emphasised by loudness or high pitch as shown by the underlining {1} in the chart below. HMR somehow recognised the salience of the misuse of an honorific expression of this remark and lowered his evaluation accordingly.

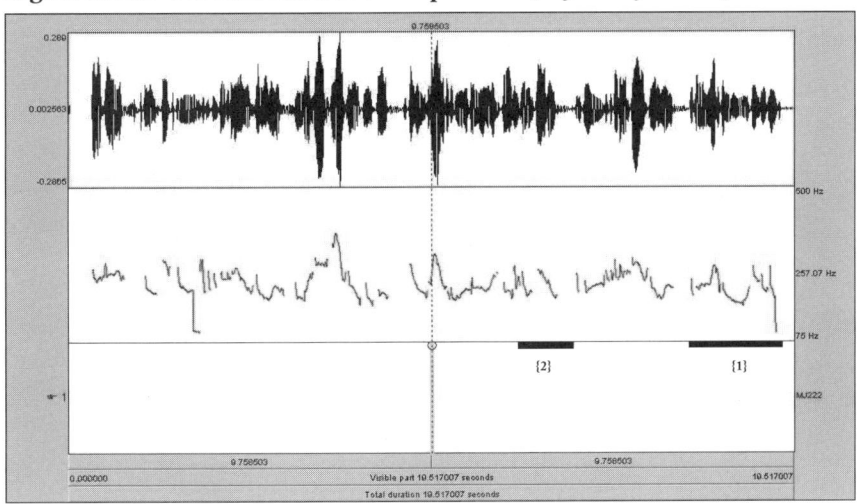

Figure 6.3.2.2   Prosodic features of Response 02 [MJ222 – JYAF02]

I suspect this phrase with the wrong honorific use is salient as it is said in the last part indicated by {1}. Furthermore, the final part has a falling tone and is therefore not an indicator of a polite request[8].

YFR, on the other hand, raised her evaluation of **politeness** from 2 to 1. She said in the interview, 'The tempo of her speech was slow and sounded polite. The part "*moshi **yoroshi**-kereba*" <if possible> was impressive'. For this rater the tempo of this response functioned to raise evaluation. The part she mentioned is underlined in the chart at {2}. This part is followed by a brief pause. The presence of the short pause seems to have helped this part to be emphasised in the utterance, although there is no strong intensity or high pitch there. The expression '*moshi **yoroshi**-kereba*' <if possible> 'gives options' and leaves the choice to *h*. In this sense *s* expressed her consideration towards *h*'s schedule. This part was evaluated highly by this rater, for it sounded prominent to her.

Response 03 (HIGH) [MJ406 – JHAF04] POL: 1.50 → 2.50 (n.s.) APP: 1.25 → 1.25 (n.s.)

While there was no change in the evaluation of **appropriateness**, three out of four raters lowered their assessments of **politeness** (the difference is not statistically significant, but it is very close to the significant level: *p*= .05). The lower evaluation in **politeness** stems from an insincere impression conveyed by the prosody of this response. HFR, although not having changed her ratings, explicated her observation as follows:

> The way this person spoke conveyed a 'perfunctory' impression. It also sounded as if she had not really meant it. I felt that she said this from a sense of duty to be polite, since she was speaking to her superior. I thought it was more polite when I read it. Still, I think this is an appropriate response to a male senior/superior.

The other raters said something more or less similar to her observation. The 'perfunctory' impression given by this response is the key factor to be investigated. The characteristics of this utterance in a spoken form are illustrated in the chart below.

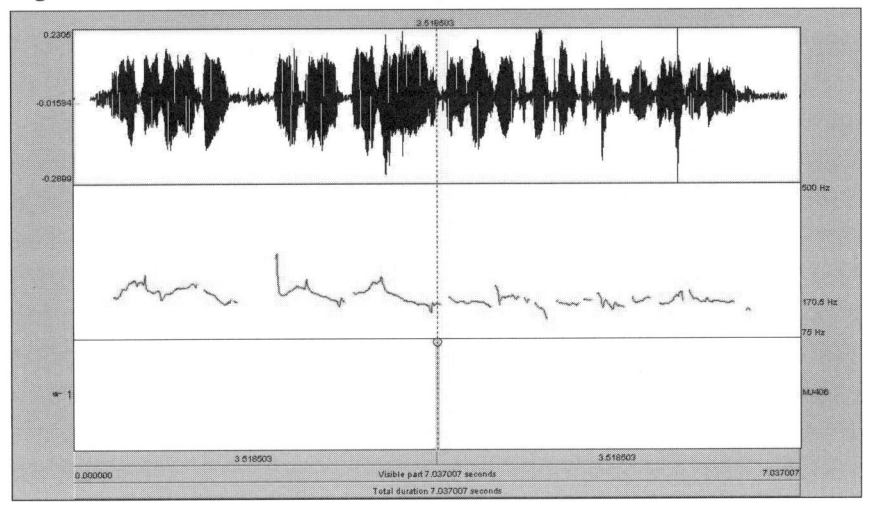

Figure 6.3.2.3 Prosodic features of Response 03 [MJ406 – JHAF04]

As can be seen, the intonation is rather flat and low, without any conspicuous accent on any specific part. The average frequency of this utterance is 170.5Hz, while that of JYAF02's described above is 257.07Hz. The difference in the pitch contour between the two is rather obvious as well. JYAF02 spoke with far more rises and falls, but JHAF04 said this in a rather flat way. With regard to voice quality, which does not appear in the above chart, her voice is not deep but rather expressionless, monotonous and toneless with shallow breaths. Therefore this response, especially the latter part, sounds as if she 'muttered' it. I suspect these features gave a 'perfunctory' impression on the raters. She failed to express sufficient 'gladness' or 'gratitude' orally. It is interesting that this aspect affected **politeness** but not **appropriateness** at all. It seems that a 'sincere impression' conveyed by prosody influences the scale of **absolute politeness**, probably in many cases, when the propositional content is the same.

Response 04 (LOW) [MJ423 – JYAF04] POL: 4.75 → 4.75 (n.s.) APP: 2.75 → 2.75 (n.s.)

This response by a young female informant is a very striking case – and the ratings for the spoken and the transcribed forms precisely correspond with each other. All the raters recognised this as more or less an impolite and inappropriate response.

YFR said 'I thought the part "*uso-baakka*" <totally a lie> was impolite in any sense. I would be offended by this'. YMR maintained that this response deserved 5 for **politeness** and 3 for **appropriateness** because it was said as if to reject *h*'s opinion altogether. HMR pointed out that a response of this kind was 'impolite' and far from behaviour associated with *wakimae*. HFR was the only one who showed a little understanding for this informant as a young undergraduate student, talking to a close, friendly *senpai*.

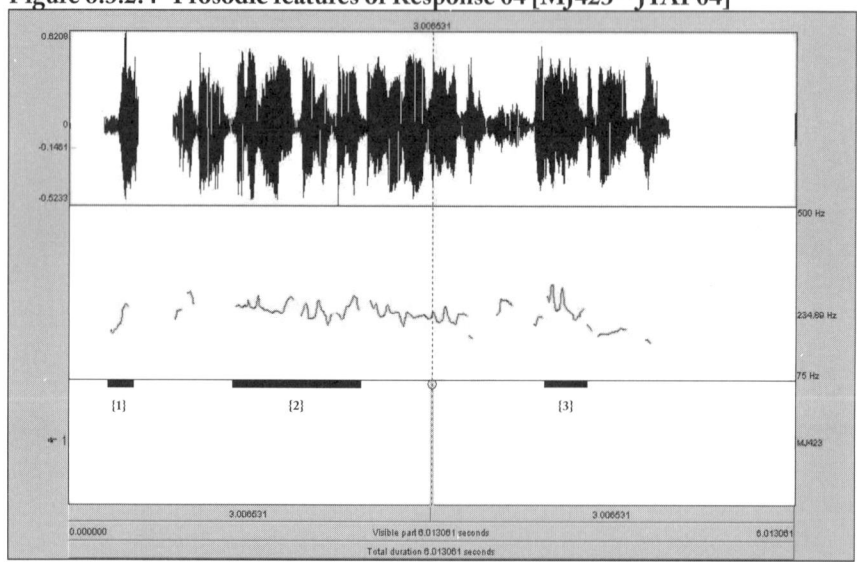

Figure 6.3.2.4 Prosodic features of Response 04 [MJ423 – JYAF04]

The chart above suggests how this response was uttered prosodically. In order to survey where an impolite impression of this response originates, I looked for the words or phrases emphasised in it. The strongest intensity is at '*E*' <hey> (indicated by the underline {1}) [81.15dB], the second strongest being at '*sonna senpai*' <such a thing, senpai> (indicated by {2}) [81.00dB], and the third strongest at '*uso (-baakka)*' <(totally a) lie> (indicated by {3}) [80.05dB]. The first accentuation emphasises this informant's surprise, which is nothing impolite. But with the second accentuation she tries to ridicule or reject the male senior's opinion, 'I was impressed', by referring to it as 'such a thing'. And by the third accentuation she challenges the senior's *quality face* and *identity face* (Spencer-Oatey, 2000c: 15): she is emphasising that what he said was 'totally a lie' and that he is 'a liar'. This part is also emphasised by the highest pitch [307.57Hz] in this response and by a sense of ridicule and sarcasm in the voice quality. It is obvious that she refused to employ the *GSP* – '*place a high value on what pertains to o*' – in prosody as well, and performed the opposite strategy for impoliteness!

Response 05 (LOW) [MJ627 – JYAF06] POL: 4.25 → 3.25 ($p<.05$) APP: 2.50 → 1.25 (n.s.)

This response received a significantly higher evaluation in **politeness** and also a rise in **appropriateness** (although of no statistical significance). As stated before I had disagreed with the raters' very low evaluation of this response, which created the motivation for this further study. Therefore this result supported my hypothesis that the spoken data would have a different impact on the assessment of **politeness** and **appropriateness**.

The two higher age raters both pointed out that the phrases '*Sokkaa*' <I see>, '*taihen-datta-nee*' <you must have been upset> and '*Sokka, sokka*' <I see, I see> showed a deep sympathy towards *h*. Prosodic marking of these phrases is indicated in the chart below with underlining and the numbers {1}, {2} and {3} respectively.

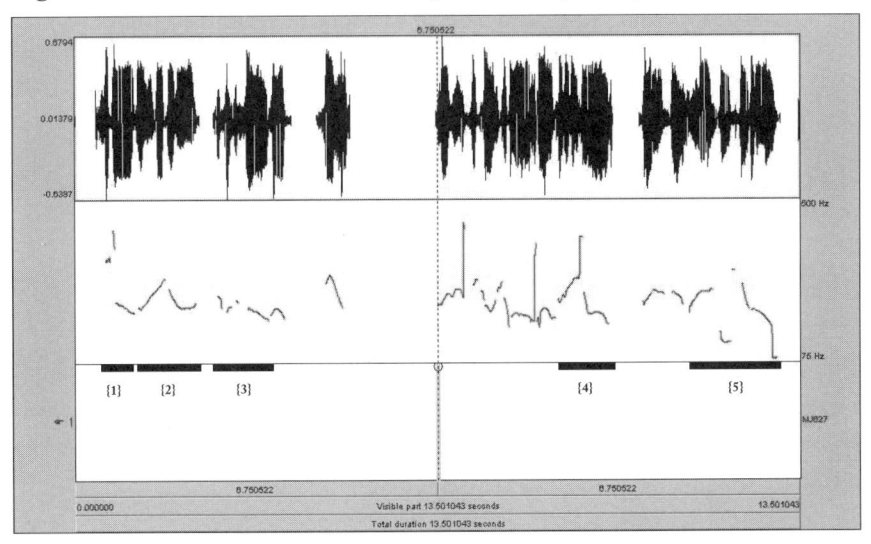

Figure 6.3.2.5 Prosodic features of Response 05 [MJ627 – JYAF06][9]

One notable thing is that these three phrases have a falling tone. The gap between the highest and the lowest pitch is very sharp in the case of {1}: the highest is approx. 395Hz and the lowest is approx. 208Hz. I assume what Aijmer (1996: 15) stated – that a fall tone when saying *sorry* signals a sincere regret – can be applied to explain the aforementioned case as well, although the speech act supposed to be performed here is commiserating and not apologising: *S*'s polite intention and her serious attitude represented by these falling tones are assumed to have raised the evaluation in **politeness**. The second phrase ends with a slight rising tone because it ends with a final particle *ne*, which usually shows familiarity or friendliness, and the rising tone expressing *s*'s sympathy more than the falling tone.

The same is true with {4} '*shooga-nai-karaa*' <as it can't be helped> and {5} '(*o-mimai-shite-kite-*) *agena-yo*' <why not offer (him your visit)>. These phrases were other sources of the impolite impression in the transcription, but when they were heard they gave a 'sympathetic impression' (according to YFR).

Prosodic attributes of this response served to raise the evaluation in **absolute politeness** (also in **relative politeness**, although the difference was not statistically significant) – mainly by the sympathetic impression created by falling tones. They have clarified *s*'s polite intention and consideration towards *h*, viz. 'sympathy' – a **positive direction** strategy of the *GSP*. Without prosody, however, the phrases mentioned above could not be identified as such. Instead, they were taken as 'inconsideration' and 'informality' in the previous stage with transcribed data – this led to its very low evaluation.

This finding also provides a striking contrast to Response 04, where the degree of **absolute politeness** declined because of the insincere impression produced by *s*'s flat and monotonous tone.

Response 06 (HIGH) [MJ629 – JYAM01] POL: 1.50 → 1.75 (n.s.) APP: 1.25 → 1.50 (n.s.)

This response did not evince a major change in the evaluation, although it showed a slight decline in both **politeness** and **appropriateness**. The decline in **politeness** was caused by HMR, who lowered his evaluation from 1 to 2. He explained the reason for this change in the interview as follows:

> When I read this response, it looked very polite. But when I heard it I didn't get such a polite impression, since it was spoken without particular stresses. The way this person said this, such as intensity or smoothness, may have

affected my judgement.

The two younger raters, both lowering their evaluation from 1 to 2 in **appropriateness**, also pointed out the 'awkwardness' and 'unnaturalness' of this response. In order to investigate how awkward and unnatural this utterance sounded, its prosodic features have been examined with the chart below.

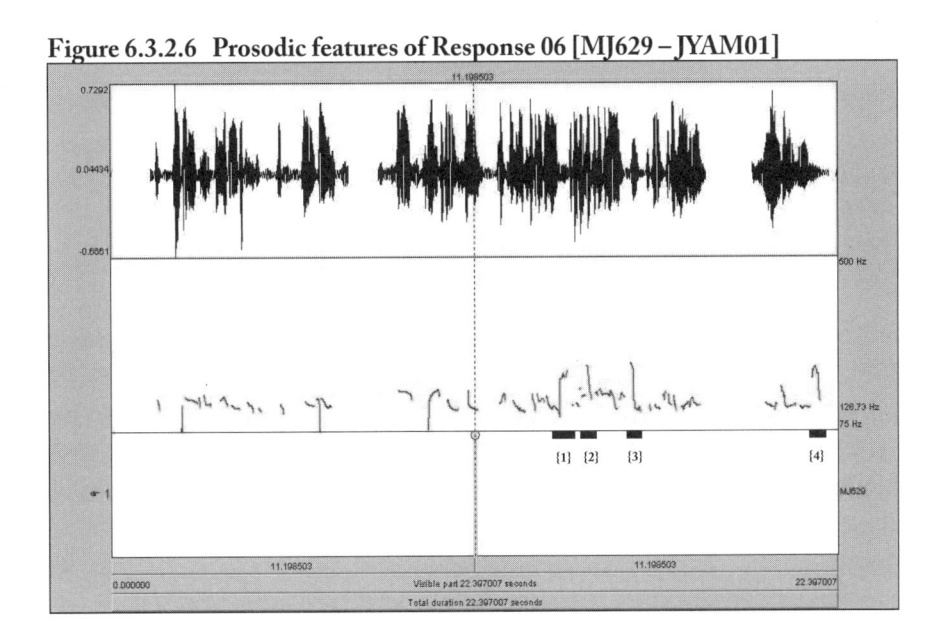

Figure 6.3.2.6 Prosodic features of Response 06 [MJ629 – JYAM01]

The intonation of this response is demonstrated in the second tier[10]. As can be seen, this informant spoke with a rather flat tone. There are some high pitches, but they were not employed to emphasise some 'key' content words or phrases to show his polite intention – {1} '*node*' <because>, {2} '*otooto*' <younger brother>, {3} '*ni*' <to> and {4} '*masu*' <[adverb] (**POL**)>. Also, there are somewhat long and unnatural pauses in the middle of some words. These pauses sound as if this informant stopped to look for further suitable words and expressions. These prosodic characteristics operated somewhat unfavourably for this response when it was heard, although other linguistic characteristics had no problem in conveying *s*'s polite intention.

It is also intriguing that the two higher age raters gave 1 for **appropriateness** of this response, whereas the younger ones rated it as 2. This seems to be because the higher age raters put more emphasis on the lexicogrammatical features and the propositional content of this utterance in this serious situation – where one is supposed to express a sense of commiseration. For the younger raters this response sounded too polite and unnatural to some extent, considering that it was said by a male undergrad of their age. This means that the information regarding *s*'s age, which was provided by the spoken data, has affected the younger judges' evaluation of **appropriateness**.

Response 07 (LOW) [MJ637 – JYAM06] POL: 4.00 → 3.25 (n.s.) APP: 2.75 → 1.25 (*p*<.05)

All the raters raised their evaluation in **appropriateness** and this caused a statistically significant difference. The main cause of the change was the information about *s*'s age and gender, judging from what the raters said in the interview. YMR, who belongs to the same generation and the same gender as the informant, gave the reason for his higher rating in **appropriateness** (from 3 to 2) as follows:

> I think this informant is a male undergrad, and the content of this utterance seems fine considering that. Although I still take the phrase '*shikata-nai-kara*' <as it can't be helped> as inappropriate, it did not stick out when the whole utterance was heard. It is taken just as an on-going phrase in the conversation. Still, the tone of this speaker sounds monotonous and cold. I don't feel he has much consideration towards *h*.

His observation of the flatness of this response is justified by the pitch contour shown in the second tier of the chart below. He did not change his assessment in **politeness** nor put 1 in **appropriateness**, while the others did so.

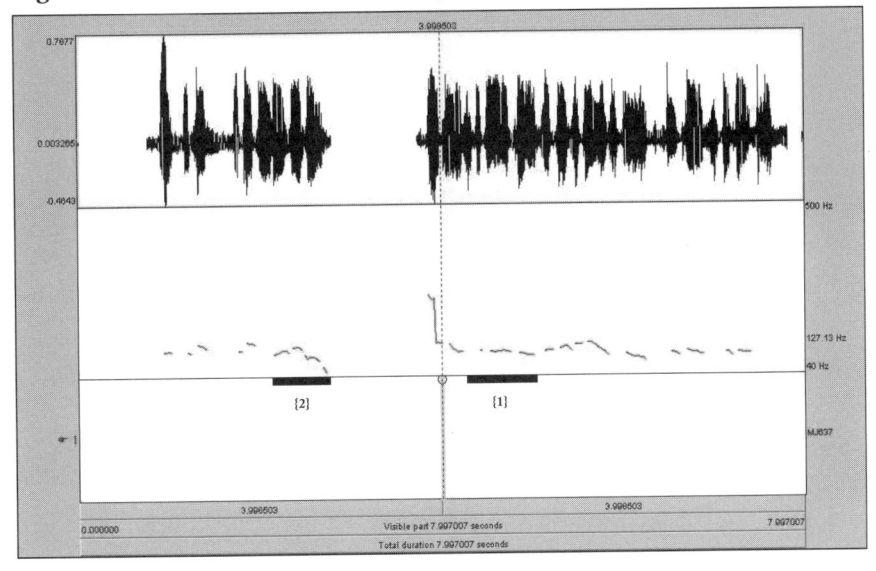

Figure 6.3.2.7 Prosodic features of Response 07 [MJ637 – JYAM06]

As can be seen in the underlined part {1}, the controversial phrase '*shikata-nai-kara*' <as it can't be helped> is not emphasised in this utterance. This prosodic feature also seems to have raised the evaluation of this utterance.

YFR, who raised her assessment in **politeness** from 4 to 2 and in **appropriateness** from 2 to 1 said the following.

> The phrase '*shikata-nai-kara*' <as it can't be helped> did not sound impolite. This response sounded natural as that of a young male student. He showed his consideration in the part '*daijoobu?*' <alright?> (shown in the underlined part {2}). When I saw this response, this impression was not conveyed. I thought it was not polite enough then.

HMR pointed out the same thing. He also said the phrase '*daijoobu?*' <alright?> had shown this person's consideration and had covered the impolite impression of the following part, '*shikata-nai-kara*' <as it can't be helped>. He said, 'It did not sound as bad as when I read this last time'.

HFR took the informant's age and gender into consideration when assessing this response this time. Her observation was similar to YMR in that she still thought this is not a polite response and did not change her evaluation in

politeness. Still, what concerned her was not the tone but the way he said 'your younger brother' – she insisted that he should have used a more polite form '*otooto-san*' <younger brother-**POL**> instead of a plain one '*otooto*' <younger brother>, as she did last time.

This response also demonstrated that prosodic features had mitigated the impolite and inappropriate impression of an utterance, especially that of a young person. It is assumed that younger Japanese people are more liberalised and therefore less concerned about the form of the language than older ones. Simplicity in the language seems to be preferred by young males nowadays. In this context prosody appears to be employed more frequently to show consideration towards *h* than lexicogrammatical devices, such as polite address terms.

Response 08 (HIGH) [MJ808 – JHAF05] POL: 1.75 → 1.75 (n.s.) APP: 1.00 → 1.25 (n.s.)

Although the average assessment of **politeness** did not change, there were some different opinions about this response. YFR raised her evaluation in **politeness** from 3 to 1, saying the following:

> The part '*o-heya-o yooi-shite-**itadaketa**-node tasukari-**masu***' <we are relieved because you will accommodate us in a room> (shown in the underlined part {1}) was outstanding. It was not conspicuous last time when I read this response. I feel this response is polite this time, since that phrase can be heard clearly.

The phrase she pointed out is illustrated by the underlined part {1} in the chart below.

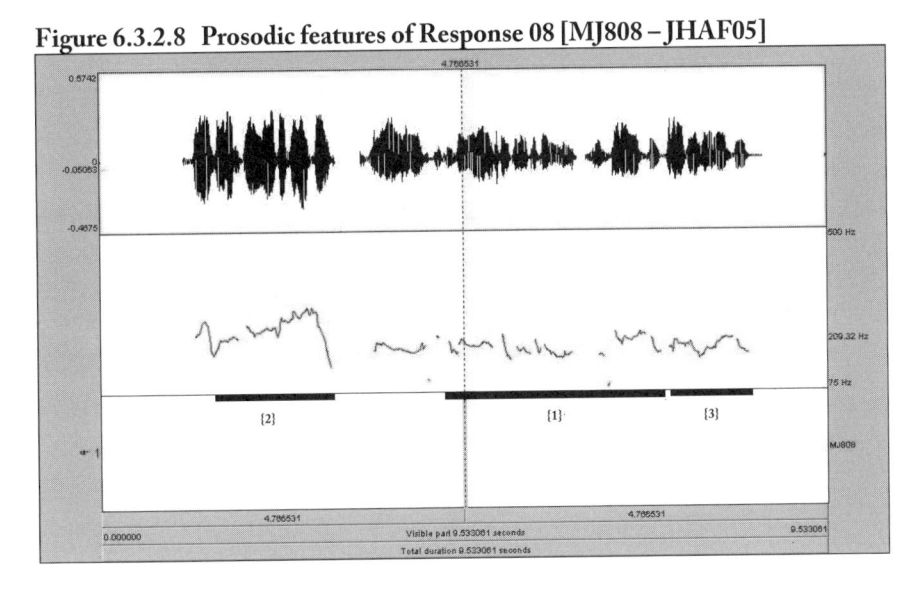

Figure 6.3.2.8 Prosodic features of Response 08 [MJ808 – JHAF05]

Although this part is not emphasised by the strongest intensity or the highest pitch, it has a considerable length (2.83 sec.). Throughout this research, YFR tended to take a phrase with a slow tempo as something polite or serious. This suggests that tempo is one of the prosodic factors which can affect the assessment of **politeness** (and **appropriateness** as well).

However YMR and HMR both lowered their evaluation from 1 to 2 in **politeness**. HMR maintained that this response 'did not sound as polite as it looked'. YMR pointed out what was missing in her response: a phrase to express apology, such as 'I thank you for such considerate treatment after our mistake', should have been included. When he read this last time, he thought the phrases '*yoroshiku o-negai-itashimasu*' <please make arrangements for us> (shown in {2}) and '*arigatoo-gozaimasu*' <I appreciate it> (shown in {3}) deserved 1 in **politeness**. He observed, however, that these phrases could not make up for a more important phrase of apology. As can be seen from the chart, the final fall in the part {3} is not emphasised by strong intensity, either. When the issue of tempo is taken into consideration, an interesting fact emerges: these parts are shorter than the phrase YFR pointed out ({1} = 1.54 sec., {3} = 1.09 sec.). For YMR, this response sounded like a superficial 'thank you', partly because of such tempo features. Although I cannot present any clear evidence as it is not possible to compare the same word to get different tempos, this finding seems to be implying that the tempo is associated with superficiality or casualness.

In contrast, HFR lowered her evaluation in **appropriateness** for a different reason. She thought the honorific expressions '*itashimasu*' and '*itadaketa-node*' were too polite for a customer to address to a worker at a restaurant. She said, 'these expressions were salient when they were heard'.

This response did not receive a major change in evaluation, but there were such various observations when the spoken response was heard. People's recognition of 'illocutionary force' may well vary according to what is emphasised or stressed syntactically, semantically, or prosodically. This observation tells us the importance of including 'prosodic features' in a pragmatic study of politeness.

Response 09 (HIGH) [MJ810 – JHAF06] POL: 1.75 → 2.00 (n.s.) APP: 1.25 → 1.00 (n.s.)

The overall evaluation of this response declined slightly in **politeness** but rose a little in **appropriateness**. The decline in **politeness** was because of the lower assessment by HMR, who dropped his rating from 2 to 3. He described the reason for the change as follows:

> When I read this, I got a more polite impression from the phrase '*o-kizukai arigatoo-**gozaimasu***' <I thank you for your consideration> (shown by the underlined part {1} in the chart). But it sounded only like a common formulaic expression for social convention, and this affected my evaluation.

As can be seen from the chart below, the phrase {1} pointed out by this rater is not emphasised by the strongest intensity or the highest pitch in this response.

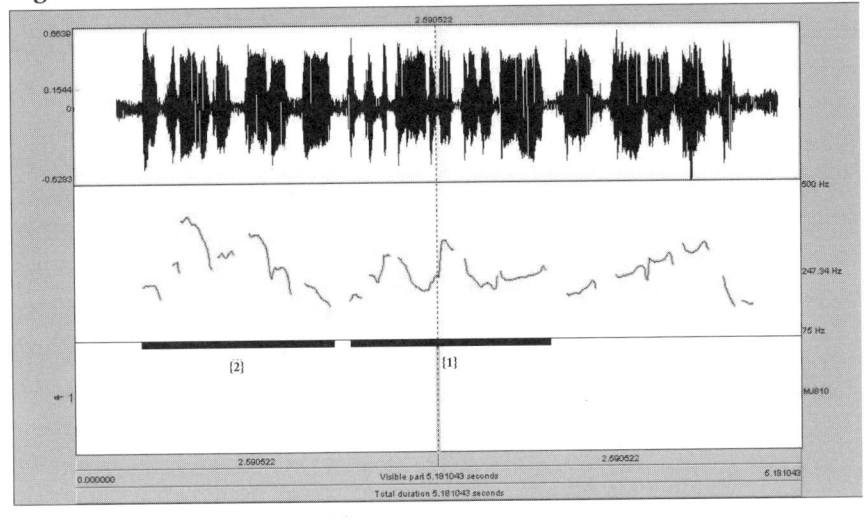

Figure 6.3.2.9 Prosodic features of Response 09 [MJ810 – JHAF06]

The first phrase '*Mochiron kekkoo-**desu***' <Of course that's fine with us> (underline {2}) has the strongest intensity [84.09dB] and the highest pitch [410.89Hz]. Consequently this phrase sounds more emphatic than {1}. This means that *s*'s satisfaction was more stressed than gratitude towards *h*. I think HMR noticed this prosodic feature, which relates to the propositional content of this utterance, and lowered his evaluation.

As for **appropriateness**, HFR raised her evaluation from 2 to 1. She stated that the phrase '*o-kizukai arigatoo-**gozaimasu***' <I thank you for your consideration> (underline {1}) had sounded appropriate this time. It looked too polite when she read it last time. This is again due to the prosodic feature described above: this part is less emphatic in the whole utterance. Interestingly she also pointed out this informant's 'successful performance' as an actress in this scenario – she had thought some other informants had been poor at performing. This suggests that how a response is uttered (i.e. fluency and naturalness) can influence the assessment of **politeness** and **appropriateness**.

Response 10 (LOW) [MJ816 – JHAM05] POL: 4.50 → 4.50 (n.s.) APP: 2.50 → 2.75 ($p<.05$)
The impolite and inappropriate impression of this response did not improve in this experiment – on the contrary the evaluation in **appropriateness** declined.

One notable phenomenon in the judgement of **politeness** is that the two female raters raised their evaluation from 5 to 4 whereas the male raters did the opposite (lowering 4 to 5).

YFR said that she understood the genuine gladness of this informant in the part '*Oo, yokatta. Tasukatta-yoo*' <Oh, that's good. We are relieved> (shown by underline {1} in the chart). She had taken this part to be impolite and inappropriate last time. HFR made a similar observation, pointing out the same phrase expressing his relief. This lady said that she had given 2, instead of 3, for **appropriateness** because such genuine gladness had been successfully expressed.

In contrast the male raters received a worse impression from this response. YMR explained the background of his evaluation as follows:

> As this response did not include any apologetic expression, I thought I should put 5 for **politeness**. I felt more impoliteness when I heard this. It sounded as if he were saying 'It is the customer's right to receive this kind of additional service'.

The above implies that an impolite impression from this response was reinforced by its prosodic characteristics. The following chart demonstrates how such a negative impression could be conveyed by prosody.

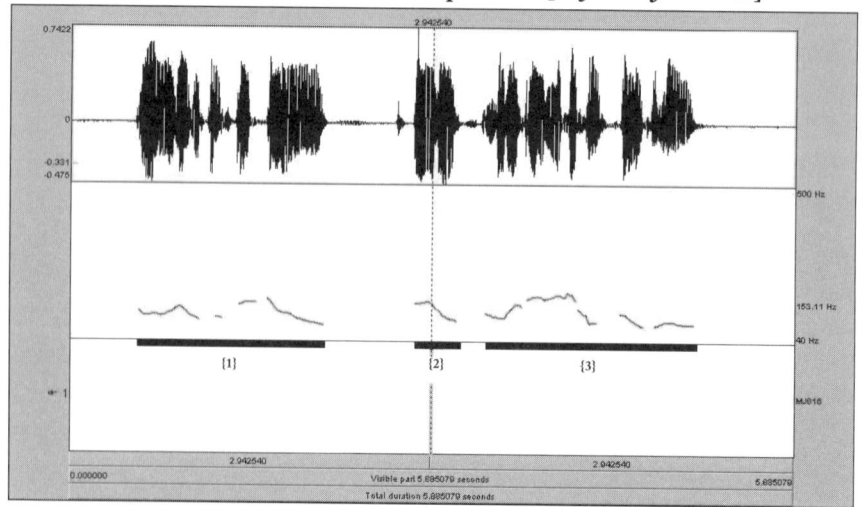

Figure 6.3.2.10 Prosodic features of Response 10 [MJ816 – JHAM05]

There are three major parts stressed by strong intensity in this utterance: the first is '*Oo*' <Oh> in {1} [79.73dB], the second is '*tokorode*' <by the way> in {2} [80.83dB] and the third lies in '*doregurai*' <how long> in {3} [81.03dB]. These characteristics suggest that this informant emphasised (1) his feeling of relief, (2) his intention to change a topic to that of his interest, and (3) his question to ask how long they will need to wait. As the male raters pointed out, this informant had not emphasised his apologetic feeling or gratitude towards *h* prosodically. What YFR said can be justified by the fact that '*oo*' in {1} '*Oo, yokatta. Tasukatta-yoo*' <Oh, that's good. We are relieved> is stressed by the highest intensity. This phrase is also emphasised by a falling tone, which is supposed to show seriousness in this context, and also by the prolonged sentence-final particle '*yo(o)*', which in this case functions to 'impose *s*'s feeling or opinion on *h*'.

HMR pointed out the inconsiderate impression expressed by this response. He was particularly concerned with the way this person uttered '*Tasukatta-yoo*' <we are relieved> (shown in {1}) and '*mateba-ii-no-ka-naa*' <do we need to wait?> (shown in {3}), especially the end of these phrases. As can be seen from the second tier of the chart, these phrases end with prolonged falling tones. It is assumed that this rater had taken the first phrase as an 'imposition', contrary to YFR's observation. The final part of the second phrase '*ka-na*' is a combination of questioning and emotive particles. As this part was pronounced with a falling tone instead of a rising one, it connotes 'directing' rather than 'asking'. He made an observation similar to that of YMR: 'this response sounded as if this informant were claiming that he is a customer'.

What this informant said in the interview is the following:

> As the problem was sorted out, I confirmed how long we needed to wait because it is most important. The manager looked young, so it's no use shouting (at her?). I don't get angry (with the manager?) about such a thing.

As I stated in Section 5.2.8, he did not have an intention to apologise for his junior's mistake and to thank the restaurant manager. On the contrary he took the offer as a matter of course and, besides that, as insufficient. Such an intention was conveyed through prosody as well.

It is interesting, however, that the way he expressed his sense of relief raised the female raters' evaluation in **politeness**. It seems that prosodic features somehow mitigated the impact of the impolite impression they received from this utterance.

6.3.3 Raters' opinions on this experimental survey

In this section I will present a summary of what the raters reported on the similarities and dissimilarities of their impressions of spoken and transcribed data.

All the raters mentioned the different impressions created by the prosodic features of the spoken responses. In this sense dissimilarity was more prominent than similarity. HMR stated as follows:

> I was surprised by the different impression of the spoken data. I think language conveys the speaker's personality, age, gender and so on. We may or may not be offended by the same phrase or expression. I think the speakers' 'image' affects our interpretation.

From this observation, we can see how comprehensive information about s (age, gender etc.) affects the interpretation of utterances. It is meaningful that he also pointed out the 'personality' of s as a factor to be taken into consideration. This implies that how polite or appropriate an illocution is also decided by our expectation of s's linguistic behaviour. Prosody does communicate some of such background information concerning s.

What HFR observed in the interview suggests that prosody can change the 'force' of an utterance:

> I have noticed many things that I was not aware of last time. Even harsh or impolite utterances sounded okay if s's consideration was communicated through the way they were uttered. I also realised what parts were or were not emphasised this time. It is easier for me to evaluate spoken responses, for they are more informative than the transcribed ones.

This statement supports the importance of spoken data in a pragmatic study. Although there were no significant differences between the two types of data sets in a general sense, inclusion of prosodic features does make a research more authentic as demonstrated here.

YMR mentioned the different tendencies he had observed in the two types of research as follows.

In the last research with transcribed responses, I tended to look at each part of an utterance. I judged 'this part looks good' or 'that part seems redundant' bit by bit. In this research I tended to recognise appropriateness of such parts in the flow of conversation and made judgements accordingly. Consequently I noticed different things this time. I got more natural impressions than I had in the last research. I think this led to my overall higher evaluation in appropriateness.

This observation is a strong piece of evidence that not only 'what is said' but also 'how it is said' contributes to the notion of **relative politeness**. Prosody can control the salience of the parts of an utterance so that its total impression can achieve social **appropriateness**.

YFR pointed out (1) the impact of the age and gender of *s* and (2) the different impressions created by different tempos as follows:

> The phrases that had looked impolite sounded less so when they were spoken by young people. The speaker's gender also affected my judgement. The expressions I had thought polite sometimes sounded too polite or less polite. Different tempos created different impressions. There were cases where I detected the speaker's consideration towards the hearer by the use of a slow tempo.

This study has been designed not only to explore the scale of **absolute politeness**, but also to examine the **appropriateness** of responses by applying the concept of **relative politeness**. I would assume **absolute politeness** mainly relates to salience of language, while **relative politeness** is composed of the comprehensive or holistic 'force' of an utterance. The comprehensive 'force' is made up of the interaction between salience and non-salience of each component. In this sense 'how an utterance is said' and 'which phrase is/is not stressed' should be included to decide how appropriate an utterance is.

I also observed in this experiment that intonation and other prosodic features had affected the scale of **absolute politeness** as well. Previous studies (e.g. Leech & Svartvik, 1975; Knowles 1987; Laver 1994) claimed that different intonations could convey different meanings. Even a simple interjection can mean different thing with a different intonation and voice quality – e.g. a young female informant's interjection *'sokka'* <I see> turned out to be an expression to communicate 'sympathy', not 'mere understanding' of *h*'s situation. This kind of information cannot be conveyed by orthographically transcribed responses.

What I could not include in this experiment is *kinesics*: this is another factor supposed to help communicate what *s* intends to say. If a video recording is made in the data collection, *s*'s appearance, facial expressions, gestures and so on can be included. This is certainly the next step in studying 'forces' of utterances in a comprehensive manner, although there will be many difficulties to overcome in carrying out such research in an ideal situation.

The strong points of spoken data in the assessment of **politeness** and **appropriateness** have thus been demonstrated. Prosody is indeed one of the key factors in the speech act performance strategy.

Notes

1 This methodology was not employed in the earlier data collection for a practical reason. I calculate it would take more than three hours if the spoken responses, instead of transcribed ones, were used. Obviously this would be too long for a rater to handle all the spoken data. The presentation of spoken data would have made the study with the raters unmanageable – it was not a practical methodology for this study of eight different speech acts with a large amount of data.

2 This publication also includes an insightful observation on 'intonation and writing', which gives a useful account for how people 'guess at' intonation patterns in the written language (Knowles, *ibid.*: 197–98).

3 He utilised *Praat 4.2* (Boersma and Weenik, 2004) for the analyses of intonation, and *Speech Analyzer 2.4* to identify vowel sounds. I will employ *Praat 4.2.0.7* in this study mainly to analyse pitch contour (intonation) and intensity (relative loudness).

4 According to Loveday, the term 'politeness' is used to cover a whole range of notions such as sincerity, demonstration of interest, warmth, deference, social recognition, etc. (Loveday, *ibid.*: 71). He included a limited range of 'politeness formulae' in the text for data collection: 'oh hello' (*aa konnichi wa*) and 'bye' (*sayonara*), with a 'thank you' (*arigato gozaimasu*) (Loveday, *ibid.*: 75).

5 Generally, the transcribed text can be shown at the bottom tier in the chart as in Culpeper (2005), but the responses of this study are too long to be input to *Praat*. In addition, there is another limitation of this experiment utilising instrumental speech analysis: there are some noises included in the chart, such as other voices or a hissing sound which some

informants produced when operating the microphone. As the fieldwork was carried out in such places as cafeterias or restaurants, these were unavoidable. I have tried to erase some of the outstanding noises from the 'intensity' and 'pitch' tiers as much as possible. Taking these weak points into consideration, I will take a holistic and practical approach in examining the data produced by *Praat*.

6   Culpeper (2005: 53) gives the following more detailed description about these two tiers:
    The first at the top is a spectrogram, representing fluctuations in air pressure. It provides indications of relative loudness (intensity) and duration. The second is a fundamental frequency graph, representing changes in pitch (fundamental frequency being expressed in Hertz) over time. It provides an indication of the intonation contour of the utterance.

7   'Creaky voice' by the use of 'creak phonation' is described as follows in Laver (1994: 194–96):
    … it [= creak phonation] provides a pulsed input of energy to the vocal tract, but the pulses occur at a very low frequency, and are usually somewhat irregularly spaced in time. … One practical way to produce creak is to pronounce the lowest pitch possible in one's range of voiced phonation, and then try to produce an even lower note. One has the impression of almost being able to hear the individual pulses, in a frequency range that is often as low as 25-50Hz. … Creak also seems to be able to occur in simultaneous combination with voicing, to give the compound phonation of **creaky voice**. … In English, termination of this sort [= termination with 'creak' or 'creaky voice'] is sometimes used for a regulative function, … with the speaker using a creaky termination as a signal of yielding the floor to the other speaker, at the end of the speaker-turn (emphasis original, annotation mine).

8   The very final part has an extraordinary low frequency, but this seems due to the noise caused by the microphone. It is not possible to separate the pitch contour of the voice from that of the noise, unfortunately.

9   I would like to mention the limitation of this experiment here again. As there were considerable noises of various kinds included in this spoken recording, the intensity and the pitch contour graphs are not precise in a strict sense. Furthermore, it was impossible to separate voice from noise in some parts.

10 As this spoken data contains another person's rather distinctive voice, I have cut off the redundant pitch contour. However, the first tier for intensity includes such superfluous sound, which is inseparable from the informant's voice.

Chapter 7

Conclusion

In order to conclude this cross-generation study of linguistic politeness strategies, I would like to present the following: (1) summary of findings; (2) retrospective evaluation of this research – a) weakness and limitations; b) strengths showing advantages over previous research; c) pointers to future research.

7.1 Summary of findings

In this research, the following findings have been confirmed.

1- General observations (for details see Section 5.1.1)
1) JHA (Japanese higher age group) achieved higher performance than JYA (Japanese younger age group) in both **politeness** and **appropriateness**. A statistically significant cross-generation difference was confirmed between JHA and JYA with regard to **politeness**, whereas this was not the case in terms of **appropriateness**. This finding proves that JHA has the higher *pragmalinguistic* competence to achieve a higher degree of **politeness**. However, that does not indicate that they have a higher *socio-pragmatic* competence: their linguistic politeness strategies resulted in *overpoliteness* in many cases[1]. JYA's performance in terms of **appropriateness** is comparable to that of JHA, in spite of its lower achievement in **politeness**.
2) JHAF achieved the highest performance in both categories. With regard to **politeness**, the rank order is (i) JHAF, (ii) JHAM, (iii) JYAF and (iv) JYAM, and that in regard to **appropriateness** is (i) JHAF, (ii) JYAF, (iii) JYAM and (iv) JHAM. These results have confirmed the traditional assumption that Japanese higher age women are the performers of sophisticated linguistic politeness strategies. While JHAF succeeded in relating **absolute politeness** to **relative politeness**, JHAM failed to do the same: they were the performers of *overpoliteness*.

3) There was a very significant correlation between **politeness** and **appropriateness** in a general sense. This finding has proven that the concepts **absolute** and **relative politeness** have a strong connection with each other.
4) No statistically significant difference was observed between higher age raters' and younger age raters' evaluations on the whole. This result indicates that there was no 'generation gap' in the rating scales of **politeness** and **appropriateness**. YFR's evaluation in general, however, was lower than the other raters' in both categories. This young female rater tended to regard linguistic features that the other raters took to be 'salient' as 'non-salient': e.g. even expressions full of honorifics were taken as 'unmarked' as long as they were formulaic and common. This tendency made her evaluations exceptional in this research.

2- Item 01 – 'offers/invitations' (for details see Section 5.2.1)
1) As for the main group classification, JHA surpassed JYA in both categories. The difference in **politeness** was confirmed as statistically significant, whereas that in **appropriateness** was not.
2) In terms of the subgroup classification, the rank order in **politeness** is (i) JHAF, (ii) JHAM, (iii) JYAF, (iv) JYAM; that in **appropriateness** is (i) JHAF, JHAM, (iii) JYAF, (iv) JYAM.

JYAM's low evaluation in both categories results from the absence/obscurity of *head acts* – this led to an impression of 'lack of consideration towards *h*'. 'Hinting' or 'indirect way of inviting' without recognisable *head acts* resulted in negative evaluation in this case. One noticeable observation in this item is that the politeness strategies employed here mostly – preserving options for *h* – belong to **negative direction**, the *constraint* of TACT, not that of GENEROSITY. This seems due to the nature of the scenario – the speech act it elicited was an invitation with a sense of 'requesting' rather than with a sense of 'offering'.

3- Item 02 – 'directives' (for details see Section 5.2.2)
1) As for the main group classification, JHA's and JYA's average scores are equal in **politeness**. JYA surpassed JHA in **appropriateness**, and the difference between the two groups is statistically significant.
2) In terms of the subgroup classification, the rank order in **politeness** is (i)

JYAF, (ii) JHAM, (iii) JHAF, (iv) JYAM; that in **appropriateness** is (i) JYAF, (ii) JYAM, (iii) JHAF, (iv) JHAM.

The high evaluation of JYAF can be attributed to their satisfying the *constraint* of TACT and to the frequent use of honorifics to show *deference* towards the teacher. JHAM informants performed both *underpoliteness* and *overpoliteness* in their responses, which resulted in the lowest evaluation in **appropriateness**. There were, however, few 'typical' formulaic expressions that contain propositional content such as 'I'm sorry to bother you, but …' or 'It's my fault that I couldn't understand some points in the lesson, but …' to '*place a low value on s's wants*'. Instead, the informants showed their modesty by the use of lexicogrammatical devices (honorifics expressing humbleness). This result also seems to stem from the scenario: making a request to a teacher may not be an issue as big as borrowing a car from a friend – it is rather a duty for a teacher to accommodate students' requests. Therefore it seems that the informants did not need to mitigate the size of imposition of the request so much by managing the propositional content of their remarks. This seems to be a case where the concepts of 'rights' and 'obligations' took a role, viz. in a teaching situation, students have certain expectations regarding their rights and teachers' obligations.

4- Item 03 – 'compliments' (for details see Section 5.2.3)
1) As for the main group classification, JHA surpassed JYA in **politeness**, while JYA's performance was better than JHA's in **appropriateness**. The difference in **politeness** was confirmed to be statistically significant, whereas that in **appropriateness** was not.
2) In terms of the sub-group classification, the rank order in **politeness** is (i) JHAM, (ii) JHAF, (iii) JYAF, JYAM; that in **appropriateness** is (i) JHAF, (ii) JYAM, (iii) JYAF, (iv) JHAM.

There was a conspicuous discrepancy between **absolute** and **relative politeness** in this item. One JHAM informant performed *overpoliteness* again here. But in JYAF's case, the levels of **appropriateness** of their responses were judged considerably highly, although their degrees of **politeness** were evaluated rather low. One JYAF informant used a *camaraderie* strategy and this is thought to have caused such a discrepancy in the two types of politeness scale.

Also, disregard of the *constraint*, '*place a high value on o's qualities*' led to low evaluations especially in terms of **absolute politeness**, but it is worth noting that the use of mere 'congratulations' or strategies for *camaraderie* were judged 'good enough' for **appropriateness**. This seems due to the closeness between the interlocutors (i.e. *s* and *h*) and the lack of information in the scenario on what honour *h* obtained in his achievement.

<u>5- Item 04 – 'self-evaluation (self-depreciation)' (for details see Section 5.2.4)</u>
1) As for the main group classification, JHA's performance was better than that of JYA in both categories. The difference in **politeness** is statistically significant, while that in **appropriateness** is not.
2) In terms of the subgroup classification, the rank order in **politeness** is (i) JHAF, (ii) JHAM, (iii) JYAM, (iv) JYAF; and that in **appropriateness** is (i) JHAM, (ii) JYAM, (iii) JHAF, (iv) JYAF.

One JHAF informant performed *overpoliteness* here this time, and the other disregarded the *constraint*, '*place a low value on s's qualities*', and made an indirect request for more compliments. These led to JHAF's lower rank in **appropriateness**. On the other hand, JHAM obtained the highest rank in **appropriateness** by expressing 'honest gratitude for *h*'s compliment' and using a 'counter-compliment' strategy (thanking *h*'s compliment), although they did not show 'self-depreciation' clearly in the propositional content of their utterances. One JYAF informant made a very unique 'impolite' response, and it was evaluated accordingly in both categories. One JYAM's response, although evaluated low in **politeness**, was judged highly in **appropriateness**, in contrast with the JYAF's. This is because he was successful in expressing his good intention and thanks to the use of sufficient number of honorifics – these covered up the negative impression of the colloquial expressions in **politeness**.

Furthermore, as a general tendency, it is confirmed that strategies for both **negative direction** (i.e. 'self-depreciation') and **positive direction** (i.e. 'thanking' and 'expressing *s*'s pleasure') are employed in this item. This contradicts the previous common assumption that **negative direction** strategies are usually preferred, if not obligatory, in Japanese in responses to a compliment.

<u>6- Item 05 – 'agreeing / disagreeing with mitigation' (for details see Section 5.2.5)</u>

1) As for the main group classification, JHA's and JYA's average scores were equal in **politeness**. JHA's performance was better than JYA's in **appropriateness**. There were no statistically significant differences.
2) In terms of the subgroup classification, the rank order in **politeness** is (i) JYAF, (ii) JHAF, JHAM, (iv) JYAM; that in **appropriateness** is (i) JYAF, (ii) JHAF, (iii) JHAM, (iv) JYAM.

JYAF informants accomplished the highest performance in both categories by 'hiding their true opinions about the topic'. They prioritised consideration towards the old lady over their sincere views on the Japanese Prime Minister. On the contrary, JYAM informants received the lowest average scores in both categories for (i) showing too much friendliness towards the old lady, and (ii) giving an abrupt impression by making a minimal response 'Ah, yes'. In assessment, male and female raters had somewhat different tendencies here: (i) seemingly due to the gender difference in the recognition of the social role of 'an old lady' – female raters required more 'respect' from informants than male ones, and (ii) male raters prioritised lexicogrammatical features over propositional content while female ones did the opposite in the scale of **absolute politeness**.

Affirmative expressions turned out to be the key formula to perform 'agreeing/disagreeing with mitigation' in this context. This corresponds to the *constraint* of AGREEMENT, *'place a high value on o's opinions'*. It should also be noted that young female informants showed a more sympathetic attitude towards the old lady than the rest of the groups, which was not the case in the previous item (conversation with a senior male student).

7- Item 06 – 'expressing feelings' (for details see Section 5.2.6)
1) As for the main group classification, JHA exceeded JYA in both categories. Statistically significant differences were confirmed in both.
2) In terms of the sub-group classification, the rank order in **politeness** is (i) JHAF, (ii) JHAM, (iii) JYAM, (iv) JYAF; that in **appropriateness** is (i) JHAM, (ii) JHAF, (iii) JYAF, (iv) JYAM.

JHAF obtained the highest rank in **politeness**, showing formality by the use of honorifics, which are usually regarded as unnecessary when speaking with a female junior under normal circumstances. JHAM was ranked highest in **appropriateness** for (i) showing enough consideration towards *h* and (ii) using all three kinds of *head acts* for the speech act(s) of this item. On the contrary, one JYA informant's 'casual' linguistic attitude and the other's 'inconsiderate' impression in her response led to the group's low evaluation in both categories.

In a general sense 'formality/seriousness' controlled the scale of **politeness** and the *constraint* for SYMPATHY functioned to control the degree of **appropriateness**. A further survey revealed that JHAF used 'politeness markers' most frequently – in all their responses (100%), whereas JYAF used them least often (30%). This sharp contrast suggests that these two groups of the same gender have different attitudes towards a female *kohai* in a serious situation. The former treat her with 'formality' and 'seriousness', whereas the latter do so with 'friendliness' and 'warmth'.

Moreover, it is confirmed that the main two alternative strategies to the *head acts* are [telling *h* not to worry] and [urging *h* to go to the hospital]. This implies that informants had several different factors to attend to in what *h* said in her report of her brother's serious condition.

<u>8- Item 07 – 'response to thanks and apologies' (for details see Section 5.2.7)</u>
1) As for the main group classification, JHA exceeded JYA in both categories. There were not statistically significant differences in either of the categories.
2) In terms of the subgroup classification, the rank order in **politeness** is (i) JHAM, (ii) JHAF, (iii) JYAM, (iv) JYAF; that in **appropriateness** is (i) JHAF, (ii) JYAM, (iii) JHAM, (iv) JYAF.

JHAM achieved the highest performance in **politeness** for the use of formal expressions, but they were ranked third in **appropriateness** for the 'cold' and 'inconsiderate' impressions given by their utterances. In contrast JHAF obtained the first place in **appropriateness** by 'giving optimistic prospect to *h*' and 'making a suggestion to sort this problem out'. JYAF was ranked at the bottom because one of the informants showed 'lack of consideration' by expressing her 'irritated emotion' and the other made a very 'informal' response with colloquial expressions and interjections despite her good intention to soothe the younger male *kohai*.

In a further survey, I found several informants that performed '(mitigated) accusation' instead of concealing their true emotion. In addition, JHAM turned out to be 'most generous' about the male *kohai*'s blunder.

As for the *head acts* to satisfy the *constraint* for OBLIGATION (of *h* to *s*), it turned out that there were no stereotypical *semantic formulae* – showing consideration in 'suppressing *s*'s strong feeling' and 'forgiving *h*'s fault' takes various forms.

9- Item 08 – 'apology, thanks' (for details see Section 5.2.8)
1) As for the main group classification, JYA's performance surpassed JHA's in both categories. Whereas no statistically significant difference was found in **politeness**, that in **appropriateness** was proven statistically significant.
2) In terms of the subgroup classification, the rank order in **politeness** is: (i) JHAF, (ii) JYAF, (iii) JYAM, (iv) JHAM; that in **appropriateness** is: (i) JYAF, (ii) JHAF, JYAM, (iv) JHAM.

JHAM's low performance in both categories can be attributed to the very inconsiderate impression of a response full of informal expressions, produced by one informant of this group. He entirely failed to perform 'apology' or 'thanks', which satisfy the *constraint* of OBLIGATION (of *s* to *h*). He actually made an indirect request to make the restaurant manager hurry to accommodate his group. JHAF, on the other hand, obtained the first position in the rank in terms of **politeness** for the sufficient use of formal forms and for the proper propositional content of their utterances with *head acts* (thanking). JYAF was ranked first in **appropriateness** with a perfect performance in this category. Both two JYAF informants showed sufficient 'consideration towards *h*' by including either one of two types of *head acts* (i.e. 'apologising' or 'thanking'). It is worth noting that the use of either one *head act* is enough to show *s*'s consideration in this case – the two JYAF informants used just one strategy each. This means that evaluation of **appropriateness** depends on the holistic impression of the utterance, rather than a single outstanding factor.

A further survey revealed that the Japanese formulaic expression in requesting '*yoroshiku o-negaishi-masu*' [*lit.* I leave it entirely on you] and its equivalents can be included in the *semantic formulae* for the speech act(s) performance in this context (to respond to an offer from *h*).

Furthermore, whereas 'apologising' and 'thanking' served as the core parts in the majority of the responses, there were some other speech acts that served as 'alternative strategies': 'polite/modest request', 'simple query for the preparation time' and 'strong request for the immediate preparation'. Again, here, there were several different situational factors that informants needed to attend to.

10- Further survey with spoken data (for details see Chapter 6)
1) In general it was confirmed that orthographic data is comparable to spoken data;
2) However, there were three responses with outstanding differences in the ratings between the two different types of data;
3) Therefore it is desirable to include prosody (and kinesics if possible) in future pragmatic studies.

The comparability of orthographic and spoken data in a pragmatic study has been confirmed. This evidence justifies its use as a practical and efficient research resource in this study. Notwithstanding, as can be seen in the discussions in Chapter 6, it is desirable to include prosody in future pragmatic studies, as prosodic features can create a different 'force' in an utterance and can give a different impression. In this study two responses received significantly higher evaluation in **appropriateness** and one did so in **politeness** – all of them had been 'low evaluation' responses in the previous research. This suggests that prosody can be employed to express s's good intention and to mitigate the impact of informality or plainness of the lexicogrammatical features or the propositional content. Still, carrying out research in an ideal situation is not an easy task: further piloting is necessary to invent a practical way to collect authentic data for such pragmatic studies.

7.2 Retrospective evaluation of this research

In this section I will indicate 'weaknesses and limitations', 'strengths and advantages over previous research' and 'pointers to future research' in retrospective evaluation of this study.

7.2.1 Weaknesses and limitations
I would like to point out (1) the limited number of informants, (2) the limited number of raters, (3) the less-than-optimal design of the scenarios, and (4) the limited amount of data used in actual research, as the weaknesses and limitations

of this study.

As for the first and the second weaknesses, they were caused mainly by the research design which had been directed towards more 'descriptive' and 'qualitative' study of speech act performance. This study of linguistic politeness strategies employed a 'spoken DCT with video prompts' and 'in-depth guided interviews' as the main methodologies to collect data to study about eight different speech acts. Obtaining spoken data, which is more 'authentic' than the orthographic type – as discussed in Section 4.3.3.4, required more time for data collection. In the first-stage informants were requested to (1) read the scenario, (2) watch the video prompt, (3) make a response, (4) go over their first responses and think of second ones, and (5) talk about the background of the responses. In the second stage the raters (1) read the scenario, (2) watched the video prompt, (3) read the selected responses (4) evaluated them using **politeness** and **appropriateness** scales, and (5) talked about the background of their evaluation. Consequently I needed more than one hour in one research session. I needed to see the informants and the raters one by one, as it was impossible to complete these procedures on a mass scale at the same time – operating the recording equipments and VCR was crucial in this study and it was necessary for the researcher himself to manipulate them. The interview also necessitated the researcher's presence: the focus points of the interview depended on what the informant said in his/her response. In the limited time framework of the PhD work, I needed to set a practical and reasonable plan with rather limited numbers of informants and raters, which would enable me to complete this study in reasonable time.

Turning to the third weakness, it has turned out that some scenarios could not elicit the core parts of the designated speech acts, which are supposed to satisfy the *constraints*. Although carefully designed, those scenarios perhaps inevitably included other factors that elicited other speech acts or excluded the factors needed to elicit the designated ones. This is a weakness and a strong point at the same time, though – the strong points will be discussed in the following section.

Furthermore, in terms of the last limitation, it was not possible to include all the responses in this thesis to discuss other interesting and noteworthy observations. While the data is collected from no more than twenty-four informants, the number of responses amounted to as many as 301. As I mentioned in Section 4.3, it was inevitable to choose responses to make the data for the second-stage research manageable. Further discussions on other observations will be presented in my future publications.

7.2.2 Strengths and advantages over previous research

I would like to point out (1) the spoken DCT methodology, (2) the video prompts, (3) the scenarios that elicited open-ended responses, and (4) the employment of two politeness scales, as strengths of this study.

Firstly, 'a spoken DCT' was proven to be a very effective tool for a pragmatic politeness study. As discussed in Section 4.3.4 and 4.3.5, it succeeded in gathering more 'authentic' spoken data in mock conversations with the video performers. The verbal responses then enabled me to carry out a further research with selected spoken responses as presented in Chapter 6. This new research has revealed the value of including prosody, in order to investigate the holistic 'force' of an utterance.

Secondly, 'video prompts' succeeded in eliciting natural responses from the informants. The performer in the video helped an informant have a real-life image of the person s/he was speaking to. Most of the informants told me that the video had helped them understand the situations and who the addressees had been. 'Video prompts' were effective in (i) giving more information of the situations than written descriptions, (ii) giving informants a cue to make a response, (iii) allowing them to 'interact' with the video performers and to extend their responses to a discourse level. Although this method has its own weak points (e.g. the performers are not available in real time so informants cannot interact with them in a true sense), it is a step ahead of a traditional DCT and has turned out to be a very useful tool for an in-depth pragmatic study.

Thirdly, the fact that the scenarios elicited many different types of responses with different lengths demonstrates that the responses obtained in this study are more authentic than the ones elicited by the previous written DCTs. In a real-life situation there are so many factors to attend to and there are various ways to realise s's intentions: the same situation can cause different reactions from different people. The scenarios used in this study, which contain various factors to attend to, succeeded in drawing such 'natural verbal reactions' from the informants. The fact that there was no problem in evaluating all the selected responses with the two politeness scales suggests that linguistic politeness strategies can be measured not only by examining the 'core part' but also by the 'total impression' created by *supportive moves*, *head acts*, etc.

Finally, the two types of politeness scales, viz. **absolute politeness** and **relative politeness**, were very powerful tools to investigate the 'illocutionary force' of an utterance from the linguistic side and from the socio-psychological side. These two concepts allow us to learn how two elements, viz. linguistic politeness and its social appropriateness, associate with and dissociate from each other. One can say 'this utterance is polite because of its linguistic features' looking at one sentence in isolation from the context, but one cannot tell if it can make an appropriate impression in a certain context. This study examined the relation between these two concepts well, as presented in the previous two chapters, employing the scales of **politeness** and **appropriateness**.

7.2.3 Pointers to future research

As a final comment on this study, I would like to suggest three 'pointers' to future pragmatic politeness studies.

Firstly, an extended cross-cultural study between these Japanese informants and informants from different countries will reveal more about the 'generation gap' in linguistic politeness strategies. This study with Japanese informants had started as a cross-cultural study with British informants as mentioned earlier, but because of some technical difficulties in data collection in the U.K., the original plan had to be cancelled, which is to my great regret. The part of the original research is presented in Suzuki (2004) utilising the data obtained in the pilot study. I would like to investigate the way in which I can pursue a similar comparative study in the near future.

Secondly, this rather qualitatively-oriented study could be extended to a mass-scale one with the aid of computer technology: if the research session could be carried out in a computer lab with quite a few PCs, it would allow a large number of informants to look at the video prompts and record their responses at the same time (headphones and microphones are also necessary). They could also record their explanations of the backgrounds of their responses using the microphone. This method could be applied to the second-stage data collection with the raters as well. Still, I assume that various kinds of technical difficulties should be overcome before realising this mass-scale research, e.g. separating informants/raters so that one informant's voice is recorded separate from others'; and finding suitable recording devices for the PCs.

Finally, I would like to point out the importance of studying 'speech act realisation patterns' with the scale of **appropriateness**. The CCSARP, carried out by Blum-Kulka *et al.* in 1989, was an innovative project that studied speech act performance patterns thoroughly. But it is difficult to know what patterns are successful in representing *s*'s intention by looking at the results there. On the other hand there are some tendencies among recent researchers to study the appropriateness of an utterance by exploring motivational and situational factors, without looking at linguistic features. This paradigm is again insufficient for the elucidation of the relation between language and *rapport management*. I postulate that in future research on pragmatic politeness, 'illocutionary force' should be studied from two sides, viz. from the *pragmalinguistic* side and from the *socio-pragmatic* side. Studies making use of these notions will enable researchers to explore the factors for politeness and appropriateness together, rather than separately (as in previous studies). I will attempt to carry out a further survey of linguistic politeness using these two concepts, which I have found to be of crucial importance in this study, to investigate the 'force' of an utterance in a given context.

Notes

1   While saying this, I would like to suggest that *overpoliteness* is a 'safe strategy' in *rapport management*, for it does not cause any friction between interlocutors under normal circumstances. In this sense the scale of **appropriateness** has its own limitation. An utterance which is rated as 'inappropriate' with a high degree of **politeness** should still be recognised as a *rapport-enhancing* or *rapport-maintaining* one. In this sense, the 'inappropriateness' caused by *overpoliteness* differs from that by *underpoliteness*. *Underpoliteness* is certainly a 'threat' to social equilibrium.

Bibliography

Agha, A. (1994). "Honorification". *Annual Review of Anthropology* 23: 277–302.

Aijmer, K. (1996). *Conversational Routines in English: Convention and Creativity*. London; New York: Longman.

Arndt, H. & Janney, R. (1985). "Improving emotive communication: verbal, prosodic, and kinesic conflict avoidance techniques". *Per Linguam* 1: 21–33.

——— (1987). *InterGrammar: Toward an Integrative Model of Verbal, Prosodic and Kinesic Choices in Speech*. Berlin: Mouton de Gruyter.

Asher, N. (ed.) (1994). *Encyclopedia of Language and Linguistics*. Oxford; New York: Pergamon Press.

Austin, J.L. (1962). *How to Do Things with Words*. Oxford: Clarendon.

Bach, K. & Harnish, R.M. (1979). *Linguistic Communication and Speech Acts*. Cambridge, MA: MIT Press.

Bardovi-Harlig, K. & Dornyei, Z. (1998). "Do language learners recognize pragmatic violations? pragmatic versus grammatical awareness in instructed L2 learning". *TESOL Quarterly* 32(2): 233–262.

Bardovi-Harlig, K. & Hartford, B.S. (1993). "Refining the DCT: comparing open questionnaires and dialogue completion tasks". In Bouton, L.F. & Kachru, Y. (eds.): 143–165.

Beebe, L.M. & Cummings, M.C. (1996). "Natural speech act data versus written questionnaire data: how data collection method affects speech act performance". In Gass, S.M. & Neu, J. (eds.): 65–86.

Beebe, L.M., Takahashi, T. & Uliss-Weltz, R. (1990). "Pragmatic transfer in ESL refusals". In Scarcella, R., Andersen, E. & Krashen, S. (eds.): 55–73.

Benedict, R. (1946). *The Chrysanthemum and the Sword: Patterns of Japanese Culture*. Boston: Houghton Mifflin.

Blum-Kulka, S. (1987). "Indirectness and politeness in requests: same or different?". *Journal of Pragmatics* 11(1): 131-146.

——— (1989). "Playing it safe: The role of conventionality in indirectness". In Blum-Kulka, S., House, J. & Kasper, G. (eds.): 37–70.

——— (1992). "You don't touch lettuce with your fingers: parental politeness in family discourse". *Journal of Pragmatics* 14: 259–288.

Blum-Kulka, S. & House, J. (1989). "Cross-cultural and situational variation in requesting behavior". In Blum-Kulka, S., House, J. & Kasper, G. (eds.): 123–154.

Blum-Kulka, S., House, J. & Kasper, G. (eds.) (1989a). *Cross-Cultural Pragmatics: Requests and Apologies*. Norwood, NJ: Ablex.

——— (1989b). "Investigating cross-cultural pragmatics: an introductory overview". In Blum-

Kulka, S., House, J. & Kasper, G. (eds.): 1–34.

Boersma, P. & Weenik, D. (2004). *Praat: Doing Phonetics by Computer*. www.praat.org

Bond, M.H., Žegarac, V. & Spencer-Oatey, H. (2000). "Culture as an explanatory variable: Problems and possibilities". In Spencer-Oatey, H. (ed.): 47–71.

Bouton, L.F. & Kachru, Y. (eds.) (1992). *Pragmatics and Language Learning, Monograph Series, Vol.3*. Urbana, IL: Division of English as an International Language, University of Illinois at Urbana-Champaign.

——— (1993). *Pragmatics and Language Learning, Monograph Series, Vol.4*. Urbana, IL: Division of English as an International Language, University of Illinois at Urbana-Champaign.

Brown, P. & Fraser, C. (1979). "Speech as a marker of situation". In Scherer, K. & Giles, H. (eds.): 33–62.

Brown, P. & Levinson, S.C. (1978). "Universals in language usage: politeness phenomena". In E.N. Goody (ed.): 56–289.

——— (1987). *Politeness: Some universals in language usage*. Cambridge: Cambridge University Press.

Byon, A.S. (2004). "Sociopragmatic analysis of Korean requests: pedagogical settings". *Journal of Pragmatics* 36: 1673–1704.

Chambers, J. (1992). "Linguistic correlates of gender and sex". *English World-Wide* 13, 2: 173–218.

Christie, C. (2000). *Gender and Language*. Edinburgh: Edinburgh University Press.

Chen, R. (1993). "Responding to compliments: a contrastive study of politeness strategies between American English and Chinese speakers". *Journal of Pragmatics* 20: 49–75.

Cole, P. & Morgan, J.L. (eds.) (1975). *Syntax and semantics 3: Speech acts*. New York: Academic Press.

Collinge, N.E. (ed.) (1990). *An Encyclopaedia of Language*. London: Routledge.

Comrie, B. (1976). "Linguistic politeness axes: speaker-addressee, speaker-referent, speaker-bystander". *Pragmatic Microfiche* 1–7. Department of Linguistics, University of Cambridge.

Coulmas, F. (ed.) (1981a). *Conversational Routine: Explorations in Standardized Communication Situations and Prepatterned Speech*. The Hague: Mouton Publishers.

——— (1981b). "Introduction: conversational routine"; In Coulmas, F. (ed.): 1–18.

——— (1981c). "Poison to your soul. Thanks and apologies contrastively viewed". In Coulmas, F. (ed.): 69–91.

——— (1992). "Linguistic etiquette in Japanese society". In Watts, J., Ide, S. & Ehlich, K. (eds.): 299–323.

——— (1994). "Formulaic language". In Asher, N. (ed.) Vol.3: 1292–1293.

Culpeper, J. (1996). "Towards an anatomy of impoliteness". *Journal of Pragmatics* 25: 349–367.

——— (1998). "(Im)politeness in drama". In Culpeper, J, Short, M. & Verdonk, P. (eds.): 83–95.

——— (2005). "Impoliteness and entertainment in the television quiz show: The Weakest Link" Journal of Politeness Research 1: 35–72.

Culpeper, J., Bousfield, D. and Wichmann, A. (2003). Impoliteness revisited: with special

reference to dynamic and prosodic aspects. *Journal and Pragmatics* 35: 1545–1579.
Culpeper, J., Short, M. & Verdonk, P. (eds.) (1998). *Studying Drama: From Text to Context*. London: Routledge.
Daly, N., Holmes, J., Newton, J. & Stubbe, M. (2004). "Expletives as solidarity signals in FTAs on the factory floor". *Journal of Pragmatics* 36: 945–964.
de Kadt, E. (1998). "The concept of face and its applicability to the Zulu language". *Journal of Pragmatics* 29: 173–191.
Drew, P. & Heritage, J. (eds.), (1992). *Talk at Work*. Cambridge: Cambridge University Press.
Edmondson, W.J. (1981). "On saying you're sorry". In Coulmas, F. (ed.): 273–287.
Eelen, G. (2001). *A critique of politeness theories*. Manchester: St. Jerome.
Eisenstein, M. & J.W. Bodman (1993). "'I very appreciate': expressions of gratitude by native and non-native speakers of American English". *Applied Linguistics* 7(2): 167–85.
Faerch, C. & Kasper, G. (1989). "Internal and external modification in interlanguage request realization". In Blum-Kulka, S., House, J. & Kasper, G. (eds.):221–247.
Ferguson, C.A. (1981). "The structure and use of politeness formulas". In Coulmas, F. (ed.): 21–35.
Ferrara, A. (1980a). "An extended theory of speech acts: appropriateness conditions for subordinate acts in sequences". *Journal of Pragmatics* 4: 233–252.
────── (1980b). "Appropriateness conditions for entire sequences of speech acts". *Journal of Pragmatics* 4: 321–340.
Fraser, B. (1981). "On apologizing". In Coulmas, F. (ed.): 259–273.
────── (1990). "Perspective on politeness". *Journal of Pragmatics* 14: 219–236.
Fraser, B. & Nolen, W. (1981). "The association of deference with linguistic form". *International Journal of the Sociology of Language* 27: 93–109.
Fukuda, A. & Asato, N. (1997). "The notion of politeness revisited". *Paper read at the Eleventh Annual International Conference on Pragmatics and Language Learning*. University of Illinois at Urbana-Champaign.
────── (2004). "Universal politeness theory: application to the use of Japanese honorifics". *Journal of Pragmatics* 36: 1991–2002.
Fukushima, S. (2000). *Requests and Culture: Politeness in British English and Japanese*. Bern: Peter Lang.
Gass, S.M. & Neu, J. (eds.) (1996). *Speech Acts across Cultures*. Berlin: Mouton de Gruyter.
Geis, M.L. (1995). *Speech Acts and Conversational Interaction – Toward a Theory of Conversational Competence*. Cambridge: Cambridge University Press.
Girke, W. (ed.) (1996). *Slavische Linguistik* 1995, Munich: Böhlan Verlag.
Goffman, E. (1967). *Interactional Ritual: Essays on Face-to-Face Behavior*. New York: Anchor Book.
Goody, E. (ed.) (1978). *Questions and Politeness: Strategies in Social Interaction*. Cambridge: Cambridge University Press.

Grice, H.P. (1975). "Logic and conversation". In Cole, P. & Morgan, J.L. (eds.): 41–58.
Gu, Y. (1990). "Politeness phenomena in modern Chinese". *Journal of Pragmatics* 14: 237–257.
Gudykunst, W.B. (2000). "Methodological issues in conducting theory-based cross-cultural research". In Spencer-Oatey, H. (ed.): 293–315.
Haig, J.H. (1991). "A phonological difference in male-female speech among teenagers in Nagoya". In Ide, S. & McGloin, N.H. (eds.): 5–22.
Hartford, B.S. & Bardovi-Harlig, K. (1992). "Experimental and observational data in the study of interlanguage pragmatics". In Bouton, L.F. & Kachru, Y. (eds.): 33–52.
Hashimoto, G. (ed.) (2003). *Shin Nihongo-no Genba*. Tokyo: Chuo Kouron Shinsha.
Hayashi, S. & F. Minami (eds.) (1974). *Keigo kooza 8: Sekai no keigo*. Tokyo: Meiji shoin.
Hill, B., Ide, S., Ikuta, S., Kawasaki, A. & Ogino, T., (1986). "Universals of linguistic politeness: quantitative evidence from Japanese and American English". *Journal of Pragmatics* 10: 347–371.
Holmes, J. (1995). *Women, Men and Politeness*. London: Longman.
House, J. (1989). "Politeness in English and German: the functions of *please* and *bitte*". In Blum-Kulka, S., House, J. & Kasper, G. (eds.): 96–119.
House, J. & Kasper, G. (1981). "Politeness markers in English and German". In Coulmas, F. (ed.): 157–185.
Hymes, D. (ed.) (1964). *Language in Culture and Society*. New York: Harper and Row.
Ide, R. (1998). "'Sorry for your kindness': Japanese interactional ritual in public discourse". *Journal of Pragmatics* 29: 509–529.
Ide, S. (1982). "Japanese sociolinguistics: politeness and women's language". *Lingua* 57: 357–385.
——— (1989). "Formal forms and discernment: Two neglected aspects of universals of linguistic politeness". *Multiliugua* 8-2/3: 223–248.
——— (1991a). "Person references of Japanese and American children". In Ide, S. & McGloin, N.H. (eds.): 43–61.
——— (1991b). "How and why do women speak more politely in Japanese?". In Ide, S. & McGloin, N.H. (eds.): 63–79.
Ide, S., Hill, B., Carnes, Y.M., Ogino, T. & Kawasaki, A. (1992). "The concept of politeness: an empirical study of American English and Japanese". In Watts, R., Ide, S. & Elich, K. (eds.): 281–297.
Ide, S. & McGloin, N.H. (eds.) (1991). *Aspects of Japanese Women's Language*. Tokyo: Kurosio Publishers.
Ikeda, R. (1993). "Shazai no taishoukenkyu – Nichibei taishoukenkyuu – face to iu shiten kara (Contrastive study of apologies – contrastive study of Japanese and American – observations from the viewpoint of face)". *Nihongogaku* 12: 7–34.
Iwamoto, M. (1998). "Young people's perceptions of honorific usage in Japanese: with case studies of Japanese students in Japan and UK". Unpublished PhD thesis. Lancaster University.
Janney, R.W. & Arndt, H. (1992). "Intracultural tact versus intercultural tact" in Watts, R., Ide, S.

& Ehlich, K. (eds.): 281–97.

——— (1993). "Universality and relativity in cross-cultural politeness research: a historical perspective". *Multilingua* 12: 7–34.

Jary, M. (1998). "Relevance theory and the communication of politeness". *Journal of Pragmatics* 30: 1–19.

Ji, S. (2000). "'Face' and polite verbal behaviours in Chinese culture". *Journal of Pragmatics* 32: 1059–1062.

Johansen, J.D. & Sonne, H. (eds.) (1986). *Pragmatics and Linguistics: Festschrift for Jacob Mey:* 103–114. Odense: Odense University Press.

Johnstone, B., Ferrara, K. & Bean, J.M. (1992). "Gender, politeness, and discourse management in same-sex and cross-sex opinion-poll interviews". *Journal of Pragmatics* 18: 405–430.

Jorden, H.H. (1991). "Overview". In Ide, S. & McGloin, N.H. (eds.): 1–4.

Kamiya, T. (1997). *Japanese particle workbook*. New York & Tokyo: Weatherhill.

Kasher, A. (1986). "Politeness and rationality". In Johansen, J.D. and H. Sonne (eds.): 103–114.

Kasper, G. (1990). "Linguistic politeness: Current research issues". *Journal of Pragmatics* 14: 193–218.

——— (ed.) (1992). *Pragmatics of Japanese as Native and Target Language: Technical Report No.3.* Honolulu: Second Language Teaching and Curriculum Center, University of Hawaii at Manoa.

——— (ed.) (1995). *Pragmatics of Chinese as Native and Target Language: Technical Report No.5.* Honolulu: University of Hawaii, Second Language Teaching and Curriculum Center.

——— (1996). "Politeness". In Verschueren, J., Östman, J.-O., Blommaert, J. & Bulcaen, C. (eds.)

——— (2000). "Data Collection in Pragmatics Research". In Spencer-Oatey (ed.): 293–315.

Kasper, G. & Blum-Kulka, S. (eds.) (1993). *Interlanguage Pragmatics*. Oxford: Oxford University Press.

Kasper, G. & Dahl, M. (1991). "Research methods in interlanguage pragmatics". *Studies in Second Language Acquisition* 13: 215–247.

Kasper, G. & Rose, K.R. (1999). "Pragmatics and SLA". *Annual Review of Applied Linguistics* 19: 81–104.

Kellar, E. (1981). "Gambits. Conversational strategy signals". In Coulmas, F. (ed.): 93–113.

Kerbrat-Orecchioni, C. (1997). "A multilevel approach in the study of talk-in-interaction". *Pragmatics* 7(1): 1–20.

Kim, M.S. (1992). *Cross-cultural variations in implicit theories of requesting behavior*. Unpublished doctoral dissertation, Department of Communication, Michigan State University.

——— (1993). "Culture-based conversational constraints in explaining cross-cultural strategic competence". In Wiseman, R.L. & Koester, J. (eds.): 132–150.

——— (1994). "Cross-cultural comparisons of the perceived importance of conversational constraints". *Human Communication Research* 21: 128–151.

Kim, M., Sharkey, W.F., & Singelis, T.M. (1994). "The relationship between individual's self-construals and perceived importance of interactive constraints". *International Journal of*

Intercultural Relations 18(1): 117–140.

Knowles, G. (1987). *Patterns of Spoken English: An Introduction to English Phonetics.* London: Longman.

Koike, D.A. (1996). "Transfer of pragmatic competence and suggestions in Spanish foreign language learning". In Gass, S.M. & Neu, J. (eds.): 257–281.

Kotthoff, H. (2000). "Gender and joking: On the complexities of women's image politics in humorous narratives". *Journal of Pragmatics* 32: 55–80.

Koutlaki, S.A. (2002). "Offers and expressions of thanks as face enhancing acts: tæ'arof in Persian". *Journal of Pragmatics* 34: 1733–1756.

Kreuz, R.J., Kassler, M.A., Coppenrath, L. & McLain Allen, B. (1999). "Tag questions and common ground effects in the perception of verbal irony". *Journal of Pragmatics* 31: 1685–1700.

Lachenicht, L.G. (1980). "Aggravating language: a study of abusive and insulting language". *Papers in Linguistics* 13: 607–687.

Lakoff, R. (1973). "The logic of politeness; or minding your p's and q's". *Papers from the Ninth Regional Meeting of the Chicago Linguistic Society*: 292–305.

——— (1975). *Language and women's place.* New York: Harper and Row.

——— (1979). "Stylistic strategies within a grammar of style". *The Annals of the New York Academy of Science*: 53–78.

——— (1990). *Talking Power.* New York: Basic Books.

Laver, J. (1994). *Principles of phonetics.* Cambridge: Cambridge University Press.

Lee-Wong, S.-M. (1999). *Politeness and Face in Chinese Culture.* Frankfurt: Peter Lang.

Leech, G.N. (1983). *Principles of pragmatics.* London: Longman.

——— (2001). "Language, culture and politeness". (paper presented at the 2nd International Humanities Conference) *Horizons of the humanities: Thoughts & critical theories of the future*: 107–129. Pusan, South Korea: The Institute of Humanities Research.

——— (2003). "Towards an anatomy of politeness in communication". *International Journal of Pragmatics 14*: 101–123. Tokyo, Japan: Pragmatics Association of Japan.

Leech, G.N. & Svartvik, J. (1975). *A Communicative Grammar of English.* London: Longman.

Leech, G. & Thomas, J. (1990). "Language, meaning and context: pragmatics". In Collinge, N.E. (ed.): 173–206.

Levinson, S.C. (1979). "Activity types and language". *Linguistics* 17(5/6): 365–399.

——— (1983). *Pragmatics.* Cambridge: Cambridge University Press.

——— (1992). "Activity types and Language". In Drew, P. & Heritage, J. (eds.): 66–100.

Lewis, D. (1969). *Convention: a philosophical study.* Cambridge, MA: Harvard University Press.

Locke, J.S. (1872). *Ladies' Book of Etiquette and Manual of Politeness.* Boston.

Loveday, L. (1981). "Pitch, politeness and sexual role: an exploratory investigation into the pitch correlates of English and Japanese politeness formulae". *Language and Speech* Vol. 24, Part 1, 71–89.

Macaulay, M. (2001). "Tough talk: indirectness and gender in requests for information". *Journal of Pragmatics* 33: 293–316.

Makino, S. (1970). "Two proposals about Japanese polite expressions". In Sadock, J. & Vanek, A.L. (eds.): 163–187.

——— (1991). "Some indication of sex differences in empathy in written Japanese discourse". In Ide, S. & McGloin, N.H. (eds.): 105–116.

Manes, J. & Wolfson, N. (1981). "The compliment formula". In Coulmas, F. (ed.): 115–131.

Mao, L.M.R. (1994). "Beyond politeness theory: 'face' revisited and renewed". *Journal of Pragmatics* 21: 451–486.

Martin, S. (1964). "Speech levels in Japan and Korea". In Hymes, D. (ed.): 407–415.

Matsumoto, Y. (1985). "A sort of speech act qualification in Japanese: chotto". *Journal of Asian Culture* 9: 143–159.

——— (1987). "Politeness and conversational universals – observations from Japanese". Paper presented at the 1987 International Pragmatics Conference. Antwarp, Belgium.

——— (1988). "Reexamination of the universality of face: politeness phenomena in Japanese". *Journal of Pragmatics* 12: 403–426.

——— (1989). "Politeness and conversational universals – observations from Japanese". *Multilingua* 8-2/3: 207–221.

McGloin, N.H. (1991). "Sex difference and sentence-final particles". In Ide, S. & McGloin, N.H. (eds.): 23–41.

Meier, A.J. (1995). "Passage of politeness". *Journal of Pragmatics* 24: 381–392.

Miller, R.A. (1967). *The Japanese Language*. Chicago, IL: Chicago University Press.

Miyake. Y. (1996). "Women and the deferential particle *o* in Japanese". In Warner, N., Ashlers, J., Bilmes, L., Oliver, M., Wertheim, S. & Chen, M. (eds.): 533–542.

Mizutani, O. & Mizutani, N. (1987). *How to Be Polite in Japanese*. Tokyo: The Japan Times.

Mochizuki, M. (1980). "Male and female variants for 'I' in Japanese: cooccurrence rules". *Papers in Linguistics: International Journal of Human Communication* 13 (3):453–74.

Nakakawaji, A. (1999). *Bijinesuman-no kanpeki-manaa*. [Perfect manners for office workers] Tokyo: Diamondo-sha.

Nakamura, M. (1991). "Woman's sexuality in Japanese female terms". In Ide, S. & McGloin, N.H. (eds.): 147–163.

Neustupný, J. (1974). "*Keigo wa Nihongo dake no mono deha nai* [The language of politeness is not peculiar to Japanese]". In Hayashi, S. & F. Minami (eds.): 8–40.

Niyekawa, A.M. (1991). *Minimum essential politeness: a guide to the Japanese honorific language*. Tokyo; New York; London: Kodansha International.

Nwoye, O.G. (1992). "Linguistic politeness and socio-cultural variations of the notion of face". *Journal of Pragmatics* 18: 309–28.

Ogino, S. (2002). *Keigo no i-ro-ha oshie masu* [I'll teach you ABC of honorifics]. Tokyo: Riyon-sha.

Olshtain, E. (1989). "Apologies across languages". In Blum-Kulka, S., House, J. & Kasper, G. (eds.): 155–173.

Olshtain, E. & Cohen, A. (1983). "Apology: a speech act set". In Wolfson, N. & Judd, E. (eds.): 18–36.
O'Neill, P.G. (1966). *A programmed guide to respect language in modern Japanese*. London: University of London.
Overstreet, M. & Yule, G. (2001). "Formulaic disclaimers". *Journal of Pragmatics* 33: 45–60.
Owen, M. (1983). *Apologies and remedial interchanges*. Berlin: Mouton Publishers.
Peng, F.C.C. & Hori, M. (1981). *Nihongo no danjosa: Male/female differences in Japanese*. Tokyo: The East-West Sign Language Association.
Philips, S.U., Steele, S. & Tanz, C. (ed.) (1987). *Language, Gender, and Sex in Comparative Perspective*, 26–49. Cambridge: Cambridge University Press.
Pizziconi, B. (2003). "Re-examining politeness, face and the Japanese language". *Journal of Pragmatics* 35: 1471–1506.
Preisler, B. (1986). *Linguistic Sex Roles in Conversation*. New York: Mouton de Gruyter.
Quirk, R. et al. (eds.) (1995 [1978]). *Longman Dictionary of Contemporary English*. (3rd ed.) London: Longman.
Rathmayr, R. (1996a). *Pragmatik der Entschuldigungen. Vergleichende Untersuchung am Beispiel der russischen Sprache und Kultur*, Cologne: Böhlau Verlag.
—— (1996b). "Sprachlliche Höflichkeit. Am Beispiel expliziter und impliziter Höflichkeit im Russischen" In Girke, W. (ed.): 362–391.
—— (1999). "Métadiscours et réalité linguistique: l'exemple de la politesse russe". *Pragmatics* 9(1): 75–95.
Rehbein, J. (1981). "Announcing – on formulating plans". In Coulmas, F. (ed.): 215–257.
Reynolds, K.A. (1991). "Female speakers of Japanese in transition". In Ide, S. & McGloin, N.H. (eds.): 129–146.
Rintell, E.M. & Mitchell, C.J. (1989). "Studying requests and apologies: An inquiry into method". In Blum-Kulka, S., House, J. & Kasper, G. (eds.): 248–272.
Robinson, M. (1992). "Introspective methodology in interlanguage pragmatics research". In Kasper, G. (ed.): 27–82.
Rundquist, S. (1992). "Indirectness: a gender study of flouting Grice's maxims". *Journal of Pragmatics* 18: 431–449.
Sadock, J. & Vanek, A.L. (eds.) (1970). *Studies presented to R.B. Lees by his students*. Edmonton, Alberta: Linguistic Research.
Sakata, M. (1991). "The acquisition of Japanese 'gender' particles". *Language & Communication: An Interdisciplinary Journal* 11 (3):117–25.
Sansom, G.B. (1928). *An historical grammar of Japanese*. Oxford: Clarendon Press.
Scarcella, R., Andersen, E. & Krashen, S. (eds.) (1990). *Developing Communicative Competence in a Second Language*. New York: Newbury House.
Scherer, K.R. & Giles, H. (eds.) (1979). *Social markers in speech*. Cambridge: Cambridge University Press.
Schmidt, R.W. (1980). "Review of Esther Goody (ed.), Questions and politeness: strategies in

social interaction". *RELC Journal* 11(2): 100–114.
Scollon, R. & Scollon, S.W. (1995). *Intercultural Communication*. Malden, MA: Blackwell.
Searle, J.R. (1969). *Speech acts*. Cambridge: Cambridge University Press.
―――― (1979). *Expression and meaning*. Cambridge: Cambridge University Press.
Sell, R.D. (ed.) (1991a). *Literary Pragmatics*. London: Routledge.
―――― (1991b). "The politeness of literary texts". In Sell, R.D. (ed.): 208–224.
Seward, J. (1968). *Japanese in action: an unorthodox approach to the spoken language and the people who speak it*. New York; Tokyo: Weatherhill.
Shibamoto, J.S. (1982). "Contributions of sociolinguistics to the language sciences: language and sex". *Language Sciences* 4 (2):115–29.
―――― (1987). "The womanly woman: manipulation of stereotypical and nonstereotypical features of Japanese female speech". In Philips, S.U., Steele, S. & Tanz, C. (ed.): 26–49.
―――― (1991). "Sex related variation in the ellipsis of *wa* and *ga* in Japanese". In Ide, S. & McGloin, N.H. (eds.): 81–104.
Shibatani, M. (1990). *The Languages of Japan*. Cambridge: Cambridge University Press.
Shiotsuki, Y. (1995). *Jouhin-na hanashi-kata*. (A refined way of speaking) Tokyo: Koubunsha. (translation mine)
Sifianou, M. (1992). *Politeness Phenomena in England and Greece*. Oxford: Clarendon.
Spencer-Oatey, H. (ed.) (2000a). *Culturally Speaking: Managing rapport through talk across cultures*. London: Continuum.
―――― (2000b). "Introduction: language, culture and rapport management" In Spencer-Oatey, H. (ed.): 1–8.
―――― (2000c). "Rapport management: a framework for analysis" In Spencer-Oatey, H. (ed.): 11–46.
―――― (2002). "Managing rapport in talk: using rapport sensitive incidents to explore the motivational concerns underlying the management of relations". *Journal of Pragmatics* 34: 529–545.
Spencer-Oatey, H. & Jiang, W. (2003). "Explaining cross-cultural pragmatic findings: moving from politeness maxims to sociopragmatic interactional principles (SIPS)". *Journal of Pragmatics* 35: 1633–1650.
Spencer-Oatey, H., Ng, P. & Dong, L. (2000). "Responding to compliments: British and Chinese evaluative judgements". In Spencer-Oatey, H. (ed.): 98–120.
Spencer-Oatey, H. & Xing, J. (2000). "A problematic Chinese business visit to Britain". In Spencer-Oatey, H. (ed.): 272–288.
Sperber, D. & Wilson, D. (1995[1981]). *Relevance: Communication and Cognition*. (2nd ed.) Oxford: Blackwell.
Steinberg Du, J. (1995). "The performance of face-threatening acts in Chinese". In Kasper, G. (ed.): 165–206.
Stenström, A.-B., Andersen, G. & Hasund, I.K. (2002). *Trends in Teenage Talk: Corpus compilation, analysis and findings*. Amsterdam; Philadelphia: John Benjamins.

Suzuki, T. (2000). *A study of pragmatic competence of Japanese EFL learners at a tertiary level*. Unpublished MA thesis. Lancaster University.

——— (2002). "The gender and politeness strategies of tertiary level Japanese EFL learners". *Lingua*. Waseda University English Language Society: 34–60.

——— (2004). "The generation gap in pragmatics: a study of linguistic politeness strategies in Britain and Japan" *CamLing Proceedings 2004*: 298–305.

——— (2005). "Versatility of the GSP (Grand Strategy of Politeness) of Leech's revised PP (Principles of Politeness): its applicability to a cross-cultural pragmatic study". *Essays on English Language and Literature*. The Engllish Language and Literature Society of Waseda University: 41–53.

Takahara, K. (1991). "Female speech patterns in Japanese". *International Journal of the Sociology of Language* 92:61–85.

Takano, S. (in press). "Re-examining linguistic power: strategic uses of directives by Japanese women in positions of authority and leadership". *Journal of Pragmatics*.

Takahashi, T. & Beebe, L.M. (1993). "Cross-Linguistic Influence in the Speech Act of Correction". In Kasper, G. & Blum-Kulka, S. (eds.): 138–157.

Takekuro, M. (1999). "Formulaic speech and social conventions in linguistic politeness of Japanese". Paper presented at the *International Symposium for Linguistic Politeness, Bangkok, 7–9 December 1999*.

Takeuchi, L. (1999). *The Structure and History of Japanese: from Yamatokotoba to Nihongo*. New York: Pearson Education (Longman Linguistic Library).

Tanaka, N. (2001). *The Pragmatics of Uncertainty: Its Realisation and Interpretation in English and Japanese*. Yokohama: Shumpūsha.

Tanaka, N., H. Spencer-Oatey & Cray, E. (2000). "'It's not my fault!': Japanese and English responses to unfounded accusations". In Spencer-Oatey, H. (ed.).

Tanaka, S. & Kawabe, S. (1982). "Politeness strategies and second language acquisition". *Studies in second language acquisition* 5(2): 18–33.

Tannen, D. & Öztek, P.C. (1981). "Health to our mouths. Formulaic expressions in Turkish and Greek". In Coulmas, F. (ed.): 37–53.

Terkourafi, M. (2002). "Politeness and formulaicity: Evidence from Cypriot Greek". *Journal of Greek Linguistics* 3: 179–201.

Thomas, J. (1983). "Cross-cultural pragmatic failure". *Applied Linguistics* 4(2): 91–112.

——— (1995). *Meaning in Interaction*. Essex: Longman.

Thorne, B. & Henley, N. (eds.) (1975). *Language and sex: difference and dominance*. Rowley, MA: Newbury House.

Trudgill, P. (1975). "Sex, covert prestige, and linguistic change in the urban British English in Norwich". In Thorne and Henley (eds.): 88–104.

Tsujimura, T. (1963). "Keigo no bunrui ni tsuite[About the classification of Japanese honorifics]". *Kokubungaku: gengo to bungei* 5-2: 35–42.

Tsuruta, Y. (1998). *Politeness, the Japanese Style: An Investigation into the Use of Honorific Forms and People's Attitudes towards Such Use.* Unpublished Ph.D. thesis. University of Luton.

Turner, K. (1996). "The principle principles of pragmatic inference: politeness". *Language Teaching* 29: 1–13.

Usami, M. (2002). *Discourse Politeness in Japanese Conversation: Some Implications for a Universal Theory of Politeness.* Tokyo: Hituzi Syobo.

Uyeno, T. (1971). *A study of Japanese modality: a performative analysis of sentence particles.* Unpublished Ph.D. dissertation. Dept of Linguistics, Univ. of Michigan, Ann Arbor.

Verschueren, J., Östman, J.-O., Blommaert, J. & Bulcaen, C. (eds.) (1996). *Handbook of Pragmatics 1996.* Amsterdam/Philadelphia: John Benjamins.

Vollmer, H.J. & Olshtain, E. (1989). "The language of apologies in German". In Blum-Kulka, S., House, J. & Kasper, G. (eds.): 197–218.

Warner, N., Ashlers, J. Bilmes, L., Oliver, M., Wertheim, S. & Chen, M. (eds.) (1996). *Gender and Belief Systems.* (Proceedings of the Fourth Berkeley Women and Language Conference) Berkeley, CA: Berkeley Women and Language Group, University of California.

Watts, R.J. (1989). "Relevance and relational work: linguistic politeness as politic behavior". *Multilingua* 8(2/3): 131–167.

——— (1992). "Linguistic politeness and politic verbal behaviour: reconsidering claims for universality". In Watts, R.J., Ide, S. & Ehlich, K. (eds.): 43–69.

——— (2003). *Politeness.* Cambridge: Cambridge University Press.

Watts, R.J., Ide, S. & Ehlich, K. (eds.) (1992a). *Politeness in Language: Studies in its History, Theory and Practice.* Berlin: Mouton de Gruyter.

——— (1992b). "Introduction". In Watts, R.J., Ide, S. & Ehlich, K. (eds.): 1–17.

Weizman, E. (1989). "Requestive hints". In Blum-Kulka, S., House, J. & Kasper, G. (eds.): 71-95.

Wetzel, P.J. (1991). "Are 'powerless' communication strategies the Japanese norm?". In Ide, S. & McGloin, N.H. (eds.): 117–128.

Wiseman, R.L. & Koester, J. (eds.) (1993). *Intercultural Communication Competence.* Newbury Park, CA: Sage.

Wolfson, N. & Judd, E. (eds.) (1983). *Sociolinguistics and Language Acquisition.* Rowley, MA: Newbury House.

Wolfson, N., Marmor, T. & Jones, S. (1989). "Problems in the comparison of speech acts across cultures". In Blum-Kulka, S., House, J. & Kasper, G. (eds.): 174–196.

Web sites
COLT (The Bergen Corpus of London Teenage Language)
    <http://www.hf.uib.no/i/Engelsk/colt/COLTinfo.html#MTTT> (2005/01/18)
    <http://www.ach.org/ACH_Posters/colt.html> (2005/01/18)
Daily Yomiuri On-Line

<http://www.yomiuri.co.jp/newse/20050107wo61.htm> (2005/01/08)
Praat 4.2.0.7
<www.praat.org> (2005/02/21)
Taishukan Shoten
<http://www.taishukan.co.jp/meikyo/0403/0403_top.html> (2005/01/18)
<http://www.taishukan.co.jp/meikyo/0403/0403_1.html> (2005/01/18)

Index

a

absolute politeness   2, 4, 12, 19, 28, 30, 66, 107, 125, 259
absolute relative politeness   18
accent   248
accentuation   260
activity type   25, 30, 68, 138
addressee   75
addressee factors   85
address term   74, 191
age   60, 84, 86, 255, 264, 272
agreeing   8, 185, 280
agreement   8, 18, 21, 119, 185, 281
alerters   47, 137
apology   8, 228, 283
approbation   8, 18, 21, 119, 162, 172
appropriateness   21, 29, 68, 131, 256, 277
assertives   41
association rights   13, 14
asymmetries of politeness   40
attitudinal warmth   23
audio data   255
authenticity   109, 115

b

banter   27, 28, 170, 182
behaviour strategies   40
bikago   78
body language   72
Bonferroni test   131

c

camaraderie   3, 4, 21, 23, 24, 25, 27, 28, 171, 256, 279
camaraderie markers   4, 5
camaraderie orientation   29
CCSARP (The Cross-Cultural Speech Act Realization Project)   46, 108, 137, 247, 288
changes in Japanese honorifics   80
changes in keigo   71
chotto   154
claims of common ground   23
clarification   17
closed role-plays   124
COLLABORATIVE   17
commissives   42
COMPETITIVE   17
compliments   8, 162, 279
conflict avoidance   57
CONFLICTIVE   17
confusion in language   1
consideration   2, 28
constraint   20, 21, 32, 40, 69, 119, 138, 278
contextual assessment norms   15
conventional DCTs   6
conventional indirectness (CI)   59
conversational-contract (CC)   54
conversational-contract view   53
conversational-maxim view   52
conversational implicature   57
conversational routine   69, 250
CONVIVIAL   17, 162, 173, 186, 197, 213, 228
Cooperative Principle (CP)   20, 30, 52
correlation   278
correlation between politeness and appropriateness   134
cost-benefit   3, 155
COST-BENEFIT SCALE   19
creak phonation   275
creaky voice   249, 256, 275
cross-generation study   277

d

D (the social distance) 60
DCT (Discourse completion test) 6, 104, 108, 120
declarations 42
deference 4, 28
deference 3, 21, 22, 25, 27, 71, 243
deference/camaraderie markers 26
deference markers 4, 5
deference orientation 29
degree appropriateness 125
degree of politeness 125
demeanour 89
directives 8, 42, 151, 278
directness 143
disagreeing 8
disagreeing with mitigation 185, 280
discernment 25, 26, 27, 51, 64, 71, 73, 96
discernment politeness 91, 93
discourse politeness 100
Dunnet test 131

e

effect of spoken data 247
ego 61
emotive communication 21
empty adjectives 88
epistemological concerns 55
equity rights 13, 14
ethnography 120
ethos 61, 62
etiquette 49
etrospective think-aloud protocol 254
exaltation of h and o 16
expletive 25
expressing feelings 8, 281
EXPRESSIVE 42, 162, 173, 186, 197, 213, 228

f

face 40, 56

face-threats 57
face-wants 57
face-work 96
face management 14
face respecting act (FRA) 95
face saving view 53
fall-rise 248
falling tone 248, 261, 271
familiarity 84
FEAs (face-enhancing acts) 20, 27, 43, 95, 143, 151, 162, 169, 186, 229
Feeling-reticence 8, 21, 119
findings 131
first-order politeness 33
first-stage data collection: scenarios 119
flatness 264
force 16, 249, 272, 284, 286
formality 24, 29, 67, 84, 85, 138, 282
formal speech 85
formulaic expression 222, 240
formulaicity 65
Fraser's taxonomy 48
friendliness 25, 26, 282
FSAs (face-saving acts) 20, 27, 43, 151, 186
FTAs (face-threatening acts) 20, 43, 57, 58, 186, 228
fundamental cultural values 15

g

gender 60, 84, 86, 88, 255, 264, 272
gender differences 2
generation gap 1, 132
GENEROSITY 8, 18, 21, 119, 138, 278
giving opinions 8
group differences 134
group membership 84
GSP (Grand Strategy of Politeness) 16, 20, 21, 30, 32, 66, 71

h

h's and o's exaltation 21

Index 303

head acts 47, 137, 151, 278, 286
hearer (h) 16
hedges 88
higher age raters 125
holistic impressions 255
honorific forms 2, 3
honorifics 19, 28, 64, 71, 92, 97
horizontal 60
horizontal distance 29, 73, 138
humble forms 160
humbleness of s 16

i

identity face 13, 14, 260
IFIDs (illocutionary force indicating devices) 47, 137
illocutionary force 17, 126, 288
illocutionary functions 17, 18, 41
illocutionary goal achievement 26, 27, 79
illocutionary goals 17, 28
impact of prosody 247
impoliteness 67, 250, 261
impoliteness strategies 250
in-depth guided interview 112, 114
in-group membership 23
inappropriateness 166
indirectness 3, 19, 40, 57, 143, 155
INDIRECTNESS SCALE 19
informality 27
informal speech(colloquial speech) 85
informants 118
intensification 17
intensity 255, 256, 260, 271
intensity (relative loudness) 274
intentional/volitional politeness 91
interviews 112
intonation 248, 249, 255, 273
inventory of rapport management strategies 15
invitations 8, 278
irony 28

j

Japanese honorific system 77
JHA (Japanese higher age group) 277
JHAF 118, 277
JHAM 118, 277
JYA (Japanese younger age group) 277
JYAF 118, 277
JYAM 118, 277

k

keigo 4, 76
kenjōgo 77, 78
kinesics 274, 284
kohai 86, 163
kotoba-no midare 82
Kruskal-Wallis test 131

l

language simplification 27
lexicogrammatical devices 3, 27
lexicogrammatical features 250
lexicogrammatical politeness markers 211
lexicogrammatical politeness strategies 16
lexicogrammatical strategies 16, 29
linguistic politeness 13, 16, 21, 22, 40, 64
linguistic politeness strategies 277
linguistic sophistication 2
linguistic strategies 40
London-Lund Corpus of Spoken English 250
loudness 248, 255

m

manners 50
markers 27
maxim 17, 20, 31, 32
methodology 101, 102
mitigation 3, 17, 18

Speech Analyzer   274
speech rhythm   248
spoken and transcribed data   247, 272
spoken data   261, 284
spoken DCT with video prompts   6, 111, 114, 119, 286
SPSS (Statistical Package for Social Science)   131, 253
stress   248
supportive moves   47, 137, 286
suppressing feelings   8
sustained high pitch   249
SYMPATHY   8, 18, 119, 172, 282
sympathy   21, 196

t

TACT   8, 18, 21, 119, 146, 151, 155, 278
tag questions   88
teineigo   77, 78
tempo   255, 258, 267, 273
thanks   8, 228, 283
think-aloud protocols(TAP)   113
tiers   275
tone   72, 248
traditional DCTs   247
triangulation   103, 114

u

underpoliteness   12, 19, 39, 133, 156, 159, 288
universality   34, 64
use of honorifics   79

v

value transaction   41, 69, 79, 80
vertical distance   29, 60, 73, 138
video prompts   119, 120, 286
videotaped scenarios   120
vocal information   254
voice quality   248, 255, 256
volition   24, 25, 27, 96, 248
volitional strategies   28

w

wakimae/discernment   24, 51, 64, 71, 73
wakimae/discernment markers   28
warmth   256, 282
W(weight)   29
wrong use of honorifics   160

y

yoroshiku o-negaishi-masu   239, 283
younger age raters   125
youth language   1

【著者紹介】

鈴木 利彦（すずき　としひこ）

1964年神奈川県横浜市生まれ
〈学歴〉早稲田大学教育学部英語英文学科（学士）、英国ランカスター大学（修士、博士）
〈職歴〉東京女学館他にて小中高等学校の英語教師として勤務。現職：上智大学一般外国語教育センター嘱託講師

【主な著書・論文】

"The gender and politeness strategies of tertiary level Japanese EFL learners". *Lingua*. Waseda University English Language Society: 34-60. (2002)

"Versatility of the GSP (Grand Strategy of Politeness) of Leech's revised PP (Principles of Politeness): its applicability to a cross-cultural pragmatic study". *Essay on English Language and Literature*. The English Language and Literature Society of Waseda University: 41-53. (2005)

Hituzi Linguistics in English No. 6

A Pragmatic Approach to the Generation and Gender Gap in Japanese Politeness Strategies

発行	2007年2月20日　初版1刷
定価	9800円＋税
著者	© 鈴木利彦
発行者	松本　功
本文フォーマット	向井裕一（glyph）
印刷所	三美印刷株式会社
製本所	田中製本印刷株式会社
発行所	株式会社 ひつじ書房
	〒112-0002 東京都文京区小石川5-21-5
	Tel.03-5684-6871　Fax.03-5684-6872
	郵便振替 00120-8-142852
	toiawase@hituzi.co.jp　http://www.hituzi.co.jp/

ISBN978-4-89476-330-2　C3082

造本には充分注意しておりますが，落丁・乱丁などがございましたら，小社かお買上げ書店におとりかえいたします。ご意見，ご感想など，小社までお寄せ下されば幸いです。